PEROGIES AND POLITICS

Canada's Ukrainian Left, 1891–1991

STUDIES IN GENDER AND HISTORY

General Editors: Franca Iacovetta and Karen Dubinsky

RHONDA L. HINTHER

Perogies and Politics

Canada's Ukrainian Left, 1891 1991

UNIVERSITY OF TORONTO PRESS
Toronto Buffalo London

ISBN 978-1-4875-0049-8

Printed on acid-free, 100% post-consumer recycled paper with
vegetable-based inks.

Library and Archives Canada Cataloguing in Publication

Hinther, Rhonda L., 1974–, author
Perogies and politics : Canada's Ukrainian left,
1891–1991 / Rhonda L. Hinther.

(Studies in gender and history)
Includes bibliographical references and index.
ISBN 978-1-4875-0049-8 (cloth)

1. Right and left (Political science) – Canada – History – 19th century.
2. Right and left (Political science) – Canada – History – 20th century.
3. Ukrainians – Canada – Politics and government – 19th century.
4. Ukrainians – Canada – Politics and government – 20th century.
I. Title.   II. Series: Studies in gender and history

FC106.U5H56 2018   971.004′91791   C2017-903097-3

This book has been generously supported by the publications program of
the Shevchenko Scientific Society of Canada and the Brandon University
Research Committee.

University of Toronto Press acknowledges the financial assistance to its
publishing program of the Canada Council for the Arts and the Ontario
Arts Council, an agency of the Government of Ontario.

Canada Council   Conseil des Arts
for the Arts   du Canada

ONTARIO ARTS COUNCIL
CONSEIL DES ARTS DE L'ONTARIO
an agency of the Government of Ontario
un organisme du gouvernement de l'Ontario

Funded by the   Financé par le
Government   gouvernement
of Canada   du Canada

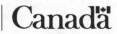

Contents

Acknowledgments

This project was completed with the support, assistance, and encouragement of many parties. It began as an oral history project at the Ukrainian Labour Temple in Winnipeg, Manitoba. The people there and others tied to the movement across Canada offered an array of assistance with the research. Special thanks go to Zenovy Nykolyshyn, Mary Semanowich, Myron Shatulsky, Lily Stearns, Brett Stearns, Gloria Gordienko, Orysia Zaporazan, Mary Skrypnyk, and John Boyd. I would also like to express appreciation to those individuals who generously shared their life stories with me by participating in the Ukrainian Labour Temple's oral history project. Without their contributions this study could never have been as rich in detail as it is. I am also indebted to the Association of United Ukrainian Canadians (AUUC) for allowing me access to its fonds at Library and Archives Canada (LAC) and to substantial uncatalogued materials housed in Winnipeg and Toronto.

At McMaster University, where this book began as my doctoral thesis, Ruth Frager served as my supervisor. I am grateful for her intellectual guidance and support. I would also like to acknowledge the other members of my doctoral supervisory committee – Ken Cruikshank and Dick Rempel – for their help and encouragement. Others at McMaster whose support aided in the successful completion of this study include Wendy Benedetti and Rita Maxwell. Two individuals deserve special mention for their friendship and encouragement: Wendy Churchill and Erika Hauschild Abbott were especially supportive during my time in the doctoral program. Dan Gorman, Mary Jo Megginson, Jessa Chupik, Greg Stott, Ken MacMillan, Dave Leeson, and Neil White also aided my efforts to complete the thesis. During this time, Myron Momyruk at LAC was extremely helpful, not only directing me to resources useful for my study but also taking the time to translate numerous documents for me. Later, he offered helpful feedback on various versions of the manuscript. I also appreciate the assistance received from Kim Foreman and Doug Luchak in LAC's Access to Information and Privacy Division.

I would like to recognize Oksana Demkiw and her family for their ongoing friendship and for hosting me when I was Lviv, Ukraine, studying the Ukrainian language. I would also like to extend my appreciation to Victor Krevs of the Ivan Franko National University in Lviv for designing an individualized program of Ukrainian language study for me. Thanks also go to my former supervisor, Nolan Reilly of the University of Winnipeg, for drawing the Ukrainian Labour Temple to my attention and for his continued advice, support, and friendship. I would like to express my appreciation to Larissa Stavroff for granting me access to the collection of her father, Peter Krawchuk, at LAC in Ottawa, and for her friendship, research assistance, and time spent tirelessly translating sources crucial to this study. Tannis Waugh also deserves special mention for her continuing friendship and support; I will always be grateful for her willingness to accommodate my unpredictable and, at times, trying research schedule by providing me with a place to stay, moral support, and many diversions with which to relieve the stress of research whenever I needed to be at the National Archives in Ottawa. Other friends and colleagues provided me with encouragement, engaging conversation, and much-needed distraction during the completion of this project. Among them are Wendy Sawatzky, Jason Hooper, Sabine Hikel, Danishka Esterhazy, Jonathan Esterhazy, Shannon Slater, Holly Lowe, Joan Trimble, Tamara Biebricht, Mike Carroll, Kristy Menzies, Leanne Dustan, Kaj Hasselriis, Sharon Reilly, Jim Mochoruk, Heather Bidzinski, Krista Cooke, Jennifer Anderson, Jennifer Lonergan, Jars Balan, Dave Cannon, Jillian Wolfe, and John Willis. I am also grateful to my colleagues at Brandon University – especially Lynn MacKay and Jim Naylor – for their words of encouragement as they bore witness to the latter stages of the manuscript's transition to publication.

Many thanks go to Len Husband and Frances Mundy at University of Toronto Press for helping to move this book forward. Thanks go as well to Angela Wingfield for her patient and careful copy-editing of the manuscript. I am also grateful to Franca Iacovetta, as the external reader on the thesis and co-editor of the Studies in Gender and History Series, who has offered much valuable feedback and encouragement along the way. I would also like to offer thanks to the four anonymous peer reviewers for their thoughtful commentary on previous versions of the text.

I am fortunate to have a supportive family, and I am especially appreciative of the encouragement received from my parents, Evelyn Hinther and the late G. Ronald Hinther. Throughout my academic career they have generously and warmly offered moral and financial support. My mother was exceptionally helpful with this project; she provided critical research assistance by helping me review mountains of organizational newspapers and RCMP surveillance files. Other members of my family whose support sustained me during this project include my grandparents Sophie and the late Fred Skolny; my cousins Lynne Onofreychuk, Peter Onofreychuk, and Keegan Onofreychuk; my aunts Gisele Skolny and Myrna Eng; and my in-laws, Helen Floresco, George Floresco, and Cathy Kennedy. Finally, special thanks must go to my partner, Aaron Floresco, and our son, Sebastian Hinther-Floresco, for their love and unwavering support.

This project has benefited from funding by a variety of sources. In addition to my parents, I would also like to thank the Department of History and the Department of Labour Studies at McMaster University for their financial assistance. Financial support was also received through the Ontario Graduate Scholarship Program and the Canadian Institute of Ukrainian Studies' Darcovich Doctoral Fellowship.

Note on Transliteration

The transliteration of Ukrainian in this project is in keeping with the modified Library of Congress system. Proper names of some individuals are included in their most frequently used spelling (as evidenced in the source materials consulted). Occasionally there may be place names and proper names that have a traditional and recognizable spelling that defies modified Library of Congress convention. These have been left intact for purposes of recognition.

PEROGIES AND POLITICS

Canada's Ukrainian Left, 1891–1991

Introduction: The Men, Women, and Children of the Ukrainian Labour Temple Movement, 1891–1991

Myron Shatulsky was born in 1930. His parents, Katherine and Matthew, both Ukrainian immigrants who had come to Canada in 1910, were active in the left-wing Ukrainian Labour Farmer Temple Association (ULFTA). The organization had developed largely in direct response to the difficult social, economic, and working conditions that most Ukrainians encountered upon coming to Canada. Although some of them (like Matthew) had been touched by left-wing politics in the old country, and even fewer had arrived in Canada already politicized, the majority of left-leaning Ukrainians (like Katherine) were radicalized by the exploitation and hardships that they experienced in Canada. A couple in politics and in life. Matthew became one of the ULFTA's most important national leaders, and Katherine helped to found the women's section, which played a critical role in mobilizing women's activism. Not surprisingly, they also involved young Myron in their activities. Like so many other children of Ukrainian leftist parents, Myron essentially grew up in the local Ukrainian labour temple, spending his formative years singing, playing mandolin, attending Ukrainian school, marching in May Day parades, and observing and engaging in the activism of his parents and of the other adults and children who surrounded him.[1]

Leftist – or "progressive" – Ukrainians like Myron Shatulsky, his parents, and their friends and families created one of the most dynamic national working-class movements in twentieth-century Canada. The founding generation belonged to the large wave of over 170,000 Ukrainian emigrants from Bukovyna and Galicia who entered Canada during the period 1891–1914. They came as part of the massive influx of immigrants whom the federal government recruited at that time to settle the Canadian prairies or to serve as cheap labour in the country's rapidly expanding resource sector. Additional support came from among the 70,000 Ukrainians who were admitted to Canada between the wars. The Ukrainian Labour Farmer Temple Association galvanized the efforts of the immigrant radicals and their offspring into a unified and influential secular movement. The institutional and cultural centres of the movement, the Ukrainian labour temples, emerged as significant activist spaces across the country from Nova Scotia to British Columbia wherever a critical mass of Ukrainian labourers or farmers existed.

These activist men and women, along with their children, accommodated themselves to a life of hardship while mounting resistance to the economic, social, and political forces that shaped their membership in a distinctly "ethnic" working or agricultural class. Socialist ideas brought from the old country, combined with the popular labour discourse that was advocated by the larger left-wing community in Canada, informed the movement's ideological and activist orientation. Embracing Marxist-Leninism[2] and consciously situating themselves in an international context of labour solidarity and burgeoning revolution, these Ukrainians developed an array of activities to express their particular brand of radical Ukrainianness, applying it to the class struggle to improve their lot in Canada and that of their comrades, Ukrainian and otherwise, locally and abroad. Their efforts bore fruit and offered them radical social, cultural, and political alternatives to the fledgling Ukrainian churches and emerging right-wing Ukrainian nationalist organizations.

The aim of this study is to explore the twentieth-century history of the Ukrainian left in Canada as a political and cultural movement and community, written from the standpoint of the women, men, and children who formed and fostered it. Especially concerned with change over time, this project considers how particular events and social, economic, and political forces in the past affected the activists and how the latter, in turn, influenced, processed, and responded to these experiences. Although it is not its main preoccupation, the project also notes the position of the Ukrainian left within the broader left, most notably vis-à-vis the Communist Party of Canada (CPC). Exploring these themes tells us much about the Ukrainian left itself and about leftist activism more broadly in Canada, while hinting at general insights that are applicable to other ethnicized and activist communities – leftist or otherwise.

This study argues that in its early decades the Ukrainian left was enormously successful because it met the needs of and spoke in meaningful, respectful, and empowering ways to its supporters' experiences and interests as an immigrant working-class community. Above all, for these Ukrainians, culture and politics were inextricably and unapologetically linked. Evident among the movement's members and supporters was a fervent desire to carry out politicized cultural activities in which their Ukrainianness could be celebrated front and centre for sheer pleasure, personal and community validation, and as a powerful activist tool. Indeed, as the research shows, Ukrainianness was a key tool in their class struggle, and they defended their right to engage it, often in the face of strong Communist Party opposition. Ultimately, a couple of key factors undermined the Ukrainian left as a cohesive movement. First, and perhaps ironically, its own success in aiding community members – and their children – to adapt to Canada, alongside the gains of the broader Canadian left of which the Ukrainian left was a critical part, meant that the movement outlived its usefulness as it had been envisioned in the interwar years. Tensions emerged from the change in community composition – that is, the transformation from an immigrant Ukrainian working-class community to a Ukrainian Canadian one as the migrants' children grew up and had children of their own. The movement failed to meaningfully reinvent itself and adapt to the needs and realities of the second and subsequent generations of left-minded Ukrainian Canadians. A number of factors combined to make this challenging: chiefly the cold-war context and the increased assimilation of young Ukrainians. Especially problematic, however, was the movement's inability to recognize and meaningfully address what would become intolerable gender and generational inequities, an outcome of the intersections of gender, class, ethnicity, and generation within the movement at key points in time. In particular, the adherence of the immigrant generation's male leaders to older political priorities and their unwillingness to pass the torch (until it was virtually too late) stood in the face of any potential reinvention and regeneration that younger, Canadian-born women and men might have driven. As such, the movement slowly fragmented; most of the young people gradually turned elsewhere – because they could. This is in many ways a testimony to the movement's ultimate success. The host of opportunities – activist or otherwise – available to these young Ukrainian Canadians could be attributed to many of the struggles and successes of the Canadian left in which the Ukrainian left had played an important part.

In line with recent scholarship, this project combines a top-down and bottom-up intersectional approach. Intersectionality as an analytic concept illuminates the interactions of gender with other categories of inequality and difference, which occur, as Kathy Davis explains, "in individual lives, social practices, institutional arrangements, and cultural ideologies and the outcomes of these interactions in terms of power." These processes are historically and spatially contingent, maintaining power in different ways in different historical times. Olena Hankivsky notes that "intersectionality conceptualizes social categories as interacting with and co-constituting one another to create unique social locations that vary according to time and place." Concurrently, it is important to note, as S.E. Smith emphasizes, that intersectionality "boils down to the idea that people experience oppressions in overlapping ways, not as separate and distinct identities that can be teased apart and viewed individually." To help illustrate, Smith offers the following example: "A person who is trans and disabled, for example, does not experience life separately as a trans person and a disabled person, but experiences life as a disabled, trans person." Smith underscores this, stating, "It is impossible to separate out these experiences of oppression, but they are also not the same oppression or equivalent oppressions." For our purposes, for instance, Katherine Shatulsky's subjectivity cannot be broken down in the individual parcels of immigrant *and* Ukrainian *and* working-class *and* woman, but her experience must be understood distinctly and specifically as that of an *immigrant Ukrainian working-class woman*. Moreover, what this means was subject to change with the passing of time, as old identities shifted and new ones emerged within (and increasingly without) the context of the Ukrainian left community. The daughters of Katherine's cohort, as we shall see, had very different experiences. Intersectionality, then, is often engaged to provide a smoother and more nuanced understanding of identity, where, as Gill Valentine notes, "social positions, identities and differences are made and unmade, claimed and rejected." These interactions, per Alison Symington, "contribute to unique experiences of oppression and privilege." Social practices are the means through which these processes of difference and inequality become manifest: "Individuals delineate themselves in social contexts, construct identities, process symbolic representations, support social structures or challenge them." Indeed, attention to resistance and resilience is essential. "These can disrupt power and oppression," underscores Hankivsky, adding that "even from so-called 'marginalized' spaces and locations, oppressive values, norms, and practices can be challenged." Intersectionality is therefore a valuable methodology for, as Davis highlights, it "initiates a process of discovery, alerting us to the fact that the world around us is always more complicated and contradictory than we ever could have anticipated."[3]

On this particular front, intersectional theory is especially valuable for illuminating the machinations of power, especially the beneficiaries and the casualties of systems of oppression, while also underscoring that these categories are by no means fixed or absolute. Rather, individuals or groups may be simultaneously privileged and oppressed depending on the spatial and/or temporal settings in which they are acting. That is, they may be concurrently oppressor in one context, oppressed in another.[4] For example, as an immigrant Ukrainian working-class man, Matthew Shatulsky was economically disadvantaged and socially marginalized relative to Anglo-Celtic men in Canada; however, as we shall see, as a leader within the context of the Ukrainian left, he and other men like him enjoyed considerable status and advantage vis-à-vis women and even some men.

The concepts of *hegemonic, complicit*, and *subordinate masculinities* and *hegemonic* and *oppositional femininities* in direct engagement with an intersectional analysis are valuable theoretical tools to deconstruct gender dynamics. In particular, they help to illuminate the co-constitutions and relationships of femininities and masculinities; power relations and difference among men; the concurrent impact on women's – and some men's – experiences of inequality; and resistance and change over time. These concepts, adopted by scholars (though not without considerable debate) for three decades,[5] build on the work of the Italian theorist Antonio Gramsci on hegemony. Mike Donaldson explains:

> Hegemony, a pivotal concept in Gramsci's Prison Notebooks and his most significant contribution to Marxist thinking, is about the winning and holding of power and the formation (and destruction) of social groups in that process. In this sense, it is importantly about the ways in which the ruling class establishes and maintains its domination. The ability to impose a definition of the situation, to set the terms in which events are understood and issues discussed, to formulate ideals and define morality is an essential part of this process. Hegemony involves persuasion of the greater part of the population, particularly through the media, and the organization of social institutions in ways that appear "natural," "ordinary": "normal."[6]

Hegemonic masculinity and hegemonic femininity, then, refer to the particular categories of masculinity and femininity that are "naturalized" and elevated above others in a given time and space. However, a crucial difference distinguishes the two. "Hegemonic masculinity is always constructed as superior to femininity," explains Justin Charlebois, which results in asymmetrical gender relations; similarly, "hegemonic masculinities always establish and sustain unequal relationships with nonhegemonic masculinities and femininities and thus involve subordination." He notes another important distinction: "While men are empowered through the embodiment of hegemonic masculinity, the celebrated characteristics associated with hegemonic femininity work to subordinate and ultimately disempower women."[7] Like other historical processes of inequality, hegemonic masculinity and hegemonic femininity are subject to challenge and change, and the maintenance of the particular gender order and the masculinist culture they facilitate and support necessitates considerable effort.[8]

From the resulting unequal gender relations is realized what R.W. Connell has termed "the patriarchal dividend." The patriarchal dividend, she explains, is "the advantage men in general gain from the subordination of women."[9] She notes: "Money is not the only kind of benefit. Others are authority, respect, service, safety, housing, access to institutional power, emotional support, and control over one's own life." Gender inequality feeds the dividend for it "is reduced as overall gender equality grows."[10]

Not all men sit at the top of the gender hierarchy, of course. R.W. Connell and James W. Messerschmidt note that "hegemonic masculinities can be constructed that do not correspond closely to the lives of any actual men," but these ideas do "express widespread ideals, fantasies, and desires."[11] Indeed, within any system of gender relations exist other non-hegemonic masculinities and femininities. Of "complicit" masculinities R.W. Connell explains that "masculinities constructed in ways that realize the patriarchal dividend, without the tensions or risks of being frontline troops of patriarchy, are complicit in this sense." She and James Messerschmidt remark that, typically, complicit masculinities often overlap with hegemonic masculinities when hegemony plays out successfully. "Marginalized" masculinities are the purview of those for whom hegemonic or complicit masculinities are inaccessible, perhaps because of processes of racialization, generation, sexual orientation, and/or the interaction of other categories of identity.[12] Finally, "oppositional" femininities are those that challenge inequalities in a given system of gender relations between hegemonic femininities and masculinities.[13] Evident in the history of the Ukrainian left are each of these gender positionalities, as we shall see. The identification and analysis of the resulting gender order as an outcome of the intersections of the processes of class, ethnicity, and generation with gender over time is fundamental to this project.

Essentially, for the purposes of this study of the Ukrainian left, we are concerned with the following questions that are meant to illuminate the heterogeneity and complexity of this activist community and to garner understanding of the ways in which power functioned therein. How did the intersections of gender, class, ethnicity, age, and generation have an impact on identity formation, opportunity, and experience? In what ways did the resulting gender order shape and motivate individual and collective action within the Ukrainian labour temples and other sites of Ukrainian leftist political and cultural activism? How and why did the interactions of these processes change over the course of the movement's twentieth-century history? What did this ultimately mean for the movement and its supporters? From this, what insights can we glean that would help to strengthen current and future social justice movements and to ensure equity in practice and with broader success? An intersectional approach is a valuable and viable analytical means by which to address these crucial questions.

Indeed, in Canada and elsewhere over the past three decades a variety of scholars – including feminist, labour, and post-colonial historians – have demonstrated well the methodological effectiveness of an intersectional approach in addressing such concerns.[14] Their research reveals how the intersection of gender with ethnicity, class, and other social categories has shaped women's, men's, and, increasingly, children's experiences within the home, workplace, neighbourhood, and community. These scholars offer key insights into female and male agency, resistance, and power, increasingly doing so by highlighting and interrogating the dynamics of different and competing femininities and masculinities. By deploying a framework of class, ethnicity, and gender, Frances Swyripa, for example, has fruitfully examined not only the differences but also the similarities in the gendered positions of the Ukrainian women who were in the rival nationalist (or conservative) and progressive political camps. Ruth Frager has shown how the uneven convergence of ethnicity, gender, and class with external social, economic, and political forces defined and eventually undermined the attempts of female and male Jewish garment workers to "bring about a fundamental socialist transformation" in the early half of the twentieth century in Toronto. Similarly, the collected articles in *Sisters or Strangers: Immigrant, Ethnic, and Racialized Women in Canadian History*, edited by Marlene Epp, Franca Iacovetta, and Frances Swyripa, focus on the particular ways in which the categories of race, ethnicity, and class (and others) mattered within historically specific situations. In so doing, they enrich our understanding of the complexities surrounding the experiences of immigration, community, and nation building and the gendered notions of newcomer, worker, and citizenship.[15]

An intersectional analysis does not mean that gender, class, ethnicity, and other categories always interacted in equal degrees or in the same way. For example, Katrina Srigley has illustrated that gender could matter less than class, race, or ethnicity to women seeking employment in Depression-era Toronto. She underscores the strength of an intersectional methodology by reminding us that "we need to make critical judgements about which identities emerge as more or less influential in shaping women's working lives in a given time and place, and at a particular phase of their life cycle." Indeed, place and space are critical variables in the processes of identity construction. "Identities are highly contingent and situated accomplishments," underscores geographer Valentine; "space and identities are co-implicated." As such, she explains, "in particular spaces there are dominant spatial orderings that produce moments of exclusion for particular social groups." This is evident in her own work on the deaf community and in historical studies like those of Craig Heron on boys in Hamilton, Ontario. Using the city as a case study, he illustrates how working-class boys "learned and practised" (and renegotiated) masculinity in a host of private and public venues. "The result," he states, "was a complex bundle of contradictory attitudes and practices in which the processes of class, ethnic/racial, and gender formation were closely interwoven."[16]

Given its commitment to dual cultural and political goals and its differently located members, the Ukrainian left community easily lends itself to an intersectional methodology – and especially to a gendered study of masculinity and femininity. The movement's organizational and spatial arrangements paralleled contemporary family structures and models of gender relations (brought from the old country and influenced by Canadian social patterns). These encompassed, in varying ways, all family members, validated and reinforced male gender privilege, and gave rise to a masculinist ideology that subordinated the activism and activities of women and youngsters. The ULFTA's strong emphasis on the retention and enrichment of Ukrainian cultural and working-class political activities, as well as its maintenance of separate slates of gender- and age-specific activities, meant that Ukrainian radicalism simultaneously contained divergent and even conflicting elements. Language skills, in particular, influenced engagement with the movement, shaped generational and gender relations, and played a key role in community restructuring. Individual participants' locations at the juncture of particular subjectivities, then, meant that experiences, opportunities, and meanings of activities, events, and activism often varied along gender and generational lines. As women, men, and youngsters asserted claims to space in the labour temples, their actions underscored identifiable systems of power relations, processes that were constantly being constituted and reconstituted over time. Working within these parameters, however, even those who were the most marginalized found or devised spaces of influence and autonomy and the means to exert control over their own activism and, at times, challenge the oppression they faced inside and outside the movement. In later decades, some (particularly the younger generations) increasingly moved on to other – often non-Ukrainian – sites of political activism or social engagement.

An intersectional approach that pays as much attention to the women and children as to the men in the Ukrainian labour temple movement during the twentieth century represents something of a departure from studies of Ukrainians in Canada. Most historical works on Ukrainians have tended to focus on immigration patterns, the early settlement period, and religion. When they have offered commentary on Ukrainian communities, institution building, and formal politics, they have generally done so from a male-centred perspective.

Studies of the Ukrainian left have been similarly limited. None has explicitly carried out a sustained gender analysis of the Ukrainian left that compares and contrasts the experiences and subjectivities of both men and women and of children and youth. Existing studies instead consider the movement narrowly, focusing mainly on its interwar relationship with the Communist Party of Canada. Many historians and others have often characterized (and at times written off) the movement as simply – and monolithically – "pro-communist." This often occurs because their analyses consider only the actions and activities of the organization's male leaders and treat these men's attitudes and experiences as representative of the entire movement. This bias has obscured nuances in political ideology and changes in political association and activism that have occurred over time, and has precluded acknowledgment and analysis of the contested terrain that was the wider Canadian left, of which the Ukrainian labour temple movement was a critical component.[17] Undeniably, it has also eclipsed the experiences of the vast majority of Ukrainian leftists (many of whom never directly associated themselves with the party), thereby falsely universalizing the experiences and activism of a small male-leadership core as representative of the broader movement. This study offers a more nuanced consideration of the relationship between the Ukrainian left and the CPC, while highlighting above all the experiences of the lion's share of these Ukrainians – rank-and-file women, men, and youngsters – who have received far less attention in the scholarship. This project, therefore, consciously avoids the use of depicters like *Communist Ukrainians* or *Pro-Communist Ukrainians*, which are often used elsewhere to describe those involved with the Ukrainian labour temples. These terms are too simplistic and obscure the diversity and significance of the various social, cultural, and political activities of these Ukrainians, not to mention their complex relationship with the broader Canadian socialist movement, including, but not limited to, the CPC.

The activism of these Ukrainians paralleled that of other contemporary immigrant groups in Canada and elsewhere. Studies of leftist Jews, Finns, Hungarians, and others have noted the rich tapestry of social and cultural activities that were central to defining the left politics and "ethnic hall" – or diaspora socialism – of these groups.[18] During the interwar years the commitment of Ukrainian radicals to social justice was manifested in many fascinating ways. Using as a home base the activist space that they had established at the Ukrainian labour temples, they engaged in traditional modes of resistance including the support of strikes, the publication of newspapers, and the endorsement of candidates (particularly CPC members) for political office. Like other "ethnic" radicals, they also expressed their activism through a diverse array of cultural activities. Ukrainian theatre, embroidery, dance, food, and music (especially from mandolin orchestras and choirs) were commonplace and exceedingly popular at the halls. Concerts, plays, and other performances routinely attracted sell-out crowds during the interwar years and drew new members to the

ULFTA. Organizers used these occasions to communicate complex political matters, encourage working-class solidarity, and further the struggle against economic and social injustice in Canada and abroad. Within the halls, rank-and-file members experienced economic and social validation and a safe and convivial space to express, share, and celebrate their Ukrainianness with their friends and family, especially their offspring.

Uncloistered, the engagement with the Ukrainian labour temple – and particularly the efforts of the movement's leaders – regularly brought the migrant community into contact and cross-ethnic collaboration with the wider national (and, indeed, transnational) socialist community. This was most noticeable during times of crisis, protest, or celebration that cut across ethnic lines; strikes (including the 1919 Winnipeg General Strike), annual May Day demonstrations, and the 1935 On-to-Ottawa Trek are some of the many instances that spurred inter-ethnic, leftist cooperation in the interwar years. Nonetheless, while recognizing and embracing the value of these connections, most Ukrainian leftists preferred to perform their activism and ethnic identity regularly together with other Ukrainians at the Ukrainian labour temples in the 1920s and 1930s. Ethnocentrism, particularly that of many Anglo-Celtic leftists, played a role; language differences too could discourage intermingling. As Ian McKay explains of the Ukrainians, Finns, and Jews, the leading diaspora socialists, their leftist practice was "both connected to and autonomous within" the Canadian left "It actually makes more sense, and aligns better with the evidence, to speak of 'Canadian' socialisms ... If all of the variations shared a common language of socialism, each had its own distinctive dialect and nurtured its own sense of history."[19] Put plainly, then, with the socialisms of the broader left, the Ukrainian labour temple movement was linked but distinct.

Enormously successful, its array of cultural, social, and political activities served to establish the Ukrainian labour temple as one of the most popular and important working-class institutions in interwar Canada, encompassing impressive numbers of members and supporters, female and male, children and adult. By the beginning of the Second World War, the ULFTA counted some fifteen thousand members working in eighty-seven Ukrainian labour temples. Its two Ukrainian language newspapers reached more than twenty thousand subscribers, and Ukrainian-language dramas and concerts routinely played to full houses in its halls across the country.[20] The interwar years were truly a golden age for Ukrainian cultural and political radicalism in Canada.

Of course, not everyone supported the Ukrainian labour temple. As historians have documented for other politically polarized ethnic communities in Canada,[21] ideology fiercely divided Ukrainians. Many of those associated with the Ukrainian churches and other more conservative Ukrainian associations in Canada condemned the Ukrainian left, especially its cooperation with the CPC and support of the Soviet Union. Indeed, though the membership base was smaller in number compared to organized nationalist Ukrainians, the Ukrainian labour temples offered an important secular, Ukrainian-oriented, cultural alternative and access to radical political activism that might (for a host of reasons) have been otherwise inaccessible. Likewise, the Ukrainian leftists posed an important challenge to those purporting to represent the views of a monolithic Ukrainian community in Canada. While an extensive discussion about the relations of Ukrainian labour temple supporters with the wider Ukrainian community in Canada is beyond the scope of this study, relevant key episodes of divergent opinion and conflict will be highlighted.

The Canadian government also considered the Ukrainian left and its support of the Communist Party to be dangerous. As it did with other radical and leftist immigrant groups, the Royal Canadian Mounted Police (RCMP) kept the community under constant surveillance, seeking evidence to suppress its activities. The state also formally persecuted the movement's members at various junctures. As we shall see, the very real possibility of arrest, imprisonment, and deportation hung over many left-wing Ukrainians (even those without official connection to the CPC) for much of the twentieth century.

This book is organized both chronologically and thematically. It starts in the earliest years of mass Ukrainian migration to Canada from 1891. The first three chapters focus primarily on the interwar era but also comment on the Ukrainian left's origins and formation as a distinct community and political movement (the genesis of its fomentation lay in the experiences of the earliest migrants). These chapters examine the distinct, divergent, and disparate opportunities, experiences, and subjectivities of men, of women, and of children, respectively. The fourth chapter outlines the strategies employed by these Ukrainian leftists to challenge the extreme political repression faced by their community at the hands of the Canadian government during the Second World War. The final two chapters of the study explore the post-war Ukrainian left. The first compares and contrasts the experiences of multiple generations of adults, highlighting continuity and change in terms of gender roles, notions and expressions of Ukrainianness, and the effects of language and intergenerational conflict on the movement's form and longevity. As their experiences remained markedly divergent from those of adults in the post-war years, youngsters comprise the focus of the final chapter. The book's conclusion offers some remarks on activities from the 1980s to 1991, with brief commentary on the effect of the fall of the Soviet Union and the advent of an independent Ukraine. It also offers a few words on the movement's direction since those events.

Organizing the project in this fashion allows us to understand clearly the outcomes of the intersections of gender, class, ethnicity, age, and generational identities, how these were concurrently understood and performed, and how they changed over time in response to internal and external influences and challenges. It also facilitates a more nuanced understanding of the distinct experiences of female and male adherents, be they adults or youngsters. For the post-war years in particular, it helps to illustrate continuity and change in gender and ethnic identity, while underscoring the critical influence of generation and language in shaping the activism of members and supporters. The arrangement also facilitates a careful examination of the movement's overall history, permitting the highlighting of especially dynamic or difficult episodes.

This study uses a variety of sources. Among the most helpful have been the extensive and detailed records maintained by the RCMP on the movement, particularly its subsections, cultural groups, and contacts. A number of other sources have also proven valuable, particularly oral histories. Forty-two individuals generously agreed to interviews, all of whom were involved with various manifestations of the Ukrainian left during the previous century. Other key sources include several vast archival collections; two of the best being the Association of United Ukrainian Canadians (AUUC) Fonds and the Peter Krawchuk Fonds housed at Library and Archives Canada. Two uncatalogued collections – the Krawchuk Collection privately maintained by Larissa Stavroff in Toronto and the Association of United Ukrainian Canadians' holdings in Winnipeg, Manitoba – have also been useful. Rounding out the source base are newspapers and other publications (in Ukrainian and in English), as well as photographs, songs, plays, and artefacts. These sources bear witness to the rich and distinctive culture and history of the Ukrainian labour temple movement, to the tenacity, resourcefulness, and varied identities and experiences of its supporters, and to its enduring legacy as a key force in Canadian left-wing history.

1 "Sincerest Revolutionary Greetings": Men and the Interwar Ukrainian Left

Mathew Popovich was born into a peasant family in Galicia in 1890. His father was active in the Ukrainian Radical Party (URP). Influenced by this and the growing climate of revolt that was evident among peasants and workers, Popovich soon joined in the socialist struggle. While training as a teacher, he became a leader of a student socialist group. His reward for this activism was expulsion from two teacher seminaries. Undaunted, Popovich continued his work by helping to organize sports and cultural groups connected with the URP and by writing for several radical newspapers. He later returned to school, studying music in Lviv at the Ukrainian Conservatory of Music. Like many Ukrainian men seeking to avoid compulsory military service in the Austrian army, Popovich left the old country in 1910 for the United States. He moved to Canada in 1911, where he promptly became involved in the fledgling socialist movement, engaging with leftists of a variety of ethnicities but choosing to focus his activism primarily with Ukrainians. He demonstrated his aptitude for leadership by assisting in the development of a Ukrainian drama group and a choir and by teaching public speaking. In August of 1916 he took over as editor of the Ukrainian Social Democratic Party's (USDP's) newspaper *Robochyi narod* (Working people). In this position he helped to "Bolshevize" the movement, encouraging Ukrainian socialists in Canada to draw inspiration from the efforts of workers and peasants engaged in the Russian revolution. When the USDP decided to build a Ukrainian labour temple in Winnipeg to serve as its cultural and educational centre, Popovich became one of the project's most active boosters. Throughout the 1920s and 1930s he remained a committed supporter, editing newspapers, giving speeches, encouraging cultural activities, and at times fuelling controversy as one of the organization's most prominent leaders. In this vein he remained a key conduit between the Ukrainian left and the larger Canadian left – especially the CPC – within which these Ukrainians played a key role.[1]

William Stefiuk, also of peasant origins, came to Canada in 1926 at the age of twenty-four, entering the country under the government's Railways Agreement (1925–30), which brought in as many as fifty-five thousand of the seventy-eight thousand Ukrainians who journeyed to Canada between the wars.[2] Like so many other immigrants, he quickly made the transition from peasant to worker and came to understand labour exploitation first-hand as a farm hand, a railroad labourer, and, most notably, as a miner. For him, as for thousands of other immigrant workers, Canada was a disappointing and dangerous place. "I left Ukraine because of the conditions of life, but I never worked so hard there as I did [for the Manitoba and Saskatchewan Coal Mine Company] in Canada," he recounted. "I found the work so hard at first that I cried like a child."[3] In Estevan, Saskatchewan, on 6 September 1931, Stefiuk was among the multi-ethnic group of miners who struck in protest over wage cuts and difficult working conditions. As the efforts to mount a parade on 29 September degenerated into a confrontation with local authorities, Stefiuk witnessed the killing of three miners and injuries to many others when the RCMP opened fire on the demonstrators.[4]

What sustained Stefiuk and countless other Ukrainian men like him was involvement in the ULFTA, the national organization that arose out of the very labour temple that Popovich had helped to build. Stefiuk had joined the association upon his arrival in 1926. It offered a safe and welcoming space in which to express his Ukrainianness, and it facilitated inter-ethnic leftist collaboration around class issues. While the 1931 strike was ongoing, for example, Stefiuk had been particularly impressed with how the organization helped to unite the miners with local farmers from a variety of ethnic backgrounds; the farmers in turn demonstrated their support by donating food to the miners' families. As historian Stephen Endicott has noted, the local Ukrainian labour temple during that time actively supported the union movement, which was under the leadership of Anglo-Celtic workers and visiting organizers.[5]

Stefiuk's transitory working life meant that he sometimes had to employ novel means to remain active in the movement. When he and some friends were living in a remote railway camp in Saskatchewan, the closest site of ULFTA activity was a rented hall in Taylorton, a town located several miles down the tracks. As Stefiuk recalled, the men so enjoyed the social, cultural, and political opportunities afforded by the association that several evenings each week they travelled to the planned events by "borrowing" a handcar from the Canadian Pacific Railway and enthusiastically pumping it down the tracks, and back again afterwards. By using the tools of the company that exploited their labour, Stefiuk and his friends assisted in fuelling the growth of the interwar Ukrainian left (and, by association, the wider Canadian left). His support was ongoing; he read the movement's newspapers avidly, attended plays and concerts, and contributed to the ULFTA's efforts to aid the Ukrainians who were resisting Polish occupation in western Ukraine. In the town of Bienfait in 1934 he even volunteered to lay the floor of the new ULFTA hall in his preciously little spare time.[6]

Although they approached the movement from different vantage points, men like Popovich and Stefiuk were critical builders of the Ukrainian left. Disenfranchised as Ukrainians and as workers or agriculturalists in Canada, these men established their own bases of authority within the Ukrainian labour temples, participating in or leading a broad range of empowering political, social, and cultural activities. Influencing this involvement was a combination of radical politics and budding Ukrainian nationalism rooted in socialist ideals that challenged capitalism and offered exploited male workers and farmers a source of dignity in the face of oppression. Leaders attempted to mobilize male workers and farmers and their families into a political and cultural movement aimed at improving their lot in Canada and the lot of fellow travellers around the world. A concerted effort to link exploited Ukrainians in Canada to an international proletarian brotherhood, as well as a wider Ukrainian brotherhood, was an especially critical element of this activism.

While the men were also taking part in many of the same or parallel activities as those of the women, youth, and children in the movement, the outcome of the interaction of gender, class, and ethnicity during the interwar meant that men enjoyed the patriarchal dividend of far greater opportunities for expression, authority, advancement, and leadership. The Ukrainian left's masculine discourse viewed the class struggle, notions of labour, and activism through a distinctly male, breadwinner lens. Men's experiences as Ukrainians and workers or farmers in Canada were thus paramount in shaping gendered relations in the movement and the engagement of participants in the halls. The masculinist ideology that permeated the Ukrainian left's interwar gender order ensured men's privilege, while simultaneously naturalizing their domination of the movement.

Within this context, Popovich and Stefiuk's narratives illustrate the presence of multiple masculinities within the interwar Ukrainian left community, relational to each other, women, and other men and masculinities outside the Ukrainian left community. Specifically, two categories of masculinity were evident during the interwar years: *hegemonic* and *complicit*. Hegemonic masculinity's characteristics encompassed a selfless devotion to the cause, evidenced by robust interconnected political and cultural activism within the halls, with strong links to the CPC (particularly its upper echelons) – a key source of relational power within the halls. Leadership was a key trait involving the exhibition of bold, uncompromising, and even self-sacrificial behaviour as necessary. The behaviour of the ULFTA's higher-level leaders – like Popovich – corresponded most with the Ukrainian left's notions of hegemonic masculinity. Rank-and-file supporters like Stefiuk embodied a complicit masculinity, characterized by strong awareness of class, engagement in the class struggle – as articulated by the Ukrainian left – and active grass-roots participation in political and cultural activism within and without Ukrainian labour temples, as warranted.

Just as they were relational to one another, so too were notions of masculinity defined in dialogue with constructions of femininity within the movement. For example, recognition of the precariousness of Ukrainian men's working lives played an important role in shaping notions of complicit masculinity, particularly as it was defined in relation to Ukrainian leftist femininities. Uneven involvement at the halls and limited ties to the CPC, for example, were accepted and viewed not as male shortcomings but as a consequence and critique of the capitalist system against which the movement struggled. Ukrainian leftist women did not fare so well; failure to live up to male activist ideals resulted in stern judgment and often in application of the label "backwards," with no recognition of the triple burden of household, paid, and activist work that they bore as supporters of the movement – also a product of capitalism. In fact, men's ability to perform hegemonic or complicit masculinities depended upon women's unpaid and unacknowledged (or unappreciated) labour in the household and the hall, a sexist practice that drew on old-country models and found reinforcement in the dominant North American discourse on gender relations.

Concurrently, the masculinities of the Ukrainian left were articulated and performed in relation to those of other men. While they shared similar concerns for cultural expression and preservation, politics distinguished Ukrainian leftist men from other Ukrainian men and the masculinities they practised, particularly the nationalists who expressed their masculinity and cultural identities as Ukrainians in Canada through conservative, religious, and, at times, pro-fascist activities. Outside the Ukrainian communities, within and without the broader Canadian left in interwar Canada was underscored the simultaneity of Ukrainian leftist men's privilege and oppression. Within the Ukrainian labour temples, the patriarchal dividend enjoyed by these men advantaged and positioned them as marginalizers and oppressors. Outside, within the context of the CPC or Canadian society more broadly, the outcome of the interactions of gender, class, and ethnicity meant that they experienced a marginalized masculinity and subordinate status vis-à-vis Anglo-Celtic men. Indeed, the Ukrainian left's interwar masculinities, the manner in which they were embodied and performed, and the power and validation that these offered to men within the context of the halls were a critical response to ethnocentrism and class discrimination. Like other "ethnic radicals," most notably the Finns and the Jews in the Canadian context, these Ukrainians were not entirely insular, and they preferred to conduct their activism primarily through the Ukrainian labour temples. For them, this preference arose in significant part from the efforts of the male leadership to carefully guard the authority and status they enjoyed; they never hesitated to challenge the CPC and others (in a variety of ways) when ethnocentrism reared its head in its many forms.

The purpose of this chapter is twofold. As a contribution to the expanding historiography of gender studies applied to masculinity, the chapter builds particularly on feminist and gender histories of the immigrant working classes and ethnic left in Canada and in North America as a whole.[7] It examines those men who built the interwar Ukrainian left, illuminating the varied ways in which these differently located men understood, negotiated, expressed, and performed their interlocking masculine, ethnic, and class identities. It also considers how male notions of authority, agency, and privilege took shape in relation to the movement's female supporters and in relation to other men, particularly the Anglo-Celtic leaders who dominated the CPC. Concurrently, the chapter explores the development of the Ukrainian left in Canada as a distinct ethno-political movement, paying particular attention to its goals and activities as framed by its male participants in the 1920s and 1930s. It also highlights how its particular brand of "ethnic hall socialism" fit and engaged with the broader Canadian left and the international socialist struggle, especially as this played out through the ULFTA's often tumultuous links to the Communist Party of Canada.

Much valuable work exists on Ukrainian men in Canada, but significant gaps in our knowledge remain. Most studies of Ukrainians focus too narrowly on the activities of community leaders, for example. While historians have paid some attention to rank-and-file workers and settler farmers and to men's labour activism, they have focused almost entirely on workplace experiences and struggles. Rarely in these studies is the process of masculinity interrogated in relation to men's experiences.[8] Similarly, when the ULFTA has been the focus of enquiry, historians have shown an almost singular preoccupation with the interactions of its leadership with the CPC and the degree to which the party controlled ULFTA leaders and activities.[9] This has precluded a broader understanding of the heterogeneous character of men's individual and collective experiences and activities in the movement. Fortunately the recent spate of masculinity studies, including those in the field of labour history, offers us useful frameworks for assessing such diversity. Whether working from materialist or postmodern principles,[10] scholars have interrogated the fluid nature of masculinity (particularly its change over space and time) and have examined well the ways in which the complex intersection of masculinity with class and ethnicity has shaped men's and women's individual and collective experiences. Important insights about competing masculinities and male agency and power – over women, children, and other men – have emerged from these works.[11] Applying such insights to the Ukrainian left allows us to recognize and understand better the complexity of male experiences, especially the differences among men, and how these contributed to the shaping of models of femininity in the movement.

Canada's first wave of Ukrainian immigration, which included more than 170,000 people, coming primarily from Galicia and Bukovyna, took place between 1891 and 1914. During the first seventeen years most émigrés came as families and settled in homesteads on the Prairies. Poor job prospects, dwindling access to land, and compulsory military service had compelled their outmigration from the Ukraine while the possibility of employment and free agricultural land had enticed them to Canada. At that time, gender balance was the norm. However, the post-1907 years saw the arrival of more men than women; many of these men identified primarily as labourers, and most journeyed as individuals, leaving immediate family behind. Responding to Canada's need for workers to feed its rapidly developing resource and industrial sectors, some never intended to stay long but planned to return to the old country with an accumulation of cash. Fed up with toiling on land owned by wealthy landlords, many hoped to establish themselves back home as independent landowners.[12]

Once in Canada, some men found themselves on the Prairies; many others sought work in urban centres or resource communities in British Columbia, Ontario, and elsewhere in the east. They were joined in many cases by some of the offspring of the homesteaders. In cities they dug sewers and constructed roads, streetcar lines, and buildings; they worked as deliverymen, toiled in restaurants, and cleared snow. Elsewhere they mined, logged, or worked on the railroad. Typically the conditions under which they laboured were difficult, dangerous, poorly paid, and offered little in the way of job security. Instability characterized their livelihoods; most tramped across the country in order to piece together a living. Many employers took advantage of the men's vulnerability by cheating on wages or underpaying.[13]

There were few options for bettering their situation. Prior to the war some men responded by returning to the old country. Others remained in Canada but "voted with their feet" when labour conditions became unbearable, and sought jobs with other employers. In other cases, the men banded together – sometimes with other foreign workers – and staged spontaneous strikes. Many, especially prior to 1905, were uninterested in formal workplace organization because they viewed themselves not as lifelong workers but as farmers, only working for wages until they could establish their farms. Those who were open to unionization often encountered, as did other recent immigrant labourers, a cold welcome from workers and labour organizations that were already established in Canada. Linguistic, cultural, and ethnic differences, coupled with xenophobia, made labour solidarity difficult. Other factors, too, reinforced division. Being unskilled, many Ukrainians were automatically excluded from labour organizations such as the American Federation of Labor (AFL) and the Trades and Labor Congress (TLC), whose priority was the protection of skilled workers. Moreover, many Anglo-Celtic workers distrusted Ukrainian and other eastern and southern European workers because of the willingness of some to work for low wages and "scab" during strikes.[14] While it sometimes did exist, workplace solidarity between Ukrainian and Anglo-Celtic workers was difficult to achieve.

Thus, many Ukrainians looked instead to the Ukrainian immigrant community for support. Some turned for solace to religious organizations such as the fledgling Russian Orthodox Church or the Ukrainian Catholic Church. Others found the idea of church involvement distasteful, often because, like Wasyl Woloshyn, a railroad worker who arrived in Canada in 1929, they had developed anti-clerical attitudes as children in the old country. Woloshyn had had a negative experience with a priest when his father had died in 1919. Unsympathetic to the difficult conditions under which Woloshyn's family lived, the priest had refused to perform the service until he was convinced that they would pay his fee. "We were so poor, we had no bread at home. I'll remember this as long as I live," Woloshyn recalled. "The priest has had a good meal and asks me, a hungry boy, who would pay for my father's burial."[15] Political ideals brought from the old country also compelled others towards non-religious organizations. Northern Bukovyna and eastern Galicia, where many of these immigrants had grown up, were hotbeds of political radicalism, and socialist groups like the Ruthenian-Ukrainian Radical Party (1890) had taken hold. Politicized by their participation in such organizations, many of the men later brought these ideas with them to Canada.[16]

The simultaneity of these men's identities as workers and Ukrainians and their pre-migration engagement in left-wing politics encouraged the development of distinctly Ukrainian socialist activities on Canadian soil. By 1906 these had begun to take formal shape, led by a core group of male intelligentsia. Among the most prominent were Pavlo Krat and Myroslav Stechishin, both of whom had become politicized back home. In Winnipeg they founded the Shevchenko Educational Society, named for the celebrated nineteenth-century Ukrainian artist, poet, and literary icon Taras Shevchenko. Both Ukrainian progressives and nationalists alike held Shevchenko in the highest regard; much of his life's work was dedicated to challenging the tsarist social and cultural oppression of Ukrainians. The society met at the Taras Shevchenko Reading Hall, the latter modelled on Ukrainian village *chytalni* (reading rooms). Shortly thereafter the group expanded, affiliated with the Socialist Party of Canada (SPC) by founding the party's first Ukrainian branch in 1907, and started publishing a newspaper, *Chervonyi prapor* (Red flag), under Krat's editorship. Ten more Ukrainian party branches soon appeared. Financial constraints compelled *Chervonyi prapor* to fold in August 1908; however, *Robochyi narod* (Working people), which Stechishin edited, soon appeared to fill the void in the spring of 1909.[17] Besides newspapers and political activism, the Ukrainian SPC branches enriched the lives of their members with drama activities, choirs, and orchestras. These popular activities offered Ukrainian immigrants the opportunity to express their cultural heritage as they negotiated and attempted to challenge their labour exploitation.

Still, the early work of the Ukrainian socialist movement was limited, characterized by instability and internal conflict. Prior to 1912 the membership of the SPC's Ukrainian branches totalled only three hundred and fifty, mostly men who were working in mining. Clashes with the Anglo-Celtic leadership of the SPC over ideology and methods of activism saw eleven of the Ukrainian SPC branches unite as a new organization in May 1909, the Federation of Ukrainian Social Democrats of Canada (FUSD). The leaders began encouraging their members and supporters to collaborate with other leftists by joining the Industrial Workers of the World, a union typically receptive to unskilled workers because it advocated organization along class lines, rather than craft or skill. The FUSD eventually defected from the SPC, in the process helping to found the Social Democratic Party (SDP) in 1910, with *Robochyi narod* acting as the new party's official paper.[18] Reorganization did little to alleviate old problems, however; the infighting continued, and splits occurred. Stechishin quit in 1912 over alleged financial improprieties; around that time the federation's headquarters moved from Winnipeg to Montreal, and then back again. The party's name was changed yet again, this time to the Ukrainian Social Democratic Party (USDP) in 1914.

Despite these problems the USDP eventually gained some momentum. Expansion into eastern Canada in 1912 had increased support to eight hundred and twenty members in twenty-eight branches. The early years of the war truncated this success, however; countless Ukrainian men lost their jobs or were interned as enemy aliens, resulting in the decimation of many USDP branches. Fortunately circumstances soon improved. By 1916 the need for wartime workers saw the release of numerous internees, many of whom found permanent, well-paying industrial jobs. Concurrently, a young cohort of recently arrived radicals, among them Danylo Lobay, John Naviziwsky, and Mathew Popovich, began revitalizing the movement.[19] As they stabilized the USDP, they also began to lay the foundation for the direction that the movement would take at the end of the Great War. They fired Krat as editor of *Robochyi narod* and booted him out of the party in 1916. Popovich, now the newspaper's editor, along with others began successfully to move the party in a pro-Bolshevik direction. Response to the USDP became tremendous. By 1917 the party could claim a membership of fifteen hundred strong; *Robochyi narod*'s circulation totalled some three thousand subscribers.[20]

The end of the war in 1918 was a watershed period for Ukrainian socialists in Canada. On the world stage monumental events were unfolding.
The 1917 revolution in Russia had struck fear in the hearts of capitalists and government officials while stirring the optimism of those who
supported working-class empowerment and worker internationalism. In
Canada a combination of circumstances gave rise to the potential for similarly tumultuous action. Inflation was rampant, pressure mounted for
accountability of wartime profiteering, unemployment was widespread,
and increasing numbers of workers (employed and jobless) were turning
to unions and organized protest in an effort to better their opportunities, wages, and working conditions. Among labour activists optimism
abounded. Many believed a new world was dawning.

Inspired by these developments but also worried about government
suppression, the party leaders began to consider new ways of reaching
more Ukrainians in Canada. Understanding that popular cultural activities could further Ukrainian socialism in Canada, the USDP leadership
decided to create a national cultural and educational society to expand
existing cultural work and, they hoped, to appeal to a broader membership base. They thus incorporated the Ukrainian Labour Temple Association (ULTA) on 14 May 1918 as an entity autonomous from the USDP,
which by then enjoyed a membership of two thousand.[21] The organization, later renamed the Ukrainian Labour Farmer Temple Association
(ULFTA) in 1924, would become the central body around which radical
Ukrainians would organize. The activism of these Ukrainians was not
insignificant: "From 1907 to 1918," notes Ian McKay, "the Ukrainian
socialist movement had, through many splits and mergers, become one
of strongest left forces in the country."[22]

The foresight shown by Popovich and the others in creating the ULTA
narrowly saved many Ukrainian leftist activities from severe circum-
scription later that year. To curb the strength of labour and prevent the
growth of a revolutionary movement, Prime Minister Robert Borden's
coalition government exercised drastic measures restricting radical
labour groups and political parties, their activities, and their newspapers. Authorities paid particular attention to groups with a substantial
constituency of so-called enemy aliens, especially Ukrainians. On 25
September 1918 the government outlawed *Robochyi narod*. On 28 September they declared the USDP, along with numerous other radical
organizations, to be illegal.

Despite this enormous setback, plans continued for the construction
of a Ukrainian labour temple in Winnipeg, the first of its kind in Canada,

to act as the cultural and educational centre of Ukrainian socialism in Canada. Hundreds of Ukrainian women and men from across the country donated their labour and money to ensure the building's rapid construction. Among the men, contributions varied according to their position in the movement. Men like Popovich, as heads of the fledging enterprise, used their notoriety and speaking skills to generate interest in the project, raise money, and encourage the assistance of other men. For example, during construction Popovich and his wife, Lisa, embarked on a fund-raising tour of western Canada. The two shared the stage: he spoke about the important role that the hall would play in the community, offering a venue for the expression of Ukrainian culture and a haven where exploited labourers might regroup to better their circumstances in Canada; she then entertained the crowd by singing traditional Ukrainian songs. Despite their low and unreliable incomes, rank-and-file men responded to these calls for support as best they could. An immigrant from 1912 who had worked on the railroad, on farms, and in construction jobs across the country, Vasyl Karcha was toiling in the mines in Cobalt, Ontario, when he heard about the labour temple from USDP representatives who regularly came to his union meetings. "There were often speakers from Winnipeg, and in 1918 they told us that Ukrainian workers there were constructing a Ukrainian labour temple," he recalled. A long way from Winnipeg, Karcha found a way to pitch in: "Bricks were being sold at 25 cents apiece, [and] I bought one even though I did not fully understand what kind of activity was going to be held in that temple."[23] In Winnipeg, rank-and-file men responded to similar calls for support by acting as volunteer labourers on the project, digging the basement, laying bricks, and hauling lumber to bring the building rapidly to fruition.

By the following spring the Winnipeg Ukrainian labour temple was completed. Activist trial by fire soon ensued. The start of the Winnipeg General Strike on 15 May 1919 saw the hall become a key coordinating centre. From there organizers nurtured inter-ethnic solidarities and kept strikers from the city's diverse and immigrant-rich north end informed and engaged. That police raided the hall during the strike testifies to its importance. Its place in the strike further established the fundamental activist role that the Ukrainian left would play locally and nationally in the larger Canadian left community in the twentieth century.

Inside, political, cultural, and social activities proliferated. In the spring of 1919 organizers began issuing a new newspaper, *Ukrainski robitnychi visty* (Ukrainian labour news). By the mid-1920s the movement was publishing several newspapers – including some specifically geared to women, youth, and farmers – from the state-of-the-art production facilities of the Worker-Farmer Publishing Association (WFPA) housed in the basement of the Winnipeg Ukrainian Labour Temple.[24] At different times male leaders like Naviziwsky, Popovich, and Lobay, along with Matthew Shatulsky, Myroslav Irchan, and, in the 1930s, John Weir (Weviursky) and John Boyd (Boychuk), acted as managers and editors. Through the press the leaders spread the movement's ethno-political and theoretical discourse, instructed the membership in activist and cultural activities, and consolidated their own authority and the Ukrainian left's masculinist culture. In defining their role as male leaders – through which they articulated and performed Ukrainian leftist hegemonic masculinity – they also proscribed roles for the ULFTA's female and male supporters (hegemonic femininity and complicit masculinity) that were in keeping with the movement's larger objectives. They disseminated national and international labour news that helped readers to understand their individual and collective experiences within the larger class struggle. Rank-and-file members contributed to the growth of the press by subscribing to the newspapers, sharing them with co-workers and neighbours (and encouraging them to subscribe), and writing to the editors to laud the movement and share their experiences.

Beyond the rhetoric, the leaders, performing the vanguard role characteristic of the movement's hegemonic masculinity, also pushed the movement's growth by establishing support networks for workers who were facing the harsher realities of working-class life in Canada. In 1922 they created a mutual benefit society, the Workers Benevolent Association (WBA), which offered insurance and other financial services to help men provide for themselves and their families in times of injury or death. To assist aged Ukrainian workers and families in which one or both parents were deceased or too ill to care for their children, the WBA purchased a large estate on the outskirts of Winnipeg in 1927 and named it Parkdale Benevolent Home. Meant to house older workers and "the poor workers' orphans whose fathers' lives were sponged out by exploitation," the home was to be run in such a way that "the old age people would not feel that they [were] getting charity, and the orphans of workers would not be obligated to be taken care of by religious charity institutions."[25] Parkdale played a key role in the lives of ordinary men, underscoring the importance of women's unpaid caring labour and the devastating impact of its absence on working-class families. Several of the children in the orphanage had lost a mother only, but their father's need to work meant that no one was at home to care for them. Men who were unable to return to the old country, were too ill, aged, or injured to work, and had no family support also turned to Parkdale. In the leaders' rhetoric, Parkdale's men and children were held up as martyrs whose circumstances reflected not some personal shortcoming but rather the flawed and exploitative capitalist system under which they had been forced to toil.

During the early 1920s the leaders also continued to work to strengthen the movement's ties with, and help build, the larger Canadian left, which was a key source of their relational power with other men and women within the Ukrainian labour temples. On 23 May 1921, Popovich and Naviziwsky were among the twenty-two delegates present in Fred Farley's Guelph (Ontario) barn when the Workers Party of Canada (later renamed the Communist Party of Canada) was formed. The ethnic hall socialists organized into separate language federations within the new party; the Ukrainians, like the Finns (the other majority group), enjoyed significant autonomy and embraced the party's "united front" strategy. The party helped to connect the Ukrainian left with personalities, organizations, and opportunities in the Soviet Union, consolidating the Ukrainian leaders' own credentials as dedicated revolutionaries who were helping to define the activism of the Workers Party as part of a larger national and international labour struggle and brotherhood. The leaders emphasized this broader significance to members through their speeches, newspapers, and activities in the halls. Relations with outside socialist groups were often cooperative. While maintaining their autonomy as distinct socio-cultural entities, they frequently staged joint activities, shared resources, and promoted and attended one another's events. In many localities the Ukrainian labour temples opened their doors to the CPC and other progressive ethnic organizations when they needed large venues for their events. Likewise, the ULFTA's print shop assisted with the final production of the newspapers and periodicals of many similarly minded organizations. Inter-ethnic interactions were not always cordial, however, particularly with the Anglo-Celtic party leaders. As we shall see, the ULFTA leaders would become embroiled in major feuds and power struggles with "Anglo" party leaders over the ULFTA's major activist strength for attracting supporters, its Ukrainianness.

The initiatives and networking efforts of the ULFTA leaders, along with the positive attention that the organization's popular cultural and social activities attracted, helped fuel the movement's rapid national expansion. The ongoing interest and involvement of the rank-and-file men, their attendance at events, their volunteer labour, and their cash outlays were critical to this growth. Such responses clearly speak to the positive meaning that men derived from their participation in the movement. It validated their experiences. It combined hope for change (and a map to it, in the form of Marxist-Leninist ideology) with concrete political and cultural activism. In 1922, Karcha, now in Timmins, volunteered his labour to help build that town's hall. Shortly afterwards, he explained, "Labour Temples in northern Ontario sprang up like mushrooms after a rain – in Kirkland Lake, South Porcupine, Ansonville, and Rouyn, Quebec."[26] Ukrainian labour temples and ULTA branches emerged in the Prairies, British Columbia, Quebec, southern Ontario, and Cape Breton – in short, wherever large communities of Ukrainian workers or farmers existed. In many localities the presence of the ULTA helped to cement the growing divide between the Ukrainian left – or "progressives" as they came to identify themselves – and the religious, right-wing "nationalist" Ukrainians. The desire of some groups' members to affiliate with the ULTA led to schisms within many *chytalni* and other cultural groups. "After the 1917 revolution in Russia, there was a sharp division in the Ivan Kotlyarevsky Drama Society: some were of one thought, others of another," recalled member Fedir Hordienko of the split Winnipeg group. Consequently, he explained, "many of its members transferred to the dramatic group of the Ukrainian labour temple," himself included.[27]

Conflict did little to stall the movement's growth, however. By 1923 the organization counted three Ukrainian farmer temples and twenty-three Ukrainian labour temples. The ULFTA's 1925 national convention welcomed delegates from fifty-eight different communities across Canada. This number increased to seventy-one in 1927. By that time, forty-six halls had been established. The men's branches had more than 2,200 members. The circulation of *Ukrainski robitnychi visty* had also grown, to 8,700 subscribers, and then to 10,000 by 1929.[28]

As the discrepancy between subscriber numbers and membership numbers suggests, not all men could be active in the halls in the same way or to the same degree. Livelihood was perhaps the most critical factor that shaped involvement. Here we note a critical difference between the rank-and-file men and the ULFTA leaders. Not surprisingly, men who worked at the national leadership level had the easiest time, particularly since their jobs frequently offered rewards in addition to wages; typical of this group was the easy embodiment of hegemonic masculinity and its concurrent pay-offs and risks. For men like Popovich,

Naviziwsky, and Shatulsky, their positions in the ULFTA and their roles as conduits to the wider Canadian left offered notoriety, extraordinary educational opportunities, and the chance to travel throughout Canada and occasionally to the Soviet Union and Ukraine. They also set the movement's agenda and shaped its ideological imperatives.[29] Such perks, however, were not without their price. These men typically worked long hours, and the most prominent among them faced frequent state harassment and risked incarceration for their activism, especially because of their open ties to the CPC. Popovich and John Boychuk, for example, were among the nine CPC activists arrested and charged for unlawful assembly, unlawful association, and sedition under section 98 of the Criminal Code in 1931. Convicted, both did time in Kingston Penitentiary.[30] Still, even in this capacity the men continued to serve the cause as martyrs and self-sacrificing male role models, acting (as the men and children of Parkdale did) as symbols of the injustice inherent in the capitalist system.

Men at the grass-roots level could find involvement seamless if they too worked for the movement, their actions being aligned with the embodiment of complicit masculinity. There were positions available in the press, teaching at the halls, or as labourers in ULFTA's various business enterprises. Ironically, the working conditions were often little better than in other jobs, characterized as they were by difficult working conditions, long hours, and poor pay. The Ukrainian left's masculine discourse and ideological bent helped to render these positions more palatable, however. For many of these men the knowledge that they were working for a cause larger than themselves, and one whose success could improve conditions for all Ukrainians and other labourers, helped them to endure these difficulties. They could take pride in themselves as men in the fact that, in a sense, they were working for themselves as workers. The movement celebrated them as committed activists and cultural role models. For many of them such feelings of satisfaction more than made up for the low wages and long hours of work.

After completing a ULFTA leadership course in 1936, John Alexiewich was hired by the movement to be a travelling newspaper agent and was given sixty-five dollars to buy a horse, buggy, and harness. "After [buying] the first two," he recounted, "there wasn't enough money left for the harness. I rode horseback for two weeks until I earned enough money to buy a harness, using thin rope for reins." Since his earnings were meagre, he relied on ULFTA supporters for help: "I did not receive a salary, only commission from the sale of newspapers and literature. There were days when I did not earn a cent, but the good will of the people I met, be they of varying character or beliefs, kept me and my horse fed." Alexiewich laboured from the fall to the spring, working on the harvest during the summer to supplement his meagre earnings."[31] For single men like him, with few responsibilities except to themselves, such devotion to the cause was easier to demonstrate. Nonetheless, many married men toiled with similar dedication, sometimes to the detriment of their familial relationships. This behaviour, too, was very much in keeping with the Ukrainian left's discourse of manly self-sacrifice, a point of occasional overlap between the hegemonic and the complicit masculinities evident in the movement. Such was Nick Mateychuk's experience. He worked as a milkman for six days a week at the People's Cooperative Dairy (which the ULFTA founded in Winnipeg in 1928), with only Tuesdays off. "When he worked," explained his wife, Kalyna, "he would get up at two in the morning and come home at four in the afternoon," which interfered with his participation in family activities. On occasion she would attend a wedding with him, but otherwise they rarely did much together because after work "all he wanted to do when he got home was eat and go to sleep." Mateychuk's children hardly saw their father. Nonetheless, he remained devoted to the cause to the end of his life. As he lay dying in hospital, he underscored his belief in the movement. "I would sit by him," Kalyna recounted, "and he would ask me why I wasn't at the hall since they needed me there."[32]

Less physically arduous but similarly demanding, particularly in terms of self-sacrifice, was the more common experience of the paid cultural teacher. Although a handful of women served as teachers, the job was primarily defined as a male occupation within the movement. In the 1930s Kosty Kostaniuk taught at the hall in Fort William, Ontario, where he worked seven days a week. "Concerts were on Sunday," he recalled, which involved much preparation: "I had to write my own or scrounge around to find music. We didn't have copiers, so I had to make copies by hand – there was a lot of work just to get an orchestra ready." This came in addition to his other duties: "I taught Ukrainian school or choir at night, and during the day I would teach English." Kostaniuk worked year round for the organization in Fort William, receiving only forty dollars a month for his efforts because, as he explained, "that was all they could afford."[33] High job satisfaction sustained him, especially since he found that "the young people got along well together and wanted to play."[34] There were other potential pay-offs. Jobs as cultural teachers offered key opportunities to gain valuable organizational experience, make contacts, develop a strong reputation as a dedicated activist, and participate actively and visibly in the movement – all of which could aid immensely the rank-and-file men who had leadership ambitions. Kostaniuk himself followed such a career trajectory and went on to become an important national figure in the movement after the Second World War.

Within the ULFTA some of the most active men were the unemployed. Lacking paid labour to fill their time, many spent their days at the Ukrainian labour temple. "We had a large male membership because of unemployment," Peter Spichka recalled of the rural Saskatchewan Ukrainian labour temple where he was a member during the 1930s.[35] Joblessness also built the hall in Sudbury, where, according to Dmytro Slobodian, "Myron Kostaniuk was chairman of our branch, and I was financial secretary, looking after the 'finances' that we did not have ... Both of us worked on the building project because we were both currently unemployed."[36] Ivan Kyfiuk pitched in, too, along with a generous carpenter, recounted Kosty Kostaniuk: "Three of us worked for nothing, and the carpenter was paid 50 cents an hour, but he donated many hours of work to the building."[37] As an alternative to idleness, the work they accomplished around the halls was an important source of pride that validated their sense of manhood in spite of their unemployment. Like other situations in the movement, this labour offered them opportunities to be role models of dedicated activists. It also allowed them to perform their masculinity through physical labour for a meaningful project, one designed to directly combat the unemployment they were experiencing and other problems they faced as Ukrainian men in Canada.

Most rank-and-file men made their living outside the ULFTA, however. This could make regular participation difficult and even create setbacks for the organization, especially when valued men had to relocate to find work. The activities of the Vegreville (Alberta) ULFTA Youth Section slowed during the summer of 1927 when its leader left the area to find work as a miner.[38] Seasonal work also made consistent participation difficult. Activity ceased during harvest season in many rural communities as farmers necessarily turned their attention to ripened crops. The harvest also drew men from halls in the city. "A great many of the Ukrainian Labor Temple members have left for the harvest and there is only a very little group left," reported an RCMP informant in August of 1921.[39] But even men unaffected by seasonal labour markets could find regular participation difficult. Born in Canada in 1915, Mike Skrynyk was an active member of the Winnipeg ULFTA Youth Section and wrote a sports column for the ULFTA newspaper *Svit molodi* (The youth's world). In 1936 things changed when at the age of twenty-four he found a job at Swift's Abattoir in Winnipeg. Working an average of seventy to eighty hours per week, he ceased participating apart from paying dues, reading organizational newspapers, and attending the occasional event. After retirement he joined the senior citizens' choir at the Winnipeg Ukrainian labour temple.[40]

Most men tried to find ways to balance their working lives (or search for work) with ULFTA involvement. Sometimes this could be tricky. While the ULFTA leaders advocated and demonstrated conspicuous support for the association, many Ukrainian men who were employed elsewhere found it necessary to hide their ULFTA allegiances at work. Employers were often quick to dismiss those presumed to harbour radical ties and have a penchant for unionization. Myron Kostaniuk experienced this first-hand in Sudbury. "In 1929 we started to organize a union of miners and smelter workers at INCO," he recalled. "They retaliated by sending spies into the union and into our Ukrainian Labour-Farmer Temple Association." Men who belonged to the ULFTA and WBA were fired, and "none were asked if he had a family or other means for a living."[41] Within the movement, political discourse, ideological objectives, and constructions of notions of manliness accounted for the firings, helping many of these men to cope with such difficulties by validating their experiences and explaining their difficulties as the product of a failed and unfair economic system. Their respectability as men, despite unemployment, thus remained solidly intact, a key characteristic of complicit masculinity within the Ukrainian left. Like other Ukrainian leftist men elsewhere, they acted simultaneously as martyrs and as role models by engaging openly in the class struggle despite potential threats to their livelihoods; their experiences served as a rallying point to draw others to the movement. These circumstances underscore the process of masculinity within the Ukrainian left, constructed as it was in relation to other men, in this case owners, bosses, spies, and other union busters. Kostaniuk's comments, for example, highlight the perceived lack of honour among this cohort of men whose actions denied other men not only dignity and a workplace free of exploitation but also the means through which to support their dependents.

The ULFTA's connection with the CPC, too, could generate vitriol on the shop floor – and not only from the bosses. Within the workplace many rank-and-file men had to negotiate their way carefully around divisions in the labour movement. Skyrnyk was active in the union at Swift's, serving as president and chief steward, but "kept [his] politics a secret at work" because "the spirit in most places was anti–[Ukrainian] labour temple. If you belonged to the labour temple, you were automatically communist, and many unions didn't approve of communists holding office."[42] In the face of such unwelcoming circumstances, many ordinary Ukrainian men performed their activism differently in the workplace than they did at the hall.

Within the halls Ukrainian-language cultural activities were particularly popular with men, and these were the sites of important opportunities for overt displays of hegemonic and complicit masculinities. Leaders infused cultural activity with radical political content and often incorporated a class analysis to explain the experiences of Ukrainians in Canada and elsewhere. Cultural activities alleviated homesickness, offered examples of positive male role models (underscoring key notions of hegemonic masculine ideals), and empowered men by keeping them linked to the class struggle in Canada and around the world. While some men participated by attending cultural performances at the halls, others actively joined the choirs and orchestras and other cultural endeavours.

Drama was a particularly important activity for some members because it allowed an individual man who was far from the upper echelons of the movement to make a significant impact on his comrades, most notably as an actor performing in front of capacity crowds hungry for Ukrainian-language entertainment. The stage was a key site where Ukrainian leftist masculinity was constructed and performed; the movement's specific masculinist culture was reinforced – and that of opposing groups was called out. On stage, men could literally act out the Ukrainian leftist masculine ideal by playing powerful and decisive characters who stood up for workers and other marginalized folk or who set up for ridicule and condemnation the bourgeoisie, bosses, nobles, priests, and other adversaries. In the friendly space of the Ukrainian labour temples such displays of radical manliness enjoyed unanimous support, giving the men who acted them a celebrated status as strong male role models. This could help to compensate exploited workers who otherwise found their sense of manhood under assault. In the workplace and in the public spaces they occupied as picketers during a strike or as demonstrators protesting injustices, Ukrainian men were exposed to various dangers and subjected to humiliation, unemployment, arrest, violence, and even deportation. In contrast to the reality of their daily experiences, acting gave them a chance to play heroic roles, bring to life the workers' dreams of a better world on the Ukrainian labour temple stage, and hopefully inspire others to action.

An indication of the enormous positive meaning that these men derived from their cultural role as actors is the great lengths to which many went in order to perform in the labour temple's theatrical productions. Some found ingenious ways of balancing their demanding workweek with their responsibilities as actors. A leading actor on the Winnipeg Ukrainian labour temple stage, Fedir Hordienko, for example, always managed to learn his lines and be available for rehearsals and performances despite his work schedule. "I was often given a difficult and important role with only a week to prepare it," he explained. "I then learned to be cunning at work, putting a piece of iron on the melting pot where it would heat up for 20 minutes, during which time I was able to study my role."[43] By doing so, Hordienko, in a sense, subverted the conditions of his employment to aid the class struggle.

As vocal boosters of cultural groups and activities at the halls and in the press, the ULTA and ULFTA leaders well understood the power of Ukrainian cultural activities – and drama in particular – to attract and politicize supporters. "In a long speech [Mathew Popovich] pointed out the importance of the proletariat to have its own musical dramatic circles, in order to inspire the working masses ... gaining members for the ULTA," reported an RCMP informant of a 1923 meeting at the Winnipeg hall. Popovich saw these activities as key – and entertaining – means to raise class-consciousness: "He pointed out that this helps to tear away the people from church going and from going to shows which the capitalists are supporting in order to occupy the minds of the working masses with nonsense."[44] Plays were also accessible, engaging, and, at times, emotional venues for introducing and explaining complex political and theoretical issues to audience members who had different levels of education, literacy, and even commitment to the class struggle. Furthermore, some leaders, including Popovich and Matthew Shatulsky, also wrote, produced, and acted in plays, at times modifying the content of existing works to fit the movement's activist priorities.[45] In 1919 the ULTA staged *John Tohobochny – Visionary Combatant*, a play about a widow and her two sons, one representing the proletariat, the other the capitalists. In addition to playing one of the sons, Shatulsky had translated the play from its original Russian into Ukrainian, even rewriting much of the piece (alleged an RCMP informant) "to suit the modern Bolshevik spirit."[46]

A particularly key figure in these drama circles was Myroslav Irchan; although he was a leader and a press editor, his playwriting and other theatrical work were perhaps his most significant contribution to the movement. Shortly after his arrival in Winnipeg from Prague in October 1923, the Ukrainian labour temple in Winnipeg presented Irchan's play *The Twelve*. It told the story of twelve Galician revolutionaries, among them Petro Sheremeta and Stepan Melnychuk, who had been executed for their part in the attacks on Polish landowners in Galicia during the First World War.[47] The sold-out play was extremely well received. At its conclusion the audience showered Irchan "with much applause," reported an RCMP informant, adding that it "lasted about 15 minutes, and broke out again at intervals."[48] In the months that followed, Irchan worked to raise the performance standards of the Ukrainian labour temple in Winnipeg. According to Hordienko, "Irchan organized a Workers Theatre Studio where we were taught acting, make up and costuming as well as the history of theatre ... The lectures at the Workers Theatre Studio," he added, "were of great help to the group. We were just ordinary people, not highly educated, but we loved the theatre."[49]

Across the country these cultural efforts were extremely popular and thus drew positive attention to the ULFTA. Since they also provided a critical source of revenue, the theatre offered to the men involved a real opportunity to help raise vast sums of money. The Winnipeg hall had performances nearly every week, and because it was filled to capacity early, people had to be turned away at the door.[50] Some halls took their shows on the road. Speaking of Sudbury, Slobodian recalled that, "having prepared a play, we presented it in our hall, then toured the near-by communities like Creighton Mine, Levack Mine, Coniston, and others ... I was sent to ahead to sell tickets," he added, "and during intermissions in the play, M. Hucaliuk appealed for donations to help pay the debt on the Labour Temple." In this manner they managed to pay the fifteen thousand dollars owing on the Sudbury labour temple within two years of construction, raising as much as three hundred dollars on a single occasion.[51]

Considering the amount of money at stake, acting was a position of great responsibility, whether one was a leader or a rank-and-file member. Actors, therefore, had to take their participation seriously. Hordienko went to extraordinary lengths one evening to demonstrate his commitment to the cause. He was set to play the leading character in a play about the eighteenth-century Ukrainian "Robin Hood," Oleksa Dovbush, when his wife went into labour. Instead of accompanying her to the hospital, he went to the hall. "I had to go on the stage for we never had understudies like professional theatres have," he explained. His wife's condition worsened during the course of the performance: "I went out on the stage, and they brought me the news that my wife was practically near death and that there were two doctors by her side." Convinced that a cancellation would mean a significant financial loss for the ULFTA, he asked rhetorically, "How could I have broken off the play and not appeared on the stage?" Hordienko was not the only man who demonstrated his dedication to the movement by putting its needs ahead of his own and those of his wife. Fortunately the evening turned out well – and not only for the labour temple's fiscal health; Hordienko's wife pulled through and successfully delivered a son at one in the morning.[52]

The gendered division of activism, and the ways in which it privileged men, was evident throughout the Ukrainian left. Nowhere was the masculinist culture of the movement more evident than in the ULFTA branches. Many (though certainly not all) men were active through a formal membership in a local ULFTA branch, and since these were dominated by men and exhibited a homo-social male culture, they were often called the "men's branch." Separate women's, children's, and youth branches also existed at the local level. However, it was the men's branch that enjoyed male privilege and dominant status; it oversaw and expected to control all facets of the local Ukrainian labour temple, directing and coordinating much of the activity that occurred therein. Organizers usually held bi-weekly executive and monthly membership meetings to plan events, discuss organizational matters, and elect executive members.[53] These typically reflected male-defined priorities, activist models, and values. Bolstering the actions were the regularly scheduled lectures called "educationals," which took place as part of the membership meetings and reinforced messages that were espoused elsewhere by the movement's intelligentsia. The educationals focused on key political issues, framed through a Marxist-Leninist lens that was designed to refine the men's radical activist identities and promote ongoing and exuberant participation in the class struggle.[54]

The structure of the ULFTA branch at the local level underscored and reinforced the masculinist ideology prevalent in the movement, subordinating the activism of the women and youngsters while supporting the power and privilege of the men at their expense. All of the other local branches, including the women's branch and children's branch, were expected to send representatives to the ULFTA branch's meetings in order to summarize and sometimes justify their activities. In many halls men from the ULFTA branch regularly attended the meetings of the women's branch and the children's branch, in some cases acting in a leadership capacity. In 1927, for example, the second issue of *Svit molodi* explained that the men were at their meetings "to teach members how to conduct meetings, organize concerts, socials, picnics, performances, how to read newspapers, magazines, books, how to present lectures, make speeches and how to behave within and outside the organization." In addition, the paper concluded, "they are to facilitate and help resolve matters in discussion," emphasizing that "their directives should be obeyed."[55] Even in some smaller localities where the membership of the men's branch was not solely male, a strict gendered division of labour existed. The women participants typically carried out activities reflecting traditional feminine domestic roles while the men led the branch, managing administrative or educational activities. The ways in which women and youngsters routinely acted to challenge and subvert this male authority is discussed in the following two chapters.

Significantly, participation in the men's branch afforded rank-and-file men a route through which they could pursue leadership positions if they so wished, an opportunity that was not extended to women. When the Point Douglas branch held a meeting in 1938 to plan for the building of the neighbourhood's first Ukrainian labour temple, those present elected a branch executive committee, a hall librarian, and a wardrobe master – all of them men.[56] Most men wishing to hold such positions could be accommodated, even those with limited formal education. Joe Sekundiak was heavily involved in the Veregin, Saskatchewan, branch. "I could not read," he explained, "so they made me chair of the meetings."[57] Branch activity offered men a possible route to provincial or national leadership opportunities in the ULFTA as well, because each branch routinely elected delegates for provincial and national conventions. Only at the Winnipeg Ukrainian labour temple, the ULFTA's national headquarters, could rank-and-file men have a more challenging time attaining these positions, a circumstance that highlights the power disparities evident among different men in the movement. There, as an RCMP report explained in 1922, "all of the management and work of the Association depends upon the local executive, which consists of [national leaders] Popowich, Kolisnyk, Shatulsky, Naviziwsky, and [unnamed man]. Ordinary men stay outside of everything unless they are asked to do something."[58]

For many men, involvement in the men's branch also functioned as a conduit to the larger Canadian radical left, specifically through the Communist Party of Canada. Ties with the CPC informed the politicized brand of Ukrainianness that was present in the labour temples' activities and supported the Ukrainian left's masculinist orientation, acting as an important source of men's relational power within the halls. Many of the ULFTA leaders were also CPC leaders, serving in executive positions at the national, provincial, and local levels. They performed their politics in a variety of ways, integrating them, as we have seen, into cultural activities and newspaper articles. Their didactic and fiery Ukrainian speeches attempted to raise class-consciousness and spur action. The rhetoric employed by these men illustrates how their construction of a certain kind of capitalist masculinity helped them to shape notions of masculinity back at the halls. "I wonder who benefits by whom?" Shatulsky asked an audience at a meeting at the Winnipeg hall in 1933, adding, "Put the Capitalist out on a secluded island with all his heaps of gold, and without the workers' toil he will die like a fly in winter. You will see how much the Capitalist will produce with his brain and gold, without the workers' sweat." Having framed wealthy elites as parasitic insects and called them out for their lack of physical strength and stamina, Shatulsky continued to highlight their avarice: "Who gives, and takes more? The Capitalist ... If it was possible they would monopolize sunshine and air and tax you workers for enjoying it."[59]

By underscoring working men's precarious position under capitalism, but simultaneously reminding them of their imposing individual and collective strength, Shatulsky and other leaders promoted a politicized gender ideal that was rooted in the workplace, the party, and the hall. The radical atmosphere nurtured by the leaders at the Ukrainian labour temples and in the press combined with the men's own experiences of exploitation and their resentment over Canada's pro-capitalist political and social values. This led many rank-and-file men to respond to the leaders' proscriptions and support the CPC. Some followed the leaders and took out formal party memberships. Many others, however, were cautious. Some who were interested in joining the party shied away out of a fear of deportation (a reasonable fear, particularly during the 1930s), police persecution, and job loss. In any case, notions of both hegemonic and complicit masculinities in the movement shaped and validated these behavioural and activist choices.

Sufficiently compelled by their individual and collective experiences with unemployment and economic hardship, rank-and-file men nevertheless found other ways to lend their support in the class struggle outside the party. One of the most important methods was supporting party candidates for public office. The ULFTA's male leaders were active components of the CPC election machine. In Winnipeg during civic elections the party assigned John Naviziwsky "the task of the organization of the campaign, especially in Ward Three (North Winnipeg)," where, "beginning in 1926, the Communist Party almost regularly elected its representatives to the city council."[60] Many of these leaders also stood as candidates, further intensifying the support that ULFTA members might offer the party. Rank-and-file Ukrainian men played important roles as boosters and voters. The first communist elected in North America, in fact, came out of the Ukrainian labour temple in Winnipeg. William Kolisnyk served two terms as a city alderman from 1926 to 1930.[61] In addition, many of the protests and causes in which the ULFTA supporters took part complemented or were coordinated in tandem with the CPC and related radical groups. Men from the ULFTA worked with other leftists to support the Canadian Labour Defence League (CLDL) in championing the cause of the CPC leaders – including Boychuk and Popovich – who were incarcerated in Ontario in 1931. They also supported the Workers Unity League (WUL) and the Farmers Unity League (FUL), joined anti-deportation efforts, took part in the 1935 On-to-Ottawa Trek, and protested Quebec's 1937 Padlock Law.[62]

These party connections, however, did not automatically mean that the ULFTA lent wholesale, unquestioning, or unified support to the CPC and the Communist International (Comintern) directives. For much of the history of the ULFTA, and especially during the interwar years, its leaders sought to work with the CPC while also actively resisting the party's repeated attempts to dictate Ukrainian labour temple activities. In ways that echoed the actions of mainstream Canadian gatekeepers and institutions, the CPC and its leaders tried to assimilate Ukrainian party supporters, pushing them towards English language work and Anglo-Celtic methods of organization, political expression, and values. Although politically radical, the CPC engaged in ethnocentric behaviour and reinforced ethnic hierarchies that were evident elsewhere in Canadian society. Like other contemporary "ethnic" radicals, these Ukrainians guarded the autonomy of their halls and their right to determine the nature of the activities carried out there. The ULFTA's Ukrainian cultural activities were a frequent target of criticism. In response, the Ukrainians, though willing to compromise and cooperate on other issues, consistently resisted total party control and worked hard to maintain their autonomy and cultural direction as an independent cohort within the larger Canadian left.

Fortunately for the ULFTA its leaders were in a strong position to stand up to the party. Owing to the organization's numerical strength, extensive network of halls, financial resources, and long-standing political tradition – and the commitment of its large base of support to guarding the independence of the Ukrainian labour temples – the Ukrainians were able to enjoy a place of relative power in relation to party authorities. Thus, the ULFTA managed to maintain its own distinct agenda, which, though in sympathy with the party, often diverged from CPC priorities. The party had to tolerate this defiance because it was dependent on the support that the Ukrainians and other ethnic hall socialist groups were able and willing to provide. The association's difficult relationship with the CPC is best characterized by a mix of negotiation and uneasy resistance rather than complacency, and its political activism did not blindly mimic but instead paralleled (to varying degrees) that of the party.

Relations began well enough with the founding of the CPC in 1921, at which time the Ukrainian party supporters, like the Finns, formed a separate and semi-autonomous language federation within the organization. Cracks, however, soon became apparent, often around issues of respect. "I beg to report that considerable dis-satisfaction exists among the Ukrainian members of the Communist Party in the Winnipeg district," indicated an RCMP informant in 1922 who had infiltrated a CPC pre-convention gathering at which Popovich and Naviziwsky had argued that their group warranted greater consideration by the party's central executive committee. "Navis stated they had about 130 dues paying members in the Winnipeg area," reported the informant, "and that as there was no English speaking group organized, more attention must be paid to the Ukrainians, as otherwise the movement would die out in the district."[63]

Threats to their autonomy also compelled the Ukrainian leaders to react. In 1924 the Comintern initiated its campaign of "Bolshevization," which called for, among other things, the dissolution of the language federations, thereby further straining relations with supporters from the ethnic halls. The Ukrainians and Finns opposed the change with some success (though not without a fight) largely because of the tremendous human and financial resources that they brought to the party. The Anglo-Celtic leaders simply did not have what these groups possessed, namely "hundreds of followers, printing presses, flourishing weeklies, and buildings."[64]

The political wrangling between the CPC and the ULFTA leaders continued into the late 1920s' "Third Period," when the association faced increased condemnation from party hierarchy. In 1928 the Comintern, now controlled by Stalin, predicted that the West was about to enter a third period of political and economic collapse. Insisting that communists had "veered dangerously toward reformism," Stalin directed them "to reinstate a revolutionary political praxis."[65] A year later, the Comintern instructed the CPC to adopt an organizational structure in which "the primacy of the English language" and a focus on "occupational and not cultural groups" were assured.[66] "It was expected," observes Kolasky, "that Ukrainian workers would abandon their language groups and commit themselves to the activities of the newly formed CPC industrial unions."[67] When they failed to comply, the party leadership disparaged the ULFTA and its activities for being inherently conservative and nationalist and accused its members in the CPC of being "right-wing deviationists," engaged in Ukrainian cultural activities that distracted Ukrainians from "real" activism. At the Ukrainian labour temples the party directives fell on deaf ears, however. Numerous individuals even abandoned the party in protest.[68] Those who remained stood up for the ULFTA. As Peter Krawchuk explains, "they pointed out that Ukrainian Communists, for their part, were putting in a great deal of effort to building the party, while the leaders of the party were neglecting the recruitment of Anglo-Saxon workers." Mathew Popovich and others were quick to suggest "that the party's CEC would be better advised to give greater attention to winning over Anglo-Saxon workers instead of rebuking Ukrainian communists for not displaying 'greater activity' in recruiting party members from among Ukrainian workers in Canada."[69] When the party's politburo sent the ULFTA leaders a letter condemning their alleged lax involvement in the class struggle, the Ukrainians rejected the document. Normally such behaviour would have resulted in immediate expulsion from the party, but with the Ukrainians making up a third of the CPC's overall membership, party leaders were forced to compromise and tolerate some of this resistance.[70]

Despite this ongoing power struggle ULFTA leaders who were also party members remained staunchly committed communists. They could disagree with the party or its leaders and challenge party policy, but they nonetheless did what they could to integrate many party initiatives into the programs of the ULFTA and its associated groups without upsetting the overall functioning of its cultural and organizational work. It was a delicate balancing act that was once again tested in 1931 when, in response to the Comintern directive to adopt "a turn to the path of general revolutionary struggle,"[71] the CPC pushed the ULFTA to further radicalize and Bolshevize all its activities. The association's leaders were more receptive to this directive because of the great suffering caused by the Depression and because they, like many other radicals, believed the worsening economic situation signalled an impending break-down of the capitalist order. They thus tried to accommodate the "turn" by advocating, among other measures, a further radicalization of existing cultural work. "All the bourgeois-urban trash, both in plays and songs, should be thrown out from our labour-farmer stage," Matthew Shatulsky implored at that year's ULFTA convention, emphasizing that the organization's choirs, orchestras, and drama groups must all take part in the turn as "real shock-troop activists [performing] art in the service of the proletariat!"[72] To adhere to such a program was not difficult for many of the association's cultural groups who had long been doing this kind of work.

It was easier still to embrace the priorities of the mid-1930s Popular Front with its increased emphasis on social and cultural activities as a means to raise awareness and develop alliances in the name of fighting the rise of global fascism. The ULFTA enthusiastically supported the Popular Front because its emphasis on neighbourhood- and community-based activism dovetailed with the work that progressive Ukrainians had always embraced. One of the most dramatic ways in which many young rank-and-file men showed support was by volunteering to fight General Franco's fascist forces in the Spanish Civil War (1936–9). They went as members of the International Brigade's Mackenzie-Papineau Division, but, as Wier recalled, they also Ukrainianized their participation by forming their own company "named after Taras Shevchenko."[73] By 1938, it was estimated that more than two hundred Ukrainian leftists were fighting in Spain.[74] Approximately one hundred of these men would die in the conflict.[75]

Scholars have offered a number of arguments to try to account for the actions of the Ukrainian leaders in the CPC who resisted the party directives that were aimed at undermining Ukrainian autonomy. Some have argued that men like Popovich and Shatulsky, in opposing the party, were seeking to protect their own authority and power as leaders of the ULFTA and its related organizations. Others have shown that the ULFTA's failure to embrace the party line – particularly in its calls for Ukrainians to take out formal membership in the CPC – was related to their fears of arrest and even deportation. A rejection of the party leaders' ethnocentric attitudes has also been cited as a source of the Ukrainian left's resentment of the party.[76] All these perspectives are valid, but the analysis is incomplete. What scholars have underestimated is the pressure that the Ukrainian leaders faced from the movement's base of members and supporters. When developing programs or policy, the leaders had to be mindful of the interests and concerns of the association's constituents, who would oppose the dissolution of a cultural mandate as well as the integration of its members into the CPC. For them, the separate space of the Ukrainian labour temple was key to their activism. The party failed to appreciate that the Ukrainians embraced a "communism" that was simultaneously a cultural and a political movement, one that combined the priorities of Ukrainian cultural preservation and expression with a Marxist-Leninist political philosophy. This is not surprising given that other ethnic hall socialists did the same, including Finns and Jews. About Jewish socialists in Toronto Ruth Frager has shown that "class consciousness and ethnic identity reinforced each other and intensified the commitment to radical social change." Most Jews, she notes, "had been radicalized not only in response to class oppression but also in response to the oppression they faced as Jews."[77] ULFTA members and supporters were not simply part of the working classes in Canada but *Ukrainian* members of the Canadian working classes and thus experienced a dual oppression as workers and as foreigners. There was a critical Canadian component to their identity, and their Canadian experiences informed a distinct brand of class-consciousness and socio-political resistance.

When trying to satisfy both party officials and ULFTA supporters, Ukrainian leaders often found themselves stuck in between a rock and a hard place. Sometimes they could reach a compromise; at other times they found themselves on the receiving end of challenges and even open revolt. For many leaders, their sense of masculinity (and the hegemonic masculinity on which it was grounded) was in part contingent upon party loyalty and the respect of party leaders. Their predicament reflected in part the success of those rank-and-file members who were opposed to party affiliation and were maintaining a distance between the movement and the CPC. Owing to language differences and discrimination, virtually no other political options existed for radical Ukrainian men who did not want to associate with the party. Disgruntled men simply stayed away from party work, choosing to express their activism through other activities at the Ukrainian labour temple. But some men reacted differently, particularly if they suspected that the leaders of the ULFTA and of the party were being deceptive. Such instances gave rise to break-away factions that threatened the credibility and support of both organizations.

By far the most serious threat to the ULFTA and its leadership arose around 1934 when Danylo Lobay, a long-time ULFTA editor and administrator, began questioning the ULFTA and CPC's account of contemporary events in the Soviet Union and Soviet Ukraine.[78] Lobay's concerns reflected broader currents of dissidence emerging elsewhere in radical circles during the 1930s. As news of Stalin's efforts at "dekulakization and collectivization,"[79] generally poor conditions in the Soviet Union, and the 1932–3 Ukrainian famine began to trickle in to Canada and ULFTA circles, many, including Lobay, began to challenge the organizations' interpretations (or denials) of these events. Both groups quickly expelled him and his supporters. Lobay responded by publishing pamphlets and later a newspaper, *Pravda* (Truth), in which he condemned the ULFTA leadership for alleged corruption; he also continued his assault on their account of Soviet conditions.[80]

A particularly damning topic emphasized by Lobay and his supporters was the disappearance of two beloved ULFTA leaders in the Soviet purges. Myroslav Irchan had returned to Ukraine in 1929 to continue his efforts for the workers' cause there, and ULFTA teacher Ivan Sembay was deported to Soviet Ukraine in 1932 after being arrested by the RCMP for "revolutionary activity."[81] Both were imprisoned in the Soviet Union for questioning the political authorities. In 1934, word began to trickle back that the two had been detained as counter-revolutionaries and been given prison sentences. According to an RCMP observer, "the news has spread among the Ukrainians here, and at the Ukrainian labour temple the common members are very bewildered, not knowing what to think."[82] The situation escalated when the news reached Canada that Sembay had died in prison.[83]

The ULFTA, continuing to support the party and Comintern's explanation of the events, became the focus of controversy. Support grew for the "Lobayists." ULFTA membership numbers, which had risen to 8,838 in 1935, began to fall, dropping to 4,415 by 1937.[84] During this time, worried that the organization was vulnerable to takeover, the leaders in 1935 cancelled the 1936 annual convention, claiming there was an urgent need to devote organizational energies instead to a higher educational course to train much needed teachers and organizers that year.[85]

In their efforts to spin the Lobay imbroglio in a number of ways, the leaders drew on the constructions of Ukrainian leftist masculinity that stressed their superiority to bourgeois men and supposedly inferior men. Their arguments in turn reinforced particular elements of the movement's hegemonic masculine discourse, in this case, loyalty to the party and adherence to the party line. The leaders continued to support the official Soviet account that Irchan and Sembay had come to Canada as counter-revolutionaries. "They were here as traitors and we, trusting them in all good faith, like comrades, we popularized them and recommended them when they returned to the USSR, so that they were taken in and entrusted with important duties," Naviziwsky told an audience at the Ukrainian labour temple in Winnipeg in 1935. He continued, saying that after they had been apprehended, "the authorities were really very lenient with them" and sentenced them to hard labour to atone for their offences. "Sembay could not bear all this," explained Naviziwsky, suggesting Sembay was effeminate and too cowardly to face the consequences of his actions: "He committed suicide and it may be better for him that he chose that." In this scenario Irchan's behaviour defied a benevolent Soviet state that was willing to forgive in the face of contrition. The playwright, Naviziwsky indicated, "was given a chance to work with his pen, helping to build up socialism, and at the very last it was proposed to him that he change his mind and become loyal, but he refused. Now he must help build Socialism with the shovel."[86]

Lobay was also written off as a counter-revolutionary. At a meeting held on 4 February 1936 in Winnipeg an unnamed speaker delivered a lecture on "how to fight against counter-revolutionary elements" and condemned Lobay "for working against the revolutionary proletariat, against the Soviet regime and for cooperating with the Ukrainian Nationalists."[87] On other occasions the ULFTA leaders labelled Lobay a Trotskyite,[88] favourably comparing his and his supporters' expulsions from the ULFTA and the party to the purges in the Soviet Union – a necessary bump on the revolutionary road. "Such ills will remain unavoidable until the last remnants of decaying capitalism are completely swept out of existence," indicated Naviziwsky and Matthew Shatulsky during a January 1937 address at the Winnipeg labour temple.[89] In discrediting Lobay, the ULFTA leaders also used the episode to link the organization to the larger international revolutionary struggle. The campaign rehabilitated the ULFTA to the extent that by 1938 its total membership had swelled to over fifteen thousand, an all-time high.[90]

Over the course of its twenty-year history in early-twentieth-century Canada the ULFTA developed into a sanctuary for countless Ukrainians. For men, in particular, it channelled their deep-seated fears and resentment over unemployment, under-employment, labour exploitation, workplace humiliation, danger, ethnocentrism, and unfulfilled expectations into a class-based analysis rooted in Marxist-Leninism that validated their experiences and offered them collective tools with which to battle ethnic and economic discrimination. The movement assured them that their dire circumstances arose not from personal shortcomings but from an unjust capitalistic system that thrived on class exploitation and ethnic prejudice. The Ukrainian labour temples mounted a variety of practical engaging and empowering activities geared towards helping these men to adjust to and challenge the difficult conditions they encountered in Canada. By defining their Ukrainianness as a source of both oppression and strength, the movement shaped an activist strategy that attracted members and offered men a source of personal meaning and validity.

From within the Ukrainian left emerged two key categories of masculinity. Hegemonic masculinity within the movement reflected the priorities, proscriptions, desires, and behaviour of the movement's intelligentsia. It was centred in engagement in ULFTA leadership, a strong commitment to the CPC and the class struggle, and a solid dedication to Ukrainian cultural activism. The men who most embraced and embodied these characteristics acted daily in myriad capacities: as newspaper editors, travelling organizers, orators, cultural teachers, and/or as liaisons with the party and the broader Canadian left. Their work could also extend to other forms of labour activism, including union organization and workplace agency. While these positions offered considerable opportunities, they also presented considerable risks, including arrest, incarceration, and even deportation.

Rank-and-file men negotiated and adopted, to varying degrees, aspects of this hegemonic masculinity, depending on their individual and collective interests and socio-economic circumstances; as a result their embodiment of a complicit masculinity was shaped not only by the movement's discourse but also by their personal interests, abilities, and priorities. Although they may have concurred with the leaders' emphasis upon intellectual engagement and full-time political commitment to the movement, their own engagement was typically circumscribed by long working hours, low wages, remote work locations, or lack of access to ULFTA activities. As such, the masculinity of these

Ukrainian leftists was rooted in and validated by an engagement with cultural activities and grass-roots political activism. These men did not hold prominent, public positions in the movement, but they were nevertheless committed members who participated in a variety of cultural, social, and political activities – on the stage, at meetings, on the picket line, in the workplace, on the street, and at home.

However, while these men may have performed a subordinate masculinity in relation to that of the leadership, they were by no means disadvantaged compared to other supporters of the movement. The patriarchal dividend resulting from the movement's masculinist culture ensured that all men enjoyed advantage – in terms of real or potential power – vis-à-vis women and children in the interwar Ukrainian left. As we shall see in the next two chapters, this authority did not go unchallenged.

2 Raising Funds and Class-Consciousness: Women and the Interwar Ukrainian Left

Anna Mokry, Teklia Chaban, and the rest of the Edmonton ULFTA women's section walked at the very front of the 19 December 1932 Hunger March of the Unemployed in Edmonton. The Workers Unity League and the Farmers Unity League, Communist Party groups with which the Ukrainian left was well acquainted, had organized the event, much to the frustration of Mayor Dan Knott. Seeking to quash the protest, Knott called in the police, whose appearance marked a bloody turn. "The savage enraged police charged into our ranks with their horses. They beat us and trampled us underfoot," Mokry recalled. "The police twisted my arm so hard that it bothers me to this day," Chaban recounted some decades later.

Mokry and Chaban followed a similar route to their leftist activism, choosing to express it not through a membership or close association with the CPC and its women's activities (as their Anglo-Celtic counterparts did) but through the Ukrainian Labour Farmer Temple Association. Their limited English-language skills would have made such CPC ties challenging, as would the ethnocentrism so prevalent within many predominantly English-speaking leftist organizations. Instead, a desire to engage as activists within a Ukrainian language and culturally centred milieu drew them towards the Ukrainian labour temples.

Chaban's and Mokry's journeys to the hall were common, shared by countless women who came to be involved with the ULFTA. Both Chaban and Mokry were born in the area now called western Ukraine, in 1893 and 1895 respectively. Neither had the opportunity to attend school. Both made their way alone to Canada at the age of nineteen, settled in Edmonton, and found employment. Mokry worked first in restaurants, later in a laundry, and eventually in a cigar factory, and

Chaban toiled as a domestic for a boarding-house keeper. They both married miners and became housewives in Cardiff, Alberta. Finding it difficult to make ends meet on her husband's inconsistent wages, Chaban baked and sold bread, did laundry for single miners, and supplemented the family's income in other ways. "For five years I hauled coal in a hand-drawn sled so as not to have to pay delivery charges," she said. "I did everything I could to help out so that we would have enough to live on."

Politicized by these experiences, both found themselves attracted to the Ukrainian left's earliest manifestations, taking part in reading societies, choirs, and theatrical productions. They eventually helped to found the ULTA women's section in 1922 – Chaban, the branch in Cardiff, and Mokry, the branch in Edmonton, where she and her husband had by then relocated (and to which Chaban would transfer in 1924). Most of their activities centred on the Ukrainian labour temple where the women raised money, cooked for conventions, and participated in Ukrainian cultural endeavours and in political activism. "We began to observe International Women's Day, held public meetings, conducted campaigns, and had well-known speakers deliver lectures," Mokry recalled. The women found their work challenging at times, she confessed, since "we had to provide leadership to other women when we ourselves were limited in our knowledge of such things." Experiences like the hunger march strengthened their commitment to the ULFTA. "By being a member of the organization, my belief in victory was confirmed," Mokry later explained, "that is, in the victory of the truth of labour over the evil of the exploiters."[1]

This chapter offers an analysis of the women, like Mokry and Chaban, who helped to build, nurture, and maintain the dynamic cultural world of Ukrainian Canadian radicalism during the interwar decades. Like the men, they were active participants in cultural, social, and political activities, including drama, the choir, the orchestra, socials, banquets, parties, political rallies, and strike support. Like other women (radical or otherwise), they performed seemingly invisible but critical roles that ensured the movement's financial, organizational, cultural, and political survival. They expressed their activism through what some have called "support" work: they raised money, cooked food, and took care of other duties that were an extension of their domestic roles at home. Like their menfolk – and often with children in tow – they walked picket lines, marched in May Day rallies, and participated in other demonstrations, peaceful and violent.

The particular location of these women at specific intersections of gender, class, and ethnicity meant that their opportunities and experiences were shaped, and differed, in key ways from those of their menfolk. As the previous chapter illustrates, men held virtually all ULFTA leadership positions and were among the most visible and celebrated supporters. Although rank-and-file men might hold lower-level positions similar to those of women, constructions of masculinities grounded in intersections with class and ethnicity – and the resulting patriarchal dividend payout – facilitated a context of opportunity benefiting all men but inaccessible to women. Notions of hegemonic femininity – shaped by male discourse and reinforced in social practice – were the crucial underpinning of the gender order. Women, for example, were expected to carry out all necessary "support" work around the halls (cooking, cleaning, and fund-raising) usually through active women's branch membership. They were to embody and exhibit strong class-consciousness, be self-sacrificing, and ideally style themselves after Soviet heroines. Likewise, they were tasked with youngsters' activities, as an extension of their domestic responsibilities to raise good, class-conscious children. At the same time they were expected to engage in intense cultural-political activism on par with that of the men and in keeping with a male-defined activist model.

The sum of these parts equalled an impossible standard of femininity for women to meet. It was fundamental to ensuring women's subordination, which was reinforced and maintained through the ongoing discourse that framed and critiqued women as less capable, less dedicated, and even less intelligent activists than were the men. Many of the women's support activities were trivialized, despite their essentiality in sustaining the movement and the men's work. Men often disparaged these women's efforts because they were less visible – mirroring women's traditional undervalued and unpaid household and reproductive labour. Likewise, virtually no credit was given for the impact that the triple burden of household, movement, and, for many women, paid labour had on their ability to be active. There were simply not enough hours in the day to meet expectations. The resulting gender order, then, served multiple concurrent functions – defining, circumscribing, and devaluing women's activism in the movement while reinforcing male hegemony. As we shall see, however, these Ukrainian women strategically negotiated the gendered parameters and masculinist culture of the interwar Ukrainian left. In doing so, they performed an oppositional femininity. They assumed aspects of hegemonic femininity that made sense, while challenging, rejecting, or reshaping the components that failed to resonate with their sensibilities, lived realities, desires, interests, and abilities.

Their responses were evident in a number of ways. To be sure, there never emerged during the interwar Ukrainian left a formal analysis of their distinct experiences of oppression as immigrant, working-class, Ukrainian women in Canada more broadly and within the movement in particular. Their actions, however, often stood as direct and indirect rejoinders to inequity. Occasionally, for example, they responded to men's policing of their activism by calling out these men for offensive behaviour and unfair criticism. Usually they simply manoeuvred and exercised agency by developing and carefully guarding spaces for autonomy where they could carry out their activism on their own terms, rejecting male prescripts and directives that failed to speak to their preferred means of activism and their distinct experiences of inequality and oppression as immigrant, Ukrainian, working-class or farm women. For most, from day to day this meant a centring of their activism around support activities, and, in doing so, these women played a critical role in building and sustaining the movement in ways that the men did not. Their embodiment of or resistance to notions of hegemonic femininity – and masculinity – was thus carefully measured, reflecting the complex processes of power and inequality.

As an outcome of the interaction of gender, class, and ethnicity in interwar Canada, the notions of Ukrainian leftist hegemonic femininity, and women's responses to it in the oppositional femininity they practised, were shaped in relation to a number of factors, most notably Ukrainian leftist masculinities. Male dominance, predicated on peasant village values, reinforced male privilege by stressing female inferiority. In the old country, as Francis Swyripa explains, women "were essential to the functioning of the family as the basic unity of production, yet they were regarded as inferior beings subject to the authority of their menfolk."[2] Although forced to endure difficult social and economic circumstances themselves, men had nonetheless enjoyed an elevated status over women. This social and political culture would be, in many ways, replicated and adapted to the circumstances that these immigrants encountered and the communities and organizations that they created in Canada. This being the case, it is important, however, that we not fall into the ethnocentric trap of viewing these women as the victims of a culture that was supposedly much more deeply patriarchal than the Anglo-Celtic culture and hence the Anglo-Canadian left. Indeed, the

Anglo-Canadian left was a hotbed of sexism, which served to validate similar patterns within the Ukrainian left in Canada.

Within the movement the proscribed and embodied notions of femininity paralleled and were shaped in relation to those of other women. "A lack of self-confidence, inexperience in meeting procedures, and fear of speaking in public" limited many immigrant Finnish women socialists, for example.[3] So too was it for Ukrainian women, a situation exacerbated by male dominance and the women's own high levels of illiteracy. Language was, for many women, an insurmountable barrier. The Ukrainian left maintained close affiliations with other radical organizations, including the CPC, that firmly situated the ULFTA as a key player in the wider Canadian left. Most of the Ukrainian women, however, often because they could not speak, read, or write English well (if at all), preferred to centre their activism, leisure, and especially their child-rearing within the ULFTA, particularly its women's section. Like other ethnicized women, few joined the party, and, given the particular work carried out by these women, the Comintern and CPC directives did little to influence their activism. Their concern for Ukrainian cultural expression and preservation most set the ULFTA women apart from other socialist women. For these women, as for their nationalist Ukrainian counterparts, Ukrainian cultural expression provided comfort, a sense of belonging, and a connection to the old country. Unlike nationalist Ukrainian women whose political bent leaned to the right, however, women like Chaban and Mokry combined their cultural work inextricably with radical political activism.

With some important and notable exceptions,[4] we know relatively little about Ukrainian women because most studies of Ukrainians in Canada have tended to emphasize male experiences of work, religion, and institutions.[5] What we do know about women is still somewhat limited. Most studies have focused on men's directives or criticism of women, proscribed gender roles, and the broader organizational structures within the nationalist progressive divide as it affected Ukrainian women in particular. Similarly, studies on women in the CPC tend to focus primarily on Anglo-Celtic women activists, there being few Ukrainian women in the party, and therefore tell us very little about them.[6] Historians of Italian, east European Jewish, Mexican, Latin American, and other militants in North America have produced multigenerational portraits of female militants whose radical lives were rooted within a deeply felt ethnic left-wing culture in which family, neighbourhood, community, and cultural ties overlapped with politics and ideology.[7]

These women often functioned within a rough and tough female radical culture in which street protests and labour militancy were normal and acceptable components of family and community life and completely consistent with women's identities as respectable wives, daughters, and mothers.[8] Such experiences parallel those of leftist Ukrainian women like Chaban and Mokry, in terms of both gendered discourse and practice. An in-depth discussion of the outcomes of the interactions of gender, class, and ethnicity in the lives of the women involved with the Ukrainian left is long overdue. This chapter examines the women themselves, their recorded activities and experiences, and, when possible, their personal recollections in order to understand how they negotiated and shaped the Ukrainian left according to their own needs and interests and in the process embraced, rejected, and reshaped proscriptions of feminine behaviour and activism.

During the early years of Ukrainian migration to Canada (1891–1905) most female migrants, like their male counterparts, came as part of family units and then homesteaded. With their arrival in the new land, and usually being ensconced on homesteads, illiterate, and unable to speak English, these women experienced isolation and a continued marginal status within the community.[9] In the years that followed, until the advent of the Great War quelled immigration, more female migrants arrived in Canada. Many women travelled on their own, with the explicit intention of finding work as labourers. Typically, along with their daughters and countless women of other ethnicities, they toiled in difficult, low-paying, low-status work (often in urban environments) as waitresses, domestic servants, or factory workers.[10] For many, this waged labour tended to end upon marriage because countless Ukrainian men seemed to feel that "working wives lowered their status" as husbands,[11] a sentiment echoed by men of other ethnicities in Canada. Much of a Ukrainian woman's adult life therefore would be centred around difficult, unpaid, labour-intensive domestic toil for her family, work that was crucial to stretching the household income garnered through the sale of farm produce (if the family had a homestead), revenue from boarders, or wages of male family members. As the majority of Ukrainian women were unpaid workers in the immigrant household, the face of Ukrainian labour – defined by consistent (or consistent attempts to find) waged work – tended to be envisioned as male.

Many of these women, like many Ukrainian men, were radicalized by the difficult and exploitative working and social conditions and other realities of working-class or farm life encountered in Canada, as

Chaban and Mokry's stories demonstrate. Other female émigrés, like their male counterparts, arrived with predisposed socialist sympathies thanks to the radical political or anti-clerical currents manifest in the regions where they had formerly lived. Such was the case for Mary Slobodyn, who arrived in 1914. "I already held progressive views when I came to Canada. My father had been a radical in the old country," she explained. "I completely disassociated myself from the church when I came to Canada because I felt drawn to progressive-minded people." By 1916 she was active in the socialist Society for Self-Enlightenment in Edmonton, where she took part in plays and concerts.[12] Across the country, in communities large and small, rural and urban, countless women did the same: supporting the Ukrainian Social Democratic Party, taking part in *chytalni* (reading halls), subscribing to the Ukrainian left's newspaper *Robochyi narod* (Working people), and participating in other manifestations of early Ukrainian radical activism. When the ULTA was founded in 1918, these women played important roles in the movement's rapid development. Many did so as members of existing halls that affiliated with the new national organization, while others bolstered the ULTA by helping to build new Ukrainian labour temples.

By the early 1920s much of their activism had become concentrated around the ULTA's women's branch, an entity with origins in a 1921 old-country crisis. That year drought and crop failure created famine conditions affecting parts of Russia, southern Ukraine, and the Volga regions of Eastern Europe.[13] The ULTA responded to calls for aid by organizing a committee of women members into the Ukrainian women's unit of the Famine Relief Committee. Maria Vynohradova took part in Winnipeg. After she had come to Canada in 1912, she had encountered poor working conditions and pay as a waitress and a bakery worker. She had her first exposure to the Ukrainian left through *Robochyi narod*, which she would read to an illiterate friend who brought it to her home. She helped at the construction site of the Winnipeg Ukrainian labour temple and later attended its cultural functions. In response to the 1921 famine, that fall she and the forty-nine other committee members went door to door to collect funds and textile goods to send overseas. They found it difficult; few women possessed outside fund-raising experience, and language was a constant barrier. "In order to cover the territory quickly, we went singly instead of in pairs," Vynohradova explained. "This was very difficult, especially when people asked questions ... None of us could speak English well."[14] In Winnipeg and elsewhere the women's committees also held concerts and lectures to support famine relief, raising some impressive sums.[15] By 1923, for example, the Timmins, Ontario, women had managed to raise six thousand dollars.[16]

This success marked a major turning point in women's activity. "At the conclusion of the campaign," Vynohradova reported, "the men saw that the women were capable of doing important work in the organization." The women began clamouring for a formal women's group, an idea to which the male leadership was receptive. Concurrently, the CPC had begun organizing women's labour leagues in 1922 to educate women and encourage their participation in the class struggle. The Ukrainian leaders saw an opportunity to channel the Ukrainian women's energies in similar educational directions, while keeping their labour focused on serving the needs of the Ukrainian left. As a reserve army of fund-raisers the women could deal with the movement's chronic debt, the costs of newspaper publishing and hall upkeep, and the leaders' travel expenses for promotional tours and meetings. The *Zhinocha sektsiya* or *Zhinsektsiya* (Section of Working Women, later renamed the Women's Section) was born on 1 March 1922 at the ULTA's annual convention in Winnipeg. There fifty-two women signed on as members; those in other communities quickly followed suit.[17]

To provide national leadership, address the needs of fledgling branches, and maintain a sense of uniformity, the central executive committee (CEC) of the ULTA soon created a central women's committee (CWC) based in Winnipeg.[18] The CWC offered one of the only routes to national leadership for women. Katherine Stefanitsky came to Canada in 1914, settled in Toronto, found work as a waitress, and soon became involved with the USDP. She married John Stefanitsky in 1915, supporting him emotionally, if not financially, while he endured state persecution in 1917 and 1918 for his USDP activities. Both became founding members of the ULTA in Toronto, and she, along with some forty other women, initiated a branch of the Women's Section there in September 1922. After taking a short hiatus to look after her young daughter, she became active again and was soon elected to the provincial women's committee. In 1928 she toured southern Ontario and organized new women's branches in Brantford, Welland, and several other communities. The following year, at the request of the CWC and the CEC of the ULFTA, she toured women's branches in north-western Ontario and Manitoba. "My task was to explain the decisions and resolutions of the [1929 ULFTA] convention and help the members of the branches draw up plans to carry out these decisions," she said.[19] Throughout the Depression Katherine Stefanitsky was a regular speaker at a variety of events.

At a meeting at the Winnipeg hall in 1937 she spoke for thirty minutes, urging those present to support the ULFTA's annual fund-raising campaign. "In her short address she [pointed] out the important and leading role which this organization is playing in the struggle for the workers' cause," an RCMP informant reported. She enumerated several key activities: "strikes, hunger marches, ... establishing kitchens to feed the workers, helping many other organizations and above all developing a great educational and cultural progress on a larger scale than any other national organization."[20]

At the local level during the early years of the Women's Section, the ULFTA male leaders attempted to direct the branch's work, making it a key site where one can note the assertion of, and women's resistance to, male authority and masculinist ideology. Founding member of the Winnipeg women's branch Mary Naviziwsky recalled the complicated and sometimes difficult relationship that the women had with these male advisers. She explained that initially "a member of the Men's Branch attended the meetings ... of the Women's Section. His task was to instruct us how to conduct meetings and to advise us in other matters."[21] Her branch's first instructor was William Panchuk, and, according to Naviziwsky, "he was a good teacher," as were "other advisers who also helped us a good deal."[22] But there were also "some persons who, in fact, were 'dictators' and ordered us around."[23] She and the other women did not appreciate this treatment and pushed back: "We decided that we no longer needed an instructor because we knew how to run our organization by ourselves."[24]

The ULFTA organizers also used other means to attempt to influence women's activism. In 1923 they began publishing a women's monthly newspaper called *Holos robitnytsi* (Voice of working women). The following year they shortened its name to *Robitnytsia* (Working woman), concurrently increasing its frequency to twice monthly. Its purpose was multifold. For potential supporters who lived in communities that were too small or isolated to sustain women's sections of their own, the organizers meant *Robitnytsia* to function as a surrogate branch. *Robitnytsia* was an important site for the communication and reinforcement of notions of hegemonic femininity, the justification of male dominance of the movement, and the policing of women's behaviour. The newspaper's editors, who were always male, geared much content towards politicizing the women, offering a basic political education in Marxist-Leninism, outlining the role that women were to play in supporting their male comrades, and encouraging their active involvement in the international proletarian struggle, especially the CPC. Many male leaders believed that women needed special educational assistance in this regard, that women were inherently conservative; some even went so far as to suggest that women were "backward." Deep-seated beliefs in female inferiority, and the women's own lack of formal education, fuelled these perceptions.[25] Also included often were articles on Soviet Russia, especially as they related to the lives of women. Improvements allegedly brought about by the revolution were emphasized to encourage women to follow the example of their Soviet sisters and to work for such change in Canada. To draw women in, the editors structured the paper's content to appeal to a broad audience and included material reflective of the wide scope of activities of the ULFTA as well as those of specific interest to women. *Robitnytsia* regularly included articles, poems, and graphics related to Ukrainian culture, literature, and tradition and frequently included news from the regions making up today's Ukraine.[26] The newspaper was also an important source of local organizational news; it routinely highlighted conferences, conventions, local controversies, and special events. Child-rearing advice, recipes, and other topics related to women's domestic role in the working-class home also enjoyed a central place in *Robitnytsia*.[27]

The women heartily embraced *Robitnytsia* and made important contributions to the newspaper, often by making their presence known through articles or letters to the editor. As the editors instructed, many branches elected *robkorky* (press correspondents), some of whom were prolific reporters, raising awareness of the women's activities and concerns.[28] Many lauded the paper for its educational, organizational, and political significance. "I believe *Robitnytsia* will lead the way for us out of this misery," wrote the *robkorka* of the Leniuk (Alberta) Section of Working Women in 1924.[29] The women supported the paper in other ways as well. Many sold *Robitnytsia* door to door. The women's branches took part in an annual fund-raising drive, held in March to coincide with International Women's Day.[30]

Women's activity blossomed because of the efforts of the women themselves, *Robitnytsia*, the central women's committee, and the Section of Working Women. The arrival of new women émigrés during the 1920s further enhanced this growth. Only one year after the inauguration of the Women's Section, women had formed some twenty-eight branches across the country, with membership totalling 600. By 1925 the Women's Section counted over 1,000 members; by 1928 fifty-two branches existed, with a membership of 1,335. In 1929 *Robitnytsia* could count 6,500 subscribers. This level of women's interest remained steady throughout the 1930s.[31]

The women used their separate branches to define their own work, picking and choosing activities that most appealed to them and spoke to their experiences as Ukrainian working-class or farm women, and discarding or reworking those that did not. Often these choices coincided comfortably with constructions of hegemonic femininity and the male leaders' ideas of appropriate women's activism. Work with children was one such area. Interestingly, men's roles as fathers contributed little to the ways in which masculinities were constructed within the Ukrainian left. Like other pockets of Canadian society, the ULFTA and the peasant culture whence these Ukrainian immigrants had come defined as a female responsibility the youngsters' education, both at home and at the Ukrainian labour temples. Notions of hegemonic femininity dictated that women were to be self-sacrificing and focus their personal and organizational energies on the sacred responsibility they possessed to raise a generation of class-conscious children. In the press and speeches at concerts or meetings the male leaders often reinforced these attitudes about femininity, implicitly legitimizing hegemonic masculinity and male privilege and power in the movement. At a 1924 concert organized by the Working Women's branch in Winnipeg, Manitoba, Matthew Shatulsky spoke in these terms by using examples from the life and death of Lenin: "When people came to mourn after Lenin, before the palace where his body was laying in state, Lenin's mother and wife went out, and speaking to the people told them not to mourn, but to continue Lenin's work." Their behaviour, Shatulsky added, "shows the courage of a revolutionary woman, who is left alone in the world and whose children gave their lives for the proletariat." In closing he emphasized, "We cannot expect a revolutionary generation if the women will stay away from the organization."[32]

Although it acknowledged women's importance in the struggle, Shatulsky's commentary clearly reinforced gendered notions of women's role and place. The ideal woman thus devoted her energies to ensuring that her children were equipped with the proper tools to take up the struggle of their fathers in the international proletarian movement. Robitnytsia's structure and practice reinforced this. In addition to articles on child-rearing, the newspaper included a children's section during its early years of publication, further centring children's activities within the female purview. In most localities the leaders encouraged women (especially mothers of young children) to undertake work with the children in the ULFTA "junior section", which typically included teaching Ukrainian language, dance, drama, and song.[33] Many women enthusiastically embraced this activism and the opportunities it entailed for leadership. However, the responsibility could be a double-edge sword as women's behaviour was carefully policed. When the Youth Section failed to achieve the desired membership growth in the early 1930s, the male leadership blamed the Women's Section. Using *Robitnytsia* as a forum for their discontent, they scolded the women for neglecting to work hard enough to win over the youth: "the Youth Section is suffering and not growing and [the youth newspaper] *Boiova molod* - is in such a bad way."[34]

Ukrainian literacy classes were another activity advocated by the male leadership that many women wholeheartedly embraced because of its practical, as well as political, relevance. Many of the leaders saw high illiteracy as a key barrier to building a strong base of class-conscious women. "Among the Ukrainian Working Women of Canada are many who cannot read. It is very important to pull such women into the working women's organizations and to educate them," argued a ULTA central committee report in 1923. "As long as they cannot read, you cannot introduce to them the cause of the workers through books or daily papers, – and such you cannot convert by talks and by collective readings."[35] They also saw literacy as crucial to sound mothering since, as *Robitnytsia* reminded its readers, "only a literate mother can bring up her children properly."[36] Literacy courses were established across the country. Vynohradova was among those who organized the course that ran from 1922 to 1928 at the Winnipeg Ukrainian labour temple. "At one time over forty women attended our school. Most of them learned to read and write," she recalled. The courses also offered other benefits: reading aloud gave participants the opportunity to practise what they had learned. Based on these passages, many of which came from *Robitnytsia*, Vynohradova explained, "we held discussions and so developed skills in public speaking." The women's branches and the ULFTA profited too. Many of the course participants soon took on secretarial and other branch executive duties, signed on for other ULFTA activities like drama for which illiteracy could be an impediment to participation, and wrote to or for *Robitnytsia* about local activities, sometimes as their branch's *robkorka*.[37]

Of course, the women did not embrace wholeheartedly or consistently all male-mandated endeavours. Among the most contentious was the "educational," a lecture with a discussion component meant to facilitate an awareness and understanding of key – and usually dry, male-defined – political issues. The educational was a critical site for the attempted reinforcement and negotiation of the movement's gender order. It also serves as a stark example of the additional burden of work borne by women in the movement. Male leaders expected the women to incorporate this activity into their regular women's branch meetings or to hold separate meetings for this purpose. Sometimes these men coordinated and led the educationals. In 1922 an RCMP surveillance report indicated that sixty women had attended a lecture delivered by a man in Winnipeg "on 'Party and classes', in which he made a distinction between Parties and classes from the radical point of view, and how they came into existence."[38] On other occasions the women took turns giving lectures and leading discussions, often basing their talks, as the male leaders encouraged them to, on content in *Robitnytsia* and other organizational newspapers and published materials.[39] The separate space of the Women's Section educational meant that the women could shape the direction of at least some of the discussions to reflect their own interests. Consequently, unlike in the Men's Section, not all talks centred on political topics. Some dealt with contemporary social issues and topics of specific interest to women, such as health, children, and food.[40] Similarly, sequestered in the Women's Section, women were also free from the male scrutiny that might have prevented them from actively participating in discussions. If a woman found a concept or theory difficult to understand, she had less to fear in admitting it here than at a general hall event where male comrades might belittle her. The women's branch also allowed women the chance to discuss issues that the men might otherwise have viewed as frivolous or detracting from the class struggle.

Like many of the rank-and-file ULFTA men, the women had mixed reactions to the educationals. Some enjoyed them, finding them useful confidence-building activities that enhanced their self-worth as members of the movement. "[Our] educational committee ... taught the women how to make brief speeches about world events at [our] meetings. We enjoyed considerable success," Anna Woynarsky recalled of her experiences with the East Windsor women's branch. "We saw that we were able not only to cook and look after children but also to take part in discussions."[41] For others, leading an educational could open interesting organizational doors. Pauline Bartko, who came to Canada in 1904, grew up in Manitoba's Interlake region, where her parents struggled to farm before they gave up and moved to Winnipeg in 1917. Although she was reluctant initially to embrace socialism because of the religious atmosphere in which she had grown up, she became acquainted with Vynohradova, who encouraged her to subscribe to *Ukrainski robitnychi visti* and eventually won her over. Less than a month after Vynohradova had enticed her to join the Winnipeg women's branch in 1923, Bartko was asked to deliver an educational on "Religion as Narcotic," using a pamphlet provided by another member, Anastasia Sydor. Over the next year, with help from the other women and from male leaders like Mathew Popovich, she continued to deliver educationals, honing her speaking abilities, such that ULFTA organizers frequently called upon her to give talks to mass audiences. She became particularly busy during the Depression, speaking alongside male leaders at election rallies and other community meetings. Bartko's work aimed to draw many Ukrainians into the broader Canadian socialist movement. "I was often asked during the thirties to speak at meetings of poor farmers in Northern Manitoba," she said. "I visited the districts in which I had once lived and explained to the farmers the consequences of capitalist exploitation and urged them to join the Farmers' Unity League."[41]

Most women's branch members demonstrated a relatively limited interest in the educationals, however. The minutes of their meetings, as well as articles in *Robitnytsia*, consistently complained that educationals were poorly attended compared to other events and activities at the halls. "It's embarrassing to read the annual reports [of the women's branches]," lamented an article in a 1927 issue of *Robitnytsia*. "What little attention is paid to educational work and what an excess is paid to 'socials.'"[43] A 1932 article in preparation for a Women's Section conference further complained, "Our women are far more eager to get involved in manual labour than to inform themselves."[44]

What was the manual labour that diverted the attention of these women away from the educationals? By far, most women's preferred forms of activism were domestic work for the Ukrainian labour temples and cultural activity. The domestic functions that they served in their working-class homes carried over to their work at the halls. There the women expressed their activism by carrying out valuable, though unappreciated, work that mirrored the domestic burden they shouldered in the home. Cooking, cleaning, sewing, mending, and washing all fell within their purview. It was largely through their work that bazaars, picnics, banquets, dances, concerts, conventions, and other special events could take place – and be lucrative money-makers.

Their contributions in this capacity highlight the critical link between politics and Ukrainian cultural identity. The women's engagement with food is one of the best examples of this phenomenon, in keeping with patterns similar to those noted by historians for women in other ethnic and activist contexts.[45] On most occasions when food was served, the menu consisted of traditional Ukrainian dishes, which were inexpensive, though labour-intensive to produce. The women kept costs down, helping events like conventions to run on a shoestring. Similarly, the minimal outlay required for supplies (and the value added by the women's labour in the preparation) maximized the cash raised by the organization at banquets, picnics, dances, and other events where this food might be served or sold. Indeed, their efforts in this regard were critical to the very existence of the labour temples. Women in Lethbridge, Alberta, cooked not only during the period of construction but also afterwards to commemorate the existence of their new gathering space and to ensure that any debt incurred would be paid off quickly. To save men the time of going home for lunch, the local women members cooked dishes like *holubtsi* and *pyrohy*, which fed the volunteers daily for twenty cents each. After the construction was completed, the women held a week-long bazaar and a concert to celebrate the opening of the new hall, raising seven hundred dollars to offset building costs.[46]

These women did not cook only to raise money, however. The connection between politics and Ukrainian culture was also evident when they cooked in times of crisis, most notably during the Depression when their work intensified in response to the economic situation and government repression. Across the country the women often organized impromptu kitchens at the Ukrainian labour temples to feed and sustain people from a variety of ethnic backgrounds who were hungry, unemployed, or involved in key protests. "During the years of economic crisis of the thirties, unemployed people, in transit from one city to another, used to sleep in our Ukrainian labour temple," explained Toronto women's branch member Anna Andreyko. "We helped them by laundering their clothes and providing food for them."[47] The women similarly supported the On-to-Ottawa trekkers. "When the On to Ottawa Trek began, we set up kitchens inside tents at the Exhibition grounds where we prepared meals for the unemployed," Anna Nahorniak recalled of the Winnipeg Ukrainian labour temple women. "Our members gathered vegetables and meat from neighbourhood farmers and we prepared meals from these."[48]

This activism serves as an instance of women most closely embodying the movement's notions of hegemonic femininity. For many women,
cooking for the class struggle was a preferred form activism, and many
understood that their culinary contributions were important. Moreover, they were good at it, they enjoyed it, and the kitchen gave them
a site away from male scrutiny and control. Here, unlike other areas
of the movement, women had the greatest autonomy over their work.
They – and not the male leaders or members of the movement – were
the experts and the leaders of this form of cultural preservation and
political activism. Most men simply could not claim or demonstrate a
superior base of knowledge or skill when it came to kitchen work.

Despite this work's importance and the critical contributions that
women made to the movement by doing it, their efforts were considerably undervalued by the men. Although the male leaders often publicly
thanked the women for providing food and other forms of domestic
service, they rarely acknowledged (and, as we shall see, even maligned)
the work's significance. Even in the physical structure of the interwar
Ukrainian labour temples this disdain was manifest; the plans always
included stages, meeting rooms, and gathering spaces, but kitchens
were rare. The physical and imagined masculinist construction meant
that space and its allocated uses were explicitly gendered, underscoring
men's exercised authority and views on what constituted legitimate,
important, and valuable activism. Nonetheless, the women worked
around this. In the absence of appropriate workspaces, they extended
their activism beyond the walls of the labour temples and into their
own kitchens.[49] They also found ways to compensate for a lack of serving equipment. The women's branch in Winnipeg in 1931 used money
from their treasury to purchase dishes, pots, and cutlery for the Ukrainian labour temple, spending $298.24 to properly outfit the hall in this
regard.[50]

Ukrainian cultural activity was the other most popular activist outlet for these women. Indeed, for many this was the main reason they
were attracted to the movement, and for some it was the only activity in
which they engaged at the halls. Nadia Tytarenko of Hamilton, Ontario,
for example, was most active in the movement on the stage in choir and
drama, in fact eschewing participation in other organizational activities.[51] Not all women made their contributions on the stage, however.
Some combined domestic and cultural work behind the scenes, back-
stage, or in their own homes. Although Paraskevia Fedosenko never
appeared in a play, the show at the Vernon Ukrainian labour temple

could not have gone on without her. "Whenever a play was performed, I sewed the costumes for the actors [and] I also looked after the wardrobe," she explained. "This was responsible work in those days, involving, among other things, tidying up, laundering and ironing after every performance."[52] This unpaid work was crucial to the success of labour temple performances; many men took it for granted that the women would do it. When the wardrobe master of the East Kildonan Ukrainian labour temple in Winnipeg reported to the ULFTA men's branch that the wardrobe area was "dirty and there is no one to clean up," the men had a "short discussion" and passed a motion "to give the job to the women."[53]

Among the women one of the most popular and easily accessible cultural activities was traditional Ukrainian embroidery work. As they were the experts, embroidery, like food, offered them a form of activism free from male dictation. Its popularity also arose from its accessibility. Embroidery required very little equipment, the materials were inexpensive, and it was easily portable. It could be worked on at home in between other household tasks or it could be brought to the hall to be carried out during meetings or as a group social activity. In addition, needlework was one of the most popular ways to draw new women and girls to the halls. The activity helped to forge intergenerational links between young and old; at nearly every Ukrainian labour temple, classes existed in which older women taught younger women and girls traditional Ukrainian embroidery methods. "I instructed in these classes for three years," recalled Ivanna Kulyk of her experiences at the hall in Port Arthur, Ontario, teaching embroidery to children. Once it had been completed, the women frequently displayed their handiwork at the Ukrainian labour temples, exhibiting it on tables, walls, and, in the case of costumes, on stage performers. As an outcome of the interaction of class and ethnicity, here too cultural work and political activism were inextricably linked as many women incorporated communist symbols like hammers and sickles into their work. Similarly, the sale of this embroidery work, like the plays and concerts, further politicized the activity. "We sold the items made by the little girls at bazaars held by the organization," said Kulyk. "The money received from the sales went for the organizational fund or some other worthy cause."[54]

As they shaped their involvement with the ULFTA on their own terms, embodying an oppositional femininity, the women rejected some forms of male-mandated activism almost entirely. Their apathy, despite repeated prodding, towards involvement with the broader Canadian left and its largely male-defined forms of activism through the CPC is perhaps the most obvious and significant example of this phenomenon. While for much of the interwar period Ukrainians were "the second largest group in the CPC,"[55] few of these Ukrainians were women. Most women chose not to channel their efforts through a formal party membership. Nor did they work directly for the party through the Women's Labour Leagues as did many other radical women during the interwar years.[56] There were several reasons for this. Party ethnocentrism – demonstrated by frequent charges in the 1920s that the ULFTA's cultural activities were trivial and by the CPC's Comintern-directed dissolution of the party's language branches that was begun in 1925 – deterred the involvement of many women. Compounding this were the many demands on their time. The activities for which the women were expected to be responsible at the Ukrainian labour temples, and the demands that this work placed on their busy lives as working-class homemakers and mothers (and, for some, as waged workers), made it hard for them to take on additional work with the party.

Added to this was the fact that few of these women spoke English. Given the ethnic character of the working-class neighbourhoods in which they lived, and the availability of radical newspapers published in the Ukrainian language, many found that they could manage by knowing only Ukrainian or a limited amount of English so long as they remained within their particular ethnic enclave. Even those women who led the ULFTA women's branches, worked with the ULFTA's central women's committee, liaised with male leaders of the Ukrainian left, and had close party ties felt most comfortable carrying out their work in the Ukrainian setting. In 1930 the party selected women's branch member Pearl Zen to join a tour to the Soviet Union "to help build support for the USSR in Canada."[57] Upon her return she wrote articles for the ULFTA press and toured Canada, describing the Soviet Union and praising conditions there, particularly as they existed for women.[58] Much to the party's chagrin, however, Zen was only comfortable doing this work in Ukrainian. She and a Finnish comrade "frustrated the Party with their reluctance to write articles or speak in English."[59] Towards the end of the 1930s a smattering of politicized young Ukrainian women began to emerge as a bilingual intermediary between the ULFTA women and other radical women. However, at this time most were still too young to bridge the language gap; this would happen much later. In these years language continued to act as an effective barrier to considerable joint activity between the Ukrainian and other women. While they may have had some experiences in common, differences in language meant that these women and their Finnish- or English-speaking comrades could not communicate effectively with one another to engage in significant political activities together on a regular basis. Nonetheless, hints of a wider Canadian leftist sisterhood and women's solidarity were certainly evident. Women's branch members, particularly, often aided other women workers in party-led strikes by donating money or participating in support pickets.[60]

Owing to this isolation the women experienced the influence of the broader Canadian left and the party differently than did their menfolk and non-Ukrainian women. Indeed, even significant changes in party policy (and related in-fighting) during the 1920s and 1930s did little to practically change the nature of the Ukrainian women's activities and activism – despite the power and influence gained overall by the party in Canada at that time. During the Third Period, for example, the Comintern called for an increased focus on the organization of female industrial workers as part of "the Turn." For their part at events at the halls (particularly in the educationals, which began employing intense revolutionary language) the ULFTA male leaders pushed the women to follow closely the party's decrees. At the same time, the male editors of *Robitnytsia* made sure that the paper took on a new, more militant tone and focus. A 1931 headline, for example, reminded women to "Build the Party of your Class: Join the Ranks of the CP!"[61] In 1934 the paper regularly published poems such as "Vanguard," "Hunger March," and "To the Fascists."[62]

While this new party line influenced the work of some women, as evidenced by their letters to the newspapers, the efforts of most women hardly shifted at all. In response, some male correspondents argued in *Robitnytsia* that the women's branch should be liquidated, a suggestion that the women virulently opposed on the pages of the newspaper. Joan Sangster suggests that for Ukrainian women the "reluctance ... to embrace the 'turn' was due in part to their occupational segregation – as housewives – from wage-earning women."[63] Added to this reluctance was likely the threat of deportation for so-called subversive activities that hung over the heads of immigrant families, as well as the problems many women faced in communicating in a language other than Ukrainian. At the same time, many of these women probably appreciated how valuable their work was to the ULFTA, suspecting quite rightly that the ULFTA male leadership's rhetoric reflected more bark than bite. Since these men feared losing the women's ULFTA-focused labour and contributions (particularly financial), much of this criticism may have served as lip service to placate the party. As faithful party members themselves, these men would have had to demonstrate at least some effort to cajole these disobedient women.

The women continued to work in the Ukrainian labour temples as they always had, infusing elements of Ukrainian culture into their activism: organizing bazaars, raising money for their press, taking part in cultural activities (despite ongoing party criticism of these), and cooking for temple functions. When they did directly support a party-related activity, they did so in ways that continued to limit control over their work by the party – and even by the ULFTA male leaders. When asked to help with a Young Communist League picnic in June of 1931, for example, the Winnipeg women's branch members volunteered to contribute a traditional Ukrainian dish of *holubtsi*.[64]

Some of this party-related criticism may have lightened with the advent of the Popular Front in the mid-1930s, a period of organization in which grass-roots activism was encouraged and "tactics were designed to politicize women around their day-to-day experiences as wives and mothers."[65] However, it is unlikely that many links were made between the ULFTA women and other women, Ukrainian or otherwise, as the party had hoped when it encouraged its female supporters to take part in mainstream women's organizations.[66] First, language remained a barrier, impeding access to English language groups. Second, links with other Ukrainian women, particularly those who participated in church activities, were difficult to forge because many were not favourably disposed to aligning themselves with so-called communists. Nevertheless, while many women found it difficult to participate in the Popular Front outside of their own organizations, they remained supportive in the halls, pursuing activities to build anti-fascist activism in Canada and around the world. One of the most celebrated of their Popular Front efforts was supporting the men, particularly the Ukrainians, who volunteered to fight in the Spanish Civil War (1936–9). Aside from an intensification of activity, the only way in which women's work changed over the course of the Depression was in the particular struggles they supported; it is here that the broader Canadian left and the party in particular played a role in shaping these women's efforts. Otherwise – and no matter what the cause – these women continued to act as they always had by cooking, cleaning, and canvassing, preferring to channel their efforts through the Ukrainian-speaking milieu of the Ukrainian labour temples and women-centred environment of the ULFTA women's branch.

This distance from the party, the wider left in Canada, non-Ukrainian radical women, and many forms of male-defined activism did not preclude these women from participating in more physically militant forms of radical activism; nor did it entirely prevent opportunities for cross-cultural solidarity. Indeed, along with other non-Ukrainian women and men, they were often at the centre of the most visible forms of labour solidarity, attending events like protests and rallies to represent the ULFTA Women's Section and their families' best interests. In Winnipeg during the Depression, Helen Kassian recalled, members of the Women's Section along with other local mothers took part in enormous multi-ethnic May Day rallies and other demonstrations. "It was a great honour for the women, pushing carriages with their babies in them, to head the parade."[67] Not all demonstrations were peaceful; when necessary, the women were not above physical force, conduct that was very much respected and in keeping with notions of both hegemonic and oppositional femininities within the movement. When strike-breakers were sent to undermine a strike of bush workers in north-western Ontario in the early 1920s, Anna Sawchuk and the local women's branch members were among the women from a variety of ethnic backgrounds who joined their menfolk to meet the train. Although police tried to hold back the protesters, "the demonstrators, especially the women, began to press forward," Sawchuk recalled. "The police gave way under the pressure, the owners of one of the sawmills fled, and the strike breakers asked to be taken back to Winnipeg."[68] Similarly in 1922 when miners struck in Cardiff, Alberta, Teklia Chaban, along with another miner's wife, Katherine Diachuk, did not hesitate to jump into the fray. Hearing that the company planned to bring in strike-breakers, the two informed the union. "A big fight broke out. Nor did the women just stand by and look on," Chaban recalled. When she and Diachuk saw a policeman trying to handcuff an Italian miner, the women reacted. "Katherine had a baseball bat," explained Chaban. "She hit the policeman across the shoulders so hard that his jacket burst." Diachuk and the miner escaped, but Chaban was arrested and eventually handed a provisional sentence of one year in jail.[69]

Despite their important – and indeed essential – contributions to the ULFTA and its associated organizations and causes, the women were the frequent targets of male criticism. This disparagement and some men's hostile behaviour had deep roots linked to traditional gender roles in Ukrainian peasant villages. Canadian society reinforced this male privilege, as did the CPC. Their policing served to reinforce the movement's gender order and the notions of hegemonic masculinity and femininity.

Typically the women were condemned for failing to measure up to male standards of legitimate and respectable types and levels of activism. From the late 1920s into the 1930s, for example, articles in *Robitnytsia* constantly berated the women and the women's branches for lacking class-consciousness, failing to educate themselves, being "backward," and neglecting to adequately inform the newspaper of local branch activities. Notwithstanding the workload and the obligations placed upon women in their own branches, groups, and homes, the newspaper also scolded the female members for working too little with the main ULFTA branches and their male counterparts in the class struggle.

Women also had to deal often with male indifference and hostility towards their work at the local level. Many men saw little need for the women's branches or found it laughable that women should hold positions as organizers. Individual self-interest motivated some men's resistance. An account in *Robitnytsia* from the members of the Sault Ste Marie (Ontario) women's branch speculated that many men opposed the women's branch, fearing that it and other ULFTA activity would make their wives "want to abandon their husbands or force them to cook and wash dishes."[70] Some men consciously stood in the way of women's initiatives. When Anna Moysiuk reported her findings after a 1927 organization tour of eastern Canada to assist in the coordination of the Women's Section, she observed first hand this widespread male apathy and hostility: "They won't let the women onto subcommittees because they fear 'trouble.' When the women want to put on a theatrical production or another event the men won't allow it because that's the work of the drama group which might take offence."[71]

Of course, not all men were unsupportive. Many were the first to introduce their girlfriends, sisters, wives, daughters, and mothers to the movement, encouraging them to take part in a variety of activities and exhibiting pride in their accomplishments when they did so. Some even shared domestic responsibilities so that their wives could attend meetings, as John Yurichuk did when his wife, Mary, wanted to join the Edmonton women's branch. "Look, you finish your supper and don't bother with the dishes," he told her as they ate dinner one evening. "[The children and I] will take care of them. You get yourself ready and go to the meeting." When she came home and announced that she had been elected branch financial secretary, he was pleased, remarking, "That's good."[72] Many other men behaved in a sufficiently contrary fashion, however, to warrant official notice. At the end of her tour Moysiuk pulled no punches. "There are, of course, no shortage of shortcomings and inadequacies in our organization," she reported. "The worst and most unforgivable is the indifference of the men toward the women's organization."[73] As a result, in many Ukrainian labour temples women's activities seemed to exist in spite of, rather than because of, the input of men.

Interestingly, these women never mounted any organized resistance to confront male interference or criticism. This was, at least in part, due to their segregation from contemporary feminism. Language and sometimes prejudice isolated these women from the feminist currents that Joan Sangster, Linda Kealey, and Varpu Lindström have examined among other socialist women.[74] Moreover, ethnocentrism, class – as Ruth Frager has shown for Jewish women – and language further precluded engagement with the middle-class women's movement.[75] As men controlled *Robitnytsia*, their ideals and values came through in the articles, and thus the feminist ideas that might have challenged male privilege never materialized on its pages. Quite simply, in terms of the "woman question," women's oppression as women was never a priority to the male leaders of the ULFTA. Only the oppression they shared with men as members of the exploited Ukrainian working class – interpreted through a male lens – was important. Theoretically, these women never articulated a formal challenge to their oppression as women or openly defined their particular interests as *female Ukrainian workers or farmers*. Therefore no distinct brand of radical Ukrainian feminism developed to challenge formally the interwar gender order and the lack of power experienced by women vis-à-vis men.

This did not mean, however, that the women kept quiet. As recent histories have shown, ethnic women on the left talked back to their male comrades, and some bravely attacked sexist behaviour.[76] Ukrainian leftist women were no different and responded in a number of ways. Sometimes they were quite publicly vocal. "Why do you take it out on us who are workers just as you?" demanded the Sault Ste Marie women of the men at their hall who "from every side ... laughed at us and mocked us instead of supporting and helping." They insisted, "It's time to stop thinking that a woman is a weak creature whom you can attack at any time because she does not have the means to defend herself."[77] When their activities were threatened, they protested; *Robitnytsia*'s demise offers a good example. The women valued the newspaper and worked hard to ensure its survival amidst some of the worst years of the Depression. When male organizers made the decision in 1937 at the annual ULFTA convention to discontinue it after fourteen years for financial reasons, the women present "insisted on the continuance of the journal," an RCMP informant observed. Unfortunately their protests were not always successful; in this instance of gender tension, after a lengthy and passionate discussion the ULFTA leaders voted to cease publication.[78] From that point on, women had to settle for news from one of the two remaining ULFTA newspapers, *Ukrainski robitnychi visti* (Ukrainian labour news) and *Farmerske zhyttia* (Farmers' life),[79] in which women's issues were limited to a few special columns.

Not all women chose to express their anger so overtly when their efforts or dedication were maligned. Effective resistance to male domination also came from the many subtle and likely unconscious ways in which women behaved to shape and direct their work and activism. Embodying and performing an oppositional femininity that simultaneously rejected some and embraced other aspects of Ukrainian leftist hegemonic femininity, women exerted agency at their labour temples by, for example, avoiding activities that failed to address their experiences, needs, and interests, and choosing carefully the causes or events to which they donated their precious time and effort. Although the women were limited in the overall power they possessed relative to men, such choices allowed them to negotiate a space for themselves and define their activism on their own terms, carving out a female niche that was rooted in activities suited to their interests, skills, and abilities. Or, as some historians put it, they redefined the political; that is, they designated their female work within the Women's Section not as secondary "support" labour but as fundamentally political terrain,[80] rejecting men's opinions to the contrary.

The work of these women was critical to the growth and influence enjoyed by the Ukrainian left – and indeed the broader left – during the interwar period. From their engagement with the movement, a distinct Ukrainian leftist woman's experience emerged, parallel to but divergent from the experiences of other women, radical or Ukrainian. With their menfolk they sang revolutionary songs in Ukrainian and took part in other activities with strong socialist intentions. With their daughters, eschewing religious symbolism, they created "traditional" Ukrainian embroidery inscribed with symbols of political resistance or cooked Ukrainian dishes to raise money and feed convention attendees, protesters, or strikers. Like other radical women in Canada, they played important roles in the left by raising and saving money and by supporting a variety of political causes through working with children, canvassing, voting, or marching in protests. Employing various forms of resistance, they also negotiated venues that were free from male interference and therefore offered the opportunity for them to exercise power and validate their experiences as working-class, immigrant housewives, mothers, farmers, and, in some cases, paid workers. As we shall see in the following chapter, their children did likewise, similarly creating spaces and experiences of personal and collective youthful authority in which to express themselves as young Ukrainians in Canada.

3 Junior Participants in the Class Struggle: Children, Youth, and the Interwar Ukrainian Left

Nadya Niechoda was born in Canada to a Ukrainian leftist family. Her parents were members of the Ukrainian Labour Farmer Temple Association in Winnipeg during the 1920s and 1930s. They often took her to events at "the hall," where she witnessed speeches by leaders like Mathew Popovich and Matthew Shatulsky, or performances of dancers, choirs, and mandolin orchestras. By the age of three, influenced by what she saw, Niechoda was ready to do her part at home for Ukrainian culture and the class struggle. "I used to sit on the bottom stair and play a make-believe mandolin on a broom, and sing 'The Internationale,'" she explained.

Twice a week after school she would go to the labour temple for Ukrainian school. There she learned to read and write in Ukrainian, and she and her fellow students honed their language skills by studying the works of nineteenth-century Ukrainian literary greats Ivan Franko and Taras Shevchenko. The children also learned about local and world affairs and history, particularly that of Ukraine and the Soviet Union, and learned where they as youngsters fit in the class struggle. "Left or right – these terms were known to me from childhood," she recalled. "Left to me was good; right was the authorities sending my dad to work in a relief camp; left was the hall ... right was a deportation order for our family." Members of the ULFTA came through for Niechoda and her family: "it was the people from this organization, supported by similar organizations, who launched a campaign so that the deportation order [was] rescinded." That same year Niechoda's father bought her a real mandolin. Soon, thanks to Saturday lessons at the hall, "I was able to play 'The Internationale' ..., though that did not stop me from playing 'Rock of Ages' or 'Swanee River,' and Ukrainian folk songs. How fortunate it was for me and the others that we were able to learn and study music at a time when it was so difficult for us to even survive."[1]

The experiences of Niechoda represent those of many children during the interwar era who were born into or introduced to the ULFTA at an early age. They viewed and participated in Ukrainian-language concerts and plays, organized protests, read ULFTA newspapers, discussed political issues, and raised money to support a variety of causes. Although they would have been very young, they contributed in significant ways to the shape of the ULFTA community during this period of the movement's history. This chapter seeks to explore such experiences and, in doing so, to expand our general understanding of the history of Canadian leftist children – by considering how class, ethnicity, age, and gender intersected in the lives of ULFTA youngsters. It combines a top-down and a bottom-up approach to explore how the youngsters, parents, and ULFTA leaders all acted – together and apart, united and in opposition to one another – to build a vibrant, radical, Ukrainian young people's movement during Canada's interwar years. The structure of activities for youngsters reflected the priorities of parents and leaders. At the same time, however, children and youth (and their desires and interests – or, in some cases, lack of interest) were crucial in shaping their own work and influencing the movement's broader policies. External factors – most notably the Canadian public school system and North American popular culture – also influenced the patterns of youngsters' activities. So too did the wider Canadian left – most notably, the CPC, a long-time ally, yet concurrently often an adversary, of the ULFTA. These youngsters' activities are an important lens through which to understand the significant role of cultural-political activism and the movement's overall efforts to challenge and resist party efforts to control and dictate the shape of the ULFTA. These Ukrainian children and youth, in fact, were among the most loyal, often voting with their feet when the CPC came calling, attempting to take over or redefine their activities. Placing the experiences of these youngsters front and centre allows us to consider this relationship from a more nuanced perspective and helps to illuminate some of the additional pressures faced by leaders when they were confronted with party policy that challenged or threatened the ULFTA's cultural or social components. From this we can gain a broader understanding of the community's political and cultural perspectives and the multifaceted ways in which members carried out their activism and understood their place within a wider Canadian – and indeed international – left.

The location of the youngsters at specific intersections of these power relationships meant that their experiences differed – at times significantly – from those of their parents, their public-school classmates, other Ukrainian children (particularly those tied to one of the developing Ukrainian churches), and other leftist children. This chapter examines how discourses of gender, class, ethnicity, and age intertwined – unevenly and unequally – to shape the activities and experiences of these children and youth. The unevenness is key to our understanding; among the very young, gender, for example, typically mattered less in defining their experiences than did age, class, and ethnicity. As children aged, however, they would become more aware of the gendered divisions that existed among adults (predicated, as has been demonstrated, on male dominance and female subordination). As youths, they would begin to be more formally trained and informally socialized (both explicitly and implicitly) – through their ongoing involvement with the movement – to take on (or challenge) similar roles as they entered young-adult activities.

This chapter builds on the work of certain scholars who have taken analytical approaches rooted in intersectionality that include (albeit not always directly) considerations of the lives of children. For example, children's experiences receive some attention in works on radical Euro-Canadian immigrant women and their daughters and in studies of the wider international diaspora of revolutionary movements. These works often attempt to locate children and parents within an intersectional analysis. Although the considerations tend to focus more on the adults than on the children, we can nonetheless learn something about children through their mother's activism and child-rearing methods. In tracing the radical bonds that developed between daughters and mothers, these historians have documented the importance of kitchens and neighbourhoods as radicalizing sites of female activism. They have shed light on how immigrant mothers passed on a radical heritage and a repertoire of strategies to their daughters (for instance, by helping children to read radical children's texts, perform in radical plays, or act as bodyguards). They explain how daughters learned their politics not only in the garment or tobacco shop but also at the kitchen table in animated debate in the company of female elders.[2] Particularly relevant examples – which describe circumstances that parallel those of Ukrainian leftist children – are the works by Ester Reiter and Mona Ayukawa in *Sisters or Strangers?*. Their articles analyse how the intersection of gender with class and ethnicity affected the lives and activism of

Jewish and Japanese mothers, respectively. Reiter explores the central role that women, particularly mothers, played in creating the radical Camp Naivelt and examines the experiences of its young campers from the 1920s to the 1950s. She illustrates that, by establishing and maintaining camping activities, these women "were nurturing both ethnic and political loyalties amongst their children, while resisting a class and ethnically based paternalism that would have seen their children's lives and values shaped by Anglo-Saxon charitable institutions."[3] Ayukawa explains how Japanese immigrants "countered oppressive situations with efforts to retain their cultural identity." Mothers were the primary custodians of these efforts, which focused on instilling "pride and self-image" in their children while encouraging them to "outperform their peers both in public school and in the workplace." Thanks to this critical reproductive labour, Ayukawa argues, "Japanese Canadians were able to resist and subvert a history of exclusion and the resultant obstacles to adaptation."[4]

This chapter also expands on the canon of children's history, particularly as it relates to working-class children. With a few exceptions,[5] the bulk of the history of children in Canada tends to focus largely on state institutions and reformers, particularly as these relate to social welfare programs, education, work, and juvenile delinquency.[6] It tells us much about the ways in which the state and adults have shaped children's lives in general. Unfortunately such a focus often precludes any meaningful sense of childhood agency. As historian Robert McIntosh argues, in these types of works "children tend to be portrayed as passive beings who are the objects of welfare and educational strategies," and as a result "the history of childhood becomes the history of the efforts of others on children's behalf."[7] Nonetheless, there are some studies that do offer important insight into the lives of working-class children. McIntosh's own study *Boys in the Pits* illustrates the critical occupational and familial roles of boys in early-twentieth-century coal mining, paying particular attention to their agency as workers. John Bullen's work highlights the significance of children's labour – both paid and unpaid – to Ontario's working-class families during the second half of the nineteenth century, and Bettina Bradbury's *Working Families* does likewise for late-nineteenth-century Montreal. In the U.S. context, David Nasaw's ground-breaking *Children of the City: At Work and Play* dynamically illustrates how working children made use of the streets and neighbourhoods as both workplace and site of leisure.[8] A particularly relevant study is Paul C. Mishler's *Raising Reds: The Young*

Pioneers, Radical Summer Camps, and Communist Political Culture in the United States. In it he examines how the American communist movement attempted to politicize children. Mishler argues, "In the programs that they organized to give their children an alternative oppositional culture, American Communists constructed a political culture of their own ... which provided a space in which the Communists could confront the tensions of their relationship with American society and with history." While the book certainly describes the children's activities in a detailed and engaging manner, Mishler's concern is not with the children themselves for, as he states, "I want to look at these activities for what they illustrate about the culture of the adults who created them."[9]

Children of ULFTA members and supporters most often had their first contact with the movement as babies or young children when they were brought by their parents to functions at or coordinated by a Ukrainian labour temple. Later, once they had begun attending public school, their parents enrolled them in after-school and weekend activities at a local ULFTA hall. Depending on age and the availability of programming in their particular locality, they would, perhaps between the ages of eleven and thirteen, graduate to participation in youth activities. The period of youth functioned as a transitional – and ambiguous – stage of movement life. The time that one ceased to be defined as a youth and began to be an adult within the context of the Ukrainian labour temple community had very little to do with age. Instead, the move from youth to adult activities had more to do with the whims, needs, and priorities of the male leadership of the movement and was contingent on the youngster's life circumstances. Life milestones such as public-school completion, injury or death of a parent, marriage, parenthood, the move into the workforce, and the socio-economic context also determined the transition point to adulthood.

Although there are clear differences that characterize the categories of children and youth, it is nonetheless appropriate to discuss them in tandem because within both age categories the activities followed a similar pattern, existed for similar reasons, enjoyed similar status within the movement, and were together often distinct from the activities of adults. When discussed together, children and youth will be referred to as *youngsters* or *young people* for the purpose of this book; otherwise, when specific age categories of youngsters are discussed, the terms *children* and *youth* will be used.

The Ukrainian left began to establish formal activities for youngsters with the opening of the Winnipeg Ukrainian labour temple in 1918. At the time leaders and parents ascribed a great deal of importance to children's involvement. When the governments of the three prairie provinces declared during the second decade of the twentieth century that English was to be the sole language of instruction in public schools,[10] Ukrainian families there were forced to turn to outside institutions to provide Ukrainian educational and cultural experiences to supplement those taught in the home. Many parents also wanted their children to be involved in activities that challenged the oppression faced by Ukrainian and other, particularly immigrant, members of the working class upon their arrival in Canada. They also sought supervised, non-religious activities for their children after school and on weekends when parents had their own cultural and political activities to attend at the halls or when they needed to be at work. In response to these concerns, at the first ULTA convention, leaders established Ukrainian worker children's schools (UWCSs). Their purpose was "to teach the children of Ukrainian workers their native language, to give them the means in their native tongue to raise the consciousness of the workers, [and] to teach them to view the world through the eyes of the working class."[11] As the ULFTA expanded nationally over the course of the early 1920s, halls across Canada opened their own Ukrainian worker children's schools. Throughout the 1920s and 1930s schools constantly expanded, both in number and size and in terms of activities offered.[12] With keen interest from both the parents and the children, the Ukrainian worker children's schools enjoyed a striking degree of popularity. By the time the 1933 ULFTA convention took place, there were forty-five schools functioning across Canada with some two thousand students attending.[13] In 1937 the number of schools had grown to fifty-four with the number of students remaining steady at 1,945.[14]

The central school board (CSB) of the ULFTA coordinated the schools at the national level and worked to ensure a standardized national curriculum. Thanks to this body, the schools tended to function in much the same manner regardless of locality (although remoteness of location could affect teacher availability and children's attendance rates). Typically school organizers grouped children by grade or age in the Ukrainian schools, although this might also depend on a child's ability and knowledge ofUkrainian.[15] In most communities the schools combined training in the Ukrainian language with musical and cultural training. "I attend the Ukrainian Workers Children's School where we learn our language, reading, writing, singing, and mandolin," said Maria Tysmbaliuk of Kamsack, Saskatchewan, in 1927. "Our teacher is D. Prodaniuk. He is now teaching us a play." She went on to explain, "We've mounted a few concerts, but the last one was cancelled because it was too cold and no one came." When organizer Toma Kobzey came to inspect her school, she recalled, "he gave us a lot of questions on grammar and musical theory. He also advised us on proper behaviour and how to set a good example for others. He then asked us if we knew how to sing, so we did so."[16]

Throughout the interwar era the CPC frequently criticized the UWCSs for being too culturally centred, claiming that an emphasis on the use of Ukrainian language and culture distracted children from activities that the party defined as having a more pressing political nature. Ongoing use of the Ukrainian language especially seemed to raise the ire of those working to anglicize the party. It is clear from its critiques, however, that the CPC understood or appreciated very little of the important ways in which the UWCSs contributed to support of the international proletarian struggle and integrated the party line into its curriculum. Children attending the UWCSs received, through cultural and language training, widespread exposure to Marxist-Leninism and analysis of the situation of the working class in Canada and abroad. This training, which became especially intense with the onslaught of the Depression, was facilitated through a variety of means. Teachers made use of pro-working-class, Ukrainian language newspapers, literature, songs, plays, and poems in their lessons. To make his classes more enjoyable and relatable, one teacher gave his students popular "children's literature to study individually," which he later interpreted for them "according to Lenin ideology."[17]

The central school board encouraged teachers to supplement classroom lessons with hands-on experiences. For example, organizers instructed teachers in the 1930s to help students understand the plight of the unemployed and impoverished by planning field trips "to soup kitchens and forced labour camps." Many on the left used the latter term to describe the "relief camps" established by Prime Minister R.B. Bennett for single unemployed men, which were characterized by low wages and abysmal, isolated working conditions. The central school board also told teachers to encourage children to analyse their home lives in the context of the Depression in order to understand what their role must be in the class struggle.[18] Organizers, teachers, and newspaper editors encouraged children to practise their Ukrainian and journalism skills by writing stories about working-class exploitation for their school's "wall gazette" and for the movement's newspapers.

Organizers did not structure the activities and roles of children along gender lines as those of the women and men were. Leaders and parents

1. ULFTA handicraft school in Port Arthur, Ontario, ca. 1925. Stavroff Private Collection.

expected girls and boys to participate equally and enthusiastically. Some activities, however, were geared more towards children of a specific gender, which served to socialize girls and boys into their future gender roles in the movement. When the women's branch members taught traditional Ukrainian handicrafts like embroidery to students, for example, it was generally only the girls who participated.

Sometimes separate orchestra groups existed as well, though not necessarily because the organizers considered a particular musical activity to be more appropriate for girls or for boys. Often it was simply a case of numbers. In Winnipeg, recalled Ollie Hillman, when mandolin instruction began in the early 1920s, significantly more girls than boys were involved in the mandolin orchestra. Eventually the UWCS teacher Vladislav Patek recruited the hall's boys into a separate "big band." Nor were the boys more advantaged in this case when it came to performance opportunities and status. In fact, the Winnipeg Girls Mandolin Orchestra was one of the most influential youngsters' cultural groups in the ULFTA nationally; they embarked on several tours of eastern and western Canada during the interwar years, raising funds, class-consciousness, and organizational awareness.[19]

Like adults, the UWCS students worked under a rigorous schedule, often attending classes and rehearsals nightly and even on weekends during the September to June cultural season. While these children certainly had friends from public school and their neighbourhoods, generally speaking few found time for much play or other activity outside the parameters of the labour temples. Nick Petrachenko attended the UWCS at the Welland Ukrainian labour temple during the 1920s, and it was there that he spent the most time with his friends. He would hurry home after public school for a quick snack before his five o'clock Ukrainian classes. At seven o'clock, the class would end, but he often remained at the hall for drama practice. On weekends there would also be meetings, concerts, plays, or social activities. Like Petrachenko, Hillman and her friends spent all of their spare time at the Winnipeg hall. "Every evening was filled – there would be Ukrainian school, orchestra, meetings," she explained. She, like many other children, loved attending and taking part in hall activities. The activities were so important to her and the others that they used to walk through all sorts of weather to participate: "it was like life and death, we had to attend dancing and the other events."[20] Also a student in the 1920s, Nick Dubas called the Winnipeg Ukrainian labour temple his second home, stating, "I was at the hall more than I was at home. Sometimes I did poorly in [public] school because I was so involved with the hall." For Dubas the close quarters of labour temple life led to the development of his most significant childhood friendships. "I had friends at [public] school," he explained, "but they weren't like my pals from the Ukrainian labour temple." Such patterns continued throughout the interwar years for children like Myron Shatulsky, Olga Shatulsky, Mary Semanowich, and Clara Babiy, who had similar experiences with the UWCS schedule in the 1930s.[21]

The students put their education to good use in the movement by helping to raise funds and ethnic and class-consciousness, as did the adult members of the Ukrainian labour temples. They frequently attended or took part in plays and concerts presented by the adult branches at the halls. In 1922, for example, in the last act of a play about the Bolshevik revolution that was performed at the Ukrainian labour temple in Winnipeg, children from the UWCS marched amidst downed telephone, telegraph, and light poles "with Red Flags singing the 'International' [sic]" among "Priests and Noblemen [who were] cleaning the streets, clothed in rags."[22] Sometimes the children were the main draw. In 1926 the Toronto Children's Mandolin Orchestra embarked on a tour of nine communities in remote northern Ontario and gave what one reviewer called "some very fine concerts."[23] Their program underscored the ULFTA's emphasis on musical rigour, its ethno-political interests, and general international leftist influences. Alongside traditional Ukrainian folk numbers like "Katerina," "Postava," and "Zaporozhets" could be found the overture to *The Barber of Seville*, "O sole mio," and, of course, "The Internationale."[24] Their repertoire also included the Ukrainian version of the popular "Razom tovaryshi v nohu" (Together comrades):

> All of us hail from the people,
> Children of labour and toil,
> "Fraternal union and freedom" –
> Let this be our battle call.
> Long have they held us in bondage,
> Starvation long did us waste,
> Our patience finally has ended,
> Now we'll ourselves liberate.[25]

In the end, according to the ULFTA newspaper *Ukrainski robitnychi visti* (Ukrainian labour news), the trip was "a great success from both a moral and financial point of view."[26] Tours like this and those of the Winnipeg Girls Mandolin Orchestra inspired many ULFTA groups wherever they played. Often in their wake during the 1920s were newly minted children's orchestras in even the most remote communities where these youngsters had performed.

The popularity and expansion of the UWCSs highlighted an important deficiency in the movement. From the earliest days it was clear that a lack of trained organizers and teachers plagued the movement. For work with youngsters to flourish, the ULFTA needed to develop a cadre of activists possessing appropriate skills and experience. To confront this serious problem the movement's national leadership in Winnipeg developed what came to be known as the Higher Educational Course (HEC) and recruited promising young people to take part. Although the first course in 1923 had only had thirteen students in attendance, subsequent courses tended to attract anywhere from twenty-five to forty-four students.[27] Between 1923 and 1938 five HECs took place, graduating more than one hundred students in total.[28] The course was so popular that organizers moved it to Parkdale, Manitoba, on the outskirts of Winnipeg where the Workers Benevolent Association owned a large facility that housed orphaned Ukrainian leftist children as well as older men who were too aged or infirm to look after themselves.[29] Organizers were optimistic about the training program, which they viewed as key to the movement's growth and influence among Ukrainian immigrants and their offspring.

"In a word – the Higher Educational Course is our forge," ULFTA leader Toma Kobzey explained in 1923, "which sends out hammer-wielding smiths to smash the rampant ignorance of the workers."[30] That Kobzey chose to use such a masculinist image is no coincidence. It speaks forcefully to the male-dominated left, its celebration of hammer-and-fist imagery, and the sexism prevalent among Ukrainian leftists (and other contemporary radical groups), concurrently naturalizing notions of hegemonic masculinity. It also calls attention to the life-cycle point at which these gendered expectations began to influence and shape more directly youth opportunities, behaviour, and activism. Young men were the most desirable HEC students. The resulting student bodies, therefore, were a physical manifestation of these views. The students of the 1923–4 HEC were all men. The 1925–6 course saw three women participants. Through the 1930s this pattern continued. Of the twenty-eight students who completed the course in 1936, only nine were women. Two years later, nine women and twenty-nine men took part.[31] Many women were selected only when they had proven themselves exceptional and often only in the absence of a suitable male candidate. Mary Skrypnyk, then of Hamilton, Ontario, was one of the few young women who attended the HEC in 1938. She became a student when the Hamilton Ukrainian labour temple's first choice, a boy, had to turn down the opportunity because his father had passed away, and he needed to remain in town to support his mother. At the time of Skrypnyk's selection, many members were displeased. "I was told the course would be wasted on me because I was a girl," she recalled; she ended up making her career with the Ukrainian left.[32] Skrypnyk and her cohort of young women in the course were among those who, by challenging gender roles and seizing opportunity, would establish themselves as important leaders in the movement during the Second World War and into the post-war period.

2. Teachers and students of the Ukrainian Labour Farmer Temple Association's Higher Educational Course, Winnipeg, from 1 February to 5 August 1928. AUUC Winnipeg Collection, Winnipeg, Manitoba.

To attend a ULFTA Higher Educational Course demanded temporal and often financial commitment from students. Once they had been selected, some students paid for the course themselves, though more often than not the individual branches, the national office of the ULFTA, and the WBA would cover the cost of transportation, teaching materials, and room and board.[33] For many participants the time they spent at an interwar HEC was worthwhile; it was likely the only opportunity they had for further education and training in Canada. The promise of a position as an organizer, a journalist, or a teacher in a Ukrainian labour temple somewhere in Canada – though still poorly paid – opened up alternative job possibilities beyond those typically available to young Ukrainian women and men in domestic service, resource industries, or agriculture. The course also gave them the opportunity to meet and mingle with a new group of like-minded young people; several even met their future spouses in this way.

A young woman or man who attended an HEC received training in a variety of subjects that were designed to develop their abilities as well-rounded teachers and organizers. Courses of a political nature were a priority. John Boyd, who studied at the 1930 HEC led by Mathew Popovich, remembered a curriculum that "included ... history and geography and ... political economy and Marxism."[34] This line of teaching, as 1936 course participant Kosty Kostaniuk explained, was "designed to give them a broad understanding of what was happening around them."[35] Students also learned various practical ways to organize branches and activities. At the 1926 HEC, for instance, classes engaged in role-playing exercises. One student, cast in the role of organizer, would be responsible for organizing the remaining members of the class, who played the parts of unorganized workers or farmers. In other situations students would conduct mock meetings or lectures to teach them how to set up and run WBA and ULFTA branches and UWCSs. Students also learned techniques to help revive faltering branches.[36]

Balanced with the political and organizational aspects of the course was the other priority of the ULFTA, the maintenance of Ukrainian cultural life in Canada. Students were educated about the Ukrainian language and Ukrainian culture. Courses in Ukrainian grammar, history, and literature were fixtures of the schools. Students also studied Ukrainian music, drama, and dance. Above all, they learned how to teach these subjects properly and how to coordinate cultural groups within the ULFTA.[37] When they had finished the course, participants often demonstrated what they had learned to the ULFTA members and supporters in halls in the Winnipeg vicinity. After their exams in 1936 the HEC students presented a revolutionary play called *Destruction of the Black Sea Squadron* at the Transcona Ukrainian labour temple; the 1938 group performed "some fine singing, duets, trios, quartets and larger groups" at their farewell concert.[38]

Most HEC graduates were immediately assigned to work in branches across Canada. Others were groomed for leadership positions in local branches or as touring organizers or journalists. Kostaniuk, for example, was assigned to the Fort William branch. Some fortunate male students in the 1930s even had the chance, once they had demonstrated their potential at the HEC, to study in Ukraine. Mike Seychuk, for example, was sent with three other students to school in Kharkiv, Ukraine after taking part in the 1929–30 HEC.[39]

The students selected for the HEC were nearly always drawn from the ranks of the ULFTA's Youth Section. Often linked to the activities of the UWCS, the Youth Section was designed to teach youngsters how to function as formal ULFTA branch members. The first incarnation of the Youth Section, the League of Ukrainian Working Youth (Spilka ukrainskoi robitnychoi molodi, SURM), had come into being in February 1924 at the ULFTA convention. Response was immediate, and over the course of that year twelve branches formed across Canada with a total membership of 445.

Despite – or perhaps because of – its immediate success, however, pressure from the CPC acted as a direct challenge to the SURM's existence. The CPC feared that the growing strength of the Ukrainian-language SURM would undermine its own English-language Young Communist League. As such, by 1925, as part of a wider push to anglicize itself and its activities, the CPC had successfully demanded that leaders of the ULFTA abolish the SURM to pressure Ukrainian youth into joining the Young Communist League (YCL). Ultimately the effort was a failure as only a few of the former leaders of the SURM ended up participating in the YCL. Resistant to the prospect of working not within the Ukrainian cultural and political milieu of the ULFTA but through the CPC, others, according to an RCMP source, "drifted away," choosing "to not belong to any of the organizations."[40] This acute rejection forced the CPC to recognize the desire for and value of a separate Ukrainian youth organization. At the 1926 ULFTA convention, CPC National Secretary Jack Macdonald urged the ULFTA to reorganize a youth branch, arguing that it should be led by Ukrainian youth who were also members of the Young Communist League. The ULFTA happily obliged, and the Youth Section (Sektsia molodi) was born.[41]

With a significant degree of autonomy from the CPC restored, the Youth Section enjoyed another wave of phenomenal growth. Over the course of the latter half of the 1920s, it, like the UWCSs, expanded into numerous communities across Canada. By 1927 the ULFTA boasted thirty-two youth branches and 1,508 members in its youth division.[42] In 1931 the association even created a Junior Section (Yunatska sektsia) modelled on the Youth Section for children aged seven to ten, who were too young for the Youth Section but eager for a branch of their own.[43]

Organizers deliberately structured both the Youth Section and the Junior Section like the adult branches in order to teach children how to run an effective organization, hold meetings, and raise funds. Skypnyk, who was assigned to the Junior Section during the late 1930s, "tried to make it a small organization for children, like a smaller model of the larger organization."[44] Membership meetings for the young people's sections, like many adult branches, generally took place on Sundays. As one former member recalled, the Junior Section children used to refer to it as their Sunday School, realizing there was a distinction between themselves and the religious – Ukrainian or otherwise – children.[45] Instead of the religious instruction that took place in church, however, youngsters would learn about Marxist-Leninism and their place in the Canadian and international proletarian struggle and how to elect executives, hold meetings, pay dues, plan events, and raise money. In this way, straddling two worlds – that of the Ukrainian left and that of the multi-class and multi-ethnic world outside the hall – they drew on their radical culture to make sense of what they were doing vis-à-vis other children in their neighbourhoods and public schools.

The branch activities for youngsters mirrored in intensity those of women and men, reflecting a combination of organizational, political, and social activity, often organized across ethnic lines. As one young member of the Youth Section branch in Sault Ste Marie, Ontario, explained in 1927, the branch had held in its three months of existence "five administrative meetings, seven group readings, [and] two concerts independently." They had also coordinated "seven concerts with their Finnish comrades, one annual meeting with the election of the new executive, [while] collecting money for a library."[46] The Youth and Junior Sections, like adult groups, were also encouraged to assist other ULFTA branches in fund-raising for the press, the organization, and other labour-movement-related projects. Many youngsters enjoyed the pace of organizational activity but also participated because of the important social elements inherent in their branches. Mike Seychuk, a Junior Section member in Winnipeg during the late 1920s and early 1930s, recalled his hectic schedule: "On weekends we would spend time at the Ukrainian labour temple in a group meeting or on an outing; we would have socials in the evening with kids from the Transcona or East Kildonan Ukrainian labour temples." A favourite winter-time activity for Seychuk's group involved making a twelve-kilometre "trek" east from their north end Winnipeg hall to meet their cohort at the Transcona hall.[47]

There were differences between youngsters' branches and adult branches, however. Most significantly, the young people's branch activities were not organized along gender lines. While organizers might, in some instances, develop activities with more appeal for girls or for boys, overall youngsters were not forced to adhere to rigid definitions of femininity or masculinity, nor were they confined, like their parents, to branches and activities based on whether they were male or female. Both girls and boys were encouraged within their groups to play executive and committee roles, and girls often held key leadership positions such as president.[48] This further underscores one of the key purposes of children's activities – to raise informed, engaged, and active adults to support the class struggle.

Like the UWCS and the HEC, the Junior Section and the Youth Section seemed to enjoy a strong following and a great deal of popularity. Growth in the 1920s continued into the 1930s. By the time of the 1933 ULFTA convention the membership of the Junior Section and the Youth Section totalled 1,528 and 1,050 respectively. At the 1937 ULFTA convention the Junior Section reported having more than 2,000 members,[49] while the Youth Section was shown to have grown to 1,800 members nationwide.[50]

Despite the sections' prolific expansion their existence continued to be precarious in some ways. Struggles with the Young Communist League and the CPC cropped up sporadically throughout the 1930s, threatening to alienate Ukrainian youngsters from ULFTA branch work. The role that the CPC wanted the YCL to play in relation to the Youth Section continued to be contentious, and leaders of both the ULFTA and the CPC had to tread carefully. In a 1935 ULFTA-published, Ukrainian-language article entitled "What the Relationship Should Be between the YCL and the YS, ULFTA," Seychuk outlined the existing tensions and attempted to find a common ground for the two organizations. He explained that a lack of understanding of the differing purposes of the YCL and the Youth Section led to "misunderstandings and antagonism between the two groups." Attempting to settle these, Sey-chuk argued that the task of the Youth Section was "to nurture culture-educational activity amongst the Ukrainian youth preparing it for the class struggle," while the YCL, particularly through its Ukrainian members, was meant "to show leadership to all revolutionary (labour) mass organizations of youth, including the Youth Section of the ULFTA." While clearly supporting the idea of a close and hierarchical connection between the YCL and the Youth Section, Seychuk went on to warn both groups, especially the YCL, to act carefully and respectfully and asserted that much antagonism had been generated by the view of YCL members that the Youth Section was "an unnecessary organization."[51]

Clearly Comintern and party policy at the time of the "turn" in the early 1930s and of the Popular Front in the mid- to late- 1930s intensified the pressure that the party placed on youngster's groups like the Youth Section. While many in the ULFTA leadership sought to follow party directives as closely as possible, most realized that this would be impossible given the continued contempt that the party had for the ULFTA's cultural mandate and interests, and the importance that ULFTA members and supporters placed on these ideals. Understanding the pressures they faced, many ULFTA leaders sought compromise between both sides. These efforts took on several forms when it came to the Youth Section, and few real shifts took place in the youth group despite the dramatic rhetoric employed by the party and ULFTA leaders. Throughout the 1930s, ULFTA leaders continued to encourage youngsters to join not only the Junior Section or the Youth Section but also the CPC's children's group (the Young Pioneers) or the YCL. In the same way that the CPC was pushing the women's and men's branches, it and the ULFTA encouraged youngsters in the Junior and Youth Sections to collaborate with other young people's organizations in order to gain new contacts and recruits for the class struggle.[52] By the period of the Popular Front in the mid-1930s little had changed as members of the Junior and Youth Sections continued to be encouraged by both the CPC and the ULFTA leadership, in the name of a "United Front against War and Fascism," to form alliances with other young people's organizations. In a gesture to the party and to conform to this new agenda, the delegates to the sixteenth national convention of the ULFTA in 1937 voted to change name of the Sektsia molodi (Youth Section) to the Federatsia kanadsko-ukrainskoi molodi (Canadian Ukrainian Youth Federation) in an effort to appeal to a wider constituency of Ukrainian youth.[53] Despite the name change, however, many of the day-to-day activities of young people remained the same – centred in the ULFTA – as they had in the 1920s and early 1930s. This sloganeering, therefore, seemed to represent an effort by Ukrainian leaders to placate the party without making any fundamental – and potentially unpopular – shifts with regard to the work of the Ukrainian children and youth. Moreover, while evidence to indicate the success of this initiative is scant, given the hostility of other Ukrainian groups to the Ukrainian left, it is unlikely that their children were drawn en masse to the Canadian Ukrainian Youth Federation.

Many young people did become more politically active and aware during the 1930s, likely from a combination of party pressure, ULFTA training, and their own real life experiences growing up in working-class, immigrant neighbourhoods. Some, like Youth Section member Fred Zwarch, actively advocated the program set out by the party. In 1936, supporting the party's calls for a Popular Front, he wrote to *Unite the Youth*, a bilingual (Ukrainian and English) magazine published in 1936 in honour of the tenth anniversary of the Youth Section. He exhorted young people to use drama, sporting events, social activities, and educationals to construct "a genuine mass non-party youth organization" made up "of not only young Communists, but also of young Socialists, Cooperative Commonwealth [Federation] youth, students and all other progressive-minded youth ... who are willing fighters against war and fascism and for the general welfare of the young generation."[54]

Most young people, unlike Zwarch, continued to centre their political expression and cultural activity in the ULFTA. Moreover, though politicization and activism throughout the 1930s took on a greater urgency in all facets of the association, the methods used by the movement to carry out these activities remained largely unchanged, as did the popularity of activities for children and youth. In addition to conducting their activism through Ukrainian school, orchestras, and plays, children and youth increasingly supported strikes, joined protests against war and fascism, marched in May Day parades, and raised funds for various causes related to both the ULFTA and the party.[55] Members of the Youth Section in Broad Valley, Manitoba, for example, took part "in the struggle against the tax sales, relief grievances, [and] bailiff sales."[56] Concerns for conditions in western Ukraine, peace, and protests against the rising clouds of imperialist war were also added to the list of issues with which the ULFTA was preoccupied during the Depression. In addition to the adults, the children and youth shared these concerns and were central to protests and actions taken in support of these causes.

While the CPC-YCL connection hung over the movement, bullying the Youth Section, the ULFTA leaders too were challenged in the field of work with youngsters. One of the reasons ULFTA organizers were reluctant to insist aggressively on children and youth towing the party line was that they were well aware that many youngsters were fully prepared to leave if the Junior or Youth Section failed to adequately address their interests. While still ensuring that the ULFTA's political and cultural objectives were being met, organizers had to work hard to hold young people's attention and keep them coming to meetings and functions. Nowhere was this more evident than where the educational was concerned.

The educational was one of the most important components of the Junior and Youth Sections' mandates. The sections' educationals were similar to those that took place in adult branches, usually consisting of a lecture by a ULFTA leader or of a group reading of a ULFTA newspaper. Speakers tried to teach youngsters how to be good, class-conscious, Ukrainian young people, by discussing Ukraine, the history of the Soviet Union, and other issues relevant to working-class Ukrainian children and youth. Like some adults, some youngsters enjoyed and were profoundly influenced and politicized by these lessons. "The Youth Section has given me a correct outlook on the world so that now I can understand the reasons for the present hardships and sufferings of the working class and the working class youth in particular," explained Youth Section member Nick Hrynchyshyn in 1936. "But more than that," he asserted, " it has shown me the way out of these present miserable conditions and the way to a happy new world."[57]

Not all youngsters were as moved by the educationals as Hrynchyshyn, however. Many youngsters found the educationals – and even many branch activities – to be dull. They demonstrated their ennui in a number of ways: by offering suggestions to improve branch life or, if this proved too difficult, by leaving the organization. Membership loss was clearly a constant problem, as a letter from Youth Section member M. Dembitski illustrates. In 1931 he wrote to an organizational newspaper on the topic "Why Are Some Members Leaving the Youth Section?" in an effort to produce change. He argued that members stayed away because the meetings were simply not interesting. He suggested that, in order to keep members engaged, the Youth Section needed to spend less time holding meetings, paying dues, and emphasizing "slogans" in terms of educational work.[58]

Others argued that, given the competition that the movement faced from popular culture in retaining children's interest, the labour temples needed to make use of new technology and present the class struggle in more novel and engaging ways. This seemed a particularly important tactic during the Popular Front period, as the movement tried to attract a greater variety of Ukrainian children to its activities. In 1936, for example, Anna Gnit suggested following the lead of a church that used lantern shows to engage its child congregants. "Instead of showing scenes of Jesus," she proposed, "we can show them scenes from the life of the workers' and farmers' children in Canada and other countries, contrasting this with the life of the people in the USSR."[59] Nor did she feel it necessary that all such spectacles be imbued with class content, suggesting that Mickey Mouse cartoons could also be shown. Similar ideas were implemented in many locales. Myron Shatulsky recalled going to the Winnipeg Ukrainian labour temple to see popular films; featuring Hollywood actors like Gene Autry or Jean Harlow, the movies were shown on the hall's 35 mm projector on Wednesdays to Fridays, and sometimes on Saturdays if there was no ULFTA play scheduled.[60]

The ULFTA leadership also turned to other means to keep children and youth engaged and active. The most important of these were sports. As sports historian Bruce Kidd has illustrated, Ukrainians did not bring to Canada "a strong sports tradition." Nonetheless, thanks to participation in sports at school or in their working-class neighbourhoods, and encouraged by the formation of the CPC- and YCL-led Workers' Sports Association (WSA), many young Ukrainians eagerly embraced a variety of hall-led sports as their favoured form of leisure and activist activity. As a result, according to Kidd, Ukrainians eventually "made up the second most numerous ethnic group within the workers' sports movement."[61]

Ukrainian labour temples organizers viewed the presence of physical-activity groups as crucial to recruiting and retaining a strong membership base of working-class-minded children and youth. Moreover, like at the Ukrainian worker children's schools, sports at the Ukrainian labour temples offered an important, labour-centred, radical alternative to those provided by religious and quasi-religious groups like the Young Men's Christian Association (YMCA), Girl Guides, or Boy Scouts. "These are bourgeoisie clubs, the youths there are being cultivated in the bourgeoisie way," explained an organizer, speaking critically of the YMCA in 1933, "They are absolutely kept in ignorance of the class struggle in the economic life of the people. Therefore we must support and build up our own Sports Club."[62] Sports were an important strategy that local branches were especially encouraged to employ during the summer months, when the ULFTA cultural season and the public-school year ended. Organizers feared that young people might drift away from the halls for good if they pursued activities (and made new non-ULFTA friends) outside the movement during their summer vacations.[63] Endeavouring to build the Comintern-mandated Popular Front during the 1930s, organizers held out great hope that sports might attract to the ULFTA young people from other Ukrainian, non-Ukrainian, and even non-leftist groups.[64] Most sports activities took place under the auspices of the Junior Section, and all halls eventually had some form of physical activity, though it varied according to locality and resources.

There is indication that some sporting activities were organized along gender lines. Organizers especially believed that sports were an important way to attract and retain boys for the movement. At certain times they believed that boys needed specific diversions because of extenuating social or economic circumstances. During the Depression in Welland, for example, Nick Petrachenko recalled, "all the young guys were unemployed at the time." Members of the Ukrainian labour temple suggested that a sports club be created for them so they would have something to do. Since there was no money to buy mats, the young men made some out of canvas and used them to perform "various exercises [and] gymnastics," and anyone in the area, "whether a member or not, could participate."[65] It is not clear whether the needs of unemployed girls were viewed in the same light. Even if they were playing the same sport, games or teams would sometimes be structured to separate the girls and the boys. As Ollie Hillman recalled, this did not always necessarily reflect attitudes that certain sports were inappropriate (because they were deemed either unfeminine or too rough) for girls or that boys needed extra attention or resources. Rather, she explained, "the boys had their own sports because they were heavier."[66] In many instances, though, gender divisions were not guaranteed; girls and boys often could and did play together.

A variety of sports was popular with these Ukrainian children. In the summer they commonly played baseball, hiked, or took organized nature walks. At ULFTA picnics the track and field events were also popular.[67] In the winter youngsters often tobogganed or skated. In Winnipeg, Mike Seychuk and the Junior Section formed a skating club: "We got a boxcar from the CPR for a vacant lot, put a heater in there, and this was our club room. We got old boards from people and built a rink. The city flooded it for us, and we had a skating rink for the whole winter."[68] Year round, by far the most popular and widely practised sporting activity was gymnastics (also called *acrobatics*). They were relatively easy to organize, and many children – from the youngest to the oldest – could take part at a single time (as opposed to team sports for which participant numbers were limited), and the activity could easily accommodate girls and boys together.[69] Moreover, gymnastics could be politicized more easily and more overtly than could other sports, which might only offer organizers the chance to teach youngsters the value of collective activity. Children often, for example, performed their routines at concerts and festivals, events that helped to raise money and generate new members for the ULFTA. At the same time it was easy to incorporate – as many groups often did – Soviet or communist symbols into these acts.[70] The performances were usually as well received and impressive as regular concerts or plays, apparently even to those who were not ULFTA boosters. "It was really marvellous and the place was packed, many went home without seeing it due to a lack of space," recounted an anonymous RCMP informant of a Winnipeg sports club's gymnastics performance in February 1933. "They had young children performing acrobatics wonderfully, boys and girls and grown-up boys and girls, together," he enthused. "The performances were astonishing and must have had careful preparation. Many membership forms were being filled out all over the audience."[71]

Although all halls across Canada attempted to integrate some degree of activity for young people into their local programming, such activities tended to vary in both consistency and size according to the nature of the Ukrainian community in the hall's vicinity. Halls in urban centres like Winnipeg, Edmonton, or Toronto typically possessed a larger membership base than did isolated farming communities or smaller resource towns from which to draw children and youth to activities. Generally the large communities were better able to support the cost of a teacher to coordinate classes and groups. Smaller halls, especially those in rural areas, tended to have a more difficult time organizing and maintaining young people's activities. Distance between farm families, inadequate financial resources (which became magnified for many halls during the Depression), and a lack of teachers who were qualified to carry out the ULFTA educational mandate meant that functions for children and youth in many areas were at best sporadic, if they existed at all.[72] One of the ways the ULFTA attempted to alleviate this problem was through the publication of a variety of Ukrainian-language newspapers to serve its various membership constituencies. Just as it did for adults, so too did the movement print a special newspaper for youngsters. *Svit molodi* (The youth's world) was created in 1927 to serve the needs of theYouth Section. Prior to the founding of *Svit molodi*, special pages in the women's newspaper, *Robitnytsia*, had been devoted to serving young people, particularly children. *Svit molodi* seemed to fill a void; by 1929 it boasted over 3,700 subscribers across the country.

Like the adult papers, *Svit molodi* was at heart a teaching and recruitment tool geared to the politicization of, in this case, youngsters. From it, young people learned about Marxist-Leninism, the fight for workers' rights (both locally and around the world), and the ULFTA's interpretation of current events. Its articles, poems, letters, and features supplemented and reinforced lessons that children and youth learned at hall schools (and, leaders hoped, undid bourgeois lessons learned in public schools), in cultural activities, and in the Junior and Youth Sections. Articles like "First of May – A Day to Fight," which appeared in the April 1932 issue, explored labour history, contemporary conditions for workers, and government oppression, encouraging youngsters to take part in the international proletarian struggle.[73] As it was in Ukrainian, *Svit molodi* provided young people with literature to practise and hone their Ukrainian language skills, opportunities not afforded them in public school. This was especially critical for children and youth living in remote rural communities where access to Ukrainian school was nearly impossible. *Svit molodi* was also interactive. Youngsters could both read features and write their own letters and articles for publication.

In addition, *Svit molodi* worked as an essential tool for inter-branch communication and for building the movement, much in the same way that the adult newspapers functioned. To carry out their responsibilities in corresponding with the newspaper, youth branches were expected to elect a press correspondent, called a Yunkor or Yunkorka (both boys and girls were encouraged to hold the position), to write to the newspaper, detailing their activities. Organizers hoped that, by reading about what other groups were doing, young people would be inspired to be active similarly in their localities. "I'm in the third grade of the Ukrainian Worker Children's School," wrote eleven-year-old Yunkor Wasyl Ravliuk of Coleman, Alberta, in 1927, "There aren't many of us, but we're doing a lot of work. We've already performed the play 'The Little Blacksmiths' and are preparing for a concert." Ravliuk went on to thank the women's branch for the post-play supper its members had prepared for the children, which helped to raise funds for a branch library. He closed with commendations for the group's instructor: "Our teacher A. Zablotsky works very hard to turn us into intelligent children who don't hang out on the streets."[74]

Svit molodi represented a further and significant attempt at autonomy from the CPC on the part of the ULFTA. It was another effort to resist party control and attempts at anglicization of the communist left. The party expected all young people, including the Ukrainians, to read its English-language organ, *The Young Worker*. As we know, however, Ukrainian leaders and parents wanted their children to be fluent in Ukrainian language and culture as well as proletarian politics. Creating a newspaper to facilitate this seemed a natural step. It is not surprising that the CPC tried to dictate the shape and content of *Svit molodi*. Again, like ULFTA leaders in other circumstances, the editors of *Svit molodi* attempted to find common ground with the party without compromising the newspaper's Ukrainian cultural and political integrity. For example, the newspaper routinely carried advertisements for *The Young Worker* and encouraged members of the Youth Section to subscribe to it and take part in its fund-raising campaigns.[75] *Svit molodi* also featured advertisements reminding youngsters to "Join the Ranks of the YCL!" and articles instructing them to "Step Up to the Ranks of the Young Communist League and Young Pioneers!"[76] As part of the early 1930s' "turn," the newspaper's name was even changed to *Boiova molod* (Militant youth) to address better the "revolutionary movement ... sweeping the world."[77] During the 1930s the newspaper took on a more radical tone, partly because of Depression conditions and partly because many of those young leaders who wrote for the newspaper held membership in both the Youth Section and the YCL.

Despite its best efforts to train youngsters in the Ukrainian language, however, the ULFTA saw signs early on that it was losing the linguistic battle. The UWCSs, cultural activities, and even *Svit molodi* were no match for North American popular culture, the public school system, and the youngsters' multi-ethnic neighbourhoods where the common language of communication among Jewish, German, Russian, Polish, Ukrainian, and other working-class young people was English.[78] Even those youth whom leaders hoped would move to the forefront of the movement often had a great degree of difficulty functioning in Ukrainian. Young Bill Philipovich, for example, struggled to compose his autobiography and application for the 1936 Higher Educational Course because it had to be in Ukrainian.[79] For many young people born to

Ukrainian immigrant parents, a language-based generation gap of sorts was created at home and at the hall.

In the interwar period the language problem was less pronounced than it would become for the movement during the post-war era. Nonetheless, during the 1930s it was becoming noticeable that there was an issue with communication in the Ukrainian language as far as many children and youth were concerned. The ULFTA recognized this problem and attempted to moderate the effects of the process of assimilation in several ways. In doing so, it continued to reassert its autonomy from the party. Although it could have simply directed young people to read the English-language CPC newspapers or join the YCL, little to no positive Ukrainian content could be found there. The ULFTA thus refused to accept this solution, hoping to keep children and youth within a Ukrainian milieu. Sometimes leaders continued to demand that youngsters try to communicate and carry out their organizational work in the Ukrainian language regardless of their comfort level or ability. This solution was awkward and ultimately ineffective, however. "While this forced the young people to learn to express themselves in Ukrainian," former Youth Section member Misha Korol recalled, "it also held back many who found the language a big obstacle."[80]

In other instances, particularly as the 1930s wore on, the ULFTA encouraged compromise between the use of English and of Ukrainian to ensure that children and youth would join and remain with Ukrainian labour temple activities. Leaders urged halls to create libraries that incorporated both English and Ukrainian materials. They also instructed youth organizers to conduct meetings and other activities in the language in which young members were most comfortable. The organizational newspaper *Ukrainski robitnychi visty* (Ukrainian labour news) even incorporated a section for youth during the mid-1930s that made use of both English and Ukrainian in articles and correspondence.[81]

At the same time, to command and hold the attention of youngsters the ULFTA encouraged the proliferation of Ukrainian cultural activities for which language skills were unnecessary. One of the most important was Ukrainian folk-dance. The first performances of Ukrainian folk dancing in the halls took place in 1926. That same year in Winnipeg the ULFTA held courses in Ukrainian folk-dance. The following year the ULFTA national convention voted to include folk dancing as a new activity for Ukrainian school students.[82] Within a year folk-dance groups and classes had sprung up among ULFTA groups across Canada, including Ottawa, South Porcupine, Edmonton, Fort Frances, to name but a

3. ULFTA dancers, West Toronto, ca. 1930. Stavroff Private Collection.

few.[83] Folk dancing offered another means through which to politicize
children and youth while imparting in them a strong sense of Ukrainianness. The folk-dances, modelled on traditional regional Ukrainian
dance styles, were not in and of themselves political. However, the fact
that children and youth danced them in a country overtly hostile to
Ukrainians and that these performances were used to raise money to
fund the ULFTA's (and sometimes the party's) activities imbued them
with a radical political purpose. Folk dancing developed and remained
as one of the most consistently popular pursuits for youngsters. It lin-
gers today as one of the few activities attracting children and youth to
the Ukrainian labour temples.

The interwar era was in many ways a period of cultural and organizational prosperity for the ULFTA, particularly where its activities for
children and youth were concerned. A youngster growing up in the
Ukrainian left during the 1920s and 1930s experienced a distinct type of
radical childhood thanks to the particular ways in which definitions of
class, ethnicity, age, and, to a lesser extent, gender converged to shape

their identities. Their sense of Ukrainianness distinguished them from other radical children in Canada, while the class-consciousness that their parents, leaders, and teachers tried to instil in them set them apart from other Ukrainian children (especially those from nationalist or religious families). At the same time, age differentiated them from their adult counterparts and offered girls some advantages over their mothers in terms of equal access with boys to organizational opportunities. Childhood – to a certain age – gave girls some freedom to pursue positions and activities in the movement that were unavailable to women. As a child reached adulthood, however, gender roles became more rigidly defined and enforced in keeping with discourses of masculinities and femininities in the movement. Young men were expected to put their skills to work for the main ULFTA branch or its related organizations. Most young women – unless they had the opportunity to teach, thanks to HEC attendance – would find their labours directed towards the women's branch and work with youngsters.

Leaders and parents worked to impart in young people a strong sense of Ukrainianness and understanding of the national and international proletarian situation. Reflected in these efforts was the adult hope and expectation that children would grow up with an intense and ongoing commitment to the Ukrainian left, the class struggle, and Ukrainian culture and history, becoming enlightened and active Ukrainian leftist adults. Young people, too, made important contributions to the shape of the movement, particularly where their own activities and experiences were concerned. Leaders had to work hard to accommodate youngsters' interests and needs – particularly their demands that activities be fun and, increasingly, in English – while still maintaining integral movement values. As a result organizers often reworked activities to keep them attractive to children and youth but remaining true to the cultural and political milieu of the radical Ukrainian community and the broader Canadian left during the interwar years.

To maintain the movement's Ukrainian integrity, leaders also continually and successfully fended off CPC efforts to anglicize and control the Ukrainian left's organizations and activities. Although the party did influence the shape of youngsters' activities to some degree, rarely did it rework these activities in any sort of dramatic or fundamental fashion. In the end, the party was fighting a battle it could not win. Communist officialdom neglected to appreciate that the party line (as manifest or proscribed) could not fully satisfy the needs of Ukrainian leftists, be they female or male, child or adult, fighting as they were not only economic but also ethnic and social oppression. It failed to address their oppression as both Ukrainians and members of the working class. Heaping ethnocentric criticism on these Ukrainians – calling them backward, conservative, "right-wing deviationists" – for their radical cultural and political pursuits only served to reinforce the need for a separate sphere of work.

Overall, the efforts of leaders and the encouragement that young people received from their parents to attend events at the hall paid off during the interwar era. From the time of their official inception with the advent of the ULTA at the end of the Great War to the early months of the Second World War, groups for leftist Ukrainian children and youth, like those for adults, thrived across the country. Many who came of age in the 1920s and 1930s continued to support the movement in which they had grown up, opting to become members of adult branches at the halls or, most often in the case of young men, leaders at the national level of the movement. The dedication of these young adults (particularly the women) would become especially crucial during the Second World War. As we shall see, aggressive state intervention would fundamentally challenge the Ukrainian left's very existence.

4 "Dear Kate, I Don't Know How You Manage!": The Ukrainian Left and the Second World War

In the wee hours of 6 June 1940 Mary Prokop and her husband, Peter, prematurely awoke to the sound of loud knocking at their North End Winnipeg door. When they opened it, the two long-time ULFTA members faced an RCMP Red Squad that was primed to raid the couple's home and arrest Peter in a deliberately public, humiliating manner. Sixteen other Ukrainian men, whose Winnipeg households had endured the same early morning encounter with the Canadian state, joined him in jail.

Unable to contact their menfolk for days, Mary, the other affected wives and families, and the community as a whole had no idea where or on what charges authorities were holding the men. "It took a few days of frantic enquiries and unbearable anxiety," Mary recalled, "before our lawyer found out that our husbands were interned at Kananaskis in Southern Alberta."[1] There, labelled "Prisoners of War," Peter and the Winnipeg men found themselves in familiar and supportive company. Seventeen additional Ukrainian and some sixty other pro-communist and communist men drawn from across Canada would come to be isolated together for nearly a year and half behind barbed wire and bars.

Their detention was part of a broader climate of repression, intimidation, and fear that hung over many leftists in wartime Canada. Supporters of the CPC and the ULFTA were targets allegedly because of the anti-war position that these organizations had assumed after Hitler and Stalin had signed the infamous German-Soviet Pact in August of 1939. Fearing disruption and looking for an opportunity to silence Canadian radical groups, which had long been a thorn in the government's side, Prime Minister William Lyon Mackenzie King, via the War Measures Act, had invoked an Order-in-Council on 4 June 1940 banning the ULFTA, along with the CPC and several other groups. The government declared the ULFTA's press and activities to be illegal and soon confiscated, closed, and even sold some of its halls, often to nationalist Ukrainian groups, the Ukrainian left's long-time enemies. It also interned some of its most prominent leaders. Of the one hundred communist or pro-communist men imprisoned and labelled "Prisoners of War" or "Enemy Aliens" at that time, Ukrainians comprised about one third. They remained incarcerated even after the Soviet Union and the ULFTA membership began to support the Allied cause.[2] The summer of 1940 saw the Ukrainian left's golden age grind to an abrupt halt.

A significant difference existed between the incarceration of these Ukrainians (and their non-Ukrainian comrades) and that of Ukrainians and other Eastern Europeans in the First World War. By the end of the 1930s the ULFTA was understood to be a key pillar of the Canadian radical left, and the men were singled out for this reason, not for their ethnicity. They continued to be viewed as "dangerous foreigners"; however, it was in their radical political ideology and activism that accusations of disloyalty were grounded, not in perceived ethnic loyalties. In 1940 the government-supported formation of the Ukrainian Canadian Committee (UCC), an umbrella organization encompassing the major (and rival) nationalist factions, further reinforced the marginalization of progressive Ukrainians.[3]

Despite the government's best efforts at repression, however, the Ukrainian left not only survived the war but also continued into the post-war period as an active and vibrant working-class Ukrainian movement. As an outcome of the intersections of class, ethnicity, and gender in the wartime context, prescriptions and performance of femininity and masculinity adjusted. Roles for women and men stretched to accommodate wartime necessity, just as they did in other contexts of contemporary North American society. Imprisoned, Peter and the other men put their organizational skills to work to recreate a strong semblance of the activist communities they had left behind. They also cheered and nurtured one another, sometimes by engaging, in the absence of women, the traditionally feminine modes of activism like cooking or caregiving as the internment conditions necessitated.

On the outside, the women adjusted their activism to sustain the imprisoned and secure their liberty, while working to ensure that upon their release Peter and his comrades could return to a movement intact in terms of principles, procedure, and direction. Women like Mary Prokop, working under conditions of state siege, worry, and economic stress (still lingering from the Depression and compounded by the internments), nurtured the remaining facets of the community. Many of them, especially those from the younger Canadian-born, English-speaking cohort to which Prokop belonged, embraced traditionally masculine forms of activism. The increased use of the English language by these women in their activism, necessitated by wartime circumstance, marked a slowly emerging shift in generational understandings and performances of Ukrainianness (and eventually Ukrainian Canadianness) within the movement, which would become most keenly felt after the war.

Leveraging the community's long entrenched relationships and engagement with the broader Canadian left where the common language of activism was English, these women, along with other non-Ukrainian women and men, supported their imprisoned men folk, while actively demanding and pursuing their release by publicly and strategically characterizing them not as dangerous radicals but as devoted family men and community leaders. They also helped to run the related redress campaign, calling for the return of the confiscated Ukrainian labour temples. At the same time they played an active part in supporting the broader war effort. All the while, they facilitated their children's involvement in these struggles. Youngsters played key roles in dealing with the wartime crisis; they assisted with the women's activism and put their cultural skills to work by participating in concerts for the troops or to raise money for the war effort, all of which helped to create positive publicity for the embattled movement.

Despite these women's and men's wartime role reversals, notions of gender remained largely and firmly intact. Hegemonic masculinity's interwar characteristics, for example, stayed entrenched, with certain facets amplified; the internees embodied most those of self-sacrifice and martyrdom, in particular. Complicit masculinity reconfigured in recognition of the potential for internment faced by all men if they engaged in public support or leadership of the movement at this time. Expectations for these men revolved around overt support of the war – through war work and wartime military service – all of which helped to bolster the image of the Ukrainian left as a respectable community, loyal and supportive of the war effort. Hegemonic femininity's characteristics broadened temporarily to incorporate increased leadership expectations prior to the internees' release, and for the most part during this time men deferred to women – those men on the outside, for reasons of safety; those who were interned, because they were cut off from any

other option. The notion of women as breadwinners was also temporarily incorporated as acceptable in internee households. Aside from
women like Mary Prokop, most women continued to embody the oppositional femininity of the interwar period, adjusting the performance
of their activism towards efforts that supported the internees, the war,
and the movement's rebuilding. Our understanding of the experiences
of Ukrainian leftists during the war is uneven. Bohdan Kordan and
Thomas Prymak have well documented the political conflicts among
nationalist groups, united (at times, precariously) as the Ukrainian
Canadian Committee during the war, and their dealings with the Ukrainian leftists, albeit solely from a top-down, community-elite-focused,
and federal government relations perspective.[4] Several studies and
memoirs also highlight the interned men's experiences.[5] Unfortunately
we know very little about the grass roots; the experiences of the non-
interned men and the work of women that was critical to sustaining
the community have received virtually no attention. Frances Swyripa's
monograph on Ukrainian women in Canada contains some brief commentary on the period. Joan Sangster's survey of left-wing women in
Canada considers how Communist Party women sought to challenge
the ban and the internments.[6] However, her book's primary focus on
Anglo-Celtic women precludes an in-depth discussion of the role of
ethnicity and the experiences of the Ukrainian women, most of whom
were not formally tied to the party. This project builds on and expands
the existing body of work by examining how both women and men
negotiated the wartime internment crisis in their day-to-day lives while
still working to maintain their communities, families, and selves.

It also builds on the growing body of literature on internment and
redress. In recent years, in tandem with the growing profile, public
debate, and political success of various redress movements, there has
been a proliferation of historical works on internment. Many feature
a widening of focus. In addition to examining the Second World War
internments through the lens of redress, recent studies have explored
the bureaucratic decision-making process that led to the arrests and
continued detainment of leftist and other men.[7] Scholars focusing on
internment in Canada and in other Allied nations have not only tried to
cover political events surrounding the internment of Japanese Canadians and those incarcerated for their political connections or beliefs; they
have also begun to explore the social history of life in the camps, gender relations between interned men and outside female relatives, the
dynamics of camp life that developed because of the mixed and often

opposing political groups that were forced to cohabit in the camps, and the experiences of interned women.[8]

Throughout these treatments scholars have taken different political positions regarding recent redress movements, offering good examples of living history and the uses of history. For example, left-wing historians Franca Iacovetta, Roberto Perin, and Angelo Principe have criticized what they see as a too sanitized version of the Italian Canadian internment narrative at the core of an elite-driven redress campaign.[9] Others have even played a leading role in redress efforts, as Lubomyr Luciuk has in the fight for recognition and reparation in the case of the internment of Ukrainians and others during the First World War.[10] As Ian Radforth recently observed, historians' perspectives on and involvement in current campaigns offer graphic examples of the complexities of doing public history, the ways we use the past, and the role of historians as public and political figures.[11]

In contrast to most ethnic groups who were interned during wartime periods and lobbied the government for apologies and financial settlements for mistreatment and lost property decades later, the Ukrainian left pursued a redress campaign immediately following the release of their internees. Strongly linked to the movement's views that the interned men were political prisoners and that the community as a whole was persecuted on the basis of ideology, the contemporary support of a variety of individual citizens, civil liberties organizations, and prominent Canadians buttressed the redress efforts of the Ukrainian left. This certainly differed greatly from the experiences of Japanese and Italian internees during the same period and of Ukrainians during the First World War.

Initially, what would become the Ukrainian left's crisis built slowly throughout the spring of 1940. At first the police detained only a handful of ULFTA men with party connections like John Weir and John Naviziwsky.[12] Soon, however, the government employed more aggressive tactics. The massive sweep of 6 June that saw Prokop detained netted the RCMP a total of seventeen Ukrainian anti-fascist leaders. Among them was Andrew Bileski, then manager of the People's Cooperative Dairy, who was sleeping when the police arrived to search his home and haul him away.[13] They also included press editors like Matthew Shatulsky and John Stefanitsky, ULFTA Manitoba organizer John Dubno, and politician William Kolisnyk.[14]

Numerous men managed to avoid the RCMP's clutches and were able to elude arrest for some time. Peter Krawchuk, a ULFTA journalist, evaded police for more than two months after the sweep by going into hiding in Winnipeg.[15] At great personal risk many of them continued political work. Krawchuk and other fugitive men formed a "directing collective" to encourage unity and continued organization. In addition to maintaining the lines of communication with supporters outside Winnipeg, the collective sought a new press organ for the floundering movement to replace the banned *Farmerske zhyttia* (Farmers' life) and *Narodna hazeta* (People's gazette). They dispatched Nick Hrynchyshyn, another wanted man, to Smoky Lake, Alberta, to edit *Holos pravdy* (The voice of truth), a newspaper published by Orthodox clergyman Michael Cependa that had, in the past, "sometimes printed articles which were progressive in spirit."[16] Forced underground, the leaders tried to maintain vestiges of a Ukrainian left during the early 1940s. For most of the rank-and-file ULFTA men, however, any participation was too difficult and dangerous to even contemplate. Many disassociated themselves entirely from the movement for these reasons. Other men disappeared as they took up work in Canada's war industries or joined the armed services. Notions and performance of both hegemonic and complicit masculinities shifted to accommodate this as acceptable in light of wartime necessity. Overall, male participation in the movement outside the internment camps was, at best, limited during the early years of the war.

Of course, the internees felt the constraints on their personal liberties most keenly. As prisoners of war they passed the two years of their incarceration in several different detainment institutions. Immediately following their arrest they spent time in a local holding facility. Soon authorities transferred most of the men to Kananaskis, Alberta, in the heart of the Rocky Mountains. After Hitler attacked the Soviet Union in June of 1941, officials moved the anti-fascists to Petawawa, Ontario, and shortly thereafter to the Hull jail near Ottawa. The men experienced treatment that ranged from harsh to sympathetic at the hands of both guards and other inmates of various political stripes. Despite the difficulty of their circumstances the Ukrainian and other anti-fascist internees made the best of the situation, managing to create semblances of cultural, social, and political activity during the period of their incarceration.

Ian Radforth argues that "while the Communists suffered the usual painful and humiliating constraints imposed on prisoners of war, life was more tolerable for them because of their left politics."[17] That is, they adapted the solidarity and organizational skills to the internment situation and developed supportive and empowering political and social activities. To build a community in prison was not difficult for the Ukrainian anti-fascists as they found themselves in good company, with which they were already well acquainted thanks to the Ukrainian left's long-time relationship with the wider Canadian left. The prison roster read like a veritable "who's who" of the radical community in Canada.[18] "Practically the entire leadership of the Ukrainian and other progressive organizations in Canada were there with me. There were more than a hundred of us altogether," recalled internee Dennis Moysiuk.[19] The presence of so many like-minded men provided support and camaraderie during the incarceration. For the Ukrainian men their keen ethnic solidarity was especially beneficial. They drew on Ukrainian cultural expression to sustain themselves and provide comfort and support to all the anti-fascist internees.

This support was necessary given the difficult conditions that the men encountered in the camps, especially in Kananaskis. To provide guards with a target should a prisoner escape, the officials forced the men to wear a uniform with a red spot on the back.[20] The possibility of violent confrontation was imminent given the presence of fascist internees. Often prison officials contributed to the climate of fear and intimidation by, for example, the way in which they organized lodging. At Kananaskis, internee Myron Kostaniuk recalled, "Camp Commandant Watson ordered that one communist be placed with 11 fascists in each of the huts or shanties that held 12 people, [instructing] the German representatives 'to wipe the floors with them.'"[21] To make matters worse, in all of the prison facilities they were isolated from their families and friends. The authorities barred visitors, severely limited and censored correspondence with family and friends, and forbade newspapers and other sources of information about the outside world.[22]

In spite of the circumstances the men at times exercised a striking degree of agency and ingenuity. In Kananaskis, for example, they forcibly occupied barrack number 47, using it as a makeshift labour temple. They organized a committee to advocate for their rights in the camp, set up a library, and held discussions and lectures on topics of a political nature just as they would have done at ULFTA or party meetings prior to the war. They even developed courses in German and English. On the cultural side, the internees organized a choir, singing traditional Ukrainian folk music as well as songs written specifically about their experiences in the camps. These songs helped to keep their spirits up and created meaning out of their internment. As John Weir's

"Kananaskis Prisoners' Song" put it, "They can't intern all the workers / They can't drown the world in blood / Though they vent their rage upon us / They can't dam the ocean's flood." The men also kept up morale by observing important labour holidays such as the anniversary of the October Revolution and May Day. These celebrations mimicked wherever possible those that would have taken place at the Ukrainian labour temples. "There were speeches read, a delicious meal (prepared by ourselves), and also a concert program which included merry joking,"[23] Peter Krawchuk recalled of these events.

When conditions became unbearable, the men used their activist skills to protest. After their move to Petawawa, for example, they staged demonstrations against the poor food and the increased hostility of the fascist prisoners. This compelled authorities to move the men to the Hull jail, where they enjoyed significantly better conditions, including relaxed attention from the guards. There, internee Andrew Bileski explained, the men even "had a lot of fun." They played sports, did their own cooking, made homebrew, had access to daily newspapers, and conducted classes in bookkeeping and political economy.[24] Using a vat of cottage cheese from the People's Cooperative Dairy and sending it on a refrigerator car from Winnipeg, supporters smuggled the men a crystal set. The gift was a boon in more ways than one. "We not only received a radio but our cook, [internee] Peter Keveryha, ... made delicious *varenyky* out of that cheese for the entire anti-fascist commune," Peter Krawchuk recounted. "It meant that the parcel from our comrades in Winnipeg was just as tasty as it was useful."[25]

On the outside the women began regrouping – individually and collectively – immediately after the sweep, trying as best as they could to hold the Ukrainian left together and come to terms with the uncertainty of not knowing when their menfolk might come home. Interestingly, unlike the non-interned men, women were able to function openly and publicly despite the repressive wartime climate for radicals. This hinged on the negative regard in which most ULFTA women's work was held prior to the war. Both the Ukrainian left's male leadership and the RCMP's surveillance officers perceived – and often denigrated – these women's efforts as mostly insignificant support work (accepting the frequent criticism of many of the women as politically "backwards"). This led the RCMP to seriously underestimate the ULFTA women as an important and competent constituency of resistance when authorities were determining the targets for arrest and internment.

Particularly damaging to the state's repressive efforts was the RCMP's failure to note the potential of the cohort of young women. As girls, they had absorbed the movement's cultural and political values through the ULFTA's cultural schools, newspapers, and Junior and Youth Sections, training that some had the opportunity to further hone through the Higher Educational Courses. Growing up in Ukrainian-speaking homes provided many with a solid grasp of the language skills that were reinforced at the hall. At the same time, their English-language public school education meant that they were bilingual and had a clear understanding of and access to mainstream Canadian society.

As few women held visible movement-valued positions and consistently found themselves in roles subordinate to men, women's activist potential went under-acknowledged. Testament to this is the fact that authorities did not detain even one during the sweep that netted Peter and the others. Thus they did not suffer the same fate as the conspicuous Anglo-Celtic party organizers Annie Buller and Gladys MacDonald and a small number of more vocal women with fascist connections whom the government detained during the earlier war years.[26]

The under-estimation of the Ukrainian women ironically permitted them the space and freedom they needed to act in the absence of the male leaders, a pattern that was common among radical women, as Anne Morelli and José Moya have shown.[27] Perceived as less dangerous, notorious, or capable, young women like Prokop were thus able to step seamlessly into the roles vacated by their menfolk and to even develop new roles to deal with the wartime internment emergency. Thanks to their English and Ukrainian language skills, they were not isolated like their foremothers were and thus were able to lead the Ukrainian left. At the same time, they were able to take advantage of the movement's long-time connections with the wider Canadian left, using their language and leadership skills to readily forge enduring cross-cultural links with outside groups and left-wing women of other ethnicities locally and across the country.

As it was for women in other communities who were faced with internment and the loss of male breadwinners,[28] one of their most pressing concerns was money. Still dealing with conditions lingering from the Depression, the Ukrainian women had to find alternative means of income to replace their husband's lost wages in order to support themselves and, in many cases, their children. To do so, they employed a variety of means. Some turned to the progressive Ukrainian community for help. Their supporters, Prokop recalled, formed a committee to aid the families of the arrested men. She explained, "The Aid Committee collected funds amongst friends of the labour movement and from time to time helped those who needed it most."[29] The wives and their supporters also challenged local authorities for financial assistance. In Winnipeg, for example, as early as August 1940 the wives of the interned united to demand material support from the local relief office.[30] Relief, however, was a double-edged sword for many women. Few, in fact, qualified; only those with dependent children or who were physically unable to work did.

Not surprisingly, as we know from studies of relief during the Depression, payments were inadequate, inconsistent, and qualifying for and receiving relief was a humiliating experience. The women had to fight – often unsuccessfully – for every dime. Anastasia Kolisnyk found herself alone with her nine-year-old daughter and an older, unemployed son when the RCMP took her husband, Bill. "I went to the relief office," she recalled, "and they gave me $13.00 for a month for my [daughter] and myself, but nothing for my son." When she returned for more the following month, those in charge refused her request. "I pleaded and begged, but all I got was insults from the men working in the government offices." Eventually, a few months later, they did provide her with two cords of wood, which were supposed to last the entire Winnipeg winter. As she was unable to pay her bills, the electric company cut off her electricity, the bank repossessed the family car, and the mortgage company foreclosed on the family home. Perhaps the most humiliating moment, however, came after her daughter experienced infected tonsils and, shortly afterwards, the measles. Kolisnyk could not afford a doctor's services, and, compounded by her lack of funds for sufficient food, her daughter lost a lot of weight. Amid this turmoil, she faced the implication that she was a negligent mother. "I received a card from the school nurse, saying: 'Audrey is 9 pounds underweight,'" which asked – as if Kolisnyk was not already struggling to do so – "would I give her more nourishing food and doctor's care."[31]

Women had to employ other strategies to survive financially if they were not "fortunate" enough to qualify for relief. As historians have demonstrated for women of other ethnicities and political stripes,[32] some turned to close friends or kin for financial assistance during the internment crisis. By default and out of necessity, many of the internees' wives became the family breadwinner, a role previously constructed as masculine and which notions of hegemonic femininity temporarily stretched to accommodate. Shut out of her work for the ULFTA,

Prokop could find only a poorly paying position in the Winnipeg needle trades. Unable to afford their apartment without Peter's wages, she found it necessary to move in with friends and give away many treasured possessions that she was unable to store.[33] Helen Weir (Weviursky) encountered similar hardship after the internment of her husband and prominent party leader John. She had spent her childhood in the mining communities of Hardieville and Lethbridge, Alberta, where she joined the ULFTA choirs and orchestras. During the Depression she had taken part in demonstrations – sometimes as a featured speaker – collected food to help striking miners and their families, and joined the Young Communist League. In 1932 she married John, with whom she would have two children. They moved to Toronto in 1932, where she continued her activism by working for the CPC's newspaper, the *Daily Clarion*. The family moved to Winnipeg in 1939, and John became editor of the *Mid-West Clarion*. His internment forced her to turn to family for help. Initially she remained in Winnipeg to work and sent her children to Lethbridge to stay with her widowed mother. Soon, finding herself with no livelihood, she joined them. "My relatives helped me to survive from day to day," Weir recalled; she supplemented this assistance with a job in a store that paid $7.50 a week.[34]

These women also had to deal with the emotional trauma brought on by their husband's absence and the constant atmosphere hanging over the working-class communities of being under state siege. The threat of further arrests and raids was persistent. Anastasia Galange had acted as recording secretary of the local Brantford, Ontario, women's branch and had been an avid cultural participant from the time she came to Canada and joined the ULFTA in 1936. During the summer immediately following the men's arrests RCMP visits frequently disrupted her household. "They came as many as three times a week and searched our house," she recalled. "They seized our photographs, our sheet music, and the children's readers. They told me to go back where I came from."[35] In Winnipeg, police cruisers were a constant presence in the North End. "The homes and apartments of the wives and families of the internees were especially watched," remembered Prokop. "We women were shadowed."[36]

Mothers of young children had to contend with not only their own anxiety but also the stress of trying to explain why, as Prokop expressed, "the police took Daddy away."[37] Katherine Shatulsky had acted as financial secretary of the Winnipeg women's branch, taught Ukrainian embroidery to the local ULFTA Junior Section, and chaperoned the ULFTA's Girls Mandolin Orchestra on its tours of Canada; she had her world turned upside down when the RCMP arrested her husband, Matthew. To cope financially and support her son, Myron, she took in boarders and worked as a seamstress in a Winnipeg factory, a situation that exacerbated the stress she was enduring in Matthew's absence. As she explained in one of her many protest letters to Justice Minister Louis St Laurent, "My young son's concern about his father and constant questions as to when he is coming home further aggravates the strain on me."[38] For many women the stress manifested itself physically. For the older ones it was particularly difficult. "Their nerves were strained to the breaking point," remembered Prokop, "and some never regained their former health." Despite her younger years, she herself developed a debilitating medical condition. Just over a year after Peter's arrest Prokop required hospitalization for a serious ulcer.[39]

The wives of the interned frequently turned to one another for emotional support. In Winnipeg they gathered once a week, using the time to share news and letters from their husbands. Prokop was an active participant. "Although not all were politically prepared for the harsh conditions we faced, we stuck together and generally the morale was high," she explained. "Our regular meetings and mutual support and the support of our friends was what kept us going."[40] Across Canada leftist women of a variety of ethnic backgrounds also gathered together and wrote to one another about their experiences and their husband's incarceration.[41] Through these local groups and national connections an organized opposition to the internment crisis soon emerged, uniting the Ukrainian women with other concerned individuals.

Together the women and their supporters employed diverse individual and collective tactics to push for the men's release, often with the younger women like Prokop at the operational helm of the Ukrainian left's efforts. The loss of the Ukrainian labour temples meant that the women had to find alternative spaces in which to congregate. Despite considerable personal risk local women generously opened their homes for socials and meetings in which the internees' wives shared information and raised awareness and money. On behalf and with the assistance of those present, the younger bilingual women often composed or translated protest telegrams and petitions destined for Ottawa. The women also organized larger, more public multi-ethnic demonstrations at these meetings, many of which featured the younger women as key speakers.[42]

The women also devoted their energies to the election campaigns of candidates who were opposed to the internment of the anti-fascists.

In Winnipeg Prokop and others volunteered their time for campaign organization, office work, and leafleting to support the candidacy of Ukrainian activists like William Kardash (a long-time ULFTA member and a Spanish Civil War veteran running for the Manitoba provincial legislature). The community's ongoing relationship with the wider radical community was evident through many of the other campaigns they supported. The women worked for the election of Joe Forkin (of British background, who was running for Winnipeg alderman to replace the interned Jake Penner) and of Rose Penner (Jake Penner's wife, of Russian Jewish background, who was running for membership in the school board).[43] The campaigns, and the speeches that the candidates made against the anti-fascists' internments, helped to draw greater public attention to the plight of the internees and their families.[44]

Many women lobbied government officials individually through letters that challenged the continued incarceration of the anti-fascists. To communicate effectively with these parties, the letters had to be written in English. As such, the younger women were especially critical to the letter-writing process because many of the older women did not possess the language or literacy skills to draft a letter in English. Prokop explained, "I wrote more letters than anyone else," not because she was particularly prolific in expressing her own disdain at the men's internment but because she "also wrote on behalf of other wives who could not write in English."[45]

Typically in their letters the women demanded justification for their husbands' internment and called for their immediate release. Mary Naviziwsky's interned husband, John, had been central figure in the ULFTA's national leadership. In his defence she wrote to Minister St Laurent in 1942, pointing out the absurdity of the situation. In particular, she demanded to know why the government continued to detain John when "the main 'offense' that he has committed ... is that he has 'visited the USSR on various occasions.'"[46] This, she argued, did not prove that "his actions were in any way 'subversive' or prejudicial to the successful prosecution of the war."[47] Many women also encouraged their children's involvement in the letter-writing campaign. "Honorable Sir," wrote young Myron Shatulsky to the minister in 1942, "may I once again ask you to release my daddy as a special birthday present to me?"[48]

Although the most common demand expressed in the women's correspondence was for the men's release, many directed their actions and letters towards other concerns. Frequently they pressured the government for improved conditions in the internment facilities. "We demanded their release," Prokop recalled, "pending that, their segregation from fascists in the concentration camps [and] that their status be that of political prisoners and not prisoners of war or enemies of Canada."[49] In addition the women tried to provide their husbands with material comforts during their time in the camps. Shatulsky, for instance, made an effort to send care packages to Matthew. Acknowledging her difficult circumstances, he wrote in September 1940, imploring, "Dear Kate! Do not spend any more money on me, you need every cent at home to keep going. I don't know how you manage!"[50] Letters were also used to aid in the men's legal defence. Three months after his arrest Matthew directed Katherine to seek for his lawyer several newspaper articles that he had written in his capacity as editor of *Narodna hazeta* (People's gazette) which would demonstrate his anti-fascist activism.[51]

Getting information to and from the men was also a priority where letter writing was concerned, as this was the only contact that existed between the men, their families, and the community during much of the internment period. It was no simple task for any of the parties involved, given the limitations put by the federal authorities on correspondence. All letters had to be in English, and regulations permitted the men to mail but one letter a week.[52] Moreover, government authorities, in the name of wartime security, often severely censored the contents of the letters.[53] As women of other communities did when they confronted the internments of their family members, they employed the ingenuity necessary for communicating and for providing comfort.[54] Some young women used their bilingualism to communicate surreptitiously about life on the outside. As Peter Prokop explained, he and especially Mary corresponded in what he described as "an Aesopian fashion," and "she became especially ingenious at outsmarting the censors."[55] For example, he recalled that when referring to meetings held at the Workers Benevolent Association" (which had not been declared illegal), Mary wrote that friends and relatives got together at Aunt Tereza's place. "From this it was easy enough for me to conclude that the word 'Tereza' meant 'RZT,' the Ukrainian for WBA." In other instances in her letters, he said, "often names of people and places were translated from English to Ukrainian or twisted around in such a way that it made sense to me but not to the censor. So, though letters seemed innocent, and perhaps at times stupid, they brought precious news to all of us."[56] Supporters relayed information to the men by other stealthy means. They wrapped produce in newspapers, for example, and on at least one occasion a well-wisher concealed pieces of a note inside unshelled walnuts.[57]

The local efforts of women grew into a national and multi-ethnic movement, which built on pre-existing relationships with the wider Canadian left. Working through a multi-ethnic organization called the Committee for the Release of Labor Prisoners (CRLP), the women were able to gain widespread support for their cause across Canada. Part of their success came from the way in which the women employed a deliberate "family man" strategy, which emphasized the men's community leadership, the role the men could be playing for the war effort, their positions as husbands and fathers, and the personal, financial, and public anguish their wives and children endured in their absence. "We, their families, suffer through their internment, great hardships and unhappiness," one pamphlet stated, "particularly ... the innocent child dependents involved, who suffer through the stigma 'prisoner of war,' by which their fathers have been branded, and whose health and strength are seriously undermined by insufficient relief."[58] This family-man strategy often involved downplaying the men's communist leanings and connections. Instead, the committee's literature stressed the men's respectability, anti-fascist ideals, patriotism (particularly their support and that of their families for the war effort despite the internment), warning that the War Measures Act represented a challenge to the democratic freedoms of all Canadians. They further suggested that the government's invocation of the War Measures Act was akin to the behaviour of fascist governments in Europe, calling it "the nearest legislation approaching Nazi practises."[59]

On 31 March 1941 representatives of the committee from across Canada converged in Ottawa to demand an audience with a parliamentary committee that had been struck to review the Defence of Canada Regulations. Supporters donated money to send Prokop, along with Helen Krechmarowsky (whose husband, Nick, was also interned) and Norman Penner (son of Rose and the interned Jake Penner), to represent the Winnipeg arm of the movement.[60] Once in Ottawa the delegates united to form a multi-ethnic contingent of fifteen strong and began demanding, through direct contact and a press conference with the supportive *Toronto Star*, a meeting with the parliamentary committee.[61] According to Prokop, the article published by the *Toronto Star* "brought country-wide recognition to our situation, [which] in itself was a victory, for the government had tried to keep the internment a complete secret from the people of Canada."[62] This attention applied the pressure necessary to get the parliamentary committee to agree to meet with the CRLP on 2 April 1941. Unfortunately the government refused to budge on its position. Instead, Prokop recalled, St Laurent "kept barking that we were communists and tried to provoke us into arguments about policies of the Soviet government."[63] It would take at least another year before the women and their supporters would begin to realize some success in their endeavours to push the government to free the interned.

In the meantime the Ukrainian left also needed women to take on other roles to ensure that its remaining institutions and activities could continue to function. The ongoing threat of arrest often made these positions too risky for the men who were not interned. Stella Seychuk replaced the interned Anthony Woytyshyn as acting national secretary-treasurer of the Workers Benevolent Association (WBA). As a child she had participated in Ukrainian school, folk dancing, gymnastics, and mandolin classes and had learned Ukrainian cross-stitch from the women at the Winnipeg Ukrainian labour temple. "To demand work for the unemployed, relief, decent pay," she recalled, she and the other Youth Section members "took part in mass protests [and] accompanied our parents in long demonstrations when they marched from Market Square to the City Administration or to the Provincial Parliament." She had also been a member of the Youth Section executive and had acted as Youth Page editor for *Ukrainski robitnychi visti* (Ukrainian labour news). This experience and her Ukrainian language skills landed her a job with the WBA in 1933 and rendered her capable of taking over in Woytyshyn's absence. Although not banned itself, the WBA still encountered difficulty during the early years of the war because it had grown out of the ULFTA and its head office was in the Winnipeg Ukrainian labour temple. Immediately following the June raids federal authorities had locked all materials related to the firm inside the confiscated building. "I had to obtain permission from ... the custodians of the building ... to enter and pick up letterheads, envelopes, receipt books and other material," she remembered. "I had to sign for every bit of paper taken out of the hall."[64]

The women, along with their children and some men in the community, also maintained a steadfast crusade of political and cultural resistance against the ban on the ULFTA. The loss of the halls, which, as we have seen, were the political, social, cultural, and – for many – emotional centre of the movement, was a tremendous blow. Ukrainian leftist identity in many ways was wrapped up in the community leisure, social, and activist space that was the Ukrainian labour temples. The loss of this critical space could be particularly difficult for those who had grown up knowing no other site for their identity and activism; for many it was a considerably unsettling experience. Eugenia Makutra was fifteen years old when she helped to build Saskatoon's Ukrainian labour temple in 1919–20. She had spent her leisure time there at women's branch meetings, singing in the choir, feeding the unemployed, and raising funds to pay the building's construction debt. When the government seized the hall in 1940, "we wept," recalled Makutra, "as we walked in front of the Ukrainian labour temple which we were forbidden to enter."[65] "I was devastated," remembered Nadia Niechoda. "How could someone close down our wonderful hall? What were we to do? Where would we spend our time? When I had to walk past the hall during those days, I crossed the street, turning my face away from the hall."[66]

While members and supporters mourned, however, they also fought back against this government repression. In many communities the federal authorities sold or rented the halls to Ukrainian nationalist groups. This move had a twofold purpose: it was an effort generally to curry the support of right-wing Ukrainians and specifically to engage their energies in helping to further demoralize the Ukrainian left. It may have also reflected a naive hope that ULFTA members might be absorbed into, and become politically neutered by, one of these Ukrainian nationalist organizations. The federal authorities under-estimated the deeply entrenched nature of the Ukrainian leftists' ethno-political identity, however. This sense of self and community was rooted, for many, not only in an embracing of radical political values and activism; as the previous chapters have shown, it was also solidly grounded in a stalwart and vehement rejection of the Ukrainian nationalists' brands of Ukrainianness, centred as it was on religious and conservative political values.

Instead the government's actions merely served to heighten the existing tensions between the right- and left-wing Ukrainians and to further strengthen the resolve of those continuing to defend the embattled ULFTA. This was the case in Winnipeg when the Custodian of Enemy Property turned the Winnipeg Ukrainian labour temple and the print shop it housed over to a nationalist Ukrainian group. These rival Ukrainians began publishing a Ukrainian-language newspaper and, using the subscriber lists from *Narodna hazeta*, sent it out to left Ukrainian households across the country. This galvanized the ULFTA supporters to action: "As soon as we received this paper of theirs, we sent it back to the point of mailing, with the notation 'Refused,'" Anna Chachkowsky recounted. Some, it was rumoured, even wrapped the paper around a brick before returning it in the post. Chachkowsky had been a member of the Winnipeg women's branch and embroidery group. She and her husband had avidly supported the ULFTA's Association to Aid the Liberation Movement in Western Ukraine and had participated in neighbourhood councils of the unemployed during the 1930s. Proudly she asserted, "Someone had spent a good deal of money to get us to read a paper that wasn't ours, but they had miscalculated, not having taken into account the class awareness of our membership."[67]

In the absence of the halls, supporters actively – and covertly – established new spaces for activism to continue. Parasia Koss had joined the Toronto women's branch at its founding in 1922. Under the auspices of the ULFTA she had learned to read and write, acted in plays, and raised money to build the Ukrainian labour temple in Toronto in 1927. She and her family, at great personal risk, responded to the ban on the ULFTA by offering their Toronto home as a makeshift print shop from which Steve Macievich and J. Ivasiuk could edit and publish an underground newspaper.[68]

Women were also critical to re-establishing new space for cultural activities, especially for children. To facilitate meetings and rehearsals, participants often rented space from organizations that were sympathetic to their plight. Nine-year-old Olga Mateychuk and her friends, for example, were able to continue their cultural activities at the rented Israel Press Building or at the Polish labour temple in Winnipeg.[69] Like Koss, many women opened their homes. This combination worked reasonably well in west Toronto. "We held banquets in houses and rehearsed plays which we put on in halls that we rented wherever we could get them," Anna Andreyko recalled. During the 1920s and 1930s she had been active in the ULFTA's women's branch, had acted in plays, and was a member of the choir and concert committee. The wartime ban curtailed but did not fully circumscribe her cultural efforts. "Although it wasn't very often," she explained, "we did manage to put on plays and we continued with our organizational work."[70] The ongoing cultural and social activity facilitated by these alternative spaces was an important form of wartime resistance that helped to raise money, boost the morale and public image of the Ukrainian left, and ultimately further the national efforts of the Committee for the Release of Labor Prisoners.

While carrying on their work elsewhere, supporters nonetheless continued to assert their rightful ownership of the halls. Here too women played key roles. They were among those who routinely showed up outside the Ukrainian labour temples to protest events organized by the nationalist Ukrainian groups who controlled the halls. "Several hundred men and women, armed with sticks, bottles and vegetables," the *Globe and Mail* reported, "attacked a group emerging" from the Winnipeg Ukrainian labour temple on 28 December 1941. Of the nine Ukrainian leftists arrested on charges of rioting, seven were women. The Toronto hall at 300 Bathurst Street was also the site of frequent demonstrations. On 18 October 1942 the Toronto police reserves found themselves faced with "a mob of men and women" gathered to protest a concert that Ukrainian nationalists had arranged to celebrate their one-year anniversary of ownership of the hall. Similar scenes took place there on 18 January 1942, 31 January 1943, and 17 October 1943.[71]

Like women across Canada and around the world, these women devoted their already divided energies to a vibrant array of war-effort work. Although the Ukrainian left, and the CPC, officially opposed the war in its early years, the presence of loved ones serving or living overseas compelled many women to become involved. Many also hoped that such demonstrations of loyalty might help to generate a more positive image of the community and help the cause of the interned. War work was most substantial at the local level, especially among the older women. As they had prior to the war, these former women's branch members took part in a variety of activities across the country. Many did what they could to lend comfort to soldiers overseas. In west Toronto the older women created a committee to gather gifts and cigarettes for Ukrainian Canadian soldiers serving in the Canadian services. Andreyko recalled that the group regularly corresponded with thirty-eight soldiers.[72] In Point Douglas, Manitoba, former members of the women's Ukrainian embroidery group shifted their focus to war-effort work with the Red Cross. Maria Vynohradova was among them. She and the others kept busy gathering and making clothing to send overseas. "We mostly knitted mitts for Canadian soldiers who were waging war against the Hitlerites," she explained. "I knitted thirty-eight pairs of such mitts."[73]

To carry out their work the younger women began to establish their own patterns of activity and authority separate from those of their mothers and grandmothers, as well as from those of their male counterparts. Testament to the increased importance that English was coming to have in the movement, and reflective of their having grown up in Canada, they instituted separate English-language organizations, called Young

Women's Victory Clubs, within the Ukrainian left to address their concerns, interests, and experiences.[74] The clubs formed across the country wherever a large enough contingent of young, usually married women (many of whom had young children) was present. The women had a special interest in supporting the war effort because many were married to men serving overseas.

One of the original and most dynamic Young Women's Victory Clubs was in Winnipeg, Manitoba. Mary Kardash was a founding member. She had grown up in the Sudbury area where she had taken part in the ULFTA Ukrainian school, played mandolin, and acted as secretary of the Youth Section. She later trained and became a ULFTA cultural teacher and held posts in Guelph, Sudbury, Niagara Falls, and Winnipeg. Her father, Myron Kostaniuk, had been an active leader in the ULFTA and the labour movement and was among those men interned. During the war she fought for the release of the interned, served on the national executive of the WBA, and took part in the Young Women's Victory Club. "We conducted cultural-educational work among Canadian women," she recalled; "we worked together with the older women members of the ULFTA in the Red Cross campaigns, ... we sent parcels to our fighting men, and so on."[75] Like the older women's branches, the Young Women's Victory Clubs knit items like mitts, socks, and scarves and raised money for cigarettes for the troops. Through this work the clubs also served an important social and support function for the young women. Eloise Popiel, who had lived at the Parkdale Benevolent Home, the WBA's orphanage on the outskirts of Winnipeg, after her miner father had died of silicosis, worked in the office of the ULFTA-founded People's Cooperative Dairy. During the war she knit for her husband who was serving in the navy. Like most of the other young women, she did this at home. Bi-weekly, however, she was grateful for the chance offered by the Young Women's Victory Club to socialize with women of a similar age and circumstance and to display her handiwork.[76]

There were several reasons that these clubs appealed to the young women. The clubs gave them a chance to meet and work with others of similar age and experience. That this work, unlike that of the women's branches, took place in the English language was particularly important. This is why Joyce Pawlyk, for example, joined the Young Women's Victory Club in Winnipeg.[77] Although many of these young women would have grown up in homes where Ukrainian was spoken, and might even have studied the language at a ULFTA Ukrainian worker children's school, they had been educated in the Canadian system, and many were most comfortable – for reasons of aptitude and identity – conducting their work in English. The Young Women's Victory Clubs also presented young women with the opportunity to shape and control their own group and activism separate from the women's branches, which the older generation of women controlled. The older women often engaged in activities that did not interest younger women. Working separately from their male counterparts, too, granted these women the space to define a program of activism free from potential male input (and interference). With the establishment of a Young Women's Victory Club the young women had autonomy over the activities that most interested them. Their war work would profoundly influence their roles and opportunities after war's end.

Optimism among members and supporters of the Ukrainian left abounded with Hitler's 22 June 1941 invasion of the Soviet Union. Many hoped that this turning point in the war – particularly with the Soviets now an ally – would boost the efforts of the Committee for the Release of Labor Prisoners. It certainly enhanced the Ukrainian left's position vis-à-vis the nationalist Ukrainian Canadian Committee. The UCC's unbending anti-communist, anti-Soviet, and pro-independent Ukraine stance placed the committee in an awkward position, particularly in relation to its connections with the federal government. In the court of public opinion the Ukrainian leftists soon usurped the UCC's place as the politically acceptable Ukrainian constituency, a position they would maintain until the end of the war.[78]

With the political winds blowing in their favour, the Ukrainian leftists moved quickly to reorganize themselves publicly. In Toronto a month after the Nazi attack they gathered to create a new national organization to stand in for the still-banned ULFTA. Called the Ukrainian Association to Aid the Fatherland (UAAF), it meant to "give more effective moral and material help to Ukraine as well as to Canada's war effort against Hitler Germany."[79] Concurrently they inaugurated a new publication, *Ukrainske zhyttia* (Ukrainian life), to fill the void left by the ban of *Narodna hazeta*. Both were received with great enthusiasm. *Ukrainske zhyttia* grew from five thousand to twelve thousand subscribers in mere weeks that summer. A year later this number had increased to fifteen thousand. By the end of the war the UAAF, which by then was called the Association of Canadian Ukrainians (ACU), counted some 315 branches. In 1944 and 1945 it attracted 1,900 and 2,579 new members, respectively.[80]

Although the interned would remain so for another year, this changed political climate made it safer for the non-interned men to express their activism openly. Signs emerged that gender roles in the movement were beginning slowly to rebound to familiar pre-war patterns. Indeed the family-man strategy, which had been employed in an attempt to secure the release of the interned men, and the wartime necessity for a temporary shift in gender roles meant that many of the women's gains in terms of leadership roles and status would likewise be temporary. These wartime circumstances thus did not represent a broader challenge to the ways in which femininity or masculinity – hegemonic, complicit, or oppositional – were understood and performed in the movement. Rather, they represented a necessary response – one with wider precedent in Canada and elsewhere in other war-affected places – to a transitory community and family need. As a result, moving forward, gender prescriptions and their embodiment began to revert to their pre-interment forms.

How was this manifest in terms of activist practice? Women had little representation in the upper echelons of the new organization, except in roles specifically designated as "female." Instead, Michael Mutzak headed it, and other men claimed key leadership positions. A few women attained positions on the national executive, but for the most part their energies centred on creating a special division, modelled on the interwar women's branch, to coordinate women's activities. Concurrently, in other areas of the movement, men reassumed the traditionally male positions. Nick Hrynchyshyn, who had managed entirely to evade arrest, became the editor of *Ukrainske zhyttia*.[81] Of course, some women were grateful to have men play a more active role. In 1941 Seychuk was able direct her energies towards the full-time care of her household and infant son, Bob, when her husband, Mike, took over her position at the WBA.[82]

Despite their diminishing access to formal power and leadership opportunities, women continued to make important contributions. With the Soviet Union now an ally, many women directed their efforts towards overtly supporting the Red Army. The Point Douglas women's branch and others across the country collected clothing and other items for refugees in the Soviet Union, while the women of Youbou, British Columbia, canvassed door to door and raised five hundred dollars to support the Red Army.[83] Women also acted to bolster the Soviet Union directly and to shape Allied efforts. Her father's influence and the hardships that homesteading entailed radicalized Wasylyna Alexiewich. She joined the ULFTA when a branch was formed in 1931 in Sunset House, Alberta, was promptly elected secretary, and helped with the eventual construction of the hall. During the Depression she helped to deliver relief supplies to area farmers. She later worked as a cultural teacher and organizer in Edmonton. During the war she and other Edmonton women supported the Soviets by handing out leaflets to pressure the Canadian government and the other Allies into opening a second front in western Europe.[84]

Children were also key to these efforts. Across Canada local groups held regular concerts featuring choirs, children's recitations, and speakers who entreated the audience to give of themselves for the war effort. Youngsters participated in blood drives, performed for the troops who were preparing to deploy, and corresponded with men who were already serving overseas.[85] Indeed the youngsters' war work took on a new importance as leaders urged them to organize new Ukrainian young people's clubs in order to not only cultivate an understanding of Ukrainian culture but also preserve democracy, defend workers' rights in industry, and conduct cultural activity to foster "better understanding and friendly mutual relations between Canadians of Ukrainian origin and Canadians in general."[86] The fund-raising events at which youngsters performed occurred often. A concert at Winnipeg's Walker Theatre, for example, featured a number of children and youth in mandolin orchestras and choirs. In this great spectacle some "200 school children paraded around the theatre bearing the Union Jack, Soviet and US Flags."[87] By the end of 1941 the Ukrainian left had raised $50,000 for the Red Cross's Russian Relief Fund. Their ongoing efforts were frequently augmented by fund-raisers like the concert held at Toronto's Massey Hall on 25 January 1942 that contributed an additional $4,110.[88] These efforts helped greatly to improve the Ukrainian left's wartime image.

In these changed circumstances the wives and supporters of the interned increased their efforts to free the men. While men may have begun to take over leadership in other areas of the movement, the wives – along with their children – remained in the forefront of the struggle for the internees' release. Now that the nation with which their husbands' internments were claimed to be associated was onside with the Allies, the leftist women were presented with an activist advantage that their Italian, German, and Japanese counterparts would not possess during the war. They demanded that the government justify the internments in light of the Soviet Union's allied status. "If the internees were being held because, as we had been told, they sympathized with the Soviet Union, which had a non-aggression pact with Germany," Prokop stated, "why keep them now that the Soviet Union was at war with Germany and was our ally?" She added that the women frequently invoked Winston Churchill in letters and public statements, reminding the Canadian government that "anyone who goes with us against Hitler is our ally and anyone who goes with Hitler against us is our enemy."[89]

At the same time the irony of having a husband interned while a son was at war fighting for the Allies was an experience that these women shared with pro-fascist women around the world.[90] As more and more leftist Ukrainian men began to sign up en masse to serve overseas after June 1941, it appeared that some women were also able to use their and their husband's relationships to these soldiers to help in the anti-internment campaign. By 1941, for example, Mary Naviziwsky had to contend not only with the absence of her imprisoned husband, John, but also with that of two of her sons who were serving overseas. One was ultimately killed in the line of duty. Their willingness to put themselves in harm's way, and John's support of their presence in the armed services despite the injustice of his continued internment, was often emphasized as a demonstration of the family's willing patriotism and sacrifice for the Canadian war effort.[91]

By the end of 1941 widespread sympathy had amassed across the country for the anti-internment cause. As Prokop recalled, they had garnered the backing of "Members of Parliament and other elected representatives, union leaders, church people, lawyers and so on, representing over 140,000 Canadians."[92] Member of Parliament Dorise Nielson, the United Church of Canada, the Canadian Congress of Labour, the Cooperative Commonwealth Federation, former Member of Parliament Agnes McPhail, Ontario Premier Mitchell Hepburn, and the mayors of Winnipeg, Regina, and Windsor all threw their support behind the cause to lift the ban on the Communist Party of Canada, the Ukrainian Labour Farmer Temple Association, and other groups. By the time Prokop and the other wives and children of the interned, now working under the auspices of the multi-ethnic National Council for Democratic Rights, returned as a delegation to Ottawa in February of 1942, the federal government was hard-pressed to listen and respond in a meaningful way to their demands. Prokop and other supporters presented briefs to Parliament's Defence of Canada Regulations Committee. The committee, citing changed wartime conditions, made several recommendations to the House of Commons on 23 July 1942. Unfortunately no debate took place, and the Mackenzie King government and Justice Minister St Laurent took no action to lift the ban. They did, however, begin quietly to release the interned. By September and October of that year all of the men saw freedom.[93]

In the atmosphere of jubilation and relief that accompanied the men's release the women found their access to power and leadership positions further diminished. Again the family-man strategy – which reinforced the men's responsibilities as breadwinners and community leaders and underscored the hardship that women faced in having to assume these obligations in their absence – and the precedent for shifts in gender roles necessitated by wartime circumstances meant that changes in gender roles were understood to be temporary. Once the familial and community need no longer existed for these women to act in a central leadership capacity, it was expected that they stand aside. In their place, celebrated as heroes and martyrs for the Ukrainian left and as symbols of government repression, the men returned home and to the positions they had held prior to their incarceration. Many, including Shatulsky and Naviziwsky, went back to leadership positions working as speakers and organizers. Krawchuk returned to journalism, moving to Toronto to work for *Ukrainske zhyttia*. Still others bolstered the movement's image by signing up for the armed services, as John Dubno and Harry Slupski did upon their release from Hull Jail.[94] Women continued to fill in as the temporary wartime need required. Stella Seychuk, for example, found that the WBA needed her services again in 1942 because male employees, including her husband, Mike, had vacated the office to answer the call to serve. The People's Cooperative Dairy promoted Eloise Popiel to office manager when accountant John Federchuk resigned the position to join the air force.[95]

Other internees had not the option to return to active engagement in the movement, however. Some never recovered physically from their incarceration. Michael Saviak, editor of *Farmerske zhyttia*, was ill at the time of his arrest, and the period and conditions of the internment worsened his health. Upon release Saviak was "unable to eat and in a state of collapse," remembered Bileski.[96] Two months later he was dead.[97] Some men, though not physically scarred, internalized the experience of the internment in other ways. Some – even those not interned – may have adjusted their activity or may have left the movement entirely, too fearful of the prospect of future government repression. Unfortunately, as evidence in this regard is limited, numbers are difficult to assess.

For those men who returned to the movement, however, their period of internment clearly served to strengthen their resolve and reinforce their belief in the need for a strong workers' movement in Canada. Although they were free from incarceration, the state still restricted their actions. One of the conditions of their release stipulated that they not take part in or advocate on behalf of the Communist Party of Canada or other groups such as the ULFTA that were deemed illegal under section 98 of the Criminal Code.[98] With the Soviet Union an ally, the (still illegal) party line had changed, rendering many Ukrainian leftist male leaders and supporters "fiercely pro-war."[99] They also reframed themselves as anti-fascists, and the Ukrainian left as a whole as an anti-fascist movement. These men thus changed the tone of their speeches and activities drastically, focusing mainly on efforts to bolster Canada's participation in the war. No longer did leaders like Shatulsky and Naviziwsky condemn the war as imperialist. Instead they encouraged members and supporters of the Ukrainian left to fight fascism by continuing to shore up the Allied war effort.[100]

While heading the push for the return of the halls (and further solidifying their control of the upper echelons of organizational power), the ULFTA leaders distanced themselves from the party. The formerly interned were especially important as living symbols of government repression and injustice. The family-man strategy, particularly with its emphasis on responsibility, respectability, and wartime patriotism, remained key to the reframing of the movement, to hegemonic and complicit masculinities, and to men's activism. Maintaining this positive image and the endorsement of the civil liberties and religious groups that had supported the anti-internment struggle was foremost. With this in mind, in March 1945, Naviziwsky cautioned members of the Ukrainian left against openly supporting the Labour Progressive Party (formerly the Communist Party of Canada), particularly in the coming federal election. An RCMP source reported that during an organizational tour of eastern Canada Naviziwsky warned supporters "that the Ukrainian societies (communists) were not yet free from suspicion or distrust [in the opinion of] certain sections of the Canadian people." He advised them to therefore avoid political activity that might "create sectionalism, bitterness and ill-feeling between them and large sections of the Canadian people" while the movement was attempting to regain its property.[101]

While the men publicly represented the redress cause, on the ground (and firmly back in their interwar "support" roles), the women were also intensely involved in the struggle. As they did in the anti-internment campaign, working with each other and at times with grass-roots male supporters, they employed a variety of tactics. They organized and spoke at meetings, maintained and forged alliances with supportive individuals and organizations, wrote letters to the press and elected officials, and continued their ongoing and widely publicized war effort campaign that was critical to underscoring the injustice of the ban. They also collected thousands of signatures for petitions. When Kalyna Bazhansky had come to Canada in the 1920s, she had been disappointed by the conditions she encountered, particularly at her difficult and poorly paying job at the Hamilton cotton mill. She found membership in the ULFTA and her role as its representative to the Canadian Labour Defence League a satisfying means to challenge her personal hardships. During the war she helped to organize the Hamilton branch of the Ukrainian left's Association to Aid the Fatherland, and in 1944 she, along with other male and female Ukrainian labour temple members, collected more than 3,600 signatures on a petition calling for the return of the Hamilton Ukrainian labour temple.[102] In total, some 330,000 signatures were amassed across the country.[103]

These efforts started to pay off in 1943. By Order-in-Council, the Mackenzie King government restored the ULFTA and several other leftist organizations to legal status on 15 October, agreeing to return the Ukrainian labour temples that were still in government possession to the Ukrainian left. By January of 1944 the association had regained all the unsold halls. It unfortunately did not mark the end of this tumultuous era. As government authorities had sold or damaged extensively many of the halls, the community continued to battle for fair financial compensation. Despite extensive public pressure, final settlement for damaged and sold buildings and equipment would only come two years later, in 1946.[104] The compensation provided by the federal government was nowhere near equivalent to the loss that the Ukrainian left had endured by being unable to access their property for much of the war. In addition, unlike later redress campaigns – fought to challenge government-perpetuated injustices against Japanese Canadians during the Second World War, Eastern Europeans (including Ukrainians) during the First World War, and the Chinese over the nineteenth and twentieth centuries – no formal apology was offered or compensation awarded in recognition of the pain, humiliation, and economic losses suffered by the interned men and their families. The Ukrainian leftists themselves never pursued this demand, either during or after the war. They likely recognized the fragility of the men's liberty, feared the potential for arbitrary re-arrest, and understood that the government was simply unlikely to ever acknowledge the incarcerations as unjust.

Nonetheless, the return of the halls was cause for celebration. "It was a great victory when we got our hall back," recalled Bazhansky, "because now we had our own quarters, our hall."[105] Women were at the helm of many of the victory celebrations, which they often coordinated as fund-raisers. Anna Andreyko presided over a concert to mark the reopening of the West Toronto Ukrainian labour temple on 29 April 1944; the event raised seven hundred dollars towards the estimated twenty thousand dollars needed to restore the hall to its prewar condition.[106]

The Ukrainian left spent the first half of the 1940s manoeuvring itself out of disarray, dealing with the internments, freeing its male leaders, and recovering its losses. The Second World War was a watershed. Within the context of calamitous circumstances, the outcome of the interaction of gender, class, and ethnicity was the stretched prescriptions and performances of gender. Owing to the negative ways in which both the male ULFTA leadership and the RCMP surveillance officers perceived and often undervalued women's essential interwar contributions, the state had failed to target the female Ukrainian leftists for detainment. This had permitted women the activist space to maintain the threatened community and, after the crisis hit, the opportunity to spring quickly into action.

As a result, women had taken on unprecedented leadership roles and, using skills obtained through their interwar activist activities, had managed to sustain the community, permitting activity and initiative amid trauma and displacement. The young women were especially critical. They used their English-language skills and the lessons learned while growing up in the Ukrainian labour temples to take over the leadership and extend their activism outside the Ukrainian left, leveraging the movement's pre-existing ties with the wider Canadian left by combining forces with other ethnic radical women. Concurrently, working similarly to the older members of women's branches, they formed their own English-speaking Young Women's Victory Clubs to support the war effort, and they encouraged their offspring towards activism that was crucial to developing a positive image of the Ukrainian left. Thus, two categories of female experiences became noticeable during the war years. The growing generational divide between the women would solidify after the war. Men, meanwhile, imprisoned or unable to work publicly for the movement, found it necessary to

recede into the background or restructure their activism to accommodate the wartime situation. Those who had avoided internment lay low,
working underground or otherwise biding their time until it was safe
to become active again. When it was, they began to repossess from the
women the movement's leadership positions. The incarcerated joined
with other like-minded prisoners and attempted to maintain whatever
vestige of radical manhood they could. They used the skills they had
learned and relationships they had built as members of the larger left in
Canada, along with their knowledge of Ukrainian cultural traditions, to
make their time in custody as agreeable and fruitful as possible. Once
released, those who were able reclaimed their former positions, acting
not only as leaders but also as important figureheads – martyrs in the
struggle for the return of the halls.

Despite the wartime upheaval, the performance of masculinities and
femininities and the discourse surrounding it remained fundamentally intact. Men's concerns still dominated and were the focus of the
movement. Although the women had to step beyond their traditional
sphere, their efforts continued to focus on men's needs, and the movement
overall continued to emphasize a male-centric model of working-class
(and political) oppression. Overcoming women's distinct experience of
oppression, as women and as members of the working class, was never
the focus of analysis or activism. Nor did their temporary increase in
power – necessitated by the war and the internment of the male leaders –
ultimately shift the movement towards more egalitarian models of
gender relations during the war. Underscoring this is the seamless-
ness with which men returned to their former positions of power
once the Soviet Union had become an ally or they had been released
from jail. If women continued in a leadership capacity, it was, like in
the interwar period, only in the absence of men or as organizers of
women's activism.

As we shall see, however, in the post-war era these gender dynamics –
and the authority of the older male leaders in particular – would not go
seriously unchallenged. Language, and its inextricable interconnections
with identity, would play a fundamental role in shifting gender and generational relations. As this chapter has shown, English came front and
centre as the language of activism and, in many cases, of activity during the war. The increased use of English necessitated by the wartime
circumstance greatly enhanced the status and position of the younger
cohort of bilingual women. This was empowering for many who were
able to take on key leadership roles, for which they were already well

prepared, having grown up in the movement. Although it failed to bring about demonstrable change during the war, having proven their leadership and activist capabilities, many women entered the post-war years with enhanced expectations of potential roles for themselves within the movement. At the same time, along with their Canadian-born male counterparts and their children, these women would begin to challenge understandings and expressions of Ukrainianness in the movement by exhibiting and demanding activist space for the performance of a distinct leftist Ukrainian Canadianness in which the common language of expression was English. As the next chapters demonstrate, these internal shifts, combined with the realities of the post-war, cold-war climate, the patterns of assimilation, improved economic conditions, and changes in Canadian and international radical activist culture (particularly the rise of new forms of feminist activism), would have profound and disquieting consequences for the Ukrainian left.

5 "If There Had Been a Siberia": Adults and the Association of United Ukrainian Canadians

Zenovy Nykolyshyn was born in 1935 and grew up in the West Toronto Ukrainian labour temple. His mother was an active member of the hall, and his father, when he was not busy running the family store, helped at plays by volunteering as a prompter. They enrolled young Zeny in the Ukrainian school at the hall. There he also took violin lessons, learned Ukrainian dances, and served a term as president of the ULFTA Junior Section. As a teenager, Nykolyshyn was an active member of its youth club and, through the labour temple, the peace movement, at times a risky pursuit in the cold-war era. "In the early 1950s I was delivering peace pamphlets to neighbourhood homes," he recalled. "A Catholic priest saw what I was distributing and came chasing after me and tried to give me a kick. Fortunately I managed to run away." In 1958 the organization sent Nykolyshyn to Ukraine to train as a leader at a Communist Party school. There he studied the Ukrainian language and the history of the culture and the party. With his studies completed, he returned to Canada and went to work as an organizer in Winnipeg.[1]

Born in 1931, Olga Shatulsky grew up similarly. Her parents were active members of the Point Douglas Ukrainian labour temple in Winnipeg, and her father worked as a milkman for the People's Cooperative Dairy. She started Ukrainian dancing at age five and Ukrainian school at six. By the age of twelve she was teaching dance at the hall, which she continued during the war in rented premises. After the war she acted as recording secretary for the teen club of the Point Douglas hall, helping to organize dances and other social activities. In 1951 the leaders of ULFTA's post-war successor, the Association of United Ukrainian Canadians (AUUC), selected her to attend a Higher Educational Course at Camp Palermo in Oakville, Ontario. There she studied

Ukrainian language, music, and folk dancing and Canadian labour history. Afterwards the organizers dispatched her to teach at the hall in Hamilton, Ontario.[2]

Nykolyshyn and Shatulsky, like many of their Canadian-born cohort, were raised to assume the reins of the AUUC. Unfortunately, as they came of age and were ready to serve in the decade following the war, many found the attainment of positions of authority impossible or the associated working conditions difficult. Outcomes of the intersections of gender, class, ethnicity, and generation shaped their experiences – and those of their immigrant-generation elders – in distinct ways. Young men especially encountered few chances for meaningful leadership positions. Young women, sometimes more easily, found opportunities but often ran up against limited power, low pay, and frequently the same deep-seated male sexism that had (and still) plagued their mothers and grandmothers. The Canadian-born women and men found too often that the older male leaders refused to share authority. Many of these men, Nykolyshyn noted, "felt that before they could pass the torch to the Canadian-born, they would have to teach them for at least two to three years," but added that it was unnecessary because they had already acquired these skills through prior – often life-long – organizational involvement. Those who did manage to find leadership positions or other employment routinely encountered frustration. In Hamilton, Shatulsky found the men's branch (which ran the hall) difficult when it came to school-related matters. "They wouldn't give me a budget and told me to ask when I needed something," she explained. When she tried to do so at their meetings, "they often told me they didn't have room for me on the agenda," she recalled. His ongoing questioning of the AUUC's distribution of power "caused problems," said Nykolyshyn, "and I was given less and less responsibility." He went so far as to suggest that "if there had been a Siberia for the older members to send the younger members, many would have been sent there."[3]

This chapter examines the broader political, social, and cultural currents (both internal and external) that contoured the Ukrainian left's post-war history. Particular attention is paid to the ways in which the processes of gender intersected with those of class, ethnicity, and generation to affect adult experiences, opportunities, and behaviour. Continuing to be manifest in the movement was the gendered discourse and masculinist ideology that privileged and valued the older men's work and activist priorities while marginalizing women's contributions and perspectives. For the most part, the notions of hegemonic masculinity and femininity remained intact, continuing to be shaped by male discourse and reinforced in social practice. The older male leaders at the top of the organization continued to embody most closely these masculine ideals. The older women persisted in performing their "pick and choose" oppositional femininity, still preferring to practise their activism through the women's branches. These relations had serious consequences for – and were contested vigorously through – the ways in which young women and men engaged with the Ukrainian left.

Young women's gender performativity introduced a new category of oppositional femininity, drawing on components of the movement's conceptions of hegemonic femininity and the older women's oppositional femininity, but retooling these to reflect and address their own Canadian upbringings and cultural and political identities as leftist Ukrainian Canadians, as well as their experiences as young adults, workers, and mothers in post-war Canada. Notions of this femininity and their performance of it still involved considerable so-called support work (often through the Young Women's Clubs) and work with youngsters (which, now as mothers themselves, they took over from their mothers and grandmothers). Like their older female relatives, these women selected and rejected activist engagement based on their own interests and experiences. For these young women, however, post-war feminism, coupled with the critical roles that many women had played (or had witnessed growing up) during the war, encouraged higher expectations for women's opportunities in the movement. Increasingly many took on important roles as leaders (though still mainly of women's activities) at the local and national level and acted as liaison with outside leftist and feminist communities. The experiences, behaviour, and activist expectations of these women, and their resulting performance of this distinct oppositional femininity, posed a serious challenge to the Ukrainian left's entrenched masculinist culture.

The role that language played in reshaping gendered generational relations – in close dialogue with class and ethnicity – in the movement in the post-war years cannot go unnoted. Specifically the young members' desires and demands for English-language activities were key. Going into the post-war years, the young women already had established many English-language Young Women's Clubs, and to work together in English, young women and men developed English-speaking branches. While these offered members an important activist, social, and leisure space, language difference that was grounded in generation contributed to a fractionalization of the movement. Among rank-and-file men this had interesting consequences. Notions and performance of interwar complicit masculinity endured among the older men and many younger men, resulting in a patriarchal dividend payout in terms of male privilege in the movement. Increasingly, however, as an outcome of the interaction of gender, ethnicity, class, and generation, some older rank-and-file men found their status and activist space diminish with the waning of Ukrainian-language cultural activities such as drama. Concurrently, although some niches of opportunity existed (in cultural work, for example), many younger men found it more and more difficult to access the sort of power and authority available to their fathers and grandfathers in the movement. Their limited Ukrainian-language abilities, coupled with negative perceptions of their generation's abilities in general – as Nykolyshyn's story illustrates – meant that many young men came to embody and perform a marginalized masculinity in the movement. Carrying out their activism in the English-speaking branches and other related activities – because the branches of their elders and other routes to power were inaccessible – was, for many, the only space for engagement in the movement. Many men were comfortable with this, to varying degrees; increasingly, as the post-war years wore on, however, more and more men were not.

The Ukrainian left's post-war history, then, was marked by deeply gendered intergenerational divisions – the outcome of a complex interaction of gender, class, ethnicity, and generation – that often promoted conflict and disunity (sometimes subtle, sometimes overt); this ultimately contributed to the movement's fragmentation and eventual decline. What did this mean in terms of lived experience? As Nykolyshyn's and Shatulsky's stories illustrate, the grown children of the founding members of the ULFTA often had a tough time finding an enduring and satisfying place for themselves in the movement. Increasingly discernable was a distinct Ukrainian Canadian (as opposed to their elders' Ukrainian) leftist experience. As a group, the young supporters were heterogeneous. An outcome of the intersections of gender, class, ethnicity, and generation, the young women and men, though sharing certain disadvantages, each had distinct but uneven advantages within certain sectors of the movement. Of the immigrant generation the older women (who had long exercised authority over their own activities in their women's branches) and the older men (both the leaders and the rank-and-file) also experienced the Ukrainian left differently; their roles, which remained rigidly gender-specific, exhibited a clear continuity with the interwar era.

Certainly in spite of these differences there was unity in terms of some causes supported and some activities embraced. At times the older and younger women banded together. At other times the young women worked with their male counterparts, expressing their identities and political activism as Ukrainian Canadians, while the older-generation women and men united around causes that spoke to their experiences as radical immigrants (and, to some, as non-citizens). Sometimes all the adult constituencies joined together to support a single cause (though, again, gender and generation nearly always influenced differently the nature of the involvement of individual groups of members). Typically, however, particularly as the post-war era wore on, gendered and generational division and decline became the dominant themes that characterized the movement. Among adults, then, four divergent but occasionally overlapping experiences emerged.

Of course, none of this occurred in a vacuum. Events at the international and national levels greatly affected the local contexts in which Ukrainian leftists constructed and practised their activism. Encouraging and affecting these shifts were broad social and economic changes within Canada and elsewhere (notably the rise of the welfare state and Canada's post-war prosperity); the advent and escalation of the Cold War; post-war feminist discourse and activism; and the transforming Canadian and international lefts (including a general decline in "ethnic hall" or diaspora socialism in North America). The changed international position of Ukraine – by then completely under Soviet rule – and events in the Soviet Union, many of which frustrated and challenged Canadian leftists and fellow travellers, likewise had a significant impact. Equally critical were the nationalist Ukrainian community's attempts to reconstruct itself and Canadian Ukrainianness generally within the context of the post-war liberal state, most notably through their struggle for recognized multiculturalism. Concurrently the Canadian state's actions and cold-war strategies – apparent through the government's active surveillance and repression of dissidents, its conscious and intentional admittance of anti-communist immigrants (including a significant number of Ukrainian displaced persons), and its eventual implementation of multiculturalism policy – posed significant challenges to the broader Canadian left.

Ukrainian leftists grappled with and responded to these dynamics in various ways. In the ensuing transformation of the immigrant working-class experience within the Ukrainian left the questions of class and social marginalization – and indeed exclusion – remained fundamental.

There was a strong tide of assimilation and pressure to conform to mainstream Canadian social norms and liberal values, particularly in the face of widespread red-baiting. Increasingly apparent became the rejection – by a variety of members and supporters for a number of reasons that will be explored here – of the old-style left politics espoused by the older male leaders of the Ukrainian left. The disenchantment with post-war Soviet actions fuelled this disconnect; these men's increasingly intolerable practices of ageism towards younger members and of sexism towards women deepened the divisions. As such, the relational power of these older men, which was grounded in their ties to the broader international communist movement, became undermined, and their influence gradually waned. By the 1960s and 1970s many young members had consciously oriented themselves within feminist and New Left discourse and activism. Turned off by the old hardliners, others drifted away from political activities entirely.

Comparing and contrasting the women and the men of these generations is a valuable methodology through which to understand the challenges faced by the Ukrainian left from the 1950s to the 1970s and 1980s. In doing so, this study expands our relatively limited understanding of post-war Ukrainians and Ukrainian Canadians (and the left in particular). It also engages and builds on the dynamic and recently growing body of literature on the Cold War, especially those works focusing on state and community repression of dissent as well as the response of dissidents to this harassment.[4]

Immediately after the war the AUUC – particularly its leaders – increasingly found it useful and necessary to categorize the movement's adult membership and base of potential adult members along strict generational lines. This was especially evident as the AUUC progressively encountered problems attracting and retaining new members. The leadership defined and used widely the two categories of ethnic identity – *immigrant generation* and *Canadian born*. Although these terms had been used somewhat in early periods of the movement's history, they became more deeply entrenched as historically specific categories of identity immediately following the war. As constructions, both were far from being discrete groupings. Between the two, overlap existed, as did an entire cohort who fit neatly in neither category but whose members reflected characteristics of both.

As has been explored in the first two chapters of this study, members of the immigrant generation were born and raised in the old country. They came to Canada as workers or homesteaders, mostly during the first wave of Ukrainian immigration (though some were drawn from the second wave). Few received any formal education in Canada, and many, particular the women, had had little education growing up. The immigrant generation tended to maintain a greater sense of attachment to the old country, having spent their formative years there. Radicalized by their negative work experiences and the ethnic discrimination they frequently encountered in Canada, they were active in the early Ukrainian socialist parties and helped to found and build the ULFTA. There they took part in a various aspects of cultural and political activism and, if they were women, may have joined the women's branch. They raised their children in the Ukrainian labour temples, hoping to impart in them a strong sense of Ukrainianness and class-consciousness. After the war the immigrant generation tended to be members of the AUUC men's or women's branches (which were Ukrainian speaking), preferring to work in Ukrainian, and typically choosing to engage in cultural or activist pursuits with other adults of their generation. They were frequently honoured as the movement's "pioneers" at concerts and anniversary celebrations in the decades following the war.

Overlapping with the immigrant generation was a middle cohort, often the children of the immigrant generation, who were born in Canada or immigrated at a very young age (usually pre-school) during the first or second wave of migration. They grew up in the movement in the 1920s, were educated in the Canadian school system, and came of age during the 1930s. Most were bilingual (as their parents often spoke only or mainly Ukrainian), though many found it difficult to work entirely in Ukrainian while growing up and later as adults. Some (especially those with leadership aspirations) joined the Young Communist League or the Communist Party of Canada. Those who would become ULFTA, and later AUUC, leaders often received their training in one of the Higher Educational Courses (especially the 1936 or 1938 classes), including many of the women who would become key leaders during and after the war. Some of these men (along with the leaders from the immigrant generation) were interned during the war, while many others served overseas in the Canadian forces. This cohort was critical to the founding, development, and maintenance of the eventual AUUC, especially as many of the key immigrant-generation leaders died during the 1950s. How this group was characterized after the war – either as immigrant generation or Canadian born – hinged on the level of commitment they displayed, their language proficiency, and the type of activities with which they involved themselves in the movement. For clarity, they will be referred to as the *early Canadian-born.*

When leaders referred to the identity category of the Canadian-born generation (particularly after the war), they were typically describing those born after 1930. This was a multigenerational "generation" made up of the children, grandchildren, and eventually great-grandchildren of the ULFTA founding members. Their public school education, exposure to and comfort with North American popular culture, and childhood training at the Ukrainian labour temples shaped what would become a distinct post-war Ukrainian Canadian outlook. Although those who were born later, in the post-war period, were different from those who came of age during or after the war, the AUUC leaders grouped them all as a single category of concern because they shared certain key characteristics. Some were bilingual, though their Ukrainian proficiency was typically limited (a skill that declined significantly among later Canadian-born cohorts), and therefore most favoured working in English. Increasingly many shied away from adult activities (but still registered their own children in AUUC activities like Ukrainian school and dance). Those who joined the AUUC adult activities did so through the English-speaking branches, and they gravitated towards cultural or social activities at the hall. Many of the earlier cohort received leadership training at the last Higher Educational Course, held in 1951. Few, however, consistently continued as leaders, largely because of the difficulties they encountered with the older AUUC leaders and their unwillingness to extend meaningful leadership opportunities and autonomy to younger members. Eventually, because of a combination of these and other factors, fewer and fewer of the Canadian-born remained active in the AUUC as the post-war period continued.

The AUUC leaders attempted, albeit unevenly, to appeal to each constituency while adjusting to the circumstances of the early post-war years. The generational shifts among the association's body of members and supporters, and the broader demographic, social, and economic changes in Canada, made this period one of rapid change and adaptation. Although in many ways it could continue to resemble the old ULFTA, in other, more significant ways the post-war Ukrainian left needed to evolve. Keen to capitalize on the momentum gained from the movement's very public displays of war-effort participation and the relative success of the redress campaign, and eager to appeal to younger generations of Ukrainian Canadians, leaders worked to develop a more mainstream and even "respectable" image. At the 1946 national convention they had changed the name of the Association of Canadian Ukrainians to the Association of United Ukrainian Canadians. Concurrently they formally dissolved the Ukrainian Labour Farmer Temple Association and transferred its assets and labour temples to the AUUC. Some of the reopened or rebuilt halls became known as Ukrainian cultural centres instead of Ukrainian labour temples.

The new nomenclature reflected broader changes in the Ukrainian community and, to a lesser degree, Canada's rapid wartime and post-war industrialization and urbanization, as well as other contemporary Canadian social currents. Also influential was the post-war shift in the immigrant rural and working-class experiences. Although many members were still "labourers," their job opportunities – and especially those of their children – had begun to improve during and after the war. Likewise, many of the farmers, and especially their children, were starting to leave the farms in search of better opportunities in urban centres. As a result many of the halls in smaller communities and rural areas did not reopen after the war. Some people moved to the province of British Columbia, to western urban centres like Winnipeg, Edmonton, or Regina, or into Montreal from Quebec's resource towns. For others, participation in the rural depopulation phenomenon represented a move to the factories and cities of southern Ontario; in fact, by war's end many key AUUC personnel had relocated to Toronto. In 1954, although Winnipeg remained a critical organizational centre, the AUUC's head office also moved to Toronto. Nearly all of the post-war national conventions – which no longer occurred annually, but every two years – were held there. Key shifts in the movement occurred, then, as a result of the social and economic changes wrought by the transition to a peacetime Canada.

At the top, however, something significant remained the same. The national leadership of the movement and that of its key affiliated organizations remained male dominated. In the early post-war years many men like Matthew Shatulsky and John Boychuk, who had been critical leaders before the war and had been interned, often resumed their prior positions and activities. Increasingly a number of younger men (several of whom had also been imprisoned during the war and thus had had the opportunity to "network" closely with key interned immigrant-generation leaders) – such as Peter Prokop, Peter Krawchuk, and William Teresio – assumed key leadership roles. These men became especially important as the first generation of leaders like Shatulsky and John Naviziwsky passed away in the 1950s. Women were not entirely excluded, however;

several who had been critically active during the war found positions. Mary Prokop and Mary Skrypnyk, both early Canadian-born, were among the most important. Their presence, though, posed no immediate threat to the movement's masculinist ideology. Despite their training and extensive experience as organizers, the two nearly always were assigned to oversee the work of women and children, activities that enjoyed a marginal status within the movement in continuity with the interwar years. No woman ever headed the AUUC.[5]

Where change was felt immediately – in terms of organizational structure, shifts in gender relations, and the influence of generational shifts and language – was at the grass-roots level following the war. By 1946 the AUUC had re-established some three hundred branches, most of whose members, according to AUUC surveys, were from the immigrant generation.[6] They typically continued to work in separate women's and men's branches. For them the organization kept publishing the Ukrainian-language newspapers *Ukrainske zhyttia* and *Ukrainske slovo* (Ukrainian word). Not all members returned, however. Scared off by what had happened to the ULFTA during the war and intimidated by the burgeoning Cold War, many shifted their energies to other preoccupations. Favourably changing economic circumstances pulled others away. "When the times were hard, every one proclaimed himself progressive. But, when the war broke out ... [and] our people here began to prosper and turned anti progressive, these became our worst enemies than the churchgoers," said immigrant-generation Wasyl Woloshyn from Saskatchewan. "When they could afford to buy new pants, and white shirts, new tractors," he bitterly recalled, "they couldn't care less."[7]

To insure continued growth in the face of these particular challenges during in the 1940s and into the 1950s the leadership aggressively sought to attract new members. In the past the movement had been able to rely on new Ukrainian immigrants. This was stymied by Canada's post-war immigration policy, one intimately shaped by its cold-war context. As Franca Iacovetta writes, "the national security state was on high alert and poised to do battle against variously defined threats to the nation's political as well as social and moral order."[8] Among these, communism ranked highly. Officials worked to block the migration of potential radicals, while supporting that of anti-communist elements, including a significant number of Ukrainian displaced persons who were fleeing territories newly under Soviet control in Ukraine as a result of the Allied victory. According to Lubomyr Luciuk, "there was a perception in Ottawa and elsewhere that these anti-communist Ukrainian political refugees would have considerable political utility inside the country in combating the influence of the Left, especially within their own ethnic constituency."[9]

Tensions ran high with the arrival in Canada of approximately thirty-four thousand Ukrainian displaced persons between 1947 and 1954. Although many took up working-class jobs in the resource and service industries – which had supplied numerous supporters for the left from prior migrant cohorts – few were favourably disposed to identify politically with their class position. Indeed, most were poised to reject and challenge any rallying points that underscored the Soviet model that they had fled. Their arrival, therefore, presented a significant class as well as political issue. As we shall see, these individuals served as some of the Ukrainian (and indeed wider) left's most active and vocal detractors. In their efforts to discredit the AUUC and its portrayal and support of the Soviet Union, these "Cold Warriors" built on and amplified the chorus of opposition that nationalist Ukrainians and other anti-communists had commenced in earlier decades. In doing so, their presence and activities in Canada contributed to the further marginalization of radical leftists, and Ukrainian leftists in particular.

Consequently membership recruitment and retention strategies came to focus squarely on the descendants of the founding generation of the movement. Here, language would come to have a critical impact on community restructuring. By war's end Canadian-born Ukrainians made up the majority of the Ukrainian population in Canada. The primarily English-speaking children and grandchildren of the AUUC's immigrant generation, then, were essential to sustaining the movement. To engage them, AUUC leaders were well aware – based on experiences with these individuals as children, youth, and young adults in the interwar and wartime eras – that the movement literally had to "speak their language." So, in an effort to capitalize on those who had been raised to be sympathetic to the movement, the 1946 AUUC convention established English-speaking branches and an English-language newspaper, the *Ukrainian Canadian*. The leadership viewed the *Ukrainian Canadian* as especially key. "So as not to lose our young generation in a sea of demoralization and inane 'assimilation,'" one leader argued, "we are waging, with the help of the 'UC,' a struggle for drawing our two generations closer together and for engaging the Canadian-born in the fight for the idea which we have been spreading for over 30 years."[10] Response to these overtures was initially favourable. By the 1948 convention the AUUC counted over one thousand members in its thirty-two English-speaking branches. By 1950 the *Ukrainian Canadian* had over five thousand subscribers.[11] The AUUC's 1950 national convention saw English as well as Ukrainian used formally, though Ukrainian remained the dominant language.[12] Out of these efforts to engage descendants, several seeming "legacies" emerged at the various levels of leadership as multiple generations of a single family actively engaged with the Ukrainian left and its close affiliates. Some of the most prominent of these were the Kostaniuks, Kardashs, Bileckis, Shatulskys, Lapchuks, and Prokops.

Despite these key demographic shifts, local hall leadership continued to be male dominated in the 1950s and 1960s, mirroring the pattern at the national level. Furthermore, most of those in charge remained the same immigrant-generation men who had belonged to the Ukrainian-speaking men's branch and run the halls prior to the war. They continued to enjoy enormous power, as this example from Calgary demonstrates: "The Men's Branch is the governing body of the other branches in Calgary," an RCMP informant reported. "In addition to controlling the activities of the Men's Branch, it is also responsible for organizing and coordinating all activities of the various AUUC branches locally."[13] The men's branch also acted as the liaison between an individual hall and the AUUC's national and provincial committees, on which many of the men's branch members held positions. Leadership opportunities and local power, therefore, typically hinged on men's branch membership. Thus, women – be they immigrant generation or Canadian-born – continued to find it difficult to rise in the organization.

At the same time, despite its inclusive-sounding name, the men's branch did not include (or welcome) all men to its ranks. Indeed, Canadian-born men often found themselves excluded, chiefly because of language. Ukrainian was typically the main language of communication as many of the immigrant generation spoke little English. Clinging tenaciously to the immigrant-generation male privilege that they had enjoyed in the decades prior to the war, many of these older men staved off Canadian-born leadership ambitions at the grass-roots level by insisting that the younger men earn desired power and opportunities by improving their Ukrainian skills. Few were willing or able to do this. Moreover, these young men generally preferred to work with the people with whom they had grown up in the youngsters' branches, which meant that they tended to gravitate (or found themselves pushed) towards the unisex English-speaking branches. The combination of their abilities and interests (and the unwillingness of the immigrant-generation men to find common linguistic ground) blocked these young men from local leadership opportunities, while denying them the most efficient route to national leadership positions.

Certainly not all immigrant-generation men reached the heights of leadership. Many at the grass roots, in fact, took part in activities similar to those of women and younger men. As older men, however, unlike the Canadian-born and the immigrant-generation women, by virtue of their gender and generation they continued to have access to this power within the AUUC even if they chose not to pursue it.

Although their opportunities to access male-gender privilege were limited in this context, most Canadian-born men seemed happy to avoid the style of intense political and educational activity espoused by the men's branch that remained closely influenced by the Communist Party of Canada and its various manifestations. Few of the young men were interested in the branch's frequent lectures and educationals. Having rebelled against these elements as children in their interwar Junior or Youth Section work, not many Canadian-born men (like their female counterparts) embraced this style of activism as adults.

Other men simply preferred to engage in grass-roots or leadership activities alongside women of their own generation. In the English-speaking branches the Canadian-born women and men attained some measure of authority and control over the type of activism they pursued. They could shape their organizational lives according to their own interests as Canadians and as workers with leisure time and disposable income, and less so on overt political work. Social and cultural activities increasingly dominated the work of the English-speaking branches, a trend that was firmly established by the 1960s. In 1962, for example, the men of the Winnipeg English-speaking branch organized a fishing club.[14] Two years later the branch's female and male members ran a bowling league, competing against other Ukrainian leftists from across Canada.[15] In 1968 the men of Toronto's "Club 326" took part in weight-lifting, while the women participated in "Keep-fit" classes.[16] In the pursuit of these leisure activities the English-speaking branches remained nonetheless politicized. To celebrate May Day in 1964, for example, the Winnipeggers planned a dinner and dance. They also took part in the annual AUUC organizational campaign by holding fund-raising bingo games and nominating branch members to compete for campaign star (an honour awarded to the AUUC member who, with the help of a team of supporters, collected the most donations).[17]

Within the English-speaking branches the young rank-and-file women maintained a niche of activity and authority separate from their male counterparts and their immigrant-generation mothers and grandmothers. Continuing their wartime Young Women's Victory Clubs as AUUC Young Women's Clubs, they carried out a variety of grass-roots activities to build the English-speaking branches and benefit the AUUC as a whole. In 1947, for example, the Winnipeg Young Women's Club took care of outfitting clubrooms for meetings and other activities at the Winnipeg Ukrainian labour temple.[18] In 1953 the Edmonton group made jackets for the labour temple's Christmas production of *Hryts*.[19] Life-cycle position contributed to the construction of certain activities as more suitable for these young women. The AUUC leaders – both female and male – often framed the activism of the younger women through their roles as mothers of young children. They were, therefore, encouraged to look after local AUUC children's activities by, for example, running the Junior Section or serving on the Mother's Auxiliary Committee of the Ukrainian school.

Though separate, the activities of the Young Women's Clubs paralleled those of the women's branches. The efforts of both cohorts of women in the decades following the war remained the mainstay of local and national funding, and their volunteer labour guaranteed the existence of many activities. Often the two groups worked together on causes of particular concern to women within the broader Canadian left, extending their activism well beyond the confines of the Ukrainian labour temples. They frequently teamed up, for example, to stage bake sales, bazaars, and teas to raise money to aid women and children in war-ravaged parts of the world. They combined their efforts to commemorate events like International Women's Day, Mother's Day, and the anniversaries of prominent Soviet or Ukrainian female writers or activists.[20] They did not, however, contribute identically to these activities; in fact, a fairly strict generational division of labour typically existed. The Canadian-born, for example, acted as liaisons between the AUUC women and other non-Ukrainian women's groups. They also often handled the bilingual program and delivered speeches at teas, fund-raisers, and other events. The immigrant generation, meanwhile, coordinated, supervised, and carried out much of the preparation of refreshments.

Indeed, few young women were much interested in kitchen work, other than helping occasionally when a special event called for extra hands. Some saw how hard the labour was and wanted none of it, especially those with full-time paying jobs (and a double day of domestic labour at home). Others simply wanted to carry out grass-roots work with women of their own generation, especially if their relationships with their own mothers were difficult. Still others – less fettered by the peasant village values that had contributed to shaping the interwar experiences of their mothers and grandmothers, and having grown up in the children and youth activities of the movement in which they had been encouraged to embrace a variety of roles and activisms – developed different expectations for how they would contribute as adult women. The older women, however, continued to gravitate to kitchen activities and general hall maintenance, choosing, as they had in the interwar years, to support the movement in these ways. Many of them found that the kitchen still offered the best opportunity to shape and control their activism. It continued to be a refuge of sorts, free from male interference. The time demanded by the kitchen and other women's branch activities also made it easier for the women to continue to reject undesirable male models of activism. This was especially still the case with the educational, which had limited grass-roots appeal but which male leaders like Teresio continued to advocate as "the key to our success."[21] In the 1950s, for example, few women in Timmins came out when, pushed by the men, the women's branch attempted to hold an educational. The group had no trouble attracting grass-roots supporters to organize the annual bazaar. The Vancouver women's branch, when pressured to develop regular educationals, promised to try but provided a qualified response to the AUUC organizers. "The problem," their correspondent argued, given their other (more popular) activities and obligations, "is there are too few evenings."[22] Few organizers were willing to press the educational issue too far because kitchen work remained one of the AUUC's most critical sources for raising and saving money.

Interestingly, the efforts of nationalist Ukrainians played a key role in enhancing the post-war status of the work of these women through their active reconstruction of Ukrainians in Canada, most notably through lobbying for formal, recognized policies of multiculturalism. Nationalists reacted to the assertion that Canada was the product of two founding nations – the French and the English – and thus bilingual and bicultural. Spurring this characterization was the rising tide of French Canadian nationalism that was evident by the early 1960s; the conversation accelerated with the advent and activities of the Bilingualism and Bicultural Commission (1963–9), which was charged with finding ways to ensure appropriate acknowledgment and servicing of this cultural dualism. "The catalytic effect of the B&B Commission," Bohdan Bociurkiw describes, "compelled Ukrainians and other ethnic groups to re-think their role in Canadian society in response to the Commission's terms of reference [which appeared to condemn] other ethnic groups to an inferior, 'non-founding' status and their cultures to eventual submersion in one of two 'official cultures.'" As Julia Lalande explains, "in the eyes of many Ukrainians, the pioneering qualities and the hard work of the early settlers put Ukrainians on the same footing as the British or French Canadians." Calling for recognition of the critical role played by those they termed a "Third Force" (primarily other "white ethnics" of European origins), Ukrainian nationalist leaders were at the forefront of the movement demanding recognition of Canada as a multicultural nation. With this recognition should come governmental support – moral, financial, and institutional – for ethnocultural groups to ensure their ongoing survival. For these Ukrainian nationalists, it was key. Many feared the decimation of Ukrainian culture that they believed was occurring within Soviet-occupied Ukraine; support was essential, then, to ensure its survival within the Canadian diaspora.[23]

The Ukrainian left, in collaboration with other leftist organizations such as the Canadian Council of National Groups, supported the aspirations of French Canadians and the concept of a bilingual and bicultural Canada. "The Anglo-Canadian Establishment is determined to defend its positions of privilege and dominance at the expense of French Canadians," Mitch Sago argued in the 1 May 1968 *Ukrainian Canadian*. "They will stubbornly resist the efforts of French Canada to achieve equal terms with their English-speaking counter-parts in any continuing union." Sago called out the lobbying efforts of the Ukrainian nationalists as being self-serving: "The idea of a 'third force' is false and reactionary in the extreme and seeks to provide the Anglo-Canadian Establishment with a mass base for diversionary attacks upon the French Canadian people." He insisted that those advocating the "third force" perspective served their own self-interest, seeking "to use it as a bargaining lever for increased political recognition and political appointments, in return for their support of the Anglo-Canadian establishment." Continuing, he asserted, "We are ethnic elements of one or the other nation in Canadian society ... there is no 'third' national community in the making."[24]

The lobbying efforts of the Ukrainian nationalists and other pro-multiculturalism constituencies met with initial success in 1971, when the Liberal government adopted multiculturalism as an official policy. Although the Ukrainian leftists stood opposed, the policy's advent and, more importantly, the widespread discourse surrounding multiculturalism in the 1960s and 1970s was nonetheless influential – in combination with other post-war social, economic, and cultural forces – in reshaping gender relations and reconfiguring gendered space to some degree within the labour temples. In many localities (particularly the larger urban centres) the halls added, remodelled, enlarged, and outfitted better the kitchens, allowing women's labour to expand. During this period and into the 1970s many women's branches added to their activities by making and selling to the public (and to AUUC members) Ukrainian food for home consumption.[25] Thanks to the discourse around multiculturalism (and the increasing acceptance of expressions of Ukrainianness, in particular), these foodstuffs were becoming increasingly renowned as delicacies. The labour intensiveness necessary to produce items like *varenyky* and *holubtsi* meant that the escalating numbers of Canadian-born women in the paid workforce had little time to produce this food themselves. Many welcomed the opportunity to purchase it at the halls, in the process supporting the AUUC.

Despite this new political and social importance, as it had been in the interwar years, the kitchen labour of the immigrant-generation women enjoyed a low status. In addition, kitchen work continued to preclude involvement in higher-status, potentially influential activities. The *Ukrainian Canadian* captured this "upstairs-downstairs" dichotomy in the following description of the AUUC national convention held in Toronto in 1948: "Toronto women who had put in so much work to feed the delegates (oh, those *vareniki* and *holubtsi*!) were given a surprise. They were called up to the stage amid ringing cheers of the delegates and had corsages pinned on them ... then they went downstairs to prepare supper."[26] Thus, while women's work kept the movement running, helped to fund newspapers and to pay the salaries of the mainly male organizers, allowed conventions to run on a shoestring, and provided the financial means for the AUUC to engage nationally and internationally with the broader left, these women activists held little sway in the broader organizational decision-making process. Nonetheless, those who worked in the kitchen and their Canadian-born women counterparts appreciated their worth and efforts. The Canadian-born female organizers of the 1972 fiftieth-anniversary celebration of the Women's Branch, in particular, took great pains to acknowledge the important contributions of physical labour made by its members over the years as they planned local and national events. Above all, they insisted that the local commemorative banquets – "at which all women AUUC members would be guests of honor" – be held at facilities other than the Ukrainian labour temples. Why? "So the women can relax for once in 50 years," scrawled an organizer in the margin of a planning document.[27]

Multicultural discourse also served to enhance another form of women's activism by the 1960s: Ukrainian handicrafts (especially embroidery). Within the Ukrainian left, handicrafts had always been well regarded as a critical expression of Ukrainianness, despite the way in which the CPC leadership might have discounted this activism as peripheral to – and possibly a distraction from – the class struggle. The rising chorus surrounding multiculturalism made it apparent that this work might have value in enhancing the image of the AUUC and the Ukrainian left generally. The seemingly apolitical or benign nature of handicraft expression within the AUUC presented a less threatening and even positive image of the Ukrainian left within wider Canadian circles. Handicrafts were also an important tool for attracting and retaining new members, especially Canadian-born women and girls, because no language skills were necessary to engage in this activism. Likewise, handicrafts could also be important for raising the much-needed money from Ukrainians and non-Ukrainians alike. As a result of these important factors, the cultural expertise and participation of the grass-roots, immigrant-generation women assumed new levels of local and national importance in the post-war decades. As a National Executive Committee memorandum acknowledged in 1965, these handicrafts "not only beautify our exhibitions, but also bring financial help as well as extend our influence among our co-citizens of other nationalities who buy them."[28]

In response to the ongoing national conversations around the contributions of Ukrainians to the development of Canada – not to mention the realities of the Cold War, changes in the broader Canadian left, and the Ukrainian left's continued marginalization – the creation and exhibiting of handicrafts shifted. In the past the women had held their handicraft displays primarily at the Ukrainian labour temples. These exhibits often included handiwork featuring distinctly leftist and communist symbols. Although these events continued, gone were the hammers and sickles. Moreover, to project a more respectable image – one that exuded loyalty to Canada and a commitment to Canadian citizenship – and to attract wider audiences, post-war displays were just as likely to take place in more mainstream venues. The AUUC used these opportunities to celebrate events with a broader Canadian purpose, to legitimize the artistry of the women's craft traditions, and to affirm the organization's place as a builder of Canada. As early as June 1947, for example, the Toronto women took part in an "Exhibit of Ukrainian Embroidery and Handicrafts" held at the Toronto Art Gallery.[29] These types of displays, which were ongoing in the following two decades, reached a fever pitch in 1967 when exhibits abounded to celebrate the Canadian Centennial. They included a display at the Canadian National Exhibition, as well as several smaller, local exhibitions that featured dolls costumed in Ukrainian regional attire and examples of traditional embroidery. The events were extremely popular. "We feel that with our project of handicraft displays throughout Canada, we carried through good public relations work in honour of the Ukrainian Canadians and our organization," reported National Women's Committee organizer Mary Prokop to the AUUC national convention of 1968.[30]

Understanding handiwork's accessibility and its appeal as a fun and creative form of cultural activism, Prokop consciously used these types of events as an opportunity to attract young women to the AUUC and its grass-roots activities. "We want to involve as many of the Canadian-born women in this handicraft project as possible," she wrote to the women's branches and Young Women's Clubs across Canada during the 1967 events-planning phase.[31] Already handicraft classes had been accomplishing this locally, uniting the Canadian-born women and girls with the immigrant-generation women, on whose skills and experience the handicraft classes typically depended.[32] Embroidery, featuring traditional Ukrainian patterns and designs, was especially popular. Many younger women appreciated its versatility and adaptability. They used it as an outlet through which to express both their Canadian and their Ukrainian identities, finding mainstream ways to incorporate it into their day-to-day lives. "Ukrainian Cross-Stitch Goes Mod" read an October 1969 headline in the Ukrainian Canadian. According to the article the Toronto Ukrainian labour temple embroidery class had decided to put on a fashion show for which the Canadian-born women were making clothes that integrated traditional Ukrainian embroidery patterns with contemporary fashions.[33]

Many of the Canadian-born women and men managed to carve out activist niches for themselves as performing arts teachers and leaders, another area of activism whose perceived value increased with the advent of the national conversation around multiculturalism. Interestingly, the ensuing enhanced status enjoyed by those members was often manifest in inverse proportion to the decreasing cultural status of the immigrant-generation men, especially in the 1950s and 1960s. Language played a major role in this shift. Prior to the war the ULFTA's Ukrainian-language drama productions were wildly popular and offered many of the immigrant-generation men (and some women) the opportunity to shine on the stage. As few younger members, whom the movement was keen to attract and retain, spoke Ukrainian well enough to participate in or enjoy watching Ukrainian-language plays after the war, the viability of these types of productions declined (a circumstance that was further compounded by the increased competition from numerous professional theatre companies and other forms of public leisure activity). While the odd Ukrainian labour temple continued to produce the odd play, most often they were in English and never reached the scale or attracted the attendance that the interwar plays had. As the emphasis, then, came to centre on the forms of Ukrainian performing arts for which neither Ukrainian-language skills nor English-language skills were necessary, the immigrant-generation men experienced a certain marginalization. Certainly many remained culturally active, singing in the AUUC choirs and participating in its other musical ensembles, but when it came to leadership opportunities in the performing arts, however, most were increasingly shut out.

The Canadian school system and Ukrainian left educations afforded the Canadian-born generation a critical understanding and experience of the cultural interests of both the immigrant generation and their own. They were able to apply this sensibility to the AUUC performing arts, making them more relevant to multiple generations of participants and to a broader Canadian public. As such, their skills were in high demand. Many of the early Canadian-born, who had received their training at the 1930s Higher Educational Courses, continued to teach, and a number (especially the men) found themselves called on to assist at the AUUC's post-war national and local teaching-training courses and workshops. Among the new cohort that was trained after the war the younger men continued to have advantages. Like their interwar HEC counterparts, they were still the preferred candidates for courses and jobs. The AUUC organizers continued to choose more men than women for training and sent more men to Soviet Ukraine for advanced cultural study. Within the AUUC it was also easier for men to move up the ranks as cultural organizers.

Two of the most notable Canadian-born men to emerge out of this training were Myron Shatulsky and Eugene Dolny. Both possessed talents that they had honed as children and youth growing up in the Ukrainian left and participating in cultural activities. The AUUC leaders recognized their potential, sending them to study first at an AUUC leadership development course in 1951 and immediately afterwards to Soviet Ukraine.[34] During his three-year stay Shatulsky studied "choral and orchestral conducting and dance."[35] Upon their return both were given teaching assignments at local AUUC branches. Shatulsky went to Winnipeg where he "organized choirs, a school of folkdancing, and conducted orchestra."[36] There he combined his experiences as a leftist Canadian-born man with Ukrainian cultural traditions, increasingly shaping cultural activities around not only Ukrainian folk culture but also mainstream contemporary folk music and traditional music from other ethnic groups. These young men also assisted in engaging grassroots supporters in one of the most significant new forms of AUUC cultural expression, the national festival. The two coordinated the cultural component of the celebrations for the Shevchenko Year, which was held in 1961 to commemorate the centenary of the death of the nineteenth-century Ukrainian literary icon Taras Shevchenko. Across the country that spring, local and provincial celebrations took place, culminating in a national festival of Ukrainian song, music, and dance and a festival picnic at the AUUC's Camp Palermo in July.[37] Dolny acted as coordinator and conductor of the main concert, and Shatulsky choreographed a "Canadian Suite."[38] According to a description of the presentation, the "original and unique work" featured over two hundred dancers performing "fragments from a number of national dances – Ukrainian, Russian, Scottish, Indian, French, Slovak."[39]

In the immediate post-war years the best opportunities for the Canadian-born women could be found at the local level. By the early 1950s, for example, Josie Hawenka and her sister Dolly were leading the Regina AUUC hall's dance group, and Anne Lapchuk was directing the choir (she would go on in the ensuing decades to become one of the most important AUUC cultural leaders in Regina).[40] Olga Shatulsky, as we have seen, was teaching in Hamilton at the time. Into the 1960s and 1970s the opportunities for women continued to open up. The increased popularity of children's folk dancing was a key reason. In 1961, then married and teaching in Winnipeg, Shatulsky had little trouble in enrolling eighty-one students in her dance class, for example.[41] More than that, however, was the fact that the AUUC was finding it difficult to retain male instructors because they were leaving for better-paying jobs outside the movement that, in Canada's expanding industrial economy, were becoming more readily available in the 1950s and 1960s. Since cultural activities like dance were rapidly becoming the only way to attract and retain the interest of young grass-roots members, the willingness of women to continue to teach and take on related responsibilities was essential to the AUUC as a whole.

Paid work within the Ukrainian left also remained available elsewhere during the 1950s to the 1970s (and, in the case of some businesses, into the 1980s and 1990s). The Workers Benevolent Association, the People's Cooperative Dairy, and the press continued to employ many. In the 1950s, as Premier Khrushchev of the Soviet Union pushed for more flexible international relations between his country and Western nations, the slate of AUUC-affiliated businesses expanded further. The organization's ties with Ukraine became more formally entrenched with a near-monopoly on business and educational relations between Ukrainians in Canada and those in Soviet Ukraine. It was manifest through several movement-owned and operated enterprises based in Canada. The most significant to get their start during the 1950s were Ukrainske Knyha, a book and parcel service, and Globe Tours, which facilitated travel to the Soviet Union and Ukraine.[42] As late as the 1980s the AUUC leaders even entertained the prospect of selling Soviet-manufactured cars in Canada. Those connected to the AUUC benefited from these international connections in a variety of ways. Travel arranged through Globe Tours afforded many of the immigrant generation their first chance to visit the old country to reconnect with kin, long separated by distance, war, and migration. Shatulsky and Dolny's aforementioned studies in Ukraine in the 1950s stand as another example of the opportunities that arose for the Canadian-born.

Many of these enterprises, especially "the Knyha" (as the Ukrainske Knyha was casually known), the WBA, and Globe Tours, had offices across Canada and thus required a good-sized workforce. Canadian-born men often fared poorly when it came to employment with these businesses. The immigrant-generation men (and some of the early Canadian-born men) continued to dominate managerial roles, in some cases into the later 1970s. As Nykolyshyn's experience earlier in this chapter demonstrated, questioning the division of power could threaten a younger man's already limited prospects. Some young men did find jobs but found them temporally demanding and poorly remunerated, offering few benefits and little opportunity for advancement. In the absence of high wages, belief in the political value of their work often sustained many. For others the conditions were unpalatable, and so they turned to more lucrative outside employment opportunities, many with pension and other benefits that the AUUC businesses could not match.

These post-war circumstances had the effect of transforming – at least somewhat – gender roles and of enhancing opportunities for some Canadian-born women in the movement. Leaders satisfied the increasing demand for more and more workers in the 1950s to the 1970s but not by improving wages or benefits significantly. Instead they began hiring more women, especially those from the earliest cohorts of the Canadian-born, who often had some high-school education (and possibly formal clerical training) and tended to be bilingual. Their ability to speak both Ukrainian and English was essential for liaising with the Ukrainian Canadian community and officials in Soviet Ukraine. More important to the AUUC bottom line was that their wage expectations were lower than men's were. Some even worked to supplement the low wages of their AUUC-employed husbands. When her sons were young, Mary Prokop worked a limited schedule that centred on her national leadership duties. Her husband, Peter, was a full-time AUUC organizer and member of the National Executive Committee. As the boys aged, the family's financial needs increased. Peter's AUUC salary alone was insufficient, so Mary took on more responsibility. "In 1965 I returned to full-time employment at Globe Tours in order to help finance the children's higher education which would have been impossible on one organizational wage," she recalled. The added obligation made for an even more demanding schedule. As she explained, "it was difficult to carry a triple burden of full-time employment, national organizational work and home responsibilities."[43]

The AUUC leadership also relied on an unofficial, unacknowledged, and often unpaid group of grass-roots immigrant-generation women to underwrite the salaries of the Canadian-born women and facilitate their ability to work outside the home. The older women who provided child-care and other domestic assistance to mothers of young children were indirectly vital to the success of many AUUC businesses. Throughout her marriage early-Canadian-born Ann Kostaniuk worked outside the home, for a time in a sewing factory and later for twenty-seven years at the People's Cooperative Dairy. Her husband, Kosty, was a high-ranking AUUC organizer in Winnipeg. When their children were young, Kosty's mother looked after them so that Ann could take on waged work. Her experience was typical of many AUUC women (as well as other women across Canada). By providing (often free) childcare and other domestic assistance for their daughters, granddaughters, and other Canadian-born women, the older women facilitated the opportunities for these young mothers to work outside the home and gave the AUUC access to their inexpensive labour.

The Canadian-born women's socialization, both within the AUUC and more broadly in Canada, the immigrant-generation men's enduring hold on organizational leadership positions, and the reality of these women's domestic responsibilities meant that they were less likely to anticipate or seek opportunities for promotion or leadership during the 1950s and 1960s. Overall challenges to the masculinist ideology of the left, and of the Ukrainian left in particular were limited in this context. Nonetheless, these changes in gender relations in the movement enabled some women to move up the ranks. A handful were pathbreakers in this respect; their success, though, hinged on a combination of key circumstances. As scholars have demonstrated with women's opportunities during other historical contexts, being child-free or single seemed critical to a woman's prospects because it allowed them to navigate the long hours, irregular schedules, and travel often required at the management level. The never-married Mary Skrypnyk, in addition to her national leadership responsibilities, also worked for the AUUC press. She began during the war as a writer and linotypist for *Ukrainske zhyttia*. She later wrote for the *Ukrainian Canadian*, with many of her pieces focusing on the activities of women and children. When she became the newspaper's editor in 1953, she was the first woman ever to hold such a position in the movement.[44] Her appointment was significant not only within the Ukrainian left but also within the broader Canadian left and indeed within the wider Canadian context (although it would likely have barely registered given the community's marginalization), because few such precedents of women holding the editorship of a national publication existed in the Canada of the 1950s. During the subsequent decade the AUUC leadership sent her to study in Soviet Ukraine. Upon her return she worked as a translator, receiving many accolades for her work.

These types of associated benefits made work with the movement very attractive and personally lucrative for a small number of women and might have made up for some of the more negative associated aspects like low wages. Betsy Bilecki, who grew up in junior and youth activities at the Winnipeg Ukrainian labour temple in the 1950s and 1960s, worked for Globe Tours in Toronto during the 1970s. Early in that decade, also single, she began making regular trips to Soviet Ukraine and to the Soviet Union, particularly Moscow, on business. "This gave me a chance to see a large part of the world," she recalled.[45] The significance of Bilecki's and Skrypnyk's experiences should not be overstated, however, as in most respects these were anomalies. Most of the women employed by the AUUC were desk or counter bound, clerking, answering telephones, or typing, and reporting to an upper managerial cohort who continued to be overwhelmingly male. Their responsibilities at home to children and husbands (and the contemporary societal expectations on women) precluded irregular paid working hours or regular extended periods away from home.

Like other areas of engagement, political discourse within the AUUC was also segmented with often overlapping intergenerational tensions and a fairly strict gendered division of interest and labour that shaped individual members' experiences and opportunities, especially in the 1950s and 1960s. The interests of the immigrant-generation men (and that of some early-Canadian-born men) continued to dominate the AUUC's primary political agenda. To them the "old left" of the Labour Progress Party or the Communist Party of Canada[46] remained central. Their connection with it continued to act as a fundamental – though increasingly contested – source of their relational power within the Ukrainian left.

As in the interwar period, a complicated and often turbulent relationship with the party endured. Likely, because of what many men had experienced during the war, in terms of rhetoric it seems that they maintained a subtler official post-war connection with the party. Nonetheless, there remained obvious linkages. For example, all high-level Ukrainian functionaries in the party were AUUC leaders, organizers, or journalists. Most of these were the same immigrant-generation or early-Canadian-born men who had been similarly active prior to the war and then were interned (or went into hiding). Although the immigrant-generation women remained largely absent, eschewing party activity for other forms of activism as they had prior to the war, among the party rank-and-file could also be found a handful of AUUC Canadian-born women and men, at least for the first decade after the war.

Through their work for the AUUC many leaders contributed directly to bolstering the party in the 1950s and 1960s. As part of his responsibilities as a touring AUUC organizer in 1950, Bill Harasym pushed local AUUC branches to set up party clubs to facilitate grass-roots activism and "to give leadership."[47] In many localities, too, the party and the AUUC often held joint meetings, like the one that occurred at the

Ukrainian cultural centre in Edmonton on 15 October 1958, where Leslie Morris spoke about his recent European visit, which had included stops in the Soviet Union.[48] Similarly, the AUUC officially endorsed party candidates (some were AUUC members) who were vying for various levels of public office. In 1945 *Ukrainske slovo* favourably profiled the Labour Progressive Party candidate and AUUC leader Nick Hrynchyshyn, who was running in the federal constituency of Selkirk, Manitoba. In 1953 *Ukrainian Canadian* highlighted eight Ukrainian leftist party candidates who were running federally, under the headline "Candidates Who Put Canada First." Similarly, in 1968 the same newspaper ran an article supporting the candidacies of AUUC leaders Andrew Bileski and William Kardash, who were running in Winnipeg for school-board trustee and metro councillor respectively.[49]

The AUUC leaders persisted in consistently presenting the Soviet Union in a positive light in the decades following the war, even when strong evidence to the contrary existed. Writing to *Ukrainske zhyttia* from the Soviet Union in 1947, Weir described the communist nation's successes, which he attributed to its leader. "Everywhere we observe intense love for the leader of the Soviet people, Stalin," Weir asserted, "and at every step we feel the certainty of the fact that it is precisely the party line, Stalin's line, which is achieving these miracles which can be vouched for by everyone who first arrives in the Soviet land." Continuing, he explained, "Such a passionate, warm, filial love for one's leader I have seen nowhere on the face of this earth."[50] Many AUUC party members saw promotion of the Soviet Union as an important responsibility with broader implications, as Misha Korol demonstrated in a letter he wrote to Mary Kardash upon his return from a 1951 tour of the Soviet Union. Contemplating his upcoming Canadian speaking tour, Korol stated, "Our job is to explain to our younger generation all about the Soviet Union, its aims and policies which are directed toward lasting peace but which has been turned and twisted so much that in the eyes of an ordinary person, it is the USSR which is the aggressor today." He continued by emphasizing that "the ability of our young people to understand the Soviet Union determines their stability in the progressive movement."[51]

Not surprisingly, this political agenda drew passionate challenges that intensified as the Cold War heated up. Some of the most notable, vocal, and visible Cold War opposition came from other organized Ukrainians. The Ukrainian nationalists and their supporters, individually and under the auspices of their political, cultural, and religious organizations like the Ukrainian Canadian Committee, the Ukrainian National Federation, and various churches, continued to condemn leaders like Weir and Korol, the AUUC generally, its leftist activities, ties to pro-communist organizations, and their characterization of communism in the Soviet Union. Some of the most vehement critics emerged from the post-war wave of nationalist Ukrainian immigrants, the displaced persons, many of whom had experienced elements of the Soviet experiment first hand. Their arrival and activities played a fundamental role in the further marginalization of the Ukrainian leftists in Canada. Explains Franca Iacovetta, among these "a core of right-wing political émigrés were highly aggressive Cold Warriors and more interested in using Canada as a base from which to regroup, defeat communism with the help of the West, and return home to regain political power." As Lubomyr Luciuk puts plain, "for them, Ukraine was enslaved and must be freed."[52] Their challenges to the AUUC leaders' portrayal of the Soviet Union and Soviet Ukraine and to the organization's radical bent served to heighten the class and social exclusion of the Ukrainian left in the decades following the war.

Further fuelling the ire of these critics was the fact that many AUUC leaders actively opposed their admittance to Canada, arguing in some instances that as members of a mainly educated and professional class they had a responsibility to remain in Soviet Ukraine to rebuild after the war. At a meeting at the Toronto Ukrainian labour temple in December 1949, John Naviziwsky warned the audience "against listening to Displaced Persons who condemned the Ukrainian government," an RCMP informant noted, adding, "He said that even if they were relatives, even so they should receive no help at all from any member of the AUUC."[53] The AUUC leaders were especially vigorous in their condemnation of the eight thousand Ukrainian men captured in Italy in Nazi uniform who had been serving in the Ukrainian SS Division Halychyna and whose applications for admission to Canada had been consistently refused by immigration agents. In press releases, newspaper articles, speeches, and letters to the federal government, Matthew Shatulsky, Naviziwsky, Teresio, and others called the men fascists, war criminals, and voluntary collaborators. The Ukrainian Canadian Committee campaigned on the soldiers' behalf, arguing, as Donald Avery explains, that this group had only fought with the Germans to liberate western Ukraine from Russian communism. Thanks to this pressure, by 1950 the immigration policy had changed, and officials began granting the men admission to Canada.[54]

This war of words translated into physical confrontation and violence on many occasions. Typical were the circumstances that Peter
Krawchuk encountered as he toured Canada in 1948, addressing grass-
roots members about his recent trip to the Soviet Union. On 10 October at an unnamed town's hall in Saskatchewan Krawchuk addressed
a crowd "which consisted of a few Displaced Persons, recent arrivals
from Europe, and district residents." According to an RCMP informant
present at the event, the displaced persons heckled and challenged
Krawchuk's praise of the Soviet Union, suggesting that he "was paint-
ing the wrong picture of the whole situation ... and that conditions
are not as" Krawchuk described. The situation escalated, and a fight
broke out among audience members. Among other acts of violence, the
informant observed, "one woman slapped another man's face." The
gathering finally broke up when "one Displaced Person [having] no
handy weapon at his disposal, took off one of his shoes and threw it"
at Krawchuk. Shortly thereafter Krawchuk and his supporters retired
to a nearby farm to finish the meeting. He had met with similar opposition earlier that month at a gathering at the Winnipeg Ukrainian labour
temple. "The meeting was turned into a riot," an RCMP informant
reported, "when some of the attending displaced persons raised objec-
tions to the manner Kravchuk [sic] answered their pertinent questions."
The trend continued into December when Krawchuk spoke at a gathering in Timmins, Ontario. Ukrainske zhyttia reported a "bloody clash ...
resulting in the injuries of several persons," including Stanley Kremyr
and Nick Hubaly, both prominent local AUUC leaders.[55]

The most violent episode alleged to involve displaced persons took
place at a Thanksgiving Day children's concert on 8 October 1950 at the
Ukrainian labour temple in Toronto. At 9:10 p.m., shortly after a group
of performers had left the stage, a bomb exploded. Filled with six-inch
used railway spikes, it had been placed on a window-sill outside the
hall, accessible by the fire escape. Few in the crowd of six hundred were
seriously injured, though many sustained cuts from the flying broken
glass. The blast caused some ten thousand dollars in estimated property damage: "The explosion damaged the fire exit doors, destroyed
the steel frame and sectioning of the window and damaged the brick
wall around the window sill. Glass in other windows of the south wall
was also broken and in all about 90 panes were destroyed. Window
panes in the rear of three houses south of the hall were broken and
a fence between the fire escape and the yard to the south was badly
damaged."[56]

The AUUC immediately blamed a "circle of former Nazi S.S. men, who have managed to enter our country in the guise of Displaced Persons, who had been trained in terrorist activities" and "who functioned during the Second World War as an agency of the German Gestapo, who organized the S.S. Division 'Halichina.'"[57] Ukrainian nationalist groups were quick to refute any accusations against the Ukrainian displaced persons and accused the AUUC of planting the bomb. "The Communists wanted to put Ukrainian displaced persons in Canada in a bad light. They wanted to make the public think that these Ukrainians were Fascist murderers while the Communists were good democratic people," asserted Roman Rakhmanny (himself a former member of the anti-communist underground in Ukraine and a displaced person) in the *Globe and Mail* days after the bombing.[58] The Toronto City Police offered a reward of five hundred dollars for information, to which the AUUC added a thousand dollars. The RCMP investigated several displaced persons as possible perpetrators, but no suspects were ever charged. In the end, although the results of their investigations were inconclusive, the RCMP seemed to favour the Ukrainian nationalists' explanation. "The bombing actually serves the purpose of the Communists to an extent incomparable to that of the Nationalists," proposed an RCMP memorandum. Embracing the displaced persons' perspective, it explained, "The Communists have an intrepid fear of the factual knowledge brought to Canada by Displaced Persons and the result it has had ... on the Communist mass language movement in this country ... This bombing will serve for months to come as grist for the propaganda mill of the Communists."[59]

Red-baiting was a common occurrence from other quarters as well. Owing to the AUUC's pro-Soviet views and connections with the party, all AUUC members, regardless of their personal feelings about or links with the party, were vulnerable to red-baiting and the social, economic, and class exclusion it could produce. The harassment came in many forms. Individual Cold Warriors took it upon themselves to monitor, question, challenge, shun, and condemn the AUUC and its members. When Olga Shatulsky, who was not a member of the party, was working for Globe Tours in the 1960s, she met with a chilly reception when she represented the company on Air Canada's inaugural flight in 1967. "Many of the other travel agents were unfriendly to me," she recalled, "because of the company I worked for."[60] Others experienced more vicious attacks. Mitch Sago, then manager of *Ukrainian Canadian*, was beaten in broad daylight on the street in Vancouver when he was in town for the newspaper's fund-raising drive in February 1962. "The attack was completely unexpected, unprovoked, and was made from behind," a *Ukrainian Canadian* article reported. Sago was "kicked repeatedly and hit about the face until a gash just below the eye bled profusely." Bypassers intervened, and Sago was taken to hospital where he received several stitches. The police concluded that the beating "was one of several ... perpetuated on leading labor figures in the community during the past recent period of time."[61]

The Ukrainian left and its members and supporters were also targets of various levels of the Canadian state during the Cold War. When she was living in St Catharines in the 1950s, Shatulsky was summoned to the local post office. "I liked to read *Soviet Literature Magazine* and *Soviet Woman* because I liked the articles and used them in my teaching [at the hall]," she explained. "When I got to the post office, the postal worker started to question me about why I subscribed, and asked if I was sure I wanted them."[62] On behalf of the Timmins AUUC branches, Nick Hubaly attempted to rent the local high-school auditorium to hold a Golden Jubilee Summer Festival in 1962. School trustee Joe Behie attacked him and the group in the local press. Dismissing the AUUC as "a Communist organization," he avowed, "To hell with that sort of thing." Calling Hubaly "one of the top Commies in town," Behie insisted that the board not rent the hall to the AUUC.[63] In Quebec, Maurice Duplessis' Padlock Law, introduced in 1937, created an especially dire situation. The statute allowed authorities to padlock any building in which communist activities were believed to be taking place and to confiscate any related material. Police raided the Montreal-area hall, searching raffle tickets, books, and other materials in an effort to link the AUUC to the Labour Progressive Party. Although the hall was never closed, these items were confiscated, and local members could not afford to pursue their return through the courts. Many at the grass-roots level were afraid to go themselves or send their children to the labour temple for activities. Although the Canadian Supreme Court struck down the Padlock Law in 1957, the damage had been done. By 1966 the Montreal branch was all but decimated, and the hall was in a deteriorating condition. "We have no place to hold meetings," a Montreal member reported to the AUUC national convention that year, "and as a result of this are unable to carry out any organizational work."[64]

The federal government was especially active, continuing, through the RCMP, to monitor closely the activities of the Ukrainian left for evidence of subversion in the decades following the war. The agency clipped and translated newspaper articles, paid informants to report on AUUC meetings, classes, and concerts, maintained detailed dossiers, and confronted individual members about their activities. Although they were unaware of the extent of this surveillance, many of those associated with the AUUC knew they were being watched. Some had officers following them, stopping them on the street, or coming to their homes to question them and their families. The spied-on embraced a number of strategies to deal with this RCMP red-baiting. Gary Kinsmen has demonstrated that members of Ottawa's gay and lesbian community employed individual and collective responses to Cold War RCMP surveillance, including being cautious about revealing their own or other people's identities to the police. They also used "humour and camp" when an officer confronted them directly or was present in their social spaces,[65] a method favoured in certain circumstances by some AUUC members. Outside many Ukrainian labour temples surveillance vehicles were regular fixtures. During an AUUC convention at the hall in Toronto in the 1960s, Nykolyshyn noticed one across the street. "I went over to their car," he said, "and invited them into the hall for a coffee ... The agents got very angry and left." Within half an hour two new agents in another car had taken their place.[66]

Other AUUC members found that they needed to employ more organized forms of resistance to deal with the consequences of state monitoring and red-baiting. The immigrant generation was particularly vulnerable to the government's attempts to silence and punish dissidents during the Cold War, and experienced the resulting social, political, and economic marginalization in distinct ways. A key example of this vulnerability surrounds the issue of Canadian citizenship. Many had earlier applied for and been denied naturalization because of their connections with the Ukrainian left. With the advent of the Canadian Citizenship Act in 1946 a good number found themselves refused citizenship because of their connections with the ULFTA and the AUUC. It took very little to be blacklisted. Reading AUUC newspapers, giving money to AUUC-supported causes, attending events at a Ukrainian labour temple, or taking part in worker demonstrations was sufficient in many cases to warrant denial. In 1961 the AUUC participated in a national campaign to fight this political discrimination. It was coordinated by the inter-ethnic Canadian Slav Committee (which was headed by several key AUUC members).[67] Their efforts highlighted the profound and dire financial and personal consequences faced by those denied citizenship and underscored the petty mean-spiritedness of many forms of state-sponsored red-baiting. Barbara Mashtalar, for example, welcomed the campaign after her application had been rejected numerous times. This prevented her from visiting her dying mother in Ukraine whom she had not seen since she herself had left Galicia many years before. Devastated, Mashtalar told the AUUC's *Ukrainian Canadian* newspaper that she "cried with the pain of knowing that Canada had prevented me from seeing my mother once again before she died." "I had given many hard years of labor to Canada. I had never once committed a criminal act and never harmed anyone consciously," she added, before rightfully demanding, "Why does Canada treat me like a cruel stepmother?"[68] While it is not known whether Mashtalar's subsequent applications were successful, accounts of the campaign suggest that it "gained citizenship for hundreds of immigrants who had been this status for many decades."[69] Despite such occasional successes, concerted red-baiting efforts from a variety of corners were wildly successful in increasing the level of social, economic, and political isolation that the Ukrainian left and its supporters came to experience over the course of the decades following the war.

Further contributing to the marginalization in this Cold War era were changes and challenges from within the broader Canadian and international left, some of which, once exposed, lent considerable credence to the claims of displaced persons and other leftist opponents. Stalin's death in March 1953 shifted the political climate in the Soviet Union. Ukrainian leftists were shocked, and many leaders discredited, when Khrushchev, at the Twentieth All-Union Congress in February 1956, confirmed the long-suspected atrocities carried out under Stalin. As we have seen, the leadership of the CPC and ULFTA had downplayed or denied this abuse during the interwar period. Then came the violent suppression of the Hungarian revolution in 1956, Khrushchev's deposition in 1964, and the invasion of Czechoslovakia in 1968. These events cast the Cold War Soviet Union in a negative light and caused many supporters, Ukrainian or otherwise, to turn away from domestic communist organizations in the West.

The international currents manifested in the local context in specific ways. Response among AUUC party members was mixed, falling, in many cases, along generational lines. Most young Canadian-born members voted against the party with their feet. When Khrushchev was deposed, Zenovy Nykolyshyn left the party for over a decade. Betsy Bilecki was among the many who left over Czechoslovakia. Others lingered but eventually departed, as Myron Shatulsky did, because of the way the party operated in Canada. He cited the anti-Semitism he had witnessed from the Ukrainian leaders in the Winnipeg Maple Leaf Club as the final straw that saw him quit in 1970. Nykolyshyn, who had rejoined the party in 1977 when he was hired to work for the WBA, left again in 1990, frustrated by what he characterized as a lack of respect on the part of the Anglo-Celtic party leadership towards the Ukrainian leaders. In this context many young Canadian-born Ukrainian leftists found associations with the party distasteful or irrelevant to their activist interests.

The immigrant generation and many of the early-Canadian-born men, especially those with leadership positions in the party or the AUUC, remained more consistently loyal to the party than did the Canadian-born and party members of other ethnicities. In the wake of so many mass resignations these Ukrainians found that their proportion and influence increased in party circles.[70] Back at the Ukrainian labour temples, however, ongoing disillusionment with the Soviets was becoming a serious liability for the older male leaders in the face of the mass defection of younger members from the party and from the old left-activist models. Less and less could these older men rely on their ties to and gatekeeping role with global communism as a basis for their relational power within the Ukrainian left.

Nonetheless, these leaders remained steadfastly loyal to the CPC, the Soviet Union, and Soviet Ukraine. Their support, however, was not unquestioning. As they had in the interwar period, they were especially willing to reject or challenge party policy and perspectives where issues of Ukrainian culture and language were concerned. The most serious shake-up between the AUUC leaders and the CPC came in 1967 over the issue of Russification in Soviet Ukraine. After the war, charges made by displaced persons, concerns brought back by tourists who had visited Soviet Ukraine (many of whom were associated with the AUUC), and accusations made by former CPC and AUUC member John Kolasky brought to the surface the Russification controversy. Many male leaders of the Ukrainian left mounted pressure on the party, and in 1967 the CPC convened a delegation made up of AUUC leaders and party officials to investigate. After a three-week tour of Soviet Ukraine the men returned and submitted an explosive report. There were many problems with Russian being the official language of use in Ukraine, they asserted. Although there had been some improvements during the previous years, they felt there was still much work to do to ensure the presence and use of Ukrainian in Ukraine. Implying that the

Ukrainian language was marginalized, they insisted, "The Ukrainian language has to be encouraged, promoted, and developed in all areas of life in Ukraine. It is not to be forced upon the people, whether of Ukrainian, Russian, or other origins, but the climate has to be created for its freest flourishing and interdevelopment with other languages and cultures."[71] Although they were heavily pressured by both the CPC and the Communist Party of the Soviet Union who were extremely displeased with the report, the Ukrainian leaders refused to back down or retract their findings.

Few Ukrainian women ever joined the CPC; those who did were more likely to be drawn from the Canadian-born, like Betsy Bilecki or Mary Prokop, who started as a teenager by working on party election campaigns in Alberta during the Depression.[72] None ever held an upper-level leadership position in the party. Instead, when it came to political engagement in the post-war period, the Canadian-born and the immigrant-generation AUUC women – especially at the grass-roots level – embraced other forms of activism, often by extending their efforts beyond the parameters of the Ukrainian left by engaging with causes of the broader Canadian left. They did so sometimes through CPC-connected groups, forging enduring alliances with like-minded women and men of other ethnicities. Julie Guard, for example, has demonstrated well that these women were critical to the post-war Housewives and Consumers Association, fighting in particular for price controls in the immediate post-war years.[73]

These women were also active in the peace movement (a cause often linked to the party) and the feminist movement immediately following the war. The AUUC as an organization officially supported the peace movement, but women were by far the most engaged members, involved as both leaders and grass-roots supporters. Again, as with other areas of activism, though the women were united in peace endeavours, the nature of a particular woman's activism fell along generational lines. It was considerably easier for the fluently English Canadian-born women to be involved because language did not pose the barrier that it had for their mothers or grandmothers in the interwar period. Often the Canadian-born coordinated efforts, acting as leaders and liaisons between the Ukrainian-speaking immigrant-generation women and the mainstream activist organizations.

In terms of their peace activism a key organization with which these women worked closely in the decade following the war was the Canadian Peace Congress, founded in 1948 and headed by James Endicott.

It conducted its work in a vein that endorsed the Soviet Union, a view that the Ukrainian left could easily support. As such, like the Ukrainian left, its opponents attempted to discredit its efforts by labelling it a communist front organization.[74] During the 1950s the AUUC supported the congress's petition to ban the bomb. Rank-and-file AUUC women carried out most of the resulting work, canvassing door to door for signatures. This was not always an easy task, especially for women of the immigrant generation. In Timmins, Ontario, for example, many of these women found that "it was very difficult for them to explain what was going on and what the petition was about because they did not speak English well."[75] Notwithstanding such problems, in terms of numerical support the national campaign was successful. Members of the Vancouver women's branch, for example, succeeded in gathering 1,450 signatures.[76]

A casualty of the Cold War and red-baiting, the Canadian Peace Congress entered a steady decline in the early 1950s.[77] This did not mark the end of peace activism by these women, however. They actively engaged with other post-war progressives to pursue peace in a variety of ways. In 1955, for example, *Ukrainske zhyttia* reported that members of the Edmonton women's branch were "taking an active part in a campaign against the rearming of West Germany [by] collecting signatures to cards and petitions, and circulating leaflets, against 'remilitarization,' thus to 'influence the government not to vote for the ratification of the London and Paris agreements.'"[78] As the threat of nuclear war intensified in the 1960s, underscored by events like the Cuban missile crisis of 1962 and the Vietnam War (1954–75), so too did the women's peace work intensify in the AUUC. While protesting the war, rank-and-file women knitted and sewed for Vietnamese women and children and raised money to aid peoples living in other war-torn areas.[79] Often, like other activist women, they explicitly framed their efforts through their roles as mothers.[80] Leader Hannah Polowy emphasized this in a 1963 report to the AUUC women's conference in British Columbia. "If we are to guarantee life to our children," she declared, "then we as women and mothers must exert every ounce of energy and support to the peace movement in Canada which is demanding that we not become a nuclear power."[81]

Like that of so many other post-war feminists, the AUUC women's interest in feminism often developed from or overlapped with their work in the peace movement. For example, AUUC women engaged as leaders and grass-roots activists with other leftist feminists through the

Congress of Canadian Women, formed on International Women's Day, 8 March 1950, as an umbrella group to encompass women's groups that were affiliated with or sympathetic to the Labour Progressive Party. As AUUC member Mary Kardash explained in 1952, at its founding, the congress "adopted a program of working and fighting for women's rights and the well-being of our children. As a section of the Women's International Democratic Federation (WIDF), it also has as its aim the mobilization of women for the cause of peace."[82] Throughout the 1950s and beyond, AUUC women participated in local chapters of the Congress of Canadian Women and joined its international delegations meant to foster peace and international understanding. Katherine Stefanitsky of the Toronto AUUC women's branch, for example, was a member of the congress's five-member delegation to China during the 1950s.[83]

Within the halls and the Ukrainian press the Canadian-born women especially began articulating a broader socialist and feminist analysis in the 1950s and 1960s, mingling the class-consciousness learned at the labour temples, their mothers' and their own experiences as women and workers, and the ideals of the rising post-war feminist movement. In 1965, for example, the women collected some three thousand signatures on a petition calling for the government to lower women's qualifying age for old age pension to sixty.[84] The AUUC, represented by four of its leading female members, was also among those groups in 1968 that delivered a brief to the Royal Commission on the Status of Women in Canada. Presented by Skrypnyk, it called for guarantees of higher education for girls; argued that daycare should be accessible for all women; and demanded equal pay for work of equal value, maternity leave without fear of firing, and readily available and Medicare-funded birth control and abortion. Finally, it demanded income tax deductions for childcare and household help, and old age security for women at age sixty.[85]

These types of activist activities increasingly redirected many women's energies outside the AUUC, a circumstance that would fundamentally challenge the strength, unity, and cohesion of the organization. Hand in hand with the application of a feminist analysis to gender relations in the movement, these changes in activist focus and practice gradually served to challenge the relational authority of the older male leadership. For example, feminist consciousness-raising efforts and the broader women's rights discourse of the 1960s and 1970s inspired some women as individuals to challenge the Ukrainian left's masculinist ideology, male gender privilege, and the specific instances of sexism that they encountered personally within the movement. Canadian-born Mary Semanowich did just that at the People's Cooperative Dairy in Winnipeg. When she first started working there in the 1960s, she found that "women did not hold the same positions as men, they were paid less, women got the smaller jobs, men got the promotions." She quit but later returned part time in 1977, finding that little had changed. Angry, she approached then-head Bill Kardash, arguing that when it came to women, "management did not practise the socialist policies they preached." Change in the movement was slow, but eventually, in the 1990s, she became the first woman to hold the position of secretary-treasurer of the WBA. Nonetheless, attitudes persisted; about her WBA post she noted in 1998, "There are still some men who have a problem with this."[86]

Considerable enthusiasm for feminism existed among women of both the immigrant and the Canadian-born generations. Together they used their jointly celebrated International Women's Day and Mother's Day teas to raise funds for and awareness of women's rights activities and other related causes into the 1970s and 1980s. Despite their keen interest, however, most women found that these issues remained peripheral to the dominant AUUC male-defined political agenda. Winnipeg Young Women's Club members Beth Krall and Mary Kardash frequently attended women's conferences and related events as AUUC representatives. From the male leadership back at the hall Krall encountered polite indifference: "Nobody cared that Mary and I went to women's meetings."[87]

Consequently many women, especially the Canadian-born, shifted their energies outside the AUUC to broader leftist activism. So too did many of the politically active Canadian-born men. As they increasingly identified more with the Canadian side of their ethnocultural heritage, the New Left, rather than the old Ukrainian left, held more appeal. The aforementioned shifts in the international communist situation and in perceptions of the Soviets in particular served to reinforce this. The advent of new sites of activism offered a venue for leadership opportunities and a chance for young Ukrainian leftists to shape more effectively their own activism.

To be fair, however, this exodus was far from limited to the Ukrainian radical community; indeed, it was part of a larger decline in ethnic-hall activism that was typical of other ethnic groups in the post-war era in North America and elsewhere. The ties between these international and national trends manifested in significant ways in affected local contexts, and the consequences were multifold. Gender relations, for example, were subsequently transformed when these young women and men rejected the activist models of their parents and grandparents – rooted as they were in the halls and the old-country models of women's and men's roles and in the centrality of notions of an old-country workers' paradise – in favour of cross-ethnic organizational strategies and world views. Although gender equity remained fleeting within many of these newly formed activist communities, sexism and prevailing notions of appropriate activist models for women and men were grounded in more mainstream Canadian attitudes. These factors posed a fundamental challenge to the old male left's relational authority, grounded as it was in their ties to and gatekeeping roles in the international and often ethnically segmented communist movement. While many younger individuals remained firmly engaged in the class struggle – as defined in the context of the post-war New Left or socialist feminist movements – an assertion and defence of ethnic identity was no longer a motivating force for young Ukrainian Canadians in shaping their activist targets, strategy, and engagement. The failure of the older male leaders to appropriately respond and adapt precipitated an irreversible fragmentation of the Ukrainian labour temple movement as a whole.

At the local levels in the Ukrainian labour temples, male privilege (most often benefiting immigrant-generation men) remained a mainstay well into the 1970s. However, gender relations and roles transformed in the face of the aforementioned internal and external challenges. As it did in other times of crisis, necessity also contributed to this shift. Quite simply, with a smaller membership pool on which to draw, leaders could no longer afford to deny women the opportunities outside their traditional activities in the movement. Here language played a key role in the transformation, notably in terms of young women's bilingualism (not to mention their willingness to work for the low wages that their male counterparts were generally unwilling to accept). As such, some women were able to move more easily into jobs and positions of leadership or to engage in forms of activism denied to their mothers and grandmothers in the past. By this point it was too little, too late in many cases. Declining membership and resources, the diminishing influence of the Ukrainian labour temple movement, not to mention the hostile Cold War climate, limited the effectiveness of what they could accomplish.

Of course, the stubbornness of the older male leaders alone cannot account for the post-war decline of the Ukrainian left. A host of other factors were also at play during the 1960s and 1970s, drawing the Canadian-born away. Many women were simply too busy balancing marriage, motherhood (with baby-boom numbers of children), and paid work outside the home (and often outside the movement) to be active. Canadian-born men were turning to more lucrative job opportunities elsewhere, in positions that paid better and offered benefits and the chance to move up the ranks. Their increasingly middle-class experiences – made possible by university educations, the resulting white-collar and professional job opportunities, and generally better job prospects in the prosperous post-war economy, especially for assimilated "white ethnics" – meant that fewer and fewer young Ukrainian Canadians had an intimate and in-depth appreciation for the class struggle as defined by their Ukrainian leftist elders. With red-baiting rampant, many young people rightfully feared the potentially negative effects and the prospects for social and economic marginalization that open affiliation with the Ukrainian left could pose, particularly in their wider working and community lives.

Proximity to the halls also posed logistical challenges to ongoing engagement. With the better wages they often earned, the Canadian-born women and men often bought cars and suburban homes and moved away from the working-class neighbourhoods surrounding the Ukrainian labour temples. Increasingly they spent their disposable income on leisure activities at venues other than the Ukrainian labour temple or stayed at home to watch television. Some still sent their children to Ukrainian school, dance lessons, and Junior or Youth Section activities. Organizers at some halls even attempted (unsuccessfully in the end) to increase adult membership numbers through these children's activities. The Edmonton Young Women's Club in 1960, for example, courted the mothers of the Junior Section members. "We have been talking individually with some of the Mothers," organizer Hazel Strashok wrote to the AUUC National Executive Committee, "but soon we will hold a tea or some other affair inviting all our members and prospective members, and then maybe we will be able to have some of them join our club."[88]

Among the immigrant generation the reasons for decline were somewhat different. Mostly it was caused by the inability to attract new members from the post-war wave of Ukrainian-speaking displaced persons and by the onslaught of old age among its primary membership base. The number of new members attracted to the women's and men's branches in the post-war period was never enough to ensure a sustained growth. As those who had joined in the early years of the movement aged, experienced ill health, or passed away, the immigrant-generation branches diminished rapidly in size.[89] Some of the members attempted to stave off the problem by merging their branches, often into "Senior Citizen's Clubs" (interestingly, many women's branch members, concerned about the possibility of male dominance, resisted unification as long as possible). By the 1970s, RCMP surveillance offi-cers characterized the AUUC as an organization "primarily ... made up of old timers."[90] In 1975 the AUUC's membership of adults and youth totalled a mere 1,995, down considerably from the 15,000 it had enjoyed prior to the war.[91] Thus, as the immigrant generation of members and supporters aged and died, and the Canadian-born turned elsewhere for political, social, cultural, and economic engagement, so too did the Ukrainian left dwindle in its overall size and influence.

Although the end of the Second World War and the resolution of the progressive Ukrainian community's difficulties with the federal gov-ernment lent an optimistic air to the efforts of the Ukrainian left, the termination of the conflict in Europe ushered in a new era of friction and change for the movement in Canada. Forces internal and external to the movement at the international and national levels transformed the Ukrainian left and its members and supporters in the local contexts in which they practised their activism. After the war men's roles could be characterized by both continuity and change, though, as we have seen, this was not experienced evenly across the board. In the interwar period an individual man's experience was dependent on whether he was a leader or an ordinary member or supporter and on his embodi-ment of hegemonic or complicit masculinities. In the post-war context the outcome of the intersection of gender with class, ethnicity, and gen-eration offered continued advantage for some men (particularly the older, immigrant generation) and diminished privilege for other men (usually the younger ones). Older men of the immigrant generation who had come of age during the interwar era were resistant to change and continued to hold on to the bulk of power in the Ukrainian left as they had prior to the war. Younger men as a result often found such power to be inaccessible and opportunities for leadership to be limited, and they discovered themselves in a marginalized masculinity position as a result. In some sectors of the movement the Canadian-born men remained active and managed to carve out a niche for themselves. In most areas, however, they found themselves excluded. Consequently many turned away from the AUUC, seeking jobs and political activity through other means. In this way a stark generational divide developed between men of the immigrant-generation and those of the Canadian-born. While other factors also contributed to the pattern of activity and ultimate decline of the Ukrainian left at this time, the pronounced generational division among men most significantly shaped their respective experiences and opportunities, as well as the overall form that the movement would assume after the Second World War.

Women's experiences too possessed elements of continuity and change. The immigrant-generation women maintained the patterns of grass-roots cultural and political activism that they had in the interwar era. Culturally speaking, however, they gained influence as traditional Ukrainian food and embroidery increased in status. This status came both within the movement and outside, thanks to the accessibility of food and crafts to non-Ukrainian speakers and the role that these activities would assume in helping to legitimize the Ukrainian left with a broader public attuned to multiculturalism. Nonetheless, their opportunities were still limited as they had been in the past because their male counterparts continued to hold the bulk of power in the movement. Increasingly, however, these women looked not to their menfolk as leaders but to the Canadian-born women. Unlike the men of their generation, some Canadian-born women had an advantage in the movement, often as a result of the gendered discourse that persisted in privileging immigrant-generation men over all other members and supporters. While their male counterparts were unable to access power in the movement, Canadian-born women were able to move into new positions, largely because they were willing, at least initially, to put up with the wage and power inequities that men of their own generation were not. While it initially presented opportunity, ultimately this situation created a great deal of dissatisfaction among the Canadian-born women (at both the grass-roots and the leadership level). It led many to challenge the movement's attitudes about gender roles with their feet, taking their talents and activism elsewhere.

The intersection, then, of the processes of gender, generation, ethnicity, and, to a lesser degree, class contoured the post-war Ukrainian left, its adult members and supporters, and defined power and opportunity. While older members (particularly the dominant male leadership) sought to engage the younger generation, they simply could not as the post-war decades passed. A number of challenging factors were at play. Externally, among the most significant at the global and national levels were the changes in the international communist situation; the transformations in the broader Canadian and international lefts; the escalation of the Cold War; and the ensuing context of red-baiting, alongside post-war upward mobility, the influence of multicultural-ism, and increased assimilation. Further compounding matters was the older men's enduring unwillingness to relinquish power and author-ity and to address significant gender-related issues, along with their often-relentless insistence on close and at times uncritical engage-ment with old left-activist models and principles. These factors ulti-mately rendered ineffective the movement's efforts to attract and retain younger Ukrainian Canadians and in the process served to undermine the older men's relational power in the movement. Only in the face of vastly diminishing membership numbers and their own old age did these men begin to concede authority by the late 1970s. By then, how-ever, it was too little, too late. With better economic, social, and activist conditions elsewhere in other areas of Canadian society, most of the Canadian-born women and men had moved on. And, as we shall see in the next chapter, their children struggled to reconcile their interests and experiences as young Ukrainian Canadians with the realities of life in post-war Canada and what seemed to be the increasingly disconnected Ukrainian left of their elders.

6 "We're Ukrainian Canadians, Not Ukrainians": Children, Youth, and the Post-War Ukrainian Left

In 1951 AUUC children's organizer Mary Skrypnyk wrote a fictional account of the experiences of a young member of the Association of United Ukrainian Canadians' Junior Section. It appeared on the children's pages of the association's English-language newspaper, *Ukrainian Canadian*. Called "Little Irene," the story centred on a girl's first performance at a Ukrainian labour temple. "Little Irene now had what she wanted most of all: she stood on the stage of the Ukrainian labour temple with the rest of the school choir, a little frightened, but very proud, dressed in her very pretty Ukrainian costume, with its bright red skirt, lovely embroidered apron and shirt, black velvet jacket, colourful beads and a wreath of flowers on her head."[1]

The story recounts Little Irene's thoughts as she and the other members of the children's choir sing peace songs and traditional Ukrainian folk songs for the audience of family and friends. In particular she reflects on the song "In Defence of Peace": "Teacher had explained the whole thing to them telling them that there were people in this world who wanted war, because they made a great deal of money out of it. They did not care that millions of people were killed and millions of little children, too. Little Irene felt very badly that anyone could be so cruel." Teacher had emphasized, though, that "most of the people all over the world, like her mummy and daddy, who worked hard for a living, did not want a war." Little Irene was sure other children also felt that way, believing "they wanted to grow up and learn all sorts of things and see all sorts of things without having to go out and kill people." She herself "liked people very much, all kinds of people ... most of all the people that came to the hall, for as mummy put it, these were 'our people,' and that made them practically relatives."[2]

The tale of Little Irene served several functions. Descriptive, it illustrated some of the major cultural and political activities available to children and youth in the post-war AUUC: Ukrainian school, youngsters' branches, musical training, and cultural performance. Enticing, it attempted, through the pleasure and excitement Little Irene expresses, to encourage young *Ukrainian Canadian* readers to avail themselves of these opportunities. Didactic, "Little Irene" personalized international political issues, making explicit their ties with the local context; it also rooted youngsters in a specific sense of Ukrainianness and community (as one of "our people" at the Ukrainian labour temple), distinguishing them from other Ukrainian and non-Ukrainian youngsters alike. Proscriptive and idealized, the story also illuminated organizers' hopes for young people's activism. AUUC leaders, particularly those like Skrypnyk who worked extensively with children, hoped to raise a progressive, politically informed, and culturally engaged generation, one fully prepared to carry the AUUC torch into the future. With a girl as its main character, "Little Irene" also underscored the more egalitarian gender relations that children, unlike their parents, continued to experience in AUUC groups (though her older sisters and brothers in the Youth Division were still expected to conform to proscribed gender roles).[3] Post-war continuity with the movement's interwar ambitions, strategies for recruitment, and the practical aspects of youngsters' engagement are, thus, evident in Little Irene's story.

Equally present, however, is evidence of change – an outcome of the interactions of gender with class, ethnicity, and generation in the postwar context. Although her costume was the same and she performed for "our people" at the hall, Little Irene shared not songs celebrating revolution, as she might have in the interwar years, but a song about peace, carrying an anti-war message shaped by the Cold War and the broader Canadian leftist context in which she was growing up. Little Irene herself would have changed too. For many of her generation the ability to speak Ukrainian, despite their Ukrainian school attendance at the labour temple, would have been limited at best. Assimilation meant that English was the prime language of communication for youngsters, be they at the hall, at school, in their neighbourhood, or, for most, at home. Increasingly, as second- and third-generation Ukrainian Canadians intermarried with individuals from other ethnic backgrounds, Little Irene's last name might likely be a non-Ukrainian one. Change was also reflected in the role of early-Canadian-born Skrypnyk, who was a journalist for the movement, the story's author, and a long-time national children's organizer. As the previous chapter illustrated, many women of her generational cohort began playing more active leadership roles after the war, though typically their only opportunities arose in the field of women's and children's activism. Nonetheless, their contributions (and those of later Canadian-born women) were essential to shaping the AUUC's agenda for children, and they and their male counterparts were also critical to developing the new post-war Youth Division.

That Little Irene, performing on the stage of the Ukrainian labour temple, had "what she wanted most of all" hints at the agency that she and other post-war youngsters exercised. Like their interwar counterparts, they continued, through demands and disinterest, to shape profoundly the Ukrainian left. In the interwar years, balancing CPC demands with youngster's interests had challenged the ULFTA leadership. Although this became less of an issue with the party's post-war decline in influence, new trials emerged. As a member of the baby-boom generation, Little Irene grew up in one of the most affluent periods of Canadian history. Her exposure to Canadian and, increasingly, American popular culture would have intensified, presenting an array of leisure options that could tempt her away from the Ukrainian labour temples. Political activism outside, to which many young members were exposed in high school and then university, challenged the Ukrainian left's traditional political mandate. Most notably, youngsters began to reject outright the perspectives and methods of the immigrant-generation male leaders, which were grounded in ties to the international communist movement. Doing so posed a fundamental challenge to these older men's relational power in the movement.

The activities in the halls were modified during the 1950s and 1960s to reflect and accommodate the youngsters' changing linguistic, social, cultural, and, to a lesser degree, political interests. Leaders emphasized and expanded Ukrainian cultural activities, like dance and embroidery, for which no Ukrainian-language skills were necessary. With the obvious exception of Ukrainian school, all meetings and other activities for youngsters took place in English. Educationals, if not dispensed with altogether, came to centre on issues of concern to youth (which sometimes overlapped with issues prioritized by adults); dances for teenagers, featuring mainstream popular music, occurred regularly at many halls, and sports became more developed. New spaces were created in response to post-war interests and needs in which young people could express their activism and explore their identities as Canadian Ukrainians; summer camps were opened or expanded, and opportunities for international education and travel proliferated. These diversions came to reflect a fascinating hybridized subculture for young people that combined elements of a Ukrainian leftist, broader leftist, and mainstream Canadian identity, one that was distinctly shaped by a variety of forces, most especially the AUUC children and youth themselves. Despite these efforts, however, by the 1970s it was becoming apparent that the AUUC was fighting a losing battle where its younger generations were concerned. By then, activities for children and youth were seriously on the wane. The AUUC simply could not compete with the multitude of other social, economic, and political options that spoke to these young people's interests and dominant identities as English-speaking Canadians. Unlike their interwar counterparts, few post-war youngsters remained active in the AUUC once they had reached their teen years and especially adulthood, contributing significantly to the marked decline faced by the movement in the latter half of the twentieth century. It is, perhaps, in this decline that their agency is most apparent.

After the war youngsters' activities in most localities centred on either the AUUC's Junior Section or Youth Section. During the war both had functioned irregularly, if at all; immediately following the war both necessitated serious rebuilding efforts. Change occurred mainly because of the AUUC's altered political character. Its orientation had shifted from overt class struggle to issues of peace, citizenship, and international understanding and reflected the Ukrainian leftists' arrival as an established – and increasingly assimilated – ethnic group. The shift also arose from the AUUC's desire for respectability and from its changed relationship with the CPC. Although the association remained linked to the CPC in some obvious and important ways, overall, as the previous chapter has demonstrated, the party diminished as a strong influence on the AUUC, as it did within the rest of the Canadian left broadly. Finally, retention of children and youth was foremost on organizers' minds; they recognized that for activities to be successful they needed to take place almost exclusively in English and be both educational and enjoyable – reflective of the lifestyles, linguistic abilities, and interests of post-war youngsters.

Change was manifest in official documents and day-to-day activity. Gone were the revolutionary slogans of class overthrow and calls for the raising of good, class-conscious children. Instead by the 1950s the Junior Section, for example, was to give children "a rich understanding of the world around them – to grow up with the deep conviction of the essential equality of all the peoples of the world, regardless of race, colour, religion or national origin."[4] Although the emphasis on the Ukrainian language had gone, Ukrainian culture remained an important staple of the Junior Section's program, and, from this, organizers hoped that participants would "know and prize the rich cultural heritage, progressive traditions and democratic aspirations of [their] own national group and the AUUC in particular."[5] This is underscored by the AUUC Junior Section pledge:

It is my duty:
to love and respect my parents
to respect all people regardless of race, colour, or religion
to be proud of the culture of Ukrainian Canadians and of all the people
    in our Canada
to co-operate and share with others
to be honest at all times
to keep my body strong and healthy
to take part in and help build the Junior Section of the AUUC
to be a good Canadian!

Class-consciousness was not entirely absent from the post-war youngsters' program; however, a kinder and gentler approach was taken on the subject of the improvement of conditions for working people. A child in the Ukrainian left was to be taught "to understand the role of labour in the struggle for human betterment" and, it was hoped, would "grow up a progressive, active citizen, interested in the affairs of his country and in international affairs, and willing to work toward the realization of his ideals and hopes and dreams."[6] To these ends, throughout the 1950s the AUUC leadership implemented a number of practical measures to revitalize the Junior and Youth Sections and make them relevant and interesting.

To manage the work of children under twelve, leaders enacted a National Junior Council, which Skrypnyk headed for a number of years. It oversaw the Junior Section, kept records on participant numbers, provided suggestions for activities, offered advice on the specific organizational and political needs of children, and developed organizational methods designed to compete directly with other post-war children's clubs like the Girl and Boy Scouts. At the local level the National Junior Council handed responsibility for the Junior Section to the Canadian-born women. Often the Young Women's Clubs organized junior councils, using them to coordinate the Junior Section as well as the Ukrainian school and other children's activities at the halls.[7] The women also acted as Junior Section teachers or recruited teenage girls from the Youth Section to fulfil these roles. In some localities the system functioned well; in others a lack of interested or suitable organizers and teachers meant sporadic Junior Section activity. Branches frequently called on the AUUC's National Executive Committee to train the teacher organizers to conduct work with children.[8] In answer to this issue the National Junior Council produced and distributed an English-language resource, the *Leader's Guide*, to local Junior Section organizers during the 1950s and 1960s. Written by several key early-Canadian-born women like Mary Kardash and Mary Skrypnyk, the *Leader's Guide* endeavoured to create a uniform national Junior Section curriculum, address problems related to the lack of teachers, and remind local organizers of the importance of this children's work. "The Junior program of the AUUC should offer children the priceless things which it seldom learns in the dictated atmosphere of the school classroom – or in the anarchy of the street," emphasized the 1959 fall/winter issue. "The future of the people's aspirations for peace, progress and security rests in the hands of the Juniors of today."[9] Supplementing the *Leader's Guide* was the "Junior *UC*" section of the post-war English-language newspaper *Ukrainian Canadian*, directed at the children themselves and also written and edited by Canadian-born women.

Both the *Leader's Guide* and the "Junior *UC*" included various suggestions for activities, such as songs, craft and woodworking projects, sports, games, poems, stories, and skits, and encouraged exhibitions or performances of the children's work. Sometimes these were simply meant to be amusing diversions. In other instances, proposed activities emphasized key elements of the AUUC's political mandate or of Ukrainian history and culture. Many organizers believed songs were especially useful in this regard. "I feel very strongly on the question of the importance of songs being taught to our children. It is one of the best mediums of conveying feelings and thoughts (in our case progressive ones)," wrote Mary Kardash to then *Leader's Guide* editor Mary Skrypnyk in 1952 to compliment her on a recent issue. "That is why it is very good that you devoted so much space to songs in my opinion."[10] The guide typically featured a variety of music including songs about the labour movement ("Hold the Fort," "Solidarity Forever") and English translations of Ukrainian folk ballads. Most frequent were songs that reflected the AUUC's and the broader Canadian and international left's concern for social justice, disarmament, and peace. Like the Junior

Section pledge, the songs often encouraged good citizenship among the children, viewed through a leftist lens rooted in an early 1960s discourse on peace. In one such song, as they sang each verse, the children spelled "CANADA"; a sample of the lyrics yields the following messages:

A – Is for strong action
Let's all act against all wars
Let's shout with loud, clear voices
"NO WAR! NO, NEVER MORE"

D – Is for Disarmament
And also Dove of Peace
Go fly around the world dear bird
And make all conflict cease.[11]

The Leader's Guide also pushed instructors to encourage children towards other forms of AUUC activism. In particular, as they had done with the interwar *Svit molodi,* organizers asked children to write to the "Junior *UC*" about their clubs' activities and the issues that concerned them. The newspaper gave many aspiring journalists their first by-lines. Lari Prokop, the long-time editor of the *Ukrainian Canadian Herald*, a later incarnation of the *Ukrainian Canadian*, got his start by writing to the *UC*. At age seven he and his mother, Mary, toured a bomb shelter set up in a local grocery store, and he wrote to the paper telling of the strange experience. "When the paper published it," he recalled, "I was very proud."[12]

Educationals remained, in the eyes of organizers, an important component of the Junior Section. In the 1950s and 1960s they were carefully structured, however, to be age appropriate, and short, in order to maintain the children's interest. Often the *Leader's Guide* provided brief lectures – to be delivered by the teachers on elements of the AUUC's history and organizational structure – or lessons on how to fund-raise.[13] These were meant to encourage children to become more engaged with the organization. Some educationals for juniors were designed to be interactive; leaders were especially pushed to hold recurrent "Club Meetings," at which dues would be collected, club business discussed, and officers elected. "Frequent elections should be held so that every child will have a chance to learn meeting procedures and the responsibility assigned to executive officers," a 1959 issue explained.[14] Educationals were also meant to impart a clear understanding to the children of their Ukrainian identity. The guide provided content on Ukrainian culture, history, and literature; Taras Shevchenko, in particular, featured regularly. To commemorate the 150th anniversary of his birth in 1964, organizers encouraged teachers to tell the children about his life, his creative endeavours, and his political activism on behalf of Ukrainians. Provided in the guide was an English translation of one of his poems for the children to memorize as part of the educational. The guide also encouraged discussion of political issues. Highlighting issues of concern to the broader left and to Ukrainian leftists in particular, the January 1953 edition, for example, suggested short sessions explaining the purpose of the upcoming 21 February "Day of International Solidarity with Colonial Youth" and the history of 8 March, International Women's Day.[15]

Individual Junior Section leaders and clubs embraced the dictates of the National Junior Council to varying degrees, depending on resources, individual teacher enthusiasm, and the children's interest. Most children attending Junior Section, especially in larger centres, found a variety of activities on offer. In 1948 the Junior Section of The Pas, Manitoba, informed the "Junior *UC*" pages about its club. The members had recently financed a sleigh ride for themselves, held a photography contest, and had active sports and knitting groups. In Toronto the children's Saturday activities in the early 1960s included film screenings, gym drills and acrobatics, Ukrainian school, woodworking, and embroidery. They also had parties to celebrate special occasions.[16] Movies were especially important for getting children to come to the Junior Section and stay for its Saturday afternoon portion. Shortly after the Second World War the AUUC in many localities began showing films to compete with those available at mainstream movie theatres, which had previously been drawing the children away after lunch.[17]

Whatever its activities, the Junior Section remained less rigidly defined along gender lines. Organizers certainly presented some diversions as more feminine or masculine; for example, they encouraged girls to learn Ukrainian embroidery so that as adults they could, in turn, produce and teach it themselves. At the same time, however, Skrypnyk, who – as we have seen – had experienced gender discrimination in the movement, through the *Leader's Guide* cautioned Junior Section leaders against denying to any child, female or male, the opportunities that interested them. "The boys can be separated for certain things: for example, the girls might be sewing while the boys are doing woodwork or playing ball," she advised in the 1959 fall/winter issue of the *Leader's Guide*. She reminded teachers, however, that "these divisions are not inevitable – some girls can play ball or use a hammer and saw as effectively as some of the boys, and some of the boys may be interested in learning to sew or knit."[18] This was certainly the case for a boy in Port Arthur; in 1951 he joined the Junior Section girls for embroidery lessons from the women of the AUUC sewing circle.[19]

Despite the national organizers' insistence throughout the 1950s and 1960s, few Junior Section clubs embraced educationals as part of their regular programming, probably because the activity was unlikely to hold the children's interest in the way other diversions could. Many clubs did elect officers, so the children of these branches would have had at least some understanding of the process of running meetings, and many wrote to the press. Similarly, other activities related to the AUUC's political education program captured the children's imagination and exposed them to the types of socio-political issues and involvement emphasized by the AUUC leaders. Most clubs held concerts or plays or participated in bazaars, as the *Leader's Guide* suggested, and thus helped to raise money for the AUUC, its press, and other associated causes. The *Ukrainian Canadian*'s junior pages often featured stories about children and events in other countries, which moved some Junior Sections, like the Toronto branch in 1948, to correspond with children in Soviet Ukraine.[20] Moreover, just as the AUUC Women's Section and Young Women's Clubs commemorated International Women's Day each year, so did many youngsters celebrate the first of June, International Children's Day, in the name of peace. "We join hands together," junior pages editor Olga Dzatko explained of International Children's Day in 1967, "to form an enormous circle around the earth, greeting all the boys and girls in the spirit of peace and friendship."[21] Together with the Congress of Canadian Women in 1952 in Winnipeg, Mary Kardash organized an elaborate International Children's Day event. "We're having the children meet in their halls and parade, ride or get down in some organized manner with peace doves, peace streamers to the Park grounds," she explained. "There we shall have little speeches by the CCW representatives, a child from each group on the significance of International Children's Day, followed by peace songs and yells." The day was to continue with a "baseball competition between clubs and games for younger children. Following that will be races and the wind-up is refreshments and a few more songs. All the groups are quite enthusiastic."[22]

When these children were older, many joined the AUUC Youth Division, which was operated for those aged twelve to twenty-one. In 1947, as part of the early post-war reorganization efforts that welcomed the rebirth of the Junior Section, the AUUC National Executive Committee had merged all existing youth groups and sports clubs into a single national English-language body called the Youth Division of the AUUC.[23] Concurrently it had also created the National Youth Council to assist with Youth Division organization. The leadership also encouraged the local English-speaking branches to provide guidance and supervision.[24] Several Canadian-born women and men played key roles on the National Youth Council by acting as advisers and leaders. For example, Mary Skrypnyk and the early-Canadian-born Misha Korol, both of whom had been active in the ULFTA Youth Section in the 1930s, toured halls across the country to encourage branch formation and local youth activities on several occasions in the years immediately following the war.[25] Similarly important were the two youth "conference-rallies" that the National Youth Council organized in Ontario and Edmonton in 1952. These drew participants from across the country,[26] helped to rejuvenate branches in Winnipeg, Toronto, and Windsor, and contributed to the formation of several new branches across the country in places like New Westminster, British Columbia.[27] The council also staged regular Youth Division conferences, often in tandem with the AUUC conventions, which took place once every two years. To help attendees understand better how the AUUC functioned in the 1960s, the National Executive Committee began inviting them to the main convention as non-voting "Participant Observer-Delegates."[28] Following these conventions the National Youth Council also attempted to host leadership courses for these Youth Division delegates.

To assist with local branch formation and development and to create program uniformity, the National Youth Council published a quarterly English-language newsletter and guide called *Forward* during the 1950s and 1960s. Unlike the *Leader's Guide*, *Forward* was directed at the youth club members themselves. Moreover, as social and economic conditions changed after the war, making it difficult to find suitable local Youth Division organizers, the National Youth Council specifically shaped *Forward* to serve as a surrogate leader.[29] Like the *Leader's Guide*, it provided scripts for plays, song lyrics, and dance choreography and encouraged the youth to consider performing them at their local halls. It also offered suggestions for fund-raising, advice on how to organize a membership drive or concert, and information on planning social and leisure activities. The editors urged club members to write to *Forward* and to the short-lived "Telescope on Teens" page of the *Ukrainian Canadian* about successful events and activities.

Many youth clubs ran with *Forward's* advice and, often with the assistance of the local English-speaking branch, developed an array of activities. Most seemed to have elected an executive and held regular executive and membership meetings at which the group planned special events and regular group diversions. Clubs also engaged in fundraising, sometimes for the AUUC but also for its own activities. For example, the Fort William youth club made money by running a coat check at the AUUC's New Year's Eve dance in 1964. In the early 1960s the Winnipeg youth club raised money for its activities by cooking and selling hot dogs at the AUUC's Friday-night bingo games.[30] Nonetheless, despite the national organizers' instructions, the interests of the youth club members themselves most often continued, as they had in the interwar years, to dictate club activities. By far, organizing and participating in social and leisure activities most occupied the youth. Typically, these activities mirrored mainstream, post-war, Canadian teenage pursuits. Dances and parties featuring popular music were especially common. "A party was held on Friday, March 14 in the AUUC club room. About sixty people were in attendance," reported the Fort William AUUC club's recording secretary at the following week's membership meeting in 1949. "There were no complaints handed into me," she continued, concluding, "The people had a lot of fun and are looking forward to another party in the near future."[31] Similarly, to promote relations among the halls in the Winnipeg area, the youth continued the interwar tradition of the "tramp." "We would get bundled up and walk to Transcona where we would be greeted with hot chocolate," recalled Winnipeg Ukrainian labour temple's Youth Section member Vera Seychuk, of the annual two-hour trek. Putting their own post-war spin on it, however, "afterwards, we would have a dance," she said.[32]

In the context of these activities, as in the interwar Youth Section, strong pressures emerged, encouraging gender-appropriate behaviour. These likely found reinforcement in post-war currents of heteronormativity to which the AUUC and the broader Canadian left were not immune. Girls and boys in AUUC Youth Division groups typically took on or were assigned certain organizational roles that closely reflected the gender divisions evident among the adults in the AUUC and in Canadian society generally. For example, labour for youth club socials, dances, and other special events typically saw girls preparing food and boys setting up tables and chairs. "Party Hints – For Boys," an article in the 1954 edition of *Forward* underscored this. "Every affair we have ever attended, where eats were served the predominant note in the evening's festivities was sounded by the girls," noted the piece, written by female members of the Youth Division. "They prepared the food while the boys waited with varying degrees of patience (or impatience) for it to be served." Providing a simple recipe for making spaghetti with mushroom sauce, the authors suggested, "How about a party where the boys prepare and serve the eats?"[33]

Although they may not have been active in the kitchen, the AUUC Youth Division boys were often most engaged on the playing field or court. The national Youth Division leaders widely encouraged clubs to establish sports activities throughout the 1950s and 1960s. "As a builder of healthy bodies and good characters," sports were crucial, leaders argued, "for the physical, mental, and moral health" of division members.[34] Sports remained extremely popular with the younger AUUC set, especially the boys, and thus, like dances and parties, were one of the most successful ways to attract youth to the movement. The leadership of the AUUC, like that of other non-progressive Ukrainian groups, recognized this. "To look upon sports as unimportant or incidental would tend to isolate us from large sections of young Ukrainian Canadians and young Canadians as a whole," argued a 1963 AUUC national youth conference resolution on sports.[35] Sports were a critical means to attract youth who were uninterested in the AUUC's other activities, the resolution emphasized. "The many and varied forms of sports are important to us in creating an atmosphere and a place in the AUUC for those young people who do not sing, dance, or play an instrument. Sports can help us recruit new members to the Youth Clubs."[36]

The youth club members happily embraced sports initiatives. During the two decades following the war many Ukrainian labour temples continued in varying degrees, as they had prior to the war, to host or facilitate activities like baseball, acrobatics, swimming, hockey, tennis, track, bowling, ping pong, badminton, and boxing. Field days were popular summer events. In fact, some youth clubs seemed to engage in little else beyond sports. "Our club meets every Saturday and our activities consist of tumbling, badminton, ping pong, darts, floor hockey and we soon hope to have volleyball," reported the Calgary club's financial secretary, Donald Kazakoff, to the National Youth Council in March 1958. The club's other activities consisted of a bowling tournament with the Edmonton branch, which was held the previous fall, and, not surprisingly, a dance.[37] In numerous localities the sporting activities even expanded into inter-ethnic leagues, linking AUUC youngsters (and sometimes adults) with those from other halls and more broadly with other leftist ethnic groups. The late 1940s Toronto Slavic Softball League, for example, included teams representing the Yugoslav Youth Club, the Russian Youth Club, the Polish Youth Club, the West Toronto AUUC Youth Club, and three English-speaking branches.[38] Friendly rivalries sometimes emerged between Ukrainian labour temples when their teams competed. The youth newsletter of Winnipeg's Point Douglas Ukrainian labour temple in 1947 taunted the club's "foes," the Winnipeg temple's baseball team, the Dynamos. "The League Champions (Dynamos) will have to hustle if they wish to retain the crown," the newsletter goaded. "Rumors around the Point have it that their team will be stronger than ever and to add to this they are out for revenge for the beatings which they received last year."[39]

Quarrels, where sports were concerned, also arose elsewhere. Local concerns sometimes overrode the national leadership's advocacy of sports, and at times the youngsters' desires for particular sports came into direct conflict with the wishes of their local hall's leadership. Sports activities taking place within the hall itself were especially subject to scrutiny. Lari Prokop, for example, recalled that, in the early 1960s when he was twelve, floor hockey, a popular activity, was banned in the West Toronto hall for fear that the floor might be ruined. Concern for the floor also caused difficulty for the youth of the Winnipeg Ukrainian labour temple in the late 1950s. They had to campaign to the hall leadership for months for permission to put up a volleyball net, and even longer to get lines painted so that they could play basketball. In the face of this type of opposition many youngsters chose not to fight the leadership but simply to leave to find other venues in which to play these sports. When the basketball permission was pending at the Winnipeg hall, Bob Seychuk, for example, played at his public school.

Leaders had a harder time getting the youth to engage in (much less fight for) the less popular forms of activity in the 1950s and 1960s; among these, the most contested remained the educational. *Forward* contained texts for educationals to facilitate regular discussion sessions. Like the *Leader's Guide*, typically provided were pieces that centred on the history and organizational structure of the AUUC, its press (and lessons on the importance of supporting the annual press campaign), and Ukrainian history and culture. These proposed topics offer insight into the sort of political and social understanding that the National Youth Council leadership hoped to impart upon the Youth Division members. In a 1957 educational commemorating the fiftieth anniversary of what organizers dubbed "the Ukrainian people's press in Canada," author

Misha Korol analysed the AUUC's publishing history by contrasting it with "the capitalist papers" like the *Globe and Mail*, the *Vancouver Sun*, and the *Winnipeg Tribune*. "Our press – the people's press is not a private business institution. It belongs to the subscribers," Korol argued. "Not so with the press of Big Business. It belongs to the rich, and, of course, it speaks in the interests of the Big Shots." He concluded by urging the members of the Youth Division to join the AUUC press campaign by recruiting new subscribers.[40] *Forward* encouraged local club members to take turns presenting these materials in regularly scheduled educationals. Sometimes this meant using only the information that the editors included in *Forward*; in other instances they promoted further supplementary research. For a 1954 educational on Taras Shevchenko, the editors encouraged presenters to use what *Forward* provided, augmented by further reading from *Ukrainian Canadian* and organizer John Weir's recent book, *Bard of Ukraine*.

It is difficult to assess to what extent – if at all – individual clubs made use of the educationals included by *Forward*'s editors. The postwar youth, like their interwar counterparts, continued to resist or avoid the educational, and it was probably one of the least incorporated directives within the local branches during the two decades following the war. Some attempted a compromise: they held educationals but reshaped the content to reflect more closely the issues encountered by their club members as post-war Canadian teenagers. On 31 March 1968 Fort William Youth Section member Donna delivered an educational to the group on "drugs, early drugs, alcohol, barbiturates, tranquillizers, opium, addictive drugs, LSD and why people take them." She concluded that it was "to relieve fatigue, to release tensions, to escape, to induce sleep and dreams."[41] The push for this type of discussion had grown out of discord with the AUUC-mandated content. When, for example, the same group had polled its members six months earlier for ideas for upcoming educationals, respondents suggested future discussions rooted in issues that preoccupied teenagers in the 1960s, calling for conversations "on delinquents, on the hippies, on Patriotism, on why kids start drinking, on discrimination of Negroes and Indians."[42] Others opposed the educationals entirely. "It was said that people shouldn't be forced into doing what they don't want to do," the club secretary recorded in the minutes. "Some said the educationals would be a drag."[43]

Despite the general lack of interest in educationals the AUUC was successful in politicizing many of its youngsters. This awareness developed in many of the same ways that it had among ULFTA children and youth: from their parents in the home; through personal experience; and through AUUC activities like reading the *Ukrainian Canadian* and participating in the Junior or Youth Sections, Ukrainian school, concerts, and fund-raising campaigns. Engagement with discourses rooted in the broader Canadian and international left in the 1950s and 1960s was also key. Hearing James Endicott speak at the Canadian Peace Congress or AUUC national organizer Bill Harasym at the Innisfree Ukrainian labour temple helped Donna Yakimovich to develop her sense of political awareness, as did reading the *Ukrainian Canadian* and *Ukrainske slovo*. "I learned a lot about the Vietnam War from those papers," she explained.[44] Vera Seychuk's childhood role model was Winnipeg AUUC leader Mary Kardash. The ideas about peace on earth and goodwill among nations that Kardash taught, Seychuk recalled, "stayed with me."[45]

The youngsters demonstrated their politicization in a number of ways, which often paralleled adult activism. "When I was younger I collected petitions on Toronto streets to ban the bomb," Olga Berketa Dzatko recalled of her activities in the late 1940s. Julie Dalkie and Olga Shatulsky assisted on the campaigns of progressive political candidates. Dalkie scrutineered for the Labour Progressive Party, Shatulsky for Joe Zuken. This sometimes exposed the children to red-baiting. "I was in grade nine when Joe Zuken was running for school trustee," Shatulsky explained. "When the principal found out that some children might be leaving school early to work for the elections, she said over the [school] loud speaker that she was sure Joe Zuken wouldn't want to employ child labour, so no one should leave early to help him."[46] Some, when they were older, joined the National Federation of Labour Youth (the Young Communist League's post-war successor) and eventually the Labour Progressive Party and later the Communist Party of Canada in the two decades following the war. Politicized by speeches at the hall and by the AUUC newspapers, Lari Prokop signed up for the party in the 1960s. When some schoolmates whom he disliked red-baited him, this furthered his resolve. "If these kids didn't like what a red was," he recalled, "then I definitely wanted to be a red."[47] Their party affiliations could provide enhanced AUUC leadership opportunities. Thanks to her eventual federation membership, for example, the AUUC leaders invited Dzatko to join the National Youth Committee as an organizer.[48] As part of their involvement with the National Federation of Labour Youth and the AUUC, many Youth Division members like Dzatko also had the chance to travel overseas to participate in the World Youth

Festival of the World Federation of Democratic Youth, which took place biennially in the capital cities of various communist countries.[49]

We have already seen how the CPC's influence declined among adults after 1956; the stark decline of the National Federation of Labour Youth began even earlier. Between 1947 and 1956 (prior to Khrushchev's revelations) the federation's membership shrunk from twenty-five hundred to six hundred. Fortunes did not improve. Many of the youth rejected the party's organizational methods; their exodus was further fuelled by the same currents that saw their elders abandon the party – especially revelations about Stalin's atrocities and the invasions of Hungary and Czechoslovakia, not to mention the climate of red-baiting that increasingly surrounded party activity. Many, including the Ukrainian youth, also found themselves pulled towards new forms of radical activism, particularly in the 1960s. "What was galling to party leaders and veterans was the fact that the overwhelming majority of those who denounced capitalism and the political system in North America were not associated with the CPC and showed no inclination towards joining it," scholar Ivan Avakumovic states.[50] Instead, many young activists aligned themselves with the burgeoning organizations of the New Left, not only rejecting but at times outright condemning the party's past and present political strategies. "In so far as the New Left paid any attention to the CPC, which was very seldom," Avakumovic contends, "it was merely to deplore the chances that the CPC had missed in previous years and to castigate the Communists for their constant support of Soviet policies."[51]

Similarly and increasingly during the 1960s many of the AUUC youth reacted to the AUUC leadership's ongoing and seemingly unquestioning support of the party and the Soviet Union. The chairman of the National Youth Council, according to an RCMP surveillance report, "advised the AUUC National Convention in 1968 that interest among the AUUC youth was at an all-time low, largely due to disaffection with the constant program of indoctrination from known Communists."[52] Indeed, when AUUC Youth Division Workshop participants – presumably some of the organization's most dedicated young people – had been polled two years earlier, their comments foreshadowed this assessment. "We always have the same lectures from one point of view," Anita complained. "We should have more of two sides of the stories being given. We are being brainwashed." Monica concurred: "By hammering [the CPC] in to the heads so much, we turn a lot of kids away and to nationalist halls." Brian agreed when he added, "Monica's point is true.

Many people won't come because we're a communist hall." Stu summed up the commonly emerging youth consensus when he stated, "No organization needs that many political ties. It's sad when you have to scrape through all of the politics to get to the basic point of our Organization. All this politics has no place in our organization ... We all know about peace and that we should fight for it. Why the constant drilling?"[53] Few young people, it seemed, were much interested in the hard-line Soviet perspective or activist methods that the immigrant-generation male leadership advocated. Many youngsters increasingly voted with their feet when it came to engagement with the movement in this respect.

However, the young people continued to embrace consistently and enthusiastically their involvement in the cultural activities at the halls. Like other facets of the organization's work with children and youth, cultural work also experienced some key changes in the post-war years. The nearly exclusive use of the English language among young people and their preference for activities for which they need not cultivate any Ukrainian-language skills meant that certain activities involving the Ukrainian language declined. "Folk dancing became the most important way to attract young people to the organization," teacher Olga Shatulsky recalled, while Ukrainian-language choral groups appealed to fewer youngsters.[54] Children had mixed reactions to Ukrainian school. Some expressed enjoyment. Young John Supyk, who attended classes at the Toronto hall, told the *Ukrainian Canadian*'s junior pages in 1953: "We like Ukrainian school just as fine as English School. I like reading and writing in Ukrainian and I like to go home at 6 pm ... Our teacher teaches us how to study nature and I don't want war."[55] Others were more apathetic. In the 1950s Lari Prokop attended Ukrainian school in Toronto but resisted speaking Ukrainian. "I would use the language at certain times," he explained, "usually when I wanted something from my parents."[56] Bob Seychuk took classes at the Winnipeg hall in the 1950s. "It bothered me being expected, forced to use the language when everyone else spoke English," he recalled. "My parents were so insistent that I speak Ukrainian," Seychuk explained, "that I may have not done it to rebel."[57]

Most halls, especially those in larger urban centres, maintained successful dance groups, orchestras, choirs, and Ukrainian schools during the 1950s and 1960s. Typically, like children had during the 1920s and 1930s, post-war youngsters involved themselves in multiple activities. "I liked to dance and took folk-dance lessons with Walter Balay," recounted Olga Berketa Dzatko, who grew up attending activities at the

West Toronto hall. Skill was not a prerequisite for participation: "I also sang with a youth choir," Dzatko explained, "in spite of the fact that I really cannot sing."[58] Participation in these activities afforded young-sters remarkable performance opportunities. Dzatko and the other AUUC troupes often took to the stage at Massey Hall in Toronto, for example, in the 1960s. Regina's Poltava Folk Dancers journeyed to Win-nipeg to participate in the AUUC's Ukrainian Festival of Music, Song, and Dance held to commemorate Manitoba's centennial in 1970.[59]

Many activities, though displaying similar characteristics to those of the interwar years, shifted to accommodate the changed political and economic culture in Canada, the broader left, and the AUUC, especially the post-war interests and ethnic identities of its children and youth. The youngsters' demands in this regard were specific and ongoing throughout the period. "We're Ukrainian-Canadians, not Ukrainian. Our content should reflect this," asserted Brian about the AUUC's cul-tural performances at the AUUC Youth Division workshop in 1967, underscoring his generation's sense of nationality and ethnicity.[60] As the previous chapter illustrates, Canadian-born cultural teachers played a fundamental role in this shift by combining Ukrainian traditions with the elements of Canadian culture with which these children would have been familiar growing up in the decades following the war. Little Irene's peace song has already been noted as one example of this shift; many AUUC youngsters' choirs, while still including some Ukrainian songs, increasingly incorporated English-language folk songs and music from other national groups.

Cultural activity nonetheless remained politicized as it had been prior to the war. For example, Ukrainian school textbooks (often procured from Soviet Ukraine) helped to develop the children's understanding of the esteem in which many AUUC leaders held the Soviet Union. "The Soviet land is the father land of the workers of the whole world. The workers of all the countries look toward the Soviet land with hope," read one grammar exercise, continuing: "Who is the enemy of the work-ers and the farmers? The enemy is the exploiter of their labour; their enemy is everyone who urges them not to go forward, not to struggle for communism."[61] Singing about peace was, for example, considered staunchly radical. The youngsters' regular performances for family and friends at the halls also continued to raise money to support the AUUC's many cultural and political endeavours. Larger halls still dispatched their cultural forces to smaller communities who were unable to sup-port cultural groups of their own. The West Toronto AUUC children in December of 1955, for example, travelled to Oshawa to present a concert at the local Ukrainian labour temple. An article reporting on their performance in *Ukrainske zhyttia* urged other small AUUC halls to similarly avail themselves of the cultural groups of large centres to raise money and interest locally in the AUUC.[62] Likewise, the youngsters also used to their talents to generate funds for and awareness of political issues of concern to leftists outside the Ukrainian labour temples. "Our orchestras and dance groups would go out and perform ... [to] help people running for election in various parts of the province," Myron Shatulsky explained, recalling his late childhood experiences immediately following the war.[63]

After the war, when the Ukrainian labour temples' regular season of cultural and social activity ended in late spring, youngsters turned to a new space for activity and activist expression, the AUUC summer camps. Post-war economic expansion and consumerism, the emphasis on heteronormativity, the nuclear family, and family togetherness, and the increasing number of women entering the full-time workforce meant that many families (particularly the Canadian-born) had disposable income for vacations or needed supervision for their children during summer holidays. In response (and in the hopes of retaining youngsters in its orbit over the summer), the AUUC extended to spaces beyond the halls, establishing several summer camps. Although the ULFTA had fostered some limited forms of camping activity in the past,[64] it was during the 1950s that summer camps really took off as the AUUC purchased or built camps near major urban centres – at Palermo, Ontario (near Oakville); Husavik, Manitoba (about an hour and a half north of Winnipeg); and Sylvan Lake, Alberta (between Calgary and Edmonton) – while smaller camps were located near Wapasu Lake, Alberta, in the Lakehead region of Ontario, and other communities.[65] These settings offered activities for young and old: sleep-away camp for youngsters, short-term summer jobs for teenagers, and the opportunity of cottage ownership or rental for adults. Leadership seminars also took place there for those hoping to expand their opportunities for employment and activism within the AUUC. On a regional and national scale, these spaces functioned in the way the Parkdale Benevolent farm had in the interwar period by providing a rural venue away from the halls where events of a more substantive nature could take place. Major festivals, holiday celebrations, and convention and organizational campaign wind-ups often took place at these retreats.[66]

Children and youth who took part in formal camping activities had experiences distinct from those of adults who might have attended events or had cottages at the camps. If they attended the formal summer camp activities, the children engaged in diversions typical of most post-war summer camps. They shared cabins with other children and took part in wiener roasts, hikes, swimming and other sports, bug catching (and other nature study), and arts and crafts. These were all key components of camp life.[67] At the same time, however, the children had experiences distinct from those of campers at non-progressive camps but parallel to those of children from other radical communities. Ester Reiter has demonstrated the centrality of secular Jewish culture and radical politics at the progressive-organized Camp Naivelt, located near Brampton in southern Ontario. Paul Mischler has similarly shown how American radicals from the 1930s to the 1950s used their summer camps "to create temporary communities organized around their own culture and values."[68] Although politics were certainly present, overt political discussions seemed limited in the post-war context of the AUUC camps. Former counsellor Lari Prokop recalled attempts to have informal discussions with children about political and social issues, and former Husavik camp director Olga Shatulsky (ca. 1954) remembered making efforts to discuss peace with her young charges.[69] Officially, however, the AUUC leadership publicly downplayed the potential for politicization of a particular stripe at the camps. "Our camp is open to anybody and there is not politics involved," Camp Palermo manager John Dubno told the *Globe and Mail* in 1964, emphasizing, "We do not try to force politics on anyone."[70] More prevalent on the camps' agendas was Ukrainian culture. At Husavik, for example, Shatulsky taught Ukrainian language and singing.[71] There and elsewhere, arts and crafts sessions often included Ukrainian embroidery lessons, and films and story time featured tales from Ukrainian literary figures like Ivan Franko and Taras Shevchenko. At Gordon Lake, Alberta, in 1963 children saw nightly movies like *Cossacks beyond the Danube* and heard talks about Ukrainian history.[72]

Activities at camp also existed for teenagers, and their presence and willingness to contribute were essential to the creation and maintenance of the AUUC camping programs in the 1950s and 1960s. Each spring, youth members volunteered their labour to help prepare the camps for the coming summer. Like other youth activities, this participation fell along gender lines. When Lucy Nykolyshyn helped to ready Camp Husavik in the early 1950s, she and the other girls cleaned the sleeping quarters and cooked while the boys cut trees and did the other outside labour.[73] Many also worked – sometimes as volunteers – in positions as camp counsellors. Without their volunteer labour the camps could not have functioned as well or for as long as they did. Youth also helped to make the camps successful in other ways – by organizing or turning out for track meets, softball games, youth festivals, and other AUUC events. Moreover, just as they did in other areas of the movement, so too did youth desires and interests do much to define their camp activities. For example, when the Ontario AUUC youth expressed a desire for "supervised sleeping dormitories and recreational-educational facilities for AUUC youth and friends during the summer months," camp organizers created a youth hostel at Camp Palermo in 1967.[74] Less confining than the halls, the camps' expansive outdoor setting for events offered teenagers at times a great deal of freedom from adult supervision. "When a group of young people went to a corn roast at the camp grounds at Palermo," Olga Berketa Dzatko recalled of one occasion, many took it as an opportunity to make out. "Almost everyone divided up in pairs and headed off to the bushes for privacy," she recollected. "I was lucky that no one did take advantage of [me,] a very naïve 16–17 year old."[75]

The camps also afforded AUUC youth other opportunities, one of the most important to the AUUC being the Higher Educational Course (HEC). After the war the AUUC, like its predecessor, the ULFTA, continued to need qualified teachers and organizers, and therefore continued to organize these longer training sessions.[76] Continuity and change characterized the post-war HEC. Since Parkdale Benevolent Home had closed, organizers used the summer camps as settings for the classes. Male youth continued to be the preferred course participants. In 1956 Vancouver organizer Hannah Polowy wrote to the AUUC's National Executive Committee about potential participants for a youth course to be held that summer. She felt the need to apologize to the national organizers, saying, "Sorry these are all girls," despite the fact that "these five girls ... are the mainstays of our youth club."[77] Political awareness and activism enhanced candidates' potential for selection, as they had during the interwar period. Many successful applicants in the early 1950s, for example, were involved with the National Federation of Labour Youth or the Labour Progressive Party.[78] The initial AUUC course also followed the ULFTA's HEC model, still expecting students to commit to several months of study during the summer. In 1950, for instance, twenty-six students attended a four-month HEC at Camp Palermo where, like their interwar counterparts, they studied Ukrainian (or Russian if they were members of the Federation of Russian Canadians), music, drama, folk dancing, political economy, and the history of the labour movement, the Soviet Union, Ukraine, and Ukrainians in Canada.[79] Finally, an indicated willingness to work afterwards for the AUUC was essential.

The 1950 course was probably the longest and the most intense of the post-war HECs, but many attendees enjoyed their time in it. Most went along with the course content, grateful for the opportunity for advanced study and the prospect of AUUC employment when the course finished. Of course, not all elements of the experience were enjoyable. Universally despised was the "Criticism and Self-Criticism" component of the curriculum. "'Criticism and Self-Criticism' was very hard," course participant Olga Shatulsky recalled. "You had to get up and talk about your faults, and others could criticize you; nobody was really mean, but it was hard to experience."[80] Students were faulted on a variety of fronts: for being too sociable or not sociable enough, for wasting time, for not reading enough, or for daydreaming. Course principal William Teresio criticized some for their "capitalist tendencies" or their "bourgeois ideas." Although students were probably told that the exercise was for the good of the collective, this unlikely softened the blow when they were informed they were "difficult to talk to," that they tended "to stick to a clique in the camp," or that they had "rugged eating habits." While some undoubtedly were able to grin and bear the criticism, others refused to accept the judgment of their peers. When student John Sharko typed the results of his assessment, he included an additional page of rebuttal. In response to Principal Teresio's criticism that he slept too long, Sharko typed: "Twelve to sixteen hours is not the average of my sleep; the approximate average is eight hours, and nine to ten hours when I am really tired. I did sleep twelve hours on certain occasions when I was very tired." Sharko went on to disagree with his fellow students' complaints as well. To one student's comments that Sharko did not like responsibility, he clarified, "I dislike responsibility only when I have a reason to dislike it."[81]

The 1951 course was the last of this sort; change in course structure, length, and content occurred for a number of reasons. The more prosperous – or at least advantageous – circumstances under which the post-war cohort of progressive Ukrainian youth grew up meant that the AUUC experienced problems recruiting students to train as leaders and organizers. Youngsters after the war tended to have greater educational opportunities, with many finishing high school and considering the prospect of attending university. Unlike the youth who had come of age during the 1920s or 1930s, teenagers in the 1950s and especially the 1960s had a wide range of occupational and educational opportunities on which to draw. Thus, by the late 1950s and early 1960s, increasingly, many students preferred to spend their summers working for money to pay for university, to help their families, or to purchase goods from the rapidly growing consumer marketplace than to attend an HEC.[82] Even those who did not go on to post-secondary education had expanded employment opportunities because of improved economic conditions as the post-war period progressed. Moreover, because the wages paid by the AUUC to cultural teachers and organizers were often considerably lower than those paid in many other enterprises, the idea of making one's career in the Ukrainian left became increasingly unattractive to many young people.

Accommodating the needs and interests of youth was critical if the courses were to be maintained. The AUUC began by adjusting the duration and timing of youth courses and even changed the course name (often to some variation on "AUUC Youth Summer School"). To accommodate young people's need to work during the summer, the association shortened many courses from several months to several weeks. As a result the average young student most likely spent two weeks studying at a camp like Palermo or Husavik, and the courses usually followed the annual youth conferences that took place early in the summer months. Organizers also adjusted course content based on the youths' interests, especially into the 1960s. A report on the 1962 Alberta AUUC Youth School, which lasted twenty-one days and featured primarily English-language classes on Marxism, democratic centralism, Canadian history, and AUUC history and a drama workshop, conceded that future seminars should include more cultural subjects and have a better balance of study and leisure. This would be of greater interest to prospective students, the report argued, because "we found that many were leery of a straight theoretical school."[83] At most courses by this time the criticism and self-criticism exercises had diminished or disappeared entirely. Multiple regional courses, rather than a single national one, were often held, which helped to offset travel costs and time away from home. Finally, cultural activities often drove the bulk of course content; dance seminars, for example, were among the more successful. Nonetheless, even with these changes, by the early 1960s the AUUC still found it difficult to attract teenagers to its advanced training programs. In 1964 the National Leadership School, an annual summer educational event for youth held at Camp Palermo, was cancelled. According to a later 1969 information brief, this cancellation was "due to a lack of response," and, as such, "it has not been held since."[84] The problem worsened into the 1970s. By then, even shorter workshops and courses were often cancelled or postponed because of a lack of interest.[85]

One area of educational activity that did attract the imagination and interest of many AUUC youth involved studies in the Soviet Union, especially Soviet Ukraine. Like the summer camps, these travel opportunities expanded the activist space available for young people into an international arena. During the interwar period organizers had visited the Soviet Union on a number of occasions, and, as has been shown, a handful of young male HEC graduates had had the opportunity to study there.[86] Beginning in the early 1950s as cultural relations expanded between the Soviet Union and the broader Canadian left, these types of trips became more frequent, and students often stayed for longer periods. The trips remained popular and sought after into the 1970s. As the previous chapter has shown, the AUUC enjoyed a special relationship with the Soviet Union during the post-war period because of its long-time history and affiliation with the Communist Party and its support of the Soviet Union and Soviet Ukraine. Through the Society Ukraina – or the Ukrainian Society for Friendship and Cultural Relations with Foreign Countries – the AUUC was able to coordinate numerous trips to Ukraine for individuals and groups wishing to pursue studies of a political and cultural nature. Society Ukraina supplied students with monthly stipends, covered their travel expenses, and aided in their adjustment to soviet life in Ukraine.[87]

Several "prerequisites" qualified students for overseas study. Having grown up in the AUUC and participated in youngsters' activities was essential. Leadership experience, prior HEC participation, and a willingness to return to work for the AUUC also enhanced a student's candidacy. Being male also helped, though increasing numbers of girls and young women were also sent in the 1960s and beyond. Extended training was the norm; many committed to two to five years of study, returning to Canada with university degrees or other forms of certification. The 1960s was a particularly busy decade. During that time some thirty AUUC members undertook studies. Most stayed in Kiev, attending classes in political economy, Ukrainian and Soviet history, dance, and music at the Conservatory of Music, the Pedagogical Institute, the University of Kiev, and other facilities .

On holidays students had the opportunity to supplement their in-class training with tours around Ukraine. "We have just returned from our winter vacation where we visited Poltava, Kharkov, and Zaporo-zhe," wrote Sunny Kowalewich, who studied for three years at the Kiev Institute of Cinematography, to then AUUC president Bill Harasym about a recent trip in 1969. In addition to tours of a steel mill and a cookie factory, Kowalewich and the other Canadians visited cultural sites and universities. "We had many interesting discussions with both the students and members of the amateur cultural groups from the fac-tories," he explained, calling the trip hectic but "well organized and extremely educational."[88]

Among the most prominent Canadian students in Kiev was Ted Kar-dash, who studied music from 1962 to 1967 and acted as the students' representative. During that time he maintained a regular correspon-dence with Harasym. Kardash wrote of his experiences, his political and cultural development, and the conclusions he was drawing about the state and future of the AUUC. "Having pulled out all the stops in an effort to become an 'expert' in the field of choral singing ... I have become very interested in this field of culture ... I also see a tremen-dous future for choral singing in Canada with our organization," he explained in 1965. Continuing, he argued, "I believe more firmly than ever now that culture can and must serve us in our struggle. And choir singing, being the most democratic and most nearest to the masses ... can do much in helping us to attain our goal."[89] Immediately following his return to Canada, Kardash became cultural director of the AUUC hall in Edmonton and put these ideas to work.

As folk-dance had supplanted all other forms of youngsters' activity by the 1970s, the AUUC acknowledged its increased importance by coor-dinating short dance seminars and schools, many of which took place in Ukraine. Ron Mokry, who had studied in Kiev in the 1960s, returned in 1971 with several of his students from the Winnipeg AUUC's School of Folkdancing. "The program of dance studies was wonderful," he later wrote to the National Executive Committee, "because the students got to work with true professionals." Even better, he argued, was the opportunity to connect with Ukraine. "Before, the Ukraine was a small section on a map from where their forefathers came, and really had no connection with the lives they lead here in Canada," he explained. "I feel that this has now changed, and they feel a much greater relation-ship between themselves, the Ukraine, and its people.[90]

During the 1970s Ukrainian Canadian nationalist groups on a number of occasions relied on the goodwill of the AUUC for this type of access to Ukraine. They tagged along on several dance seminar trips – much to the chagrin of some AUUC participants.[91] These occasions became a microcosmic reflection of broader Cold War tensions and of the long-standing, lingering rivalry between leftist and nationalist Ukrainians, which played out in the groups. After the 1974 Kiev dance seminar, participant Terry Polowy, claiming to represent the views of the majority of the students, wrote to the National Executive Committee to express her outrage at the nationalists' behaviour. "Those five people should never have accompanied us. It is most fortunate that our AUUC people were as strong and mature as they were!" she insisted. "Under snide remarks, digs and jabs, downright doublefacedness ... our kids really made an effort not to openly let their frustration show. We were indignant!"[92] Donna Machuik and Joanne Laslo voiced similar protest to Harasym: "We felt that during this seminar the five individuals from the Nationalist Federation had disappointed our organization and the representation of our country, Canada, by not being present at most of the scheduled tours, appearing late at meals, being late for the occasional tour they did come on, and last but not least one individual from Winnipeg delayed our flight from Paris to Montreal."[93] Polowy expressed similar grievances about the 1976 nationalist participants; she voiced particular frustration at their political savvy (and her implicit regret at the AUUC youths' diminished politicization): "The nationalists know who they are as a group and can defend their right-wing views and organizations, while the AUUC youth only have a loose understanding of belonging to a national group that is leftist."[94]

Despite the array of activities and activism available for youngsters, increasingly into the 1960s and 1970s the organizers found it extraordinarily difficult to attract children and teenagers to the AUUC. Junior and Youth Section numbers are especially hard to uncover and are often inconsistent. Many of the clubs writing to the *Ukrainian Canadian* during the 1950s and early 1960s reported relatively stable memberships, ranging from twenty-seven children in smaller communities to a hundred and twenty-five in larger centres like Toronto. Many former participants recall being extremely busy with offered activities during the 1950s, like the interwar youngsters had been, hurrying to eat dinner and do homework every evening before heading to the Ukrainian labour temples.[95] Many children expressed pleasure with their involvement. "I go to the club and I like it," nine-year-old Mike Wos wrote to the newspaper in 1953; "I hope I will not get sick and miss any time."[96] Concurrently, however, many localities found it challenging, if not outright impossible, to maintain consistently functioning youngsters' clubs. "There is still too much fluctuation with clubs established one season failing to begin work again the next season," reported a resolution on AUUC Junior Section work in 1960, a commonly heard refrain.[97] Even if they had taken part consistently in children's activities, many as youth left the association. Lari Prokop witnessed this first hand. As a child in the 1950s he played in the West Toronto hall's mandolin orchestra with twenty-nine other children. As teenagers by the 1960s only he and two others signed on to the AUUC orchestra.[98] Decline was uneven, however; cultural activities like folk dancing remained (and in some urban centres still are) popular, while the Ukrainian schools, Junior and Youth Divisions, and sports fluctuated before gradually shutting down completely by the 1970s. By 1968, for example, the National Youth Council had record of "only one active club and [reported] the almost total collapse of the AUUC youth program."[99] As the previous chapter illustrated, few of those individuals who had grown up in the association stayed as adults. As early as 1964 the National Youth Council reported "that sixty percent of its youth club members (150 members and eleven clubs) dissociate from the organization without joining the senior [adult] branches."[100] If they did stay involved with the AUUC, it was most likely through its English-language cultural activities. Most of the summer camps had closed by the early 1980s; at the same time, AUUC-sponsored educational travel to Ukraine ceased, having too few activities for which to train organizers by this time. Today only a few halls offer activities for youngsters.

A number of factors contributed to this decline among the youngest generations. Internally a lack of leadership plagued the organization. What came to be called the "cadre problem" was a recurring topic of discussion at the national convention, one noted as a serious problem as early as 1956. The dwindling interest in the AUUC's courses meant that few new teachers were trained. Concurrently, few members of the English-speaking branches displayed an interest in coordinating or carrying out youngsters' activities. This left existing organizers scrambling to fill leadership posts or stretching themselves thin in attempting to fulfil too many organizational roles. Even if children or youth wanted to be active in the association, finding consistent activities in which to participate could have been difficult. By the early 1970s the problem reached epic proportions as those who had been trained in the interwar HECs began retiring or cutting back significantly on their level of involvement owing to their advancing age. Concurrently other teachers quit because of the AUUC's poor wages. At that time the AUUC leadership attempted to address the cadre problem by recruiting Ukrainian students from Kiev, an initiative that soon proved a failure because of the students' unfamiliarity with the association, the Canadian context in which it developed and functioned, and Canadian youngsters' culture generally.[101] Ultimately the cadre problem would never be resolved.

There were other, more serious and profound causes for the decline, some of which have already been highlighted. The post-war social, economic, and political climate, with its host of diversions, was especially key, as was the Canadian educational system, which contributed to increased levels of assimilation among these youngsters. As such, those born and raised in Canada did not feel the same loyalty or attachment to Ukraine or define themselves with the same sense of Ukrainianness as their older relatives did. While they were interested in their Ukrainian roots, they were also interested in being Canadian. To this end, many simply became too busy – pursuing an array of other post-war activities, opportunities, and obligations – to engage actively with the AUUC. "I have too much school work and my marks have gone down," teenaged Carol Petrachenko wrote to the National Junior Council in 1965, explaining that she could no longer run the Welland Ukrainian labour temple's Junior Section because school had to be her focus.[102] Part-time jobs, as was noted earlier, drew others away, and university attendance completed their drift from the AUUC. "When my friends and I went to university, that became our life," explained Julie Dalkie of her experiences in the 1960s and 1970s; at the time, she stopped playing violin and left the hall for many years. She returned years later as a parent but only to watch her own daughter's Ukrainian folk-dancing performances or attend other special events.[103]

That the post-war children were as likely to come from middle-class homes as from working-class homes further compounded the AUUC's increasing irrelevance among the young. Few experienced the social, ethnic, or economic alienation that their parents or grandparents had, which had driven them to found the movement. Similarly, as baby boomers, their identification and relationship with the post-war climate of consumerism and conformity increasingly obscured the ability of many children and youth to understand or relate to the association's particular political bent. Within the immigrant-generation male leadership, concepts of class-consciousness remained rooted in interwar analyses that were based on particular notions of working-class positionality. By the 1960s this perspective was failing to resonate with many young people, making the organization increasingly irrelevant politically. "The AUUC failed to see the change in composition of its membership (occupation, class) and failed to recognize what the white collar elements could contribute and their needs," responded Stella, a thirty-six-year-old secretary and bookkeeper, in an AUUC membership questionnaire of the Canadian-born in the mid-1960s. She asserted, "The organization has to not only give these members culture, but also help them to see where they fit in the capitalist economy .... [as] they face different working issues, like automation."[104] Those youngsters and young adults who remained politically engaged as radicals in a broader leftist context often did so by abandoning their parents' and grandparents' old left for the youth-based New Left and 1960s counterculture that spoke to them in ways that the AUUC did not.

Other youngsters, however, internalized or embraced the anti-progressive, anti-communist, anti-AUUC, Cold War political messages that were so prevalent in Canadian and North American society and rejected to varying degrees any type of overtly political activity, if not the AUUC completely. "The attitudes of the younger people to the USSR were more often influenced by school and society than by their parents," John Kolasky has asserted. "Some became indifferent and others hostile to anything pro-Soviet."[105] As they did for the adults discussed in the previous chapter, their own (or witnessed) red-baiting experiences pushed youngsters away, initially from certain activities and later entirely. "It seems to me as if some of our members are ashamed that their friends might call them 'Communists' or 'Reds' if they were seen at peace demonstrations," the Dynamo Youth Club secretary reported of its members' low turn-out for rallies and marches during the 1961–2 program year.[106] Similarly, in 1966, an Alberta father wrote to the National Executive Committee about his daughter (a former Youth Section member) and her reasons for leaving the AUUC, in response to a survey of the Canadian-born members that she had been sent by the AUUC leadership. After completing grade twelve, she had moved to Edmonton to take a medical filing course, and her studies allowed her no time for AUUC activities. More than that, her father explained, she was concerned that continued membership might negatively affect her job prospects. She had reason to be nervous; her brother Donald, the father asserted, "due to discrimination ... went through a lot" because of his ties to the association.[107]

The leaders' rigidity and the youth's mobility as it played out in the context of the escalating Cold War are critical factors that shaped the post-war face of the Ukrainian left when it came to young people's engagement or abandonment of the movement. Their behaviour challenged the relational power of the older leaders, grounded as it was in the latter's ties with the communist context internationally. In these ways the international context closely interacted with the local; the political was personal, though, for the youth, not in the ways the older leaders understood it. This disconnect had profound consequences for the Ukrainian labour temple movement.

Young Ukrainian Canadians of the baby-boom generation held considerable sway, given their increased numbers. They pushed the AUUC to cater to their wishes and interests in order to maintain their attention. As a result they were an important force that helped to shape and shift the post-war Ukrainian left and to bring about change in the ways in which the movement defined and expressed ethnicity, as well as the methods through which the movement carried out its mandate. In the end, while the organization and its leadership responded (well in some instances, poorly or not at all in others), their efforts were no match for the tide of assimilation, increased opportunity, and Cold War pressure felt by young people growing up after the Second World War. Although many youngsters continued to ascribe to the values espoused by the Ukrainian labour temple movement, on the whole – and for a variety of reasons – children and youth growing up in the AUUC had less commitment and attachment to the association than their parents and grandparents had had in the interwar period. This decline in interest among young people was key to the overall weakening in influence that the Ukrainian left experienced throughout the latter half of the twentieth century, and it also illustrates one of the most significant – and unfortunate – ways in which young people shaped the post-war Ukrainian left.

Conclusion: "If I Can't Dance, It's Not My Revolution"

That an enemy of the state could make the transition to a nationally recognized historical entity is exactly what officially occurred on 5 July 2010. On that day the federal government of Canada designated the Winnipeg Ukrainian labour temple a national historic site. "This commemoration will help to ensure that this site and its association with pivotal events in Canada's history will be remembered and appreciated by generations to come," remarked Conservative cabinet minister Vic Toews.[1] The possibility of this sort of designation would have been ridiculous even thirty years prior during the lingering Cold War, and unfathomable seventy years earlier when the federal government was not fêting but openly persecuting the Ukrainian left. Now, with Toews's words, on the hall and the national movement it represented was bestowed a national legitimacy and respectability that had been lacking for much of its history. The founders and their activities, always contemporarily controversial, were now firmly ensconced within the Canadian multicultural historical record.

The hard-fought recognition was deserved. These Ukrainians succeeded in creating a vibrant and distinctive Ukrainian working-class movement, an important cornerstone of the wider twentieth-century Canadian left. Their presence – and tenacity – ensured that perspectives of marginalized "ethnics" became a critical part of the social justice conversation. The Ukrainian left community attracted countless members and supporters – young and old, female and male, immigrant and Canadian-born – through a range of social, cultural, and political activities that combined elements of the Canadian working-class experience with components of traditional Ukrainian culture. For these activists, politics and culture were inextricably linked. These Ukrainian leftists focused their energies on two major priorities: improving the circumstances of workers and farmers in Canada and around the world and preserving and expressing Ukrainian cultural traditions in their adopted Canadian homeland. At times certain constituencies of the community valued and supported these priorities differently. Nonetheless, no matter how or when they were manifest, the concerns were reflective of both the adaptation and the resistance that the immigrant generation and its children employed to adjust to and improve their personal and community circumstances as well as to negotiate personally and collectively a sense of Ukrainianness and, later, Ukrainian Canadianness.

The women and men who founded the movement brought with them from the old country their modes of political organization, gender relations, and ethnic expression and resistance. They did not merely transplant these uprooted models, however. Rather, the founding generation of the Ukrainian left adapted these traditions to the working-class circumstances in which they found themselves upon their arrival in Canada. Concurrently they engaged with and viewed their personal and local community struggles through the lens of the international communist movement. Subsequent generations challenged these activist models, pushing the movement to adjust and change to meet their new interests and concerns. Both past and present, and the local and the international, then, influenced greatly the kinship, organizational, and community structures that developed. Nor was this activism solely confined to a traditional political arena. For these Ukrainians the political was manifest in numerous ways: on the stage at the Ukrainian labour temple, at the meetings of the Communist Party of Canada, on the front lines of strikes, in organizational newspapers (both Ukrainian and, later, English), in internment-camp barracks, in private living rooms, in hall kitchens, at summer camps, and at dances for teenagers.

The location of individuals and individual cohorts of members and supporters at specific intersections of the processes of gender, class, ethnicity, age, and generation, set against changing national and international political and social contexts, made for varied experiences in and responses to the Ukrainian left. As such, there was no universal experience but rather a multitude of distinct experiences. This meant that, even in the face of seeming unity, internal tensions and conflicting membership priorities (not to mention inequality) challenged – and ultimately contributed to the decline of – the movement. Women and men, youngsters and senior citizens, while sharing a sense of a common political and ethnic community, all had different engagements with and distinct impacts on the Ukrainian left.

In practice, this informed a masculinist culture in which men enjoyed relational power over women and children. Constructions of hegemonic masculinity and hegemonic femininity in dialogue with class and ethnicity in the interwar years ensured inequity; this was continually reinforced through social practice. Activities, structures of authority, the movement's hierarchy, and even the physical space of the Ukrainian labour temples reflected and supported these power dynamics. The Ukrainian left's masculinist ideology served to privilege men, at the same time naturalizing their domination of the movement and disadvantaging other members.

Not all men benefited equally, however. In the interwar years two categories of masculine performance existed. The ideals of hegemonic masculinity most closely corresponded to the Ukrainian left's male intelligentsia and national leadership corp. Among the leadership the discourse on masculinity was predicated on energetic participation in political activism (often through membership in the CPC) and the active preservation of Ukrainian culture. Underpinning their relational authority vis-à-vis other members were these men's close ties to the international communist movement, which informed and inspired, though not in an uncontested fashion, much of the Ukrainian left's activism in the 1920s and 1930s. The rank-and-file men embraced this model to varying degrees, depending on their interests, employment, and locality, often rejecting the strident political tendencies of the male leadership in favour of social and cultural activism. As such, they performed a complicit masculinity, whereby they benefited from the patriarchal dividend without assuming many of the risks that came with hegemonic masculine practice.

In spite of these processes of inequality arising out of the Ukrainian left's masculinist culture, even the seemingly most powerless managed to find ways to shape their own engagement and compel the movement as a whole to address their particular experiences and activist interests. This was certainly the case for the movement's women. With notions of hegemonic femininity nearly impossible to meet, they picked and chose aspects of it, incorporated others, and, in doing so, performed an oppositional femininity, one co-constituted in relation to the movement's masculinities as well as the femininities external to the movement. During the interwar years language and preoccupation with Ukrainian cultural expression set the immigrant generation of these women apart from other radical (particularly Anglo-Celtic) women, making for different (at times parallel) experiences; this precluded the development of a wider feminist discourse that challenged their oppression as women. Nonetheless, the Ukrainian women still managed to establish for themselves spaces of autonomy within the Ukrainian labour temples. During the interwar years they expressed their activism through cultural activities, work with children, and what some have labelled "support work" – an iniquitous designation for this crucial labour on which the movement so heavily depended for its very survival. The women carefully guarded these spaces, especially their women's branch and, when established, their kitchens, from male encroachment. They likewise stood up to men's criticism that questioned their dedication when they failed to live up to proscribed male activist standards. In doing so, they redefined their support work as fundamental and critical political territory. While no formal response emerged at this time to their oppression as women, their practice of an oppositional femininity indicates agency – careful, deliberate, and strategic negotiation of gendered discourse and practice within the movement.

Children and youth acted similarly in the 1920s and 1930s. They could be found studying in music and language classes, playing sports, discussing political issues, and reading organizational newspapers, among other diversions. The structure of these pursuits reflected the hopes that the adults had for their children's politicization and Ukrainian cultural engagement; they are also indicative of the young people's own interests and experiences growing up simultaneously in the Ukrainian labour temple and in mainstream Canadian society (the public schools, urban neighbourhoods, and rural communities in which they lived, learned, and played). If activities failed to please youngsters, they walked away; interwar organizers thus employed great care to meet the needs and desires of these youngest members.

The advent of the Second World War challenged the movement. During the war, as an outcome of the intersection of the processes of gender, class, ethnicity, and generation, the Ukrainian left's gendered discourse stretched (but did not fundamentally shift). The male leadership's internment circumscribed male activism across the movement; many men, because of war-industry work, service overseas, or fear of arrest, absented themselves from the Ukrainian left's organizational activities. Not targeted for arrest themselves, thanks to the Canadian state's sexist assessment of their value to the movement, the women, particularly the founding generation's bilingual daughters who had grown up in the youngsters' activities of the halls, assumed the leadership reins, fought for the men's release, and laid the foundation for the movement's rebirth. Children and youth, displaced by the seizure of the labour temples (and, in some cases, the arrests of their fathers), regrouped with the women's help. Their concerts and other displays of patriotism enhanced critically the public image of the beleaguered Ukrainian left.

These changes – to women's activism in particular – did not at the time fundamentally challenge the Ukrainian left's masculinist discourse or gender notions, proscriptive or in practice. Notions of hegemonic masculinity and femininity, their performance, and the oppositional femininity and complicit masculinity established and practised prior to the war remained relatively intact. By the end of the war the men, now released, had returned to their former positions of authority and activity, and the immigrant-generation women continued their activism along the familiar interwar lines. Occasionally these women and men united around causes that reflected their experiences as radical immigrants and, increasingly, elderly persons, but most often they continued to work in spaces and activity exclusive of one another.

Among the younger generations, however, a subtle challenge to the movement's masculinist culture began to smoulder as an outcome of the intersection of ethnicity, gender, and generation in the post-war context. With subtle and overt manifestations it gradually came to bear significant consequences. Language played an important role in this. Cultural activities for which no Ukrainian-language skills were needed grew in popularity; the most notable of these included Ukrainian folk-dance and embroidery, the latter further enhancing women's positions. A conspicuous wane was evident in activities for which Ukrainian was critical; theatrical productions, for example, declined markedly, eroding the status and authority of the older men for whom drama had been a key activity. The Canadian-born adults formed their own unisex English-language group, officially known as the English-speaking branch.

Under the auspices of the English-speaking branch, young women carved out space for themselves by maintaining the Young Women's Clubs. There they often employed activist methods similar to those of their mothers and grandmothers. At the same time, however, many young women began to perform a new category of oppositional femininity, incorporating elements of hegemonic femininity and the oppositional femininity of their female elders. In doing so, they pushed the boundaries of the movement's discourse on femininity by striking out in new directions to pursue leadership opportunities (though usually working with women and children) and paid positions within the Ukrainian left. Their organizational and language skills, the absence of older women in these positions, and their willingness to work for lower wages than those of their Canadian-born male counterparts opened some interesting employment and activist doors for these younger women. Through this work they often succeeded in uniting the Canadian-born and immigrant-generation women in the peace and feminist movements, forging important links with radical women outside the Ukrainian left. They often did so in the face of recurring sexism or indifference on the part of the AUUC's male leadership, factors that eventually pushed many to other activist outlets. Their activism and, for many, their departure acted in direct challenge to the entrenched masculinist culture of the Ukrainian left.

Like their female counterparts, many of the Canadian-born men found themselves in challenging circumstances within the movement. They were shut out of the leadership because of age, generation, and, for some, language skills as the immigrant-generation men refused to relinquish the most elite and politically lucrative positions. Around this challenge emerged a third category of masculinity – a marginalized masculinity – as more and more men came of age and attempted (often unsuccessfully) to find a place for themselves in the movement. Most, if they remained involved with the AUUC, did so through social and cultural activities. Many simply chose to leave, availing themselves of opportunities – activist, cultural, and otherwise – in mainstream Canadian society where as men they could enjoy relative privilege and greater possibilities.

The behaviour of children and youth also posed a challenge to the masculinist culture of the Ukrainian left. Youngsters continued to engage in activities patterned on those of the interwar years, but they rejected the ones that, for a host of reasons, they found unappealing. In increasing numbers they exhibited their rejection by drifting away from the AUUC in favour of mainstream Canadian social, political, cultural, and educational pursuits. These were attractive for they reflected better the interests and experiences of the young people who had grown up in Canada.

The failure of the Ukrainian left's leaders to respond in meaningful and inclusive ways to the needs and interests of these young members played a fundamental role in fuelling the movement's decline. Other factors also contributed. External forces, national and international, had an impact on the Ukrainian left's history and challenged internal gender and generational relations. Among the most influential were the actions of the Canadian state. Ongoing state surveillance and repression, the persecution and incarceration of the Ukrainian left's leaders and supporters, post-war federal immigration policy (including the active recruitment of passionate anti-communist, Ukrainian Cold Warriors), and the discourse around and advent of official multiculturalism, among other moves, presented strong challenges to the movement. In addition they contributed many difficult personal, social, and economic consequences for individual members and supporters. Various nationalist Ukrainians also took on Ukrainian leftist activism. Most significant, particularly during the Cold War, was their consistent – and not-unfounded – calling out of the labour temple leaders for their portrayal of the Soviet Union and the situation in Soviet Ukraine. Within the Ukrainian left many members joined suit, questioning the loyalties of the older male leaders to the international communist movement and resenting their inflexibility when it came to political organizing. With the credibility of the Soviets diminished, the older men's power that was grounded in key international relationships irreversibly waned. This furthered the weakening of their influence over other members, particularly women, younger men, and children.

Other important factors also contributed to gendered shifts in the community and its ultimate decline: the post-war decline in ethnic-hall socialism generally, increased post-war upward mobility, intensified assimilation, and a growing identification with the Canadian side of their Ukrainian Canadian heritage that many of the Canadian-born experienced. These combined forces drove and drew away many of the younger generations of women, men, and children. The movement was dealt further blows by the concurrent diminishment of activity among the immigrant generation due to old age and often accompanying ill health. Less relevant and influential, the Ukrainian left had entered into a pronounced decline by the 1970s.

Although still concerned with radical activism and the preservation of Ukrainian culture, those members who remained into the 1980s became increasingly preoccupied with researching and sharing the movement's history. This led, in 1984, to the founding of the Canadian Society for Ukrainian Labour Research (CSULR), an organization charged with the task of ensuing the movement's place in the broader history of Ukrainians, Canada, and international leftist activism.[2] This included the preservation of many important archival collections related to the movement's history. Some of these materials found their way to Library and Archives Canada, a large collection exists at the hall in Winnipeg, and still others remain cared for in private hands.

The fall of the Soviet Union and the advent of an independent Ukraine in 1991 presented additional challenges to the movement. Gone was its privileged connection to the old country, along with many personal and political ties with Ukrainians and others. The movement received virtually no new recruits from the small wave of Ukrainian immigrants who made their way to Canada following these monumental events. Cultural activities nonetheless continued, as did a conscious, albeit diminished (due to continually declining membership numbers), engagement with the broader Canadian left. In many ways the 1990s became a period of introspection; participants at CSULR symposia explored aspects of the movement's history that were both riveting and difficult, shared personal reminiscences of their own political and cultural activism, and collaborated with professional scholars of the Canadian left to explore a host of issues. Among the most notable and profoundly unsettling conversations, growing out of the work of Professor Greg Kealey and others, focused on the intense degree of surveillance under which the Canadian authorities had kept the movement. Many felt it ironic, in fact, that the RCMP had done a better job in documenting the movement's history than its own supporters often had. The commemoration of the Winnipeg Ukrainian labour temple as a national historic site was a direct result of the tremendous, hard work of the remaining members to preserve the movement's past and ensure its recognition as an important component of Canadian ethnic and labour history.

There exists today in the remaining Ukrainian labour temples an active and extremely dedicated core of Canadian-born members, who still run Ukrainian folk-dance classes, hold special events to commemorate Ukrainian holidays, organize the occasional concert, and engage in political activism. Halls exist in larger centres like Winnipeg, Edmonton, Calgary, Regina, and Toronto, though many branches have downsized from their original Ukrainian labour temples to smaller facilities. The movement continues to publish a national bilingual (Ukrainian and English) newspaper, the *Ukrainian Canadian Herald*.[3] Support, though tenacious, continues to decline, however, as new members are difficult to attract and remaining supporters age and pass away.

The Ukrainian left's history – including its decline – shares many parallels with other contemporary diasporic, socialist communities. Its leadership and the rank-and-file possessed a keen awareness and a desire to engage with the wider Canadian and international lefts, as manifest in various formations during the twentieth century. And, this study argues, they did so staunchly on their own terms. To paraphrase an adage attributed to radical Emma Goldman, if these Ukrainians could not dance, it was not going be their revolution. Their leftist, socialist practice was inseparably cultural and political. Like that of other ethnic-hall socialists, their class-consciousness was informed by a close intersection of class and ethnicity – rooted in the discrimination faced as a result of their dual identity as Ukrainians and members of a marginalized social class. They consciously challenged the discrimination, ethnocentrism, and alienation they encountered within the wider left and Canadian society by continually centring their efforts within their own community, specifically the activist spaces of the Ukrainian labour temples. When challenged, particularly for dancing, embroidering, cooking, or playing mandolin – activities that some other leftists, including many leaders of the Communist Party of Canada, deemed frivolous and irrelevant to the class struggle – the Ukrainian leftists pushed back, defending their right to apply their Ukrainianness as key tools in the class struggle. Working in a collaborative, parallel, but often separate manner, these Ukrainians made a tremendous contribution to the Canadian left. Without their mass of financial, moral, and numerical support – coming often at great risk, given the vulnerability of many of the movement's members as non-naturalized migrants – many of the left's most celebrated twentieth-century gains might have been harder fought.

While the goals of the movement's founders were met only to some degree and not always in the forms they envisioned, the movement as a whole had a tremendous and profound effect on those who came to embrace the Ukrainian labour temples as a second home. As such, studying the Ukrainian left enriches our understanding of the various ways to be Ukrainian in Canada's past; it likewise extends our knowledge of Canadian working-class, immigrant life generally and its related political, social, and cultural components, lending nuance to our understanding of the broader Canadian left. However, the implications of this study are not just for the past. The Ukrainian left's history – and the complex experiences of the women, men, and youngsters who passed through the Ukrainian labour temples – stands as an important reminder to those of us who engage in social justice activism. Specifically, it points to our need to be mindful of how the processes of inequality function – to include and exclude, to empower and marginalize, to uplift or demean – and their implications for the genuine success of our initiatives. We must explicitly and consciously strive to avoid reproducing inequality in our activist practice, ensuring that the perspectives of all supporters are encouraged, heard, respected, and integrated and that their needs are met. If an injury to one is an injury to all, meaningful change cannot be realized with anything less. It could be said that the Ukrainian left's legacy is one of resistance and accommodation. Indeed, it is a remarkable testament to the ingenuity and determination of a small group of outsiders who sought to empower themselves and their children to challenge the oppression of their class and culture and to defend their dignity, while contributing to the broader Canadian and international left's struggle to build a more just society for all. In the end, then, despite the founders' unmet revolutionary objectives, these Ukrainians achieved some important victories. They skilfully and unapologetically navigated their adaptation as immigrants on their own terms, and they creatively resisted and challenged the oppression they faced as ethnic workers and radicals, both within and without the broader Canadian and international lefts. In doing so, they contributed to and reinforced Canada's complicated and contradictory social and democratic fabric in critical and compelling ways.

Appendix: Key Ukrainian Leftist Organizations

Incarnations of the Ukrainian Labour Temple Movement's Central Body (In Order of Founding)

Ukrainian Labour Temple Association (ULTA), 1918–24
Ukrainian Labour Farmer Temple Association (ULFTA), 1924–46
Ukrainian Association to Aid the Fatherland (UAAF), 1941–2
Association of Canadian Ukrainians (ACU), 1942–6
Association of United Ukrainian Canadians (AUUC), 1946–Present

Other Key Ukrainian Leftist Organizations

Workers Benevolent Association (WBA), 1922–2006
Canadian Society for Ukrainian Labour Research (CSULR), 1984–Present

Notes

Introduction

1 Myron Shatulsky, interviewed by the author, June 1998; Katherine Shatulsky, in Krawchuk, Peter, ed., *Reminiscences of Courage and Hope* (Toronto: Kobzar Publishing, 1991), 331–2.

2 An expanded form of Marxist ideology, articulated in and applied to the Soviet Union under Lenin. It became the dominant ideological strand on which many communists (both in the Soviet Union and abroad) based their activism, the Ukrainian left's intelligentsia included.

3 The articles quoted here offer excellent practical and accessible explanations of intersectionality and its implications for social justice activism. Kathy Davis, "Intersectionality as Buzzword: A Sociology of Science Perspective on What Makes a Feminist Theory Successful," *Feminist Theory* 9, no. 1 (1 April 2008), 68,79; Olena Hankivsky, *Intersectionality 101* (Vancouver: Institute for Intersectionality Research and Policy, SFU, 2014), 9, 11; S.E Smith, "Push(back) at the Intersections: Defining (and Critiquing) 'Intersectionality' | Bitch Media," *Bitchmedia*, http://bitchmagazine.org; Gill Valentine, "Theorizing and Researching Intersectionality: A Challenge for Feminist Geography," *The Professional Geographer*, 59: 1, 14; Alison Symington, "Intersectionality: A Tool for Gender and Economic Justice," *Women's Rights and Economic Change*, no. 9 (August 2004), 1, http://www.awid.org/eng/Library/Intersectionality -A-Tool-for-Gender-and-Economic-Justice. Similarly, see also Gabriele Winker and Nina Degele, "Intersectionality as Multi-level Analysis: Dealing with Social Inequality," *European Journal of Women's Studies* 18, no. 1 (1 February 2011): 51–66; Devon W. Carbado, "Colorblind Intersectionality," *Signs: Journal of Women in Culture & Society* 38, no. 4,

Summer 2013 (9 July 2013): 1–42; Hae Yeon Choo and Myra Marx Ferree, "Practicing Intersectionality in Sociological Research: A Critical Analysis of Inclusions, Interactions, and Institutions in the Study of Inequalities," *Sociological Theory* 28, no. 2 (June 2010): 129–49; Sarah Chown and Jaedyn Starr, "Thinking Intersectionally: Understanding the Individual and Structural Contexts of Gay Men's Lives," http://cbrc.net; Aphrodite Kocięda, "Marginalization Is Messy: Beyond Intersectionality | Rabble. ca"; Jennifer C. Nash, "Re-Thinking Intersectionality," *Feminist Review* 89, no. 1 (2008): 1–15; Stephanie A. Shields, "Gender: An Intersectionality Perspective" *Sex Roles* 59, no. 5–6 (September 2008): 301–3; Evelyn M. Simien, "Doing Intersectionality Research: From Conceptual Issues to Practical Examples," *Politics & Gender* 3, no. 02 (2007): 264–71; Joan Z. Spade and Catherine G. Valentine, introduction to *The Kaleidoscope of Gender: Prisms, Patterns, and Possibilities* (Los Angeles, CA: Sage Publications, 2008), xiii–xxiv, 2014.

4 Hankivsky, *Intersectionality 101*, 9; Chown and Starr. "Thinking Intersectionally"; Shields, "Gender," 301–11; Smith, "Push(back) at the Intersections."

5 For a comprehensive exploration and critique of the "genealogy" of hegemonic masculinity as theoretical lens, consult R.W. Connell and James W. Messerschmidt, "Hegemonic Masculinity: Rethinking the Concept," *Gender & Society* 19, no. 6 (December 2005): 829–59. Other valuable discussions of hegemonic masculinities and femininities include Mike Donaldson, "What Is Hegemonic Masculinity?", in "Masculinities," special issue, *Theory and Society* 22, no. 5 (October 1993): 643–57, 1; Karen D. Pyke and Denise L. Johnson, "Asian American Women and Racialized Femininities: 'Doing' Gender across Cultural Worlds," in *The Kaleidoscope of Gender: Prisms, Patterns, and Possibilities* (Los Angeles, CA: Sage Publications, 2008) , 76–88; R.W. Connell, "The Social Organization of Masculinity," in *The Masculinities Reader*, ed. Stephen Whitehead and Frank J. Barrett (Cambridge: Polity Press, 2001), 30–50; Mimi Schippers, "Recovering the Feminine Other: Masculinity, Femininity, and Gender Hegemony," *Theory and Society* 36, no. 1 (1 March 2007): 85–102; Justin Charlebois, "Geographies of Femininities," in *Gender and the Construction of Hegemonic and Oppositional Femininities* (Lanham, MD: Lexington Books, 2011), 21–41.

6 Donaldson, "What Is Hegemonic Masculinity?" 646; for further discussion, see Arthur Brittan, "Masculinities and Masculism," in Whitehead and Barrett, *The Masculinities Reader*, 51–76.

7 Charlebois, "Geographies of Femininities," 22, 25, 31.

8 Connell and Messerschmidt, "Hegemonic Masculinity," 844.
9 Connell, "The Social Organization of Masculinity," 40.
10 Raewyn Connell, *Gender: In World Perspective* (Cambridge: Polity, 2009), 142.
11 Connell and Messerschmidt, "Hegemonic Masculinity," 844.
12 Connell, "The Social Organization of Masculinity," 40; Connell and Messerschmidt, "Hegemonic Masculinity," 839.
13 Charlebois, "Geographies of Femininities," 41.
14 Feminist scholars working in a variety of disciplines have embraced intersectionality. Two key developments influenced this ascension. The first, Leslie McCall explains, was the late-twentieth-century development of postmodernist and post-structuralist critique within the academy generally. The second, she notes, came from criticism by feminists of colour of white feminism and white feminist scholarship. Specifically, Joan Acker writes: "Feminist scholars of colour have argued for 30 years, with the agreement of most white feminist scholars, that much feminist scholarship was actually about white middle-class women, ignoring the reality that the category gender is fundamentally complicated by class, race/ethnicity, and other differences." Indeed, it was Kimberlé Crenshaw, an African American legal scholar, who first articulated the term *intersectionality* in 1989 in an essay exploring the simultaneity of sexism and racism. As such, Gill Valentine points out, "the specific concept of intersectionality is attributed to critical race theorists who, rejecting the notion of race, gender, ethnicity, class, and so forth as separate and essentialist categories, developed the term intersectionality to describe the interconnections and interdependence of race with other categories" ("Theorizing and Researching Intersectionality: A Challenge for Feminist Geography," *Professional Geographer* 59, no. 1 (February 2007): 12). See also Leslie McCall, "The Complexity of Intersectionality," in *Signs: Journal of Women in Culture and Society* 30, no. 31 (2005); Joan Acker, "Inequality Regimes: Gender, Class, and Race in Organizations," in *Gender and Society* 20, no. 4 (August 2006): 441–64; Kimberlé Crenshaw, "Demarginalizing the Intersection of Race and Sex: A Black Feminist Critique of Antidiscrimination Doctrine, Feminist Theory, and Antiracist Politics," *University of Chicago Legal Forum*, 1989, 139–67. See also Gudrun-Axeli Knapp, "Race, Class, Gender: Reclaiming Baggage in Fast Travelling Theories," in *European Journal of Women's Studies* 12 (2005): 249. Each of these essays offers an invaluable discussion of the challenges and promises of using intersectionality as a methodological approach.
15 Frances Swyripa, *Wedded to the Cause: Ukrainian-Canadian Women and Ethnic Identity, 1891–1991* (Toronto: University of Toronto Press, 1993);

Tina Loo, "Of Moose and Men: Hunting for Masculinities in British Columbia, 1880–1939," *Western Historical Quarterly* 32 (Autumn 2001): 296–319; Ruth Frager, *Sweatshop Strife: Class, Ethnicity, and Gender in the Jewish Labour Movement of Toronto, 1900-1939* (Toronto: University of Toronto Press, 1992), 216; Marlene Epp, Franca Iacovetta, and Frances Swyripa, eds., *Sisters or Strangers? Immigrant, Ethnic, and Racialized Women in Canadian History* (Toronto: University of Toronto Press, 2004). Other key examples include Deborah Cohen, "From Peasant to Worker: Migration, Masculinity, and the Making of Mexican Workers in the US," *International Labor and Working-Class History* 69 (Spring 2006): 81–103; the collected essays in *Gendered Pasts: Historical Essays in Femininity and Masculinity in Canada*, ed. Kathryn McPherson, Cecelia Morgan, and Nancy M. Forestell (Toronto: Oxford University Press, 1999); Karen Hunt, "'Strong Minds, Great Hearts, True Faith, and Ready Hands'? Exploring Socialist Masculinities before the First World War," *Labour History Review* 69, no. 2 (August 2004): 201–17; Ronnie Johnston and Arthur McIvor, "Dangerous Work, Hard Men and Broken Bodies: Masculinity in the Clydeside Heavy Industries, c. 1930–1970s," *Labour History Review* 69, no. 2, August 2004,): 135–151; Marlene Epp, "Heroes or Yellow-bellies? Masculinity and the Conscientious Objector," in *Journal of Mennonite Studies* 17 (1999): 107–17; Steven Penfold, "'Have You No Manhood in You?' Gender and Class in the Cape Breton Coal Towns, 1920–26," in *Gender and History in Canada*, ed. Joy Parr and Mark Rosenfeld (Toronto: McClelland & Stewart, 1996), 270–93; Gillian Creese, "The Politics of Dependence: Women, Work, and Unemployment in the Vancouver Labour Movement before World War II," in *Class, Gender and Region: Essays in Canadian Historical Sociology*, ed. Gregory S. Kealey (St John's, NL: Athabasca University Press, 1988), 121–42.

16 Katrina Srigley, "'In Case You Hadn't Noticed!': Race, Ethnicity, and Women's Wage-Earning in a Depression-Era City," *Labour/Le Travail* 55 (Spring 2005): 69–105; Gill Valentine, "Theorizing and Researching Intersectionality," 19; Craig Heron, "Boys Will Be Boys: Working-Class Masculinities in the Age of Mass Production," *International Labor and Working-Class History* 69 (Spring 2006): 7.

17 The communist question is evident in Jaroslav Petryshyn, *Peasants in the Promised Land: Canada and the Ukrainians, 1891–1914* (Toronto: Lorimer, 1985); John Kolasky, *The Shattered Illusion: The History of Ukrainian Pro-Communist Organizations in Canada* (Toronto: PMA Books, 1979); Kolasky, *Prophets and Proletarians: Documents on the History of the Rise and Decline of Ukrainian Communism in Canada* (Edmonton: Canadian Institute of

Ukrainian Studies Press, 1990); Marco Carynnyk, "Swallowing Stalinism:
Pro-Communist Ukrainian Canadians and Soviet Ukraine in the 1930s,"
in *Canada's Ukrainians: Negotiating an Identity*, ed. Lubomyr Luciuk and
Stella Hryniuk (Toronto: University of Toronto Press, 1991), 187–205;
Orest Martynowych, *The Ukrainians in Canada: The Formative Years,
1891–1924* (Edmonton: CIUS, 1991); Donald Avery, "Divided Loyalties:
The Ukrainian Left and the Canadian State," in *Canada's Ukrainians*,
ed. Luciuk and Hryniuk, 271–87; and Paul Yuzyk, "The Ukrainian
Communist Delusion," in *The Ukrainians in Manitoba: A Social History*
(Toronto: University of Toronto Press, 1953), 96–112. For more recent and
nuanced accounts that examine conflict between Ukrainian leftists and
the Communist Party of Canada and among Ukrainian leftists, refer to
Jim Mochoruk's "'Pop & Co' versus Buck and the 'Lenin School Boys':
Ukrainian Canadians and the Communist Party of Canada," and Andrij
Makuch's "Fighting for the Soul of the Ukrainian Progressive Movement
in Canada: The Lobayites and the Ukrainian Labour-Farmer Temple
Association," in *Reimagining Ukrainian Canadians: History, Politics, and
Identity*, ed. Rhonda L. Hinther and Jim Mochoruk (Toronto: University of
Toronto Press, 2011).

18 For some examples, see Carmela Patrias, *Patriots and Proletarians:
Politicizing Hungarian Immigrants in Interwar Canada* (Montreal: McGill-
Queen's University Press, 1994); Patrias, "Relief Strike: Immigrant
Workers and the Great Depression in Crowland, Ontario, 1930–35," in
*A Nation of Immigrants: Women, Workers, and Communities in Canadian
History*, ed. Franca Iacovetta, Paula Draper, and Robert Ventresca
(Toronto: University of Toronto Press, 1998), 322–58; Paul Mishler,
*Raising Reds: The Young Pioneers, Radical Summer Camps, and Communist
Political Culture in the United States* (New York: Columbia University
Press, 1999); Ester Reiter, "Secular *Yiddishkait*: Left Politics, Culture, and
Community," *Labour/Le Travail* 49 (Spring 2002): 121–46; Reiter, "Camp
Navelt and the Daughters of the Jewish Left," in *Sisters or Strangers?:
Immigrant, Ethnic, and Racialized Women in Canadian History*, ed. Marlene
Epp, Franca Iacovetta, and Frances Swyripa (Toronto: University
of Toronto Press, 2004), 365–80; Varpu Lindström, *Defiant Sisters: A
Social History of Finnish Immigrant Women in Canada* (Beaverton, ON:
Aspasia Books, 2003); Ian Radforth, *Bushworkers and Bosses: Logging
in Northern Ontario, 1900–1980* (Toronto: University of Toronto Press,
1987). For a compelling overview of late-nineteeth and early-twentieth-
century manifestations of the diaspora socialism of the Finns, Jews,
and Ukrainians, consult Ian MacKay, *Reasoning Otherwise: Leftists and*

the People's Enlightenment in Canada, 1890-1920 (Toronto: BTL, 2008), 398–415.

19 McKay, *Reasoning Otherwise*, 415; McKay, *Rebels, Reds, Radicals: Rethinking Canada's Left History* (Toronto: Between the Lines, 2005), 91.

20 For more information on the ULFTA's general history see Peter Krawchuk, *Our History: The Ukrainian Labour-Farmer Movement in Canada, 1907–1991* (Toronto: Lugus, 1996), and my doctoral thesis, "'Sincerest Revolutionary Greetings': Progressive Ukrainians in Twentieth-Century Canada" (McMaster University, 2005).

21 Again, see Patrias's *Patriots and Proletarians*. Also see Frager's *Sweatshop Strife*.

1. Men and the Interwar Ukrainian Left

1 For more detailed commentary on Popovich see Peter Krawchuk, *Mathew Popovich: His Place in the History of Ukrainian Canadians* (Toronto: CSULR, 1987). See also John Weir, "Among our Pioneers: Matthew Popovich," *Ukrainian Canadian*, 1 May 1948.

2 For a detailed discussion on the Railways Agreement, its impact on interwar immigration generally, and how it affected Ukrainians specifically, consult Myron Gulka-Tiechko, "Ukrainian Immigration to Canada under the Railways Agreement, 1925–30," *Journal of Ukrainian Studies* 16, nos. 1–12 (Summer–Winter 1991): 29–59.

3 William Stefiuk, interviewed for "Towards a New Path: The History of the Progressive Ukrainian Community in Saskatchewan Oral History Project (1976)," interviews and translations by Clara Swityk, accession #R80–550, Saskatchewan Archives Board, University of Regina, Saskatchewan.

4 For detailed analysis of the 1931 Estevan strike and its fallout consult Steve Hewitt, "September 1931: A Re-interpretation of the Royal Canadian Mounted Police's Handling of the 1931 Estevan Strike and Riot," *Labour / Le Travail*, no. 39: 159–78; Stephen Endicott, *Bienfait: The Saskatchewan Miners' Struggle of '31* (Toronto: University of Toronto Press, 2002), "Bienfait: Origins and Legacy of the Coal Miners' Strike of 1931," *Prairie Forum* 31, no. 2 (2006): 217–31, and "The Estevan Story, 1931 to 1970," *Canadian Labour* 16, no. 1 (1971): 10.

5 For an engaging and detailed account of this relationship consult Endicott, *Bienfait: The Saskatchewan Miners' Struggle*.

6 Stefiuk, interviewed for "Towards a New Path."

7 This literature includes Franca Iacovetta, *Such Hardworking People: Italian Immigrants in Postwar Toronto* (Montreal: McGill-Queen's University

Press, 1992); Nancy M. Forestell, "All That Glitters Is Not Gold: The Gendered Dimensions of Work, Family, and Community Life in the Northern Ontario Goldmining Town of Timmins, 1909–1950" (PhD diss., University of Toronto, 1994); Penfold, "'Have You No Manhood in You?'; and Creese, "The Politics of Dependence"; Frager, *Sweatshop Strife*. For American examples see Katherine Benton-Cohen, "Docile Children and Dangerous Revolutionaries: The Racial Hierarchy of Manliness and the Bisbee Deportation of 1917," *Frontiers: A Journal of Women Studies* 24, no. 2 (2003): 30–50; Nancy Hewitt, "'The Voice of Virile Labor': Labor Militancy, Community Solidarity, and Gender Identity among Tampa's Latin Workers, 1880–1921," in *Work Engendered: Toward a New History of American Labor*, ed. Ava Baron (Ithaca, NY: Cornell University Press, 1991); and Nancy Hewitt, *Southern Discomfort: Women's Activism in Tampa, Florida, 1880s–1920s* (Urbana: University of Illinois Press, 2001).

8 Martynowych's *The Ukrainians in Canada* is a key example of this phenomenon. The book is comprehensive, outlining the variety of Ukrainian institutions that emerged in Canada and the experiences that Ukrainian men had with waged labour and agricultural work. It also contains significant information on the early Ukrainian socialist movement in Canada and the development of one of the key institutions of the Ukrainian left, the Ukrainian Labour Temple Association (ULTA). Although much valuable insight is demonstrated about the movement's leadership, little is said about the role of rank-and-file men and their everyday experiences with the ULTA. Additional examples can be found in Krawchuk's *Our History* and in chapter 11 of Petryshyn's *Peasants in the Promised Land*. Vadim Kukushkin's *From Peasants to Labourers: Ukrainian and Belarusan Immigration from the Russian Empire to Canada* (Montreal: McGill-Queen's University Press, 2007) offers crucial detail on the ways in which male sojourners from areas that are now part of eastern Ukraine arrived in Canada and engaged with the socialist movement during the first two decades of the twentieth century; he examines especially some of these men's ties to the ULFTA and its fellow traveller organization, the Federation of Russian Canadians (FRC). For our purposes here, however, the usefulness of this important analysis is limited. The vast majority of those who flocked to the Ukrainian labour temples (like the majority of Ukrainian migrants to Canada) came from regions that are now part of western Ukraine, they had a different type of ethnocultural background, and their migration was motivated by a host of oft-combined social, cultural, political, economic, and

religious factors. Kukushkin's Russian empire émigrés were primarily economically motivated, arriving with an intention to return to the old country, a desire that deeply shaped their limited engagement with the host society. As such, most seldom put down more than tenuous roots in Canada, and, aside from a handful like Matthew Shatulsky (who would go on to become one of the ULFTA's key leaders), few made a significant impact on the Ukrainian left.

9 Often written by those opposed to the Ukrainian left, many such studies are hostile in tone. Paul Yuzuk's slant becomes apparent in his book *The Ukrainians in Manitoba* (Toronto: University of Toronto Press, 1953) when one reads the title of the chapter on the Ukrainian left. In "The Ukrainian Communist Delusion" Yuzuk sets out to discredit the movement as "a small but active and vociferous minority, directed by Moscow-trained leaders," frames it as a communist front organization, and thus obscures the influence and significance of all but its political elements. For additional examples see Avery, "Divided Loyalties," and Kolasky, *The Shattered Illusion*. See also Kolasky's *Prophets and Proletarians*, and Carynnyk's "Swallowing Stalinism." More recent and nuanced accounts include Mochoruk's "'Pop & Co'" and Makuch's "Fighting for the Soul of the Ukrainian Progressive Movement in Canada."

10 As Franca Iacovetta observes, while many assume that gender history is necessarily written from a postmodern perspective, historians working within different paradigms, including a material feminist one, have developed gendered approaches. See Franca Iacovetta, "Defending Honour, Demanding Respect: Manly Discourse and Gendered Practice in Two Construction Strikes, Toronto, 1960–1961," in *Gendered Pasts: Historical Essays in Femininity and Masculinity in Canada*, ed. Kathryn McPherson, Cecilia Morgan, and Nancy M. Forestell (New York: Oxford University Press. 1999), 199–222, and "Gendering Trans/National Historiographies: Feminists Rewriting Canadian History," *Journal of Women's History* 19.1 (2007): 206–13.

11 Some key examples include Cohen, "From Peasant to Worker," 81–103; Heron, "Boys Will Be Boys," 6–34; Hunt, "'Strong Minds, Great Hearts'"; Johnston and McIvor, "Dangerous Work, Hard Men, and Broken Bodies"; Loo, "Of Moose and Men," 296–319; Marlene Epp, "Heroes or Yellow-Bellies? Masculinity and the Conscientious Objector," *Journal of Mennonite Studies* 17 (1999): 107–17.

12 Swyripa, *Wedded to the Cause*, 3, 5, 21; Jaroslav Petryshyn, "The Labouring Frontier," in *Peasants in the Promised Land*, 122; Martynowych, *The Ukrainians in Canada*, 252; and Donald Avery, *Reluctant Host* (Toronto:

McClelland & Stewart, 1995), 20–1. For a thorough discussion of the first wave of immigration, migrant statistics, and settlement and labour patterns, consult Martynowych's *Ukrainians in Canada*, particularly chapters 4–6.

13 Petryshyn, *Peasants in the Promised Land*, 124; Avery, *Reluctant Host*, 38.
14 Petryshyn, *Peasants in the Promised Land*, 126, 155–60.
15 Wasyl Woloshyn, interviewed for "Towards a New Path."
16 Swyripa, *Wedded to the Cause*, 4; Martynowych, *The Ukrainians in Canada*, 521; Petryshyn, *Peasants in the Promised Land*, 161.
17 Petryshyn, *Peasants in the Promised Land*, 163–5; Martynowych, *The Ukrainians in Canada*, 253–4; Krawchuk, *Our History*, 298.
18 Martynowych, *The Ukrainians in Canada*, 253; Petryshyn, *Peasants in the Promised Land*, 165–7.
19 Martynowych, *The Ukrainians in Canada*, 254, 427–8; Petryshyn, *Peasants in the Promised Land*, 167–8.
20 Petryshyn, , *Peasants in the Promised Land*, 168–9; Krawchuk, *Our History*, 28.
21 Krawchuk, *Our History*, 32. Krawchuk's *Our History*, pages 3–30, provides a thorough account of the complicated history of the early Ukrainian socialist organizations in Canada. For additional details on how these events and early ethnic-hall socialism in Canada fit within a broader Canadian and transnational socialist context please consult McKay's *Reasoning Otherwise*, 398–415.
22 McKay, *Reasoning Otherwise*, 403.
23 Vasyl Karcha, "Pages from My Life Story," translated by Nadia Niechoda, *Ukrainian Canadian*, April 1990, originally published in *Ukrainske zhyttia*, 1951.
24 "The Ukrainians in Canada, Part II: Communist Organizations," n.d., in Records of the Canadian Security Intelligence Service, National Archives of Canada (hereafter referred to as Records of CSIS), RG 146, vol. 128.
25 *Friends in Need: The WBA Story* (Winnipeg: Workers Benevolent Association, 1972), 141; Records of CSIS, "AUUC – Winnipeg, Manitoba," RG 146, vol. 3792, file part 5; Records of CSIS, "ULFTA, 7th National Convention, 1926," RG 146, vol. 3835; and M. Popovich, *Yak robitnyky dopomahaiut sobi v neshchasti: Do 15-richchia isnuvannia i dialnosti robitnychoho zapomohovoho tovarystva* (Winnipeg: Workers Benevolent Association, 1937). For more information on Parkdale Benevolent Home consult my doctoral thesis, "'Sincerest Revolutionary Greetings.'"
26 Vasyl Karcha, "Pages from My Life Story," translated by Nadia Niechoda, *Ukrainian Canadian*, April 1990, originally published in *Ukrainske zhyttia*, 1951.

27 Fedir Hordienko, "Pages from a Life in Canada," as told to Peter Krawchuk, *Ukrainian Canadian*, September 1988, originally published in *Ukrainske zhyttia*, 1951.

28 See Krawchuk, *Our History*, 363–387, 303. For additional details on the movement's activities, reach, and growth to 1929, consult *Almanakh TURFDim, 1918–1929* (Winnipeg: Labour-Farmer Publishing Association, 1930).

29 Report dated 12 November 1927, "Ukrainian Labour-Farmer Temple Assn. – re J. Navizowsky," in Records of CSIS, RG 146, "John Navis."

30 John Weir, "Among Our Pioneers: Matthew Popovich," *Ukrainian Canadian*, 5 January 1948. For a discussion of the arrests, court proceedings, and campaign for the men's release see Ivan Avakumovic, *The Communist Party in Canada: A History* (Toronto: McClelland & Stewart, 1975), 87–90.

31 John Alexiewich, "Sketches from a Lifetime," *Ukrainian Canadian*, October 1991, originally published in *Ukrainske zhyttia*, 1951.

32 Kalyna Mateychuk, interviewed by the author, 1999.

33 Kosty Kostaniuk, interviewed by the author, 1999.

34 Ibid.

35 Peter Spichka, interviewed by Clara Swityk, 1976.

36 Dmytro Slobodian, "From a Life's Experiences," *Ukrainian Canadian*, June 1991, originally published in *Ukrainske zhyttia*, 17 April 1952.

37 Myron Kostaniuk, "Recollections from a Life of a Ukrainian Pioneer," *Ukrainian Canadian*, October 1990.

38 *Robitnytsia*, 1 September 1924, translated by L. Stavroff. See also *Svit molodi*, October 1927, translated by L. Stavroff.

39 Report re Ukrainian Labor Temple Association, dated 17 August 1921, Winnipeg, in CSIS, RG 146, vol. 4677, "Matthew Shatulsky," part 1; See also Mike Seychuk, interviewed by the author, 1998.

40 Mike Skrynyk, interviewed by the author, 1998.

41 Kostaniuk, "Recollections from a Life of a Ukrainian Pioneer."

42 Mike Skrynyk, interviewed by the author, 1998.

43 Ibid.

44 Report dated 19 September 1923, "Ukrainian labour temple Association – Dramatic Singing Circle Meeting, 16 Sept 1923," Records of CSIS, RG 146, vol. 3792, "AUUC: Winnipeg, Manitoba," part 2. See also report dated 5 April 1920, "Ukrainian Labor Party," Records of CSIS, RG 146, vol. 3792, "AUUC: Winnipeg, Manitoba," part 1.

45 Myron Shatulsky, interviewed by the author, 1998.

46 Report dated 8 December 1919, Edmonton, "Ukrainian in the Edmonton District – Samo-Oyrazowania Society," Records of CSIS, RG 146, vol. 4677, "Matthew Shatulsky," part 1.

47 Report dated 10 November 1923, "Ukrainian Agitator – Speaker at Ukrainian labour temple," Records of CSIS, RG 146, vol. 3792, "AUUC: Winnipeg, Manitoba," part 2. See also Peter Krawchuk, ed., *Our Stage: The Amateur Performing Arts of the Ukrainian Settlers in Canada* (Toronto: Kobzar, 1984), 61.

48 Report dated 10 November 1923, "Ukrainian Agitator – Speaker at Ukrainian labour temple," Records of CSIS, RG 146, vol. 3792, "AUUC: Winnipeg, Manitoba," part 2.

49 Ibid.

50 Fedir Hordienko, "Pages from a Life in Canada," as told to Peter Krawchuk, *Ukrainian Canadian*, September 1988, originally published in *Ukrainske zhyttia*, 1951.

51 Dmytro Slobodian, "From a Life's Experiences," *Ukrainian Canadian*, June 1991, originally published in *Ukrainske zhyttia*, 17 April 1952.

52 Ibid.

53 See for examples the discussion at a meeting of ULT Executive, October 14, 1938, minutes, Point Douglas Hall, 1938, Association of United Ukrainian Canadians Archives, Winnipeg, Manitoba (hereafter referred to as AUUC Archives).

54 Educationals for ULFTA members also occurred outside the regular meetings. "For men who wish to increase their knowledge," national leader Mathew Popovich taught classes on Tuesday evenings and Sunday mornings at the Winnipeg hall in 1922; see report dated 7 May 1922, "Ukrainian labour temple Night School," Records of CSIS, RG 146, vol. 3792, "AUUC: Winnipeg, Manitoba," part 1.

55 *Svit molodi*, April 1927. Members of the women's branches and youth branches responded to and tolerated the presence and directives of these representatives to varying degrees. This will be discussed at greater length in the following two chapters on women's and youngsters' experiences with the ULFTA.

56 All members meeting, 6 September 1938, minutes, Point Douglas Hall, 1938; found in room 6, AUUC Archives.

57 Joe Sekundiak, interviewed by Clara Swityk, 1976.

58 Report dated 23 August 1922, "Ukrainian labour temple Association," in Records of CSIS, RG 146, "John Navis."

59 Report dated 20 April 1933, "Ukrainian Labour-Farmer Temple Association – Winnipeg – (Todowyrnazu)," Records of CSIS, RG 146, vol. 4677, "Matthew

Shatulsky," part 2. For additional examples see report dated 21 December 1927, "John Navisowski," in Records of CSIS, RG 146, "John Navis."

60 Peter Krawchuk, "One of the First" [biography of John Navis], translated by William Kardash, *Ukrainian Canadian*, June 1984, originally published in *Ukrainske zhyttia*, 1951.

61 For a detailed account of his experiences as an elected official, see Stefan Epp, "A Communist in the Council Chambers: Communist Municipal Politics, Ethnicity, and the Career of William Kolisnyk," *Labour/Le travail*, 63 (Spring 2009): 79–103.

62 The WUL and the FUL were both CPC-linked organizations. The WUL (1929–35) sought to organize unorganized workers, relief recipients, and the unemployed, advocating for militant trade unionism to battle employers' wage cuts, refusals to bargain with existing unions, and conditions in relief camps. The FUL did likewise for farmers; it was most active organizing fights against evictions and advocating for better relief payments. Quebec's Padlock Law, or the "Act Respecting Communist Propaganda," was enacted in 1937. Under the statute, authorities could lock up for a year any building that was believed to be used for Bolshevik or communist propagation; any documents believed to be of a communist nature found therein could be ordered destroyed. Avery, "Divided Loyalties," 278. See also Peter Krawchuk, "One of the First" [biography of John Navis], translated by William Kardash, *Ukrainian Canadian*, June 1984, originally published in *Ukrainske zhyttia*, 1951, and obituary of John Weir, *Ukrainian Canadian*, January 1984; Paul Hawrylkiw, interviewed by Clara Swityk, 1976; Myron Shatulsky, interviewed by the author, 24 June 1998; monthly meeting, 3 August 1931, Women's Branch, Winnipeg, 1931 minute book, AUUC Archives; Peter Krawchuk in *Ukrainske slovo*, 12 March 1958; and report dated 22 February 1938, "ULFTA – Winnipeg," Records of CSIS, RG 146, vol. 3792, "AUUC: Winnipeg, Manitoba," part 8.

63 Report dated 20 February 1922, "CP of Canada, Ukrainian Branch, Winnipeg, Manitoba," in Records of CSIS, RG 146, "John Navis."

64 Avakumovic, *The Communist Party in Canada*, 11.

65 Joan Sangster, *Dreams of Equality: Women on the Canadian Left, 1920–1950* (Toronto: McClelland & Stewart, 1989), 55–6.

66 Avery, "Divided Loyalties," 278.

67 Kolasky, *The Shattered Illusion*, 16.

68 Avery, "Divided Loyalties," 278.

69 Krawchuk, *Our History*, 156.

70 Kolasky, *The Shattered Illusion*, 16; Krawchuk, *Our History*, 167.
71 Kolasky, *Prophets and Proletarians*, xxiv. For more on the official dialogue between the leaders of the ULFTA and the CPC, consult M. Popovich, L. Morris, S. Carr, M. Lenartovych, and I.I. Boichuk, eds., *Za bilshovyzatsiu: Polityko-ekonomichnyi ta kulturno-propagandystskyi misiachnyk tsentralnoho vykonavchoho komitetu komunistychnoi partii Kanady, 1931, issues 1-6* (Winnipeg: Labour-Farmer Publishing Association, 1931).
72 Extracts from the "Reports and Resolutions of the 12th Convention of Ukrainian Labour Farmer Temple Association in Canada held from July 15th to 20th in the Ukrainian labour temple at Winnipeg," Records of CSIS, RG 146, vol. 3792, "AUUC: Winnipeg, Manitoba," part 12.
73 John Weir, "The Flaming Torch," *Ukrainian Canadian*, 1 and 15 October 1957, reprinted *Ukrainian Canadian*, 1987.
74 Report dated 14 January 1938, "ULFTA – Winnipeg," Records of CSIS, RG 146, vol. 3732, "AUUC: Winnipeg, Manitoba," part 8.
75 Kolasky, *The Shattered Illusion*, 169.
76 For more detailed discussion of the CPC-ULFTA connection consult the standard sources cited above authored by Sangster, Avery, and Avakumovic. See also Ian Angus, *Canadian Bolsheviks: The Early Years of the Communist Party of Canada* (Victoria, BC: Trafford, 2004), and especially Jim Mochoruk's "'Pop & Co.'"
77 Frager, *Sweatshop Strife*, 212. For more on the Finnish experience consult Radforth, *Bushworkers and Bosses*, and Lindström, *Defiant Sisters*.
78 "The Ukrainians in Canada: Pt. II: Communist Organizations," n.d., Records of CSIS, RG 150, vol. 128; and *Labour-Farmer Almanac for the Leap Year of 1928*, RCMP translation, Records of CSIS, RG 146, vol. 4677, "Matthew Shatulsky," part 4.
79 Robert Conquest, *The Harvest of Sorrow: Soviet Collectivization and the Terror Famine* (New York: Oxford University Press, 1986), 165.
80 Report dated 28 November 1935, "ULFTA – (Workers and Farmers Cooperative Creamery – Winnipeg)," Records of CSIS, RG 146, vol. 3792, "AUUC: Winnipeg, Manitoba," part 7; report dated 18 December 1935, "[ULFTA] – Winnipeg," Records of CSIS, RG 146, vol. 3792, "AUUC: Winnipeg, Manitoba," part 7; report dated 17 January 1936, "ULFTA – Winnipeg – Re D. Lobay's Pamphlet," Records of CSIS, RG 146, vol. 3792, "AUUC: Winnipeg, Manitoba," part 7.
81 *Svit molodi*, June 1929, translated by L. Stavroff; and Krawchuk, *Our History*, 196–7.
82 Report dated 11 October 1934 re ULFTA, Records of CSIS, RG 146, vol. 3792: "AUUC: Winnipeg, Manitoba," part 7.

83 Report dated 7 December 1934, "Ukrainian Labour-Farmer Temple Ass'n re I. Irchan and J. Sembay," in Records of CSIS, RG 146, "John Navis."

84 Krawchuk, *Our History*, 398.

85 Report dated 2 January 1936 re ULFTA, Records of CSIS, RG 146, vol. 3792, "AUUC: Winnipeg, Manitoba," part 7; report dated 31 December 1935, "ULFTA – Winnipeg," Records of CSIS, RG 146, vol. 3792, "AUUC: Winnipeg, Manitoba," part 7; and Krawchuk, *Our History*, 396. For more information on the ULFTA higher educational courses consult chapter 3 of this book.

86 Report dated 2 January 1935, "Ukrainian Labour-Farmer Temple Association," in Records of CSIS, RG 146, "John Navis."

87 Report dated 7 February 1936, "ULFTA – Winnipeg," Records of CSIS, RG 146, vol. 3792, "AUUC: Winnipeg, Manitoba," part 7.

88 Report dated 16 February 1937, "ULFTA – Winnipeg," Records of CSIS, RG 146, vol. 3792, "AUUC: Winnipeg, Manitoba," part 7.

89 Extract from communication dated 29 January 1937, "ULFTA Winnipeg, Man.," Records of CSIS, RG 146, vol. 4677, "Matthew Shatulsky," part 2. For further reflections on the Lobay incident as well as discussion on other topics of key concern to the Ukrainian leftists during the 1930s, consult P. Prokopchak, *Za myr – proty viiny: Syla ukrainskoho narodu v yoho yednosti*, a paper delivered at a convention of the Ukrainian Labour-Farmer Mass Organizations on 22 June 1937 (Winnipeg: Central Executive Committee of the Ukrainian Labour-Farmer Temple Association, 1937).

90 Carynnyk, "Swallowing Stalinism," 198–9.

2. Raising Funds and Class-Consciousness

1 Anna Mokry and Teklia Chaban, in *Reminiscences*, ed. Krawchuk, 151–6 and 128–31.

2 Swyripa, *Wedded to the Cause*, 26.

3 Lindström, *Defiant Sisters*, 144.

4 Swyripa, *Wedded to the Cause*; Joan Sangster, "'Robitnytsia,' Ukrainian Communists, and the 'Porcupinism' Debate: Reassessing Ethnicity, Gender, and Class in Early Canadian Communism, 1922–1930," *Labour / Le Travail*, 2005: 51–89.

5 See the bulk of the essays in *Reimagining Ukrainian-Canadians*, ed. Hinther and Mochoruk, which represent recent preoccupations of scholars writing about Ukrainians in Canada. The exceptions in this book are the pieces by Rhonda L. Hinther, Stacey Zembrzycki, and Jennifer Anderson,

all of which offer commentary on Ukrainian women's experiences and activities. For additional examples see Martynowych, *The Ukrainians in Canada*, and Luciuk and Hryniuk, *Canada's Ukrainians*.

6 Swyripa, *Wedded to the Cause*; Sangster, "'Robitnytsia.'"

7 Donna R. Gabaccia and Franca Iacovetta, *Women, Gender and Transnational Lives: Italian Workers of the World* (Toronto: University of Toronto Press, 2002); Jennifer Guglielmo, "Italian Women's Proletarian Feminism in the New York City Garment Trades, 1890s–1940s," in *Women, Gender and Transnational Lives*, ed. Gabaccia and Iacovetta; and Caroline Merithew, "'Love and Solidarity': Generation and Women's Radicalism," Labouring Feminism Conference, University of Toronto, 29 September–2 October 2005. At the 2005 Labouring Feminism Conference in Toronto, where activism, transnationalism, decentring Anglo-American experiences, and cross-generational perspectives were key themes, participants addressed the subject from a variety of angles; see for example Ginetta Candelario, "Working Class Women's Activism in the Dominican Republic, 1881–1960," paper presented at the "Labouring Feminism and Feminist Working Class History in North America and Beyond" conference; and Susana Miranda, "An Unlikely Collection of Labour Militants: Portuguese Immigrant Cleaning Women on Strike, Toronto, 1984"; a number of these papers have since been published – see for example *Atlantis: A Women's Studies Journal* 32, no.1 (2007), a special issue devoted to scholarship derived from this first Labouring Feminism conference.

8 Gabaccia and Iacovetta. *Women, Gender and Transnational Lives*; Donna Gabaccia, Franca Iacovetta, and Fraser Ottanelli, "Labouring across National Borders: Class, Gender and Militancy in the Proletarian Mass Migration," *International Labor and Working Class History* 66 (Fall 2004): 57–77.

9 Swyripa, *Wedded to the Cause*, 21.

10 Swyripa, *Wedded to the Cause*, 68, 70–1; and Martynowych, *The Ukrainians in Canada*, 252.

11 Swyripa, *Wedded to the Cause*, 72.

12 Mary Slobodyn, in *Reminiscences*, ed. Krawchuk, 165–7.

13 Richard Pipes, *Russia under the Bolshevik Regime* (New York: Vintage Books, 1994), 411.

14 Maria Vynohradova, in *Reminiscences*, ed. Krawchuk, 265–72.

15 Report dated 30 December 1921, "Famine Relief Committee for Soviet Russia, Women's Unit," in Records of CSIS, RG 146, "John Navis."

16 Krawchuk, *Our History*, 367.

17 In *Our History* Krawchuk outlines the financial costs associated with running the ULTA, in his section on early conventions, 363–79. For more information on the Women's Labor Leagues and the origins of the Section of Working Women, see Maria Vynohradova in *Reminiscences*, ed. Krawchuk, 265–72; Sangster, *Dreams of Equality*, 28; "The Fiftieth Anniversary of the Women's Branches of the Association of United Ukrainian Canadians (1922–72)," in "Conventions," in Association of United Ukrainian Canadians Fonds, MG 28, V 154, National Archives of Canada (hereafter referred to as AUUC Fonds); *Robitnytsia*, 1 April 1925, translated by L. Stavroff, and *Holos robitnytsi*, January–February, 1923, translated by L. Stavroff.

18 Mary Naviziwsky, in *Reminiscences*, ed. Krawchuk, 461–3.

19 Katherine Stefanitsky, in *Reminiscences*, ed. Krawchuk, 489–96.

20 Report dated 17 February 1936, "Ukrainian Labour-Farmer Temple Association – Winnipeg," in LAC, Records of CSIS, RG 146, "John Navis."

21 Mary Naviziwsky, in *Reminiscences*, ed. Krawchuk, 461–3.

22 Ibid.

23 Ibid.

24 Ibid.

25 Introduction to, and Likeria Danylchenko in, *Reminiscences*, ed. Krawchuk, 22, 286–90; "The Ukrainians in Canada, Pt. II: Communist Organizations," Records of CSIS, RG 150, vol. 128, file AH-1999/00263; Sonia Maryn, "The Kiew ULFTA Hall: Narrative History," (Ukrainian Cultural Heritage Village Project No. 24 (Edmonton, 1984), 136; Report dated 24 September 1923, "'Golos Robitnyci' (The Voice of Working Women) – Ukrainian Monthly Magazine – Winnipeg. Re: Activities of the Working Women's Section of ULTA; Semi-annual Report of the Central Committee at the Ukrainian labour temple," Records of CSIS, RG 146, vol. 3792, "AUUC: Winnipeg, Manitoba," part 2; and Sangster, *Dreams of Equality*, 36–7.

26 *Robitnytsia*, 1 October 1927, translated by L. Stavroff.

27 For example see *Robitnytsia*, 1 March 1928.

28 In 1931, for example, the *robkorka* for the Winnipeg women's branch reported to the annual membership meeting that she had contributed eleven articles to the newspaper over the course of the previous year, detailing the group's work for the Ukrainian left. Membership meeting, 12 January 1931, Women's Branch, Winnipeg, in 1931 minute book, AUUC Archives, translated by L. Stavroff.

29 *Robitnytsia*, July–August 1924, translated by L. Stavroff.

30 Sophie Sawchuk, in *Reminiscences*, ed. Krawchuk, 387–91. Report dated
    29 November 1927, "Ukrainian Labor Farmer Temple Assn., Edmonton,
    Alta.," Records of CSIS, RG 146, vol. 3814, "AUUC Women's Branch,
    Edmonton, Alta. corresp. to 11.6.58 incl."; and *Robitnytsia*, 15 March 1928,
    translated by L. Stavroff. See also Joint Meeting of the New and Old
    Executive on 16 January 1931, Women's Branch, Winnipeg, 1931 minute
    book, AUUC Archives, translated by L. Stavroff.
31 *Robitnytsia*, 1 March 1928; Krawchuk, *Our History*, 376, 379; and "The
    Ukrainians in Canada, Pt. II: Communist Organizations," Records of
    CSIS, RG 146, vol. 128, file AH-1999/00263.For a sense of the number of
    new members gained as well as those lost in the women's branch in the
    1930s see convention reports in Krawchuk's *Our History*.
32 Report, "Ukrainian labour temple Association – Winnipeg. Re ULT
    Concert, Feb. 3, 1924," Records of CSIS, RG 146, vol. 4677, "Matthew
    Shatulsky" file, part 1.
33 Executive meeting, 3 July 1931, Women's Branch, Winnipeg, 1931 minute
    book, AUUC Archives, translated by L. Stavroff; and Mary Skrypnyk,
    interviewed by the author, 1999.
34 *Robitnytsia*, 15 January 1932 and 15 June 1926, translated by L. Stavroff.
35 Report dated 24 September 1923, "'Golos [sic] Robitnyci' – (The Voice
    of Working Women) Ukrainian Monthly Magazine – Winnipeg. Re:
    Activities of the Working women's section of the ULTA, Semi Annual
    Report of the Central Committee at the Ukrainian labour temple,"in
    LAC, Records of CSIS, RG 146, vol. 3792, "AUUC: Winnipeg, Manitoba,"
    part 2.
36 *Robitnytsia*, 15 January 1928, translated by L. Stavroff.
37 Maria Vynohradova, in *Reminiscences*, ed. Krawchuk, 265–72; see also
    Mary Naviziwsky (461–3), Parasia Koss (449–51), and Olena Holowchuk
    (256–7).
38 Report dated 30 June 1922, "Ukrainian Labor Temple Association – Women's
    Branch, Winnipeg and District," Records of CSIS, RG 146, vol. 3792, "AUUC:
    Winnipeg, Manitoba," part 1.
39 *Robitnytsia*, 1 June 1924, translated by L. Stavroff.
40 Membership meeting, 12 January 1931, and Joint Meeting of the New and
    Old Executive, 16 January 1931, Women's Branch, Winnipeg, 1931 minute
    bookAUUC Archives, translated by L. Stavroff. For additional examples
    see *Robitnytsia*, 1 January 1929, translated by L. Stavroff.
41 Anna Woynarsky, in *Reminiscences*, ed. Krawchuk, 507–8.
42 Pauline Bartko, in *Reminiscences*, ed. Krawchuk, 29–32.
43 *Robitnytsia*, 1 February 1927, translated by L. Stavroff.

44 *Robitnytsia*, 15 June 1932, translated by L. Stavroff.
45 For some recent examples of feminist scholarship related to food history, including food and ethnicity, food activism, and the meanings and politics of food consumption, consult Marlene Epp. "The Semiotics of Zwieback: Feast and Famine in the Narratives of Mennonite Refugee Women," in *Sisters or Strangers?*, ed. Epp, Iacovetta, and Swyripa; Julie Guard, "A Mighty Power against the Cost of Living: Canadian Housewives Organize in the 1930s," *International Labor & Working-Class History* no. 77 (Spring 2010): 27–47; Karen Hunt, "The Politics of Food and Women's Neighborhood Activism in First World War Britain," *International Labor and Working-Class History* 77, no. 1 (2010): 8–26; Franca Iacovetta and Valere J. Korinek, "Jell-O Salads, One-Stop Shopping, and Maria the Homemaker: The Gender Politics of Food," in Epp, Iacovetta, and Swyripa, *Sisters or Strangers?*, 190–230; and Stacey Zembrzycki, "'We Didn't Have a Lot of Money, But We Had Food': Ukrainians and Their Depression-Era Food Memories," in *Edible Histories, Cultural Politics: Towards a Canadian Food History*, ed. Franca Iacovetta, Marlene Epp, and Valerie Joyce Korinek (Toronto: University of Toronto Press, 2012), 131–9.
46 *Robitnysia*, 15 January 1934, translated by L. Stavroff.
47 Anna Andreyko, in *Reminiscences*, ed. Krawchuk, 517–21; see also Eugenia Makutra (457–60) and Mary Swityk (251–2).
48 Anna Nahorniak, in *Reminiscences*, ed. Krawchuk, 316–18.
49 See for example Maria Vynohradova, in *Reminiscences*, ed. Krawchuk, 265–72.
50 Membership meeting, 12 January 1931, Women's Branch, Winnipeg, 1931 minute book, AUUC Archives, translated by L. Stavroff. See also Anna Andreyko, in *Reminiscences*, ed. Krawchuk, 517–21.
51 Nadia Tytarenko, in *Reminiscences*, ed. Krawchuk, 376–8.
52 Paraskevia Fedosenko, in *Reminiscences*, ed. Krawchuk, 35–6.
53 Monthly meeting, 5 June 1926, minutes, ULFTA, East Kildonan Branch, 1926–8, translated by Larissa Stavroff.
54 Regular executive meeting, "28/2/27 Minutes," ULFTA, East Kildonan Branch, 1926–8, AUUC Archives; translated by L. Stavroff; program from "Canadian-Ukrainian National Music Festival, Toronto, July 15th–16th, 1939," Records of CSIS, RG 146, vol. 4677, "Matthew Shatulsky" file, part 2; Mary Naviziwsky, Serafina Romak, Waylyna [Wasylyna] Alexiewich, and Ivanna Kulyk, in *Reminiscences*, ed. Krawchuk, 461–3, 26–8, 119–27, and 399–400, respectively.
55 Avakumovic, *The Communist Party in Canada*, 35.
56 Sangster, *Dreams of Equality*, 148.

57 Sangster, *Dreams of Equality*, 69–70.
58 Meeting of Women's Section, 26 January 1931, Women's Branch, Winnipeg, 1931 minute book, AUUC Archives, translated by L. Stavroff.
59 Sangster, *Dreams of Equality*, 70.
60 Executive meeting, 23 January 1931, Women's Branch, Winnipeg, 1931 minute book, AUUC Archives, translated by L. Stavroff.
61 *Robitnytsia*, 15 May 1931, translated by L. Stavroff.
62 *Robitnytsia*, 1 November 1934, translated by L. Stavroff.
63 Sangster, *Dreams of Equality*, 5.
64 Membership meeting, 22 June 1931, Women's Branch, Winnipeg, 1931 minute book, AUUC Archives, translated by L. Stavroff.
65 Sangster, *Dreams of Equality*, 137.
66 Ibid.
67 Helen Kassian, in *Reminiscences*, ed. Krawchuk, 441–8.
68 Anna Sawchuk, in *Reminiscences*, ed. Krawchuk, 51–4.
69 Teklia Chaban, in *Reminiscences*, ed. Krawchuk, 128–31.
70 *Holos robitnytsi*, March 1923, translated by L. Stavroff.
71 *Robitnytsia*, 1 October 1927, translated by L. Stavroff.
72 Mary Yurichuk, in *Reminiscences*, ed. Krawchuk, 170–9.
73 *Robitnytsia*, 1 October 1927, translated by L. Stavroff.
74 Sangster, *Dreams of Equality*; Kealey, *Enlisting Women for the Cause*; Lindstrom, *Defiant Sisters*.)
75 Frager, *Sweatshop Strife*, 178.
76 Donna R. Gabaccia and Franca Iacovetta. *Women, Gender and Transnational Lives: Italian Workers of the World*. Toronto: University of Toronto Press 2002.
77 *Holos robitnytsi*, March 1923, translated by L. Stavroff.
78 Report dated 30 July 1937, "ULFTA Convention, Winnipeg, 1937," Records of CSIS, RG 146, vol. 3792, "AUUC – Winnipeg, Manitoba," part 7.
79 Ibid.
80 For a discussion of this in other activist contexts, see Guglielmo, "Italian Women's Proletarian Feminism."

3. Junior Participants in the Class Struggle

1 Nadya Niechoda, "Autobiography," in *Forgotten Legacy: Contributions of Socialist Ukrainians to Canada* (Winnipeg: CSULR, 1996), 7–11.
2 The relevant publications include *Women, Gender, and Transnational Lives: Italian Workers of the World*, ed. Donna R. Gabaccia and Franca Iacovetta (Toronto: University of Toronto Press, 2002), especially essays by Jennifer

Guglielmo, Caroline Merithew, and José Moya; Ardis Cameron, *Radicals of the Worst Sort: Laboring Women in Lawrence, Massachusetts, 1890–1912* (Urbana and Chicago: University of Illinois Press,1993); Lindström, *Defiant Sisters*; Mercedes Steedman, *Angels of the Workplace: Women and the Construction of Gender Relations in the Canadian Clothing Industry, 1890–1940* (Toronto: Oxford University Press, 1997); Ester Reiter, "First-Class Workers Don't Want Second-Class Wages: The Lanark Strike in Dunnville," in *A Diversity of Women: Ontario, 1945–1980*, ed. Joy Parr (Toronto: University of Toronto Press, 1995).

3 Reiter, "Secular *Yiddishkait*," and "Camp Navelt."

4 Mona Ayukawa, "Japanese Pioneer Women: Fighting Racism and Rearing the Next Generation," in *Sisters or Strangers?* ed. Epp, Iacovetta, and Swyripa, 233–47.

5 A rare exception is Neil Sutherland, *Growing Up: Childhood in English Canada from the Great War to the Age of Television* (Toronto: University of Toronto Press, 1997).

6 See for examples Joy Parr, ed., *Childhood and Family in Canadian History* (Toronto: McClelland & Stewart, 1982); Patricia Rooke and R.L. Schnell, eds., *Studies in Childhood History: A Canadian Perspective* (Calgary: Detselig Enterprises, 1982); Russell Smandych, Gordon Dodds, and Alvin Esau, eds., *Dimensions of Childhood: Essays on the History of Children and Youth in Canada* (Winnipeg: Legal Research Institute, 1990); and Craig Heron, "The High School and the Household Economy in Working-Class Hamilton, 1890–1940," *Historical Studies in Education [Canada]* 7, no. 2 (Fall 1995): 217–59.

7 Robert McIntosh, "Constructing the Child: New Approaches to the History of Childhood in Canada," *Acadiensis* 28 (Spring 1999): 126–40.

8 Robert McIntosh, *Boys in the Pits: Child Labour in Coal Mines* (Montreal and Kingston: McGill-Queen's University Press, 2000); John Bullen, "Hidden Workers: Child Labour and the Household Economy in Late Nineteenth-Century Urban Ontario," in *Canadian Family History: Selected Readings*, ed. Bettina Bradbury (Toronto: Copp Clark Pitman, 1992), 199–220; Bettina Bradbury, *Working Families: Age, Gender and Daily Survival in Industrializing Montreal, 1876–1914* (Toronto: University of Toronto Press, 1993); and David Nasaw, *Children of the City: At Work and at Play* (Garden City: Anchor Press/Doubleday, 1985).

9 Mishler, *Raising Reds*, 2.

10 Mary Ashworth, "Ukrainian Children," in *Children of the Canadian Mosaic: A Brief History to 1950* (Toronto: Ontario Institute for Studies in Education, 1993), 77–80.

11 "Report on the State of Study and Education in the Ukrainian Worker-Children's Schools," tenth ULFTA convention, 4–6 February 1929, translated by L. Stavroff; and Krawchuk, *Our History*, 245.

12 In 1927, for example, the ULFTA national convention voted to include folk dancing as a new activity for Ukrainian schoolchildren. "Re AUUC – Montreal, P. Que.," 20 January 1956, Library and Archives Canada, Records of CSIS, RG 146, vol. 3757, "AUUC: Case History Canada," part 1.

13 Translation of Ukrainian Labour News, 18 March 1933, LAC, CSIS, RG 146, vol. 3758: "AUUC, Women's Section, Canada," Part 1.

14 "Sixteenth Convention of ULFTA," 8 May 1937, LAC, Records of CSIS, RG 146, vol. 3792: "AUUC: Winnipeg, Manitoba," part 8.

15 Ollie Hillman, interviewed by the author, August 1999.

16 *Svit molodi*, March 1927, translated by L. Stavroff.

17 "Report on the 1931 Convention, ULFTA," LAC, Records of CSIS, RG 146, vol. 3792, "AUUC: Winnipeg, Manitoba," part 12; *Svit molodi*, March 1927, translated by L. Stavroff; *Programa Pratsi i navchannia v URD shkolakh* [Teaching guide for Ukrainian Worker Children's Schools] (Winnipeg, 1932), Stavroff private collection (Toronto), translated by L. Stavroff; and Krawchuk, *Our History*, 191.

18 *Programa Pratsi i navchannia v URD shkolakh* [Teaching guide for Ukrainian Worker Children's Schools].

19 Ollie Hillman, interviewed by the author, August 1999; and Krawchuk, ed., *Our Stage*, 71–9.

20 *Programa Pratsi i navchannia v URD shkolakh* [Teaching guide for Ukrainian Worker Children's Schools]; Nick Petrachenko, interviewed by the author, December, 1999; and Ollie Hillman, interviewed by the author, August 1999.

21 Nick Dubas, interviewed by the author, June 1998. For other examples see Pearl Milan, interviewed by the author, August 1999; and Olga Shatulsky, interviewed by the author, May 1998; held by the Association of United Ukrainian Canadians in Winnipeg.

22 "Re Ukrainian Labor Temple Association, Winnipeg, Concert Given at the Ukrainian Labor Temple, 25 November 1922," LAC, Records of CSIS, RG 146, vol. 3792, "AUUC: Winnipeg, Manitoba," file part 1.

23 *Ukrainski robitnychi visti*, 14 September 1926, as quoted in *Our Stage*, ed. Krawchuk, 77.

24 *Ukrainski robitnychi visti*, 21 September 1926, as quoted in *Our Stage*, ed. Krawchuk, 77.

25 Translated from Ukrainian by L. Stavroff.

26 *Ukrainski robitnychi visti*, 21 September 1926, as quoted in *Our Stage*, ed. Krawchuk, 77.

27 LAC, Records of CSIS, RG 146, vol. 3792, "AUUC: Winnipeg, Manitoba," part 10; Peter Krawchuk, "The Education of Leading Cadres by the ULFTA, 1920s–1930s," in *The Tenth Anniversary Publication of Conference Proceedings ...* (Toronto: CSULR, 1996), 32–6. Though similar in intention, the 1923 course was not called an HEC; it was only post-1925 that the course was formalized and the term *Higher Educational Course* widely used.

28 Kolasky, *The Shattered Illusion*, 10.

29 For more detailed discussion of the Parkdale orphanage, see Hinther, "Sincerest Revolutionary Greetings."

30 T. Kobzey, "What We Are Studying at the Higher Educational Course," in *Nashi sproby* [Our endeavours] (Winnipeg, 1926), a publication of the students of the Higher Educational Course of the ULFTA, translated by L. Stavroff.

31 "Re ULFTA – Winnipeg, Higher Educational Course," 20 January 1937, and "Re ULFTA, Winnipeg," 14 January 1938, LAC, Records of CSIS, RG 146, vol. 3792, "AUUC: Winnipeg, Manitoba," parts 7 and 8.

32 Olga Shatulsky, interviewed by the author, May 1998; and Mary Skrypnyk, interviewed by the author, December 1998.

33 "Re: Foreign Bolshevik-Communist Organizations," n.d. [ca. 1938], LAC, Records of CSIS, RG 146, vol. 3792, "AUUC: Winnipeg, Manitoba," part 8; and "Re Seventh Convention of ULFT Assn., held in Winnipeg on January 25–26–27, 1926," LAC, Records of CSIS, RG 146, vol. 3835, "ULFTA, Seventh National Convention, 1926," part 8.

34 John Boyd, *A Noble Cause Betrayed ... But Hope Lives On: Pages from a Political Life; Memoirs of a Former Canadian Communist* (Edmonton: CIUS, 1999), 7.

35 Kosty Kostaniuk, interviewed by the author, July 1999.

36 T. Kobzey, "What We Are Studying at the Higher Educational Course," in *Nashi sproby* [Our endeavours].

37 "Report re Seventh convention of the ULFT Assn., held in Winnipeg on January 25–26–27, 1926," LAC, Records of CSIS, RG 146, vol. 3835: "ULFTA Seventh National Convention, 1926." Also see Nick Dubas, June 1998; ; Kosty Kostaniuk, July 1999; Mary Skrypnyk, December 1998; and Bill Philipovich, May 1998, all interviewed by the author.

38 "Ukrainian Labour Farmer Temple Association – Winnipeg, Higher Educational Course," 26 October 1938, LAC, Records of CSIS, RG 146, vol. 3787, "ULFTA: Winnipeg," part 8; and "Report re ULFTA-Winnipeg,"

28 October 1936, LAC, Records of CSIS, RG 146, vol. 3792, "AUUC: Winnipeg, Manitoba," part 7.

39 Mike Seychuk, interviewed by the author, June 1998; and Krawchuk, "The Education of Leading Cadres," 32–6.

40 "Report re Ukrainian Labour Farmer Temple Association Annual Convention, 1926," LAC, Records of CSIS, RG 146, vol. 3835, "ULFTA, 7th National Convention, 1926."

41 "Youth, a Focal Point of Pride and Concern," *Ukrainian Canadian*, 15 April 1968.

42 *Svit molodi*, March 1927, translated by L. Stavroff.

43 Krawchuk, *Our History*, 389; and *Boiova molod*, September 1932, translated by L. Stavroff.

44 Mary Skrypnyk, interviewed by the author, December 1998.

45 Joyce Pawlyk, interviewed by the author, August 1999.

46 *Svit molodi*, March 1927, translated by L. Stavroff.

47 Mike Seychuk, interviewed by the author, June 1998. See also Pawlyk and Skrypnyk, interviewed by the author, AUUC Archives, Winnipeg, Manitoba.

48 *Svit molodi*, October 1927; and *Ukrainian Canadian*, 15 May 1952.

49 Krawchuk, *Our History*, 394, 399.

50 "Report on 1937 Convention, ULFTA," LAC, Records of CSIS, RG 146, vol. 3792, "AUUC: Winnipeg, Manitoba," part 8.

51 Mike Seychuk, "What the Relationship Should Be between the YCL and the YS ULFTA," *Nasha pratsia* [Our work], 5 February 1935, organizational bulletin of the central committee of the Youth Section, ULFTA, Stavroff Private Collection (Toronto), translated by L. Stavroff.

52 "Extracts from the 'Reports and Resolutions of the Twelfth Convention of Ukrainian Labour Farmer Temple Association in Canada' held 15–20 July 1931, in the Ukrainian labour temple at Winnipeg," LAC, Records of CSIS, RG 146, vol. 3792, "AUUC: Winnipeg, Manitoba," part 11.

53 "Report re: ULFTA Convention 1937," LAC, Records of CSIS, RG 146, vol. 3792, "AUUC: Winnipeg, Manitoba," part 7.

54 Fred Zwarch, "Towards a United Front of Youth against War and Fascism," *Unite the Youth*, ca. 1936, Stavroff Private Collection (Toronto).

55 See for example Niechoda, "Autobiography," 4–7.

56 J.O., "Five Years," *Unite the Youth*, ca. 1936.

57 Nick Hrynchyshyn, "What the Youth Section ULFTA Has Given to Me and What It Can Give to You," *Unite the Youth*, ca. 1936.

58 Letter written by M. Dembitski, *Svit molodi*, February 1930, translated by L. Stavroff.

59 Anna Gnit, "For a Progressive Children's Movement," *Unite the Youth*, ca. 1936.
60 Myron Shatulsky, interviewed by the author, June 1998.
61 Bruce Kidd, "Workers' Sport, Worker' Culture," in *The Struggle for Canadian Sport* (Toronto: University of Toronto Press, 1996), 164.
62 Report dated 3 February 1933, "Ukrainian Labour Farmer Temple Ass'n, Winnipeg – Sports Club Performance, Feb 2," LAC, Records of CSIS, RG 146, vol. 3792, "AUUC: Winnipeg, Manitoba," part 6.
63 *Svit molodi*, March 1927 and May 1929, translated by L. Stavroff.
64 *Resolutions of the Provincial Conference of ULFTA Youth Section, September 1–2, 1934* (Toronto: Provincial Secretariat of the Youth Section of the ULFTA, 1934), Stavroff Private Collection (Toronto), translated by L. Stavroff; and "Report re Ukrainian Labour-Farmer Temple Ass'n Schools and Instructional Methods," 2 October 1934, LAC, Records of CSIS, RG 146, vol. 3792, "AUUC: Winnipeg, Manitoba," part 7.
65 Nick Petrachenko, interviewed by the author, December, 1999.
66 Ollie Hillman, interviewed by the author, August 1999.
67 Vera Woremiuk, interviewed by the author, June 1998. Also Seychuk, Hillman, and Petrachenko, interviewed by the author.
68 Mike Seychuk, interviewed by the author, June 1998.
69 John Boyd, email to the author, 19 July 2007.
70 See *Album of the Workers Trading Cooperative Limited* (Toronto: Workers Trading Cooperative Limited, 1933).
71 Report dated 3 February 1933, "Ukrainian Labour Farmer Temple Ass'n, Winnipeg – Sports Club Performance, Feb 2," LAC, Records of CSIS, RG 146, vol. 3792, "AUUC: Winnipeg, Manitoba," part 6.
72 "Report re Seventh convention of the ULFT Assn., held in Winnipeg on January 25-26-27, 1926," LAC, Records of CSIS, RG 146, vol. 3835: "ULFTA, Seventh National Convention, 1926."
73 *Svit molodi*, April 1932, translated by L. Stavroff.
74 *Svit molodi*, March 1927, translated by L. Stavroff.
75 *Nasha pratsia [Our Work]*, ca. 1930.
76 *Svit molodi*, June 1930, translated by L. Stavroff.
77 *Boiova molod*, June 1932, translated by Orysia Zaporazan.
78 Myron Shatulsky, interviewed by the author, June 1998.
79 Bill Philipovich, interviewed by the author, May 1998.
80 Michael Korol, "AUUC Youth Discussion: 28 Years' Experience of Youth Movement," *Ukrainian Canadian*, 1 May 1953.
81 *Resolutions of the Provincial Conference of ULFTA Youth Section, September 1-2, 1934*; and *Nasha pratsia [Our Work]*, ca. 1930.

82 "Re AUUC – Montreal, P. Que.," 20 January 1956, LAC, Records of CSIS, RG 146, vol. 3757, "AUUC: Case History Canada," part 1.
83 Krawchuk, *Our Stage*, 86–8.

4. The Ukrainian Left and the Second World War

1 Mary Prokopchak, in *Reminiscences*, ed. Krawchuk.
2 Krawchuk, *Our History*, 307. The ban also covered a variety of other groups, including some alleged to be fascist in nature. That June, in all the government had declared twenty-four groups to be illegal, with an estimated total membership of 80,730 (this number did not include supporters or subscribers to related newspapers). See also Avakumovic, *The Communist Party in Canada*, 140; and Kolasky, *The Shattered Illusion*, 30. For more information on the internees' experiences see Peter Krawchuk, *Interned without Cause: The Internment of Canadian Antifascists during World War Two* (Toronto: Kobzar Publishing, 1985).
3 For detailed commentary on the UCC's formation, activities, relationship with the federal government, and slant on Ukraine's independence, see Bohdan Kordan, *Canada and the Ukrainian Question, 1939–1945: A Study in Statecraft* (Montreal and Kingston: McGill-Queen's University Press, 2001); and Thomas M. Prymak, *Maple Leaf and Trident: The Ukrainian Canadians during the Second World War* (Toronto: Multicultural History Society of Ontario, 1988).
4 Kordan, *Canada and the Ukrainian Question*; and Prymak, *Maple Leaf and Trident*.
5 See for example Ben Swankey, "Reflections of a Communist: Canadian Internment Camps," *Alberta History* 30, no. 2 (April 1982): 11–20; Krawchuk, *Interned without Cause*; Kathleen M. Repka and William Repka, eds., *Dangerous Patriots: Canada's Unknown Prisoners of War* (Vancouver, BC: New Star Books, 1982); and Ian Radforth, "Political Prisoners: The Communist Internees," in *Enemies Within*, ed. Franca Iacovetta, Roberto Perin, and Angelo Principe (Toronto: University of Toronto Press, 2000), 194–224.
6 Swyripa, *Wedded to the Cause*; Sangster, *Dreams of Equality*.
7 For examples see Reg Whitaker, "Official Repression of Communism during World War II," *Labour/Le Travail* 17 (1986): 135–66; and John Stanton, "Government Internment Policy, 1939–1945." *Labour/Le Travail* 31 (1993): 203–41.
8 For examples of various viewpoints on redress campaigns and the experiences of Japanese and Japanese Canadian internees and forced

migrants during the Second World War see Megan Heitrich, "WWII Japanese Internment Camps along the Upper Fraser," *British Columbia History* 44, no. 2 (2011): 5; Iyko Day, "Alien Intimacies: The Coloniality of Japanese Internment in Australia, Canada, and the U.S.," *Amerasia Journal* 36, no. 2 (2010): 107–24; Yuukichi Niwayama, "Caught In-Between: The Life History of a Japanese Canadian Woman Deportee," *Journal of American & Canadian Studies*, no. 28 (2010): 3–28; Pamela Sugiman, ""Life Is Sweet": Vulnerability and Composure in the Wartime Narratives of Japanese Canadians," *Journal of Canadian Studies* 43, no. 1 (2009): 186–218; Pamela Sugiman, ""A Million Hearts from Here": Japanese Canadian Mothers and Daughters and the Lessons of War," *Journal of American Ethnic History* 26, no. 4 (2007): 50–68; Steve Turnbull, "Letters from Afar," *British Columbia History* 40, no. 3 (2007): 13–15; Stephanie Bangarth, "The Long, Wet Summer of 1942: The Ontario Farm Service Force, Small-Town Ontario and the Nisei," *Canadian Ethnic Studies* 37, no. 1 (2005): 40–62; Stephanie D. Bangarth, "Religious Organizations and the 'Relocation' of Persons of Japanese Ancestry in North America: Evaluating Advocacy," *American Review of Canadian Studies* 34, no. 3 (2004): 511–40; Namiko Kunimoto, "Intimate Archives: Japanese-Canadian Family Photography, 1939–1949," *Art History* 27, no. 1 (2004): 129–55; Pamela Sugiman, "Memories of Internment: Narrating Japanese Canadian Women's Life Stories," *Canadian Journal of Sociology* 29, no. 3 (2004): 359–88;Mona Oikawa, *Cartographies of Violence: Japanese Canadian Women, Memory, and the Subjects of the Internment.* Toronto: University of Toronto Press, 2000; Masumi Izumi, "Lessons from History: Japanese Canadians and Civil Liberties in Canada," *Journal of American & Canadian Studies* no. 17 (1999): 1–24; Patricia Roy, *Mutual Hostages: Canadians and Japanese during the Second World War* (Toronto: University of Toronto Press, 1990); Ken Adachi, *The Enemy That Never Was* (Toronto: McClelland & Stewart, 1991); and Audrey Kobayaski, "Within the Barbed Wire Fence: A Japanese Man's Account of His Internment in Canada," *American Review of Canadian Studies* 11, no. 3 (1981): 93–5. Information on Italian internees can be found in Franca Iacovetta and Roberto Ventresca, "Redress, Collective Memory, and the Politics of History," in *Enemies Within*, ed. Iacovetta, Perin, and Principe, 379–412 (Toronto: University of Toronto Press, 2000). For more on Ukrainians and other Eastern Europeans interned during the First World War see Bohdan Kordan, *Enemy Aliens, Prisoners of War: Internment in Canada during the Great War* (Montreal: McGill-Queen's University Press, 2002); and Frances Swyripa, "The Politics of Redress: The Contemporary Ukrainian-Canadian

Campaign," in *Enemies Within*, ed. Iacovetta, Perin, and Principe, 355–78. For examples of camp experiences and political strategies employed in order to comfort and free internees see Pamela Sugiman, "Passing Time, Moving Memories: Interpreting Wartime Narratives of Japanese Canadian Women," *Histoire Sociale* 37, no. 73 (2004): 51–79; Radforth's "Political Prisoners," Lucio Sponza's "The Internment of Italians in Britain," Rose D. Scherini's "When Italian Americans were 'Enemy Aliens,'" and Marlene McBride's "The Curious Case of Female Internees," all in *Enemies Within*, ed. Iacovetta, Perin, and Principe. Marlene Epp's article "Heroes or Yellow-Bellies?" considers strategies employed by conscientious objectors' wives who chose to relocate and live outside the camps where their menfolk were confined for much of the war. Information on the experiences of German prisoners of war who were interned in Canada can be found in Nicole M.T. Brunnhuber, "After the Prison Ships: Internment Narratives in Canada," *Yearbook of the Research Centre for German & Austrian Exile Studies* 7, (2005): 165–78; Paul Jackson, "The Enemy within the Enemy Within: The Canadian Army and Internment Operations during the Second World War," *Left History* 9, no. 2 (2004): 45–83; Martin F. Auger. "The Harikari Club: German Prisoners of War and the Mass Escape Scare of 1944–45 at Internment Camp Grande Ligne, Quebec," *Canadian Military History* 13, no. 3 (2004): 49–67; and Sylvia Bjorkman, "Report on Camp 'W': Internment Camp '100' North of Lake Superior in World War II," *Ontario History* 89, no. 3 (1997): 237–43. For more information on experiences of Jews and other refugees interned in Canada consult Brunnhuber, "After the Prison Ship"; and Walter E. Reidel, "Exiled in Canada: Literary and Related Forms of Cultural Life in the Internment Camps," *Yearbook of German-American Studies* 24 (1989): 73–88.

9 See *Enemies Within*, ed. Iacovetta, Perin, and Principe.
10 For some examples of Luciuk's work in this regard see Lubomyr Y. Luciuk, *Without Just Cause: Canada's First National Internment Operations and the Ukrainian Canadians, 1914–1920* (Kingston, ON: Kashtan Press, 2006); *In Fear of the Barbed Wire Fence: Canada's First National Internment Operations and the Ukrainian Canadians, 1914–1920* (Kingston, ON: Kashtan Press, 2001); and "Ukrainians and Internment Operations in Ontario during the First World War," *Polyphony* 10 (October 1988): 27–31.
11 Ian Radforth, "Ethnic Minorities and Wartime Injustices: Redress Campaigns and Historical Narratives in Late Twentieth-Century Canada" (unpublished manuscript, 2005). I am grateful to Radforth for sharing this early draft of the manuscript with me; a revised version is

244 Notes to pages 107–111

featured in *Settling and Unsettling Memories: Essays in Canadian Public History*, ed. Nicole Neatby and Peter Hodgins (Toronto: University of Toronto Press, 2011).

12 Kathleen M. Repka and William Repka, "John Weir," in *Dangerous Patriots*, 59–60; and Krawchuk, *Interned without Cause*, 31.

13 Andrew Bileski, interviewed by Doug Smith, 1984–5, Provincial Archives of Manitoba, C391–C410.

14 Krawchuk, *Interned without Cause*, 20.

15 Ibid., 22–9.

16 Ibid., 24.

17 Radforth, "Political Prisoners," 196.

18 For more information on communists who were interned during the Second World War, see Radforth's "Political Prisoners."

19 Dennis Moysiuk, "A Life's Experiences in a New Land," *Ukrainian Canadian*, December 1988, originally published in *Ukrainske zhyttia*, 1951.

20 Krawchuk, *Interned without Cause*, 36; and Andrew Bileski, interviewed by Doug Smith, 1984–5, Provincial Archives of Manitoba, C391–C410.

21 Myron Kostaniuk, "Recollections from a Life of a Ukrainian Pioneer," *Ukrainian Canadian*, October 1990.

22 John Alexiewich, "Sketches from a Lifetime," *Ukrainian Canadian*, October 1991, originally published in *Ukrainske zhyttia*, 1951; letter from Matthew Shatulsky to Louis St Laurent dated 10 June 1942, Records of CSIS, RG 146, vol. 4678, "Department of Justice File Re: Matthew Shatulski and Aliases," part A.

23 Krawchuk, *Interned without Cause*, 68–72.

24 Andrew Bileski, interviewed by Doug Smith, 1984–5, Provincial Archives of Manitoba, C391–C410.

25 Krawchuk, *Interned without Cause*, 100–1.

26 Several Anglo-Celtic women with ties to the CPC were arrested and imprisoned in the Portage la Prairie jail. For more information on these women see Sangster, *Dreams of Equality*, 166–9. For a more detailed discussion on the topic of female internees consult McBride, "The Curious Case of the Female Internees," in *Enemies Within*, ed. Iacovetta, Perin, and Principe, 148–70.

27 For examples of this phenomenon see Anne Morelli's "Nestore's Wife?: Work, Family, and Militancy in Belgium," and José Moya's "Italians in Buenos Aires's Anarchist Movement: Gender Ideology and Women's Participation," in *Women, Gender, and Transnational Lives*, ed. Gabbaccia and Iacovetta.

28 For examples of how women and families in other ethnic communities dealt with the financial ramifications of internment see Sponza, "The Internment of Italians in Britain," R.J.B. Bosworth, "The Internment of Italians in Australia," and Enrico Carlson Cumbo, "'Uneasy Neighbours': Internment and Hamilton's Italians," in *Enemies Within*, ed. Iacovetta, Perin, and Principe, 256–79, 227–55, 99–119, respectively.

29 Mary Prokop, in Repka and Repka, *Dangerous Patriots*, 96–117.

30 Report dated 1 August 1940, "Ukrainian Labour Farmers Temple Association," Records of CSIS, RG 146, vol. 3792, "AUUC: Winnipeg, Manitoba," part 9.

31 Committee for the Release of Labor Prisoners, *They Fought for Labor – Now Interned!* (Winnipeg: Committee for the Release of Labor Prisoners, 1941), 25.

32 Cumbo shows how Italian women in Hamilton, Ontario, turned to family and community when their husbands were interned during the Second World War for their support of fascism – see Cumbo, "'Uneasy Neighbours,'" 107.

33 Mary Prokop, in *Dangerous Patriots*, ed. Repka and Repka, 96–117.

34 Helen Weir-Hale, in *Reminiscences*, ed. Krawchuk, 503. See also Alice Bilecki's story in *"Forgotten Legacy,"* 3–6; and Alice Bilecki, interviewed by the author, 1998.

35 Anastasia Galange, in *Reminiscences*, ed. Krawchuk, 347.

36 Mary Prokop, in *Dangerous Patriots*, ed. Repka and Repka, 105.

37 Mary Prokopchak, in *Reminiscences*, ed. Krawchuk, 476.

38 Letter from Mrs M. Shatulsky to Louis St Laurent, Minister of Justice, dated 26 August 1942, LAC, Records of CSIS, RG 146, vol. 4678: "Department of Justice File Re: Matthew Shatulski and Aliases," part A; Katherine Shatulsky, in *Reminiscences*, ed Krawchuk, 331–2.

39 Mary Prokop, in *Dangerous Patriots*, ed. Repka and Repka, 101.

40 Ibid.

41 Committee for the Release of Labor Prisoners, *They Fought for Labor – Now Interned!*

42 Mary Prokop, in *Dangerous Patriots*, ed. Repka and Repka, 96–117.

43 Ibid.

44 Ibid.; "Anti-Fascists Unjustly Interned," in *Manitoba's Program for Total War*, report of the speech delivered by Lieut. W. A. Kardash, MLA, in the Legislature, 16 December 1941 (issued by the Workers' Election Committee, Winnipeg, Manitoba).

45 Mary Prokop in *Dangerous Patriots*, ed. Repka and Repka, 103.

46 Letter from Mary Navis to Hon. L. St Laurent, Minister of Justice, dated 14 August 1942, in Records of CSIS, RG 146, "John Navis."

47 Ibid.
48 Letter from Myron Shatulsky to Minister of Justice Louis St Laurent, dated 2 April 1942, Records of CSIS, RG 146, vol. 4678, "Department of Justice File re: Matthew Shatulsky and Aliases," part A.
49 Ibid.
50 Letter from Matthew Shatulsky to Kathleen and Myron Shatulsky dated 2 September 1940, Records of CSIS, RG 146, vol. 4677, "Matthew Shatulsky," part 2.
51 Ibid.
52 Ibid.
53 Mary Prokop, in *Dangerous Patriots*, ed. Repka and Repka, 100.
54 As Lucio Sponza has shown, women with relatives interned on the Isle of Man during the Second World War devised numerous creative methods for avoiding censors and smuggling food into the camp. For more information see Sponza's "The Internment of Italians in Britain."
55 Peter Prokop, in *Dangerous Patriots*, ed. Repka and Repka, 93.
56 Ibid.
57 Kathleen M. Repka and William Repka, "John Weir," in *Dangerous Patriots*, 62.
58 *They Fought for Labor – Now Interned!*, 14.
59 Ibid., 13–14.
60 Mary Prokop in *Dangerous Patriots*, 108.
61 Committee for the Release of Labor Prisoners, *They Fought for Labor – Now Interned!*; Mary Prokop, in *Dangerous Patriots*, ed. Repka and Repka, 96–117; and Mary Prokopchak, in *Reminiscences*, ed. Krawchuk, 468–82.
62 Mary Prokop, in *Dangerous Patriots*, ed. Repka and Repka, 109.
63 Mary Prokopchak, in *Reminiscences*, ed. Krawchuk, 109.
64 *Friends in Need*, 200.
65 Eugenia Makutra, in *Reminiscences*, ed. Krawchuk, 459.
66 Niechoda, *Autobiography*, 10. Julie Dalkie recalled feeling similarly, interviewed by the author, 1999.
67 Anna Chachkowsky, in *Reminiscences*, ed. Krawchuk, 427.
68 Parasia Koss, in *Reminiscences*, ed. Krawchuk, 451.
69 Olga Shatulsky and Myron Shatulsky, interviewed by the author, 1998; and Maria Vynohradova and Anna Lapchuk, in *Reminiscences*, ed. Krawchuk, 272, 241–2.
70 Anna Andreyko, in *Reminiscences*, ed. Krawchuk. For other examples in *Reminiscences of Courage and Hope* see Eudokia Yakimchuk, Pauline Malanchuk, and Anna Semanova. See also Mary Prokop, in *Dangerous Patriots*, ed. Repka and Repka, 96–117.

71 *Globe and Mail*, 10 January 1942, 19 January 1942, 14 October 1942, 1 February 1943, and 18 October 1943.

72 Anna Andreyko, in *Reminiscences*, ed. Krawchuk, 520.

73 Maria Vynohradova, in *Reminiscences*, ed. Krawchuk, 272.

74 Beth Krall, "40th Anniversary Tribute," *Ukrainian Canadian*, 15 June 1962; and Mary Kardash, in *Reminiscences*, ed. Krawchuk, 300.

75 Mary Kardash, in *Reminiscences*, ed. Krawchuk, 301.

76 Eloise Popiel, interviewed by the author, 1998.

77 Joyce Pawlyk, interviewed by the author, 1999.

78 For additional commentary on this period of the war see Prymak, *Maple Leaf and Trident*, and Kordan, *Canada and the Ukrainian Question*.

79 *The Globe and Mail*, 28 July 1941; and Krawchuk, *Our History*, 402. To reflect the Canadian face of the movement and its support base and likely to compete with the rival Ukrainian Canadian Committee, the UAAF in 1942 changed its name to the Association of Canadian Ukrainians. The name was later changed to the Association of United Ukrainian Canadians (AUUC) in 1946.

80 Kolasky, *The Shattered Illusion*, 33.

81 Krawchuk, *Interned without Cause*, 24.

82 *Friends in Need*, 200.

83 Maria Vynohradova and Anna Holyk, in *Reminiscences*, ed. Krawchuk, 272, 39–40.

84 Waylyna [Wasylyna] Alexiewich, in *Reminiscences*, ed. Krawchuk, 126.

85 "What the Ukrainian Youth of Canada Can Do to Achieve Victory over Fascism," sent "To All Independent Canadian-Ukrainian Youth Clubs," dated 5 January 1942, from the Provincial Committee of the Ukrainian Youth Clubs in Toronto. Stavroff Private Collection.

86 Ibid.

87 RCMP intelligence report dated 10 June 1942, "Ukrainian Association to Aid the Fatherland – 1st National Convention, Winnipeg, June 4th, 5th, 6th, 1942, Changed to Association of Ukrainian Canadians," LAC, Records of CSIS, RG 146, vol. 3792, "AUUC, Winnipeg, Manitoba," part 11, page 50. For additional examples of wartime fund-raising efforts among youngsters see "What the Ukrainian Youth of Canada Can Do to Achieve Victory over Fascism," sent "To All Independent Canadian-Ukrainian Youth Clubs," dated 5 January 1942, from the Provincial Committee of the Ukrainian Youth Clubs in Toronto. Stavroff Private Collection.

88 *The Globe and Mail*, 29 December 1941 and 26 January 1942.

89 Mary Prokop, in *Dangerous Patriots*, ed. Repka and Repka, 111.

90 For examples see Sponza, Scherini, and others in *Enemies Within*, ed. Iacovetta, Perin, and Principe.

91 See Mary Naviziwsky, in *Reminiscences*, ed. Krawchuk, 463; Krawhuck, *Interned without Cause*; and records of John Navis's internment, in Records of CSIS, RG 146, "John Navis."

92 *The Globe and Mail*, 24 July 1942 and 12 August 1942; and Mary Prokop, in *Dangerous Patriots*, ed. Repka and Repka, 96–117.

93 Mary Prokop, in *Dangerous Patriots*, ed. Repka and Repka, 116.

94 Raymond Arthur Davies, *This Is Our Land: Ukrainian Canadians against Hitler* (Toronto: Progress Books, 1943), 33.

95 Eloise Popiel, interviewed by the author, 16 June 1998; and Stella Seychuk, in *Reminiscences*, ed. Krawchuk, 329.

96 Andrew Bileski, interviewed by Doug Smith, 1984–5, Provincial Archives of Manitoba, C391–C410.

97 Ibid.

98 Document dated 28 August 1942 from Louis St Laurent, Minister of Justice, Records of CSIS, RG 146, vol. 4678, "Department of Justice File re Matthew Shatulsky and Aliases," part A.

99 Radforth, "Political Prisoners: The Communist Internees," 219.

100 Report dated 1 February 1943 re John Navizowski, Records of CSIS, RG 146, "John Navis."

101 Memorandum re John Navizowsky alias Navis dated Ottawa, 19 March 1945, Records of CSIS, RG 146, "John Navis."

102 Kalyna Bazhansky, in *Reminiscences*, ed. Krawchuk, 354; see also Kalyna Mateychuk, in *Reminiscences*, 262-3.

103 Kalyna Bazhansky, in *Reminiscences*, ed. Krawchuk, 354.

104 Kolasky, *The Shattered Illusion*, 40, 42. For the contemporary AUUC perspective on the struggle consult P. Prokopchak, *Slavnu istoriiu i tradytsiiu maie TURFDim*, Boichuk I., *Borotba za lehalizatsiiu TURFDim*, speeches at the 17th Convention of the Ukrainian Labour-Farmer Temple Association in Winnipeg, Manitoba, 11–12 January 1946 (Toronto: CEC ULFTA, 1948).

105 Kalyna Bazhansky, in *Reminiscences*, ed. Krawchuk, 354; see also Kalyna Mateychuk, in *Reminiscences*, 262–3.

106 N. Kobil, "We Resume Activities in the Ukrainian Labor Temple," *Ukrainske zhyttia*, 8 June 1944, Records of CSIS, RG 146, vol. 4677, "Matthew Shatulsky," part 2.

5. "If There Had Been a Siberia"

1 Zenovy Nykolyshyn, interviewed by the author, August 1998.

2 Olga Shatulsky, interviewed by the author, 25 May 1998.

3 Zenovy Nykolyshyn and Olga Shatulsky, interviewed by the author.
4 Some key monographs include Reg Whitaker and Steve Hewitt,
   Canada and the Cold War (Toronto: Lorimer, 2003); Steve Hewitt,
   Spying 101: The RCMP's Secret Activities at Canadian Universities,
   1917–1997 (Toronto: University of Toronto Press, 2002); and Franca
   Iacovetta, *Gatekeepers: Reshaping Immigrant Lives in Cold War Canada*
   (Toronto: Between the Lines, 2006). Iacovetta's detailed examination
   of the activities of "gatekeeper" Vladimir Kaye stands as one of the
   best examples of post-war Ukrainian Canadian history to date. Two
   notable collections of articles featuring the work of some of the best
   cold-war scholars are Richard Cavell, ed., *Love, Hate, and Fear in*
   Canada's Cold War (Toronto: University of Toronto Press, 2004), and
   Dieter K. Buse, Mercedes Steedman, and Gary William Kinsman,
   Whose National Security? Canadian State Surveillance and the Creation of
   Enemies (Toronto: Between the Lines, 2000).
5 "Alberta School Principal Heads Ukrainian Canadians," *Winnipeg Free*
   Press, 1 January 1946; and report dated 15 February 1946, "Ukrainian-
   Canadian Association – National Convention – Winnipeg, Man., January
   11th to 16th, 1945," Records of CSIS, RG 146, vol. 4677, "Matthew
   Shatulsky," part 2. See also "Conventions and Conferences," in
   Krawchuk's *Our History,* 405–83.
6 Krawchuk, *Our History,* 407.
7 Interview with Wasyl Woloshynfor "Towards a New Path: The History
   of the Progressive Ukrainian Community in Saskatchewan Oral History
   Project (1976)," interviews and translations by Clara Swityk, accession
   #R80–550, Saskatchewan Archives Board, University of Regina,
   Saskatchewan.
8 Iacovetta, *Gatekeepers,* 18.
9 Lubomyr Y. Luciuk, *Searching for Place: Ukrainian Displaced Persons,*
   Canada, and the Migration of Memory (Toronto: University of Toronto
   Press, 2000), 199.
10 Letter from the National Executive Committee to All Committees,
   Branches, and Members of the AUUC, re "5th Anniversary of *Ukrainian*
   Canadian," dated 8 September 1952, AUUC Fonds, MG 28 V 154, vol. 5,
   " National Executive Committee – Minutes," file 1, "AUUC Committee,
   Minutes and Other Materials, 1951–52."
11 *Ukrainian Canadian,* May 1950.
12 Letter from the National Executive Committee to All Committees,
   Branches, and Members of the AUUC, re "5th Anniversary of *Ukrainian*
   Canadian," dated 8 September 1952. See also Krawchuk, *Our History,*
   407, 409, 415. For more on efforts to engage the younger generations

consult *Narady i ukhvaly 4-oho vsekraiovoho zizdu TOUK v ukrainskomu robitnychomu domi, 25-29 sichnia, 1950* (Toronto: Association of United Ukrainian Canadians, 1950).

13 Report dated 13 July 1962, "AUUC – Calgary, Alberta," Records of CSIS, RG 146, vol. 3818, "AUUC: Women's Branch, Calgary, Alta.," part 2.

14 Executive meeting, 13 February 1962, and annual membership meeting of English-speaking branch, 11 February 1962, in AUUC English-Speaking Branch [Winnipeg] minutes, 1960s, AUUC Archives.

15 Executive meeting, 13 February 1962, and annual membership meeting of English-speaking branch, 11 February 1962, in AUUC English-Speaking Branch [Winnipeg] minutes, 1960s, AUUC Archives.

16 "Club 326 Calendar of Activities for 1968," AUUC Fonds, MG 28, V 154, vol. 13, file 3.

17 Executive meeting, 27 February 1962, and annual membership meeting of English-Speaking Branch, 11 February 1962, in AUUC English-Speaking Branch [Winnipeg] minutes, 1960s, AUUC Archives.

18 Executive meeting, 30 November 1947, minutes, 1947–8, English-Speaking Branch #324, Winnipeg, Manitoba, AUUC Archives.

19 "AUUC Doings by Rose Mickoluk," *Ukrainian Canadian*, 15 December 1953.

20 For examples of activities see letters from Mrs Victoria Kassian and Emma Shewchuk, in AUUC Fonds, MG 28, V 154, vol. 13, file 7, "AUUC: English-Speaking Branches, Edmonton, 1956"; report from delegate from Winnipeg English-speaking branch, AUUC Fonds, MG 28, V 154, container 2, "Conventions," file 20, "AUUC: 8th National Convention" [1958]; and letter from Hazel Strashok, Young Women's Club, Edmonton, AUUC Fonds, MG 28, V 154, vol. 13, file 4, "Correspondence: AUUC – English-Speaking Branches, 1961–62."

21 Letter dated 29 January 1951 from William Teresio, AUUC Fonds, MG 28, V 154, vols. 11–12, "Correspondence – Women's Branches,"file 20, "Branches," translated by Myron Momryk.

22 Letter dated 29 January 1951 from William Teresio, and letter dated 1 December 1956 from Women's Branch, Vancouver, AUUC Fonds, MG 28, V 154, vols. 11–12, files 19–34 and 1–5, "Correspondence – Women's Branches," translated by M. Momryk.

23 Bohdan Bociurkiw, "The Federal Policy of Multiculturalism and the Ukrainian-Canadian Community," in *Ukrainian Canadians, Multiculturalism, and Separatism: An Assessment* (Edmonton: CIUS, 1978), 104–5; Julia Lalande, "The Roots of Multiculturalism: Ukrainian-Canadian Involvement in the Multiculturalism Discussion of the 1960s as

an Example of the Position of the 'Third Force,'" *Canadian Ethnic Studies* 38, no. 1 (2006): 47–64.

24 Mitch Sago, "The Third Element," *Ukrainian Canadian*, 1 May 1968. See also "Policy Statement of the 13th Convention on the Crisis of Confederation," *Ukrainian Canadian*, 1 May 1968. For more on the AUUC's perspective on this issue and others of contemporary concern at the time of the Ukrainian left's sixtieth anniversary (dated from the founding of the ULTA), consult *Six Decades of Progress, 1918–1978: Our Commitment to the Future in a United Canada*, proceedings of the special joint convention, Association of United Ukrainian Canadians and the Workers Benevolent Association of Canada (Winnipeg: AUUC and WBA of Canada, 1978).

25 See for example a report, "Oshawa, Ontario," *Ukrainske zhyttia*, 17 December 1958, Records of CSIS, RG 146, vol. 128, "AUUC: Oshawa"; "On Organizational Activity of the Women's Branch of the AUUC in Calgary in 1954," *Ukrainske slovo*, 16 February 1955, translated by RCMP, Records of CSIS, RG 146, vol. 3818, "AUUC: Women's Branch, Calgary, Alta.," part 1; Minutes, National Women's Committee Meeting, 11 Jan 1967, in LAC, AUUC Fonds MG 28 V 154, file 4: "AUUC: National Women's Committee, 1963–69," vol. 4, "National Committee."

26 Mary Skrypnyk, "Highlights of the Convention," *Ukrainian Canadian*, 1 March 1948.

27 Letter dated 31 January 1972 to National Women's Committee AUUC, Toronto, Ontario, from Mary Kardash in an envelope labelled "50th Anniversary Women's Branches, AUUC," 1972 pile of envelopes held together with an elastic band and labelled "Provcom Women's Committee," room 6, AUUC Archives; and meeting, NWC, 15 November 1967, AUUC Fonds MG 28 V 154, vol. 4, "National Committee," file 4, "AUUC: National Women's Committee, 1963–69." Contemporary commemorations of the women's branch's history include *Almanakh piatdesiatyrichchia zhinochykh viddiliv Tovarystva obiednanykh ukrainskykh kanadtsiv, 1922–1972*, ed. Petro Prokopchak (Toronto: Kobzar, 1976).

28 Memorandum from National Executive Committee to Women's Branch and Clubs dated 19 October 1965, translated by RCMP, Records of CSIS, RG 146, vol. 128.

29 Mary Prokopchak, in *Reminiscences*, ed. Krawchuk, 468–82. See also Mike Mokry, "Manitoba AUUC Plans Geared to Centennial," *Ukrainian Canadian*, 1 April 1967; and a letter dated 2 December 1965 from Mary Prokop, Secretary of National Women's Committee, and minutes of

National Women's Committee meeting, 12 June 1967, in AUUC Fonds, MG 28, V 154, vol. 4, "National Committee," file 4, "AUUC: National Women's Committee, 1963–69."

30 Mary Prokop, "Introduction and Discussion of Resolution on Work in the Women's Field," AUUC Fonds MG 28 V 154, vol. 2, "Conventions," file 29, "AUUC: 13th National Covention, 1968."

31 Letter dated 2 December 1965 from Mary Prokop, secretary of AUUC National Women's Committee, sent to AUUC Provincial Women's Committee in Winnipeg, AUUC Fonds MG 28 V 154, vol. 4, "National Committee," file 4, "AUUC: National Women's Committee, 1963–69."

32 See for example *Zhyttia i slovo*, 2 March 1970, translated by RCMP, Records of CSIS, RG 146, vol. 3818, "AUUC: Women's Branch, Calgary, Alta.," part 3.

33 "Ukrainian Cross-Stitch Goes Mod," *Ukrainian Canadian*, October 1969.

34 These opportunities will be discussed in greater detail in the next chapter.

35 Myron Shatulsky, interviewed by the author, 1998.

36 Ibid.

37 Krawchuk, *Our Stage*, 278.

38 Ibid., 280.

39 Steve Macievich, as quoted in Krawchuk, *Our Stage*, 280.

40 Letter from Regina English-Speaking Branch dated 8 February 1951, AUUC Fonds, MG 28, V 154, vol. 12, file 28, "AUUC: English-Speaking Branches, 1951." See also Mary Skrypnyk, "Windsor Festival – A Triumph," *Ukrainian Canadian*, 1 April 1961.

41 English-Speaking Branch membership meeting, 9 October 1962, AUUC English-Speaking Branch [Wpg] minutes, ca. 1960, room 6, AUUC Archives.

42 For more information on the organizational structure and a polarized indictment of the AUUC leadership and their involvement with these enterprises see Kolasky, "The Great Dilemma," in *The Shattered Illusion*, 200–20.

43 Mary Prokop, in *Reminiscences*, ed. Krawchuk, 468–82.

44 Mary Skrypnyk, interviewed by the author, 1999; see also the experiences of Eloise Popiel and Mary Semanowich, interviewed by the author, 1998.

45 E.A. Bilecki, interviewed by the author, 1999.

46 The Labour Progressive Party came to be called the Communist Party of Canada again, in 1959.

47 Report on Regina dated 7 November 1950, sent to William Teresio from Bill Harasym, AUUC Fonds MG 28 V 154, vol. 24, "Correspondence – Individuals," file 10, "Harasym, William, 1950–51, 1962–65."

48 Report dated 6 November 1958, "Labour-Progressive Party, Edmonton, Alta.," Records of CSIS, RG 146, vol. 3818, "AUUC Men's Branch No. 2, Edmonton, Alta. corresp. to 6-6-58 to 9-5-62," part 2.
49 Biography of Nick Hrynchyshyn, *Ukrainske slovo*, 30 May 1945; "Candidates Who Put Canada First," *Ukrainian Canadian*, 1 August 1953; and "Name Labour Candidates for Winnipeg Elections," *Ukrainian Canadian*, 1 October 1968.
50 *Ukrainske zhyttia*, 20 March 1947, Records of CSIS, RG 146, vol. 4677, "Matthew Shatulsky," part 4.
51 Misha Korol to Mary Kardash, letter dated 2 January 1951, AUUC Fonds, MG 28 V 154, vol. 12, file 29, "AUUC: English-Speaking Branches, 1951."
52 Iacovetta, *Gatekeepers*, 9; and Luciuk, *Searching for Place*, xxiii. For additional analysis of these post-war émigrés, particularly their political activities, their interpretation of Ukrainian history, and constructions and performance of Ukrainianness in Canada, consult John Paul Himka's insightful article "A Central European Diaspora under the Shadow of World War II: The Galician Ukrainians in North America," *Austrian History Yearbook* 27 (2006): 17–31. Luciuk's *Searching for Place* includes an important and nuanced discussion of the ways in which the displaced persons' sense of Ukrainianness, connection to Ukraine, and activism differed from those of prior cohorts of Ukrainian migrants, so much so that it gave rise to considerable rivalry within the nationalist factions of the Ukrainian community in Canada.
53 Report dated 20 December 1949, "AUUC, Toronto, Ontario meeting held at 300 Bathurst, Sunday 11th December," in Records of CSIS, RG 146, "John Navis."
54 Matthew Shatulsky, "Inner Politics of the DP's," *Ukrainian Canadian*, 15 December 1948, Records of CSIS, RG 146, vol. 4678, "Matthew Shatulsky," part 5(2); press release, dated 4 May 1949 from Teresio, President, and Prokop, Secretary, to Prime Minister Louis St Laurent, AUUC Fonds, MG 28, V 154, vol. 24, "Correspondence – Individuals," file 26, "Teresio, William, 1948–49"; and Avery, *Reluctant Host*, 157.
55 Report dated 28 October 1948, "Association of United Ukrainian Canadians, Saskatchewan, General," in RCMP files, "AUUC: Saskatchewan, Correspondence," vol. 3742, part 4; "Concerning the Visit of Peter Kravchuk in Winnipeg," *Ukrainske slovo*, 26 October 1949, as translated in Records of CSIS, RG 146, vol. 4678, "Matthew Shatulsky," part 5 (3); and "Put an End to Gangsterism of DP's: Canada Is Not Hitlerite Germany," *Ukrainske zhyttia*, 15 December 1949, in Records of CSIS, RG 146, "John Navis."

56 RCMP report dated 14 October 1950, "Association of United Ukrainian Canadians, 300 Bathurst St., Toronto, Ontario," Records of CSIS, RG 146, vol. 2623.

57 "These Are the Criminals" and "The Indictment," in undated AUUC pamphlet, Records of CSIS, RG 146, vol. 2623. See also "Former SS Troops Blamed for Blast at Labor Temple," *Globe and Mail*, 10 October 1950.

58 Roman Rakhmanny, as quoted in "Holds Bomb Blast Work of Reds to Mislead Public," *Globe and Mail*, 11 October 1950; and "Deny Red Insinuations on Planting of Bomb," *Globe and Mail*, 14 October 1950.

59 Memorandum for the monthly letter, n.d., Records of CSIS, RG 146 vol. 2623.

60 Interview with Olga Shatulsky.

61 "'UC' Manager Brutally Attacked During Recent Campaign Tour," *Ukrainian Canadian*, 15 Feb 1962.

62 Olga Shatulsky, interviewed by the author, May 1998.

63 Joe Behie, quoted in "Timmins AUUC Battles for a Concert Hall," *Ukrainian Canadian*, 15 April 1962. See also the experiences of Mitch Sago who was attacked while on tour in Vancouver, *Ukrainian Canadian*, 15 February 1962.

64 Letter to the Editor (no newspaper listed), 1949, AUUC Fonds, MG 28, V 154, vol. 38, "National Executive Committee – Circulars and Newsletters," file 29; Zenovy Nykolyshyn, interviewed by the author, August 1998; report, "2nd Session on March 21, 1966," in RCMP report, "AUUC, 12th National Convention, 1966," Records of CSIS, RG 150, vol. 128.

65 Gary Kinsmen, "The Canadian Cold War on Queers," in *Love, Hate, and Fear in Canada's Cold War*, ed. Richard Cavell (Toronto: University of Toronto Press, 2004), 121.

66 Zenovy Nykolyshyn, interviewed by the author, August 1998.

67 The *Ukrainian Canadian* throughout 1962 carried articles and features on the campaign; see for examples the issues of 15 November, 1 June, and 1 March. See also John Weir, *The Case of Canada's Stepchildren: Foreign-Born Canadians Discriminated Against by the Department of Citizenship and Immigration* (Toronto: Canadian Slav Committee, 1961).

68 Barbara Mashtalar, "Story of a Second Class Citizen," *Ukrainian Canadian*, 15 June 1962.

69 Joseph Zuken, "Memorandum to Minister Bell and MP's," *Ukrainian Canadian*, 15 November 1962; and obituary of Mitch Sago, *Ukrainian Canadian*, September 1989.

70 Avakumovic, *The Communist Party in Canada*; report dated 28 October 1948, "Association of United Ukrainian Canadians, Saskatchewan, General," Records of CSIS, RG 146, vol. 3792, "AUUC: Saskatchewan, Correspondence," part 4; "Concerning the Visit of Peter Kravchuk in Winnipeg," *Ukrainske slovo*, RCMP translation, Records of CSIS, RG 146, vol. 4678, "Matthew Shatulsky," part 5(3); and Bilecki, Shatulsky, and Nykolyshyn, interviewed by the author. For a detailed discussion of party relations in this period see Kolasky, "Relations with the Communist Party," in *The Shattered Illusion*, 140–54.

71 "Report of the Delegation to Ukraine: Central Committee Meeting – September 16, 17, and 18, 1967," *Viewpoint* [discussion bulletin issued by the central executive committee, Communist Party of Canada], January 1968.

72 Mary Prokopchak, in Krawchuk, *Reminiscences*, 468–82.

73 Julie Guard, "Canadian Citizens or Dangerous Foreign Women?" in *Sisters or Strangers?*, ed. Epp, Iacovetta, and Swyripa (Toronto: University of Toronto Press, 2004), 161–89.

74 For an extensive discussion of the policies of the Canadian Peace Congress and the views and work of Endicott see Victor Huard's "The Canadian Peace Congress and the Challenge to Postwar Consensus, 1948–53," *Peace and Change* 19, no. 1 (1994): 25–49.

75 Letter from Timmins women's branch dated 24 May 1955 to National Women's Committee, AUUC, translated by Myron Momryk, AUUC Fonds, MG 28, V 154, vol. 11, "Correspondence – Women's Branches," file 24, "Branches."

76 Letter from Vancouver women's branch dated 18 May 1955 to National Women's Committee, AUUC, translated by Myron Momryk, AUUC Fonds, MG 28, V 154, vol. 11, "Correspondence – Women's Branches," file 24, "Branches."

77 Huard, "The Canadian Peace Congress," 46.

78 *Ukrainske zhyttia*, 20 January 1955, RCMP translation, Records of CSIS, RG 146, vol. 3814, "AUUC Women's Branch, Edmonton, Alta. corresp. to 11.6.58 incl."; for an additional example see a letter from the Young Women's Club dated 8 March 1959 to Duff Roblin and the Mayor of Winnipeg in an envelope labelled "AUUC Women's Committee, Handicraft Display and Baking Sale," in a collection of envelopes labelled "Provcom Women's Committee," AUUC Archives.

79 Mary Prokop, "Introduction and Discussion of Resolution on Work in the Women's Field," AUUC Fonds, MG 28, V 154, vol. 2, "Conventions," file 29, "AUUC: 13th National Convention, 1968"; and a letter dated 18

December 1968 from Beth Krall and Mary Kardash, Provincial Women's Committee, Manitoba, to National Women's Committee, AUUC, Toronto, in an envelope marked "Correspondence: Provincial Women's Committee, AUUC, 1969–70," in a collection of envelopes marked "Provcom Women's Committee," AUUC Archives.

80 For a detailed and thoughtful discussion of post-war women's activism framed though a motherhood lens consult Tarah Brookfield's *Cold War Comforts: Canadian Women, Child Safety, and Global Insecurity, 1945–1975* (Waterloo, ON: Wilfrid Laurier University Press, 2012).

81 Hannah Polowy, "Report to the Women's Conference, AUUC, BC, 1963," in "AUUC Women's Committee Correspondence, Mailing List," AUUC Archives.

82 Mary Kardash, "March 8 – Women's Day," *Ukrainian Canadian*, 1 March 1952.

83 Katherine Stefanitsky, in *Reminiscences*, ed. Krawchuk, 489–96.

84 Memorandum dated 10 November 1965, "Upcoming Campaign," from National Women's Committee, NEC, AUUC, to Women's Branches and Club, Records of CSIS, RG 146, vol. 128.

85 "Free Education Important Point in AUUC Brief on Status of Women," *Ukrainian Canadian*, 15 June 1968.

86 Mary Semanowich, interviewed by the author, May 1998.

87 Beth Krall, interviewed by the author, July 1998.

88 Letter dated 23 January 1960 from Hazel Strashok, Young Women's Club, Edmonton, AUUC Fonds, MG 28 V 154, vol. 13, "Correspondence – English-Speaking Branches," file 4, "Correspondence: AUUC – English-Speaking Branches, 1961–62."

89 See for examples vol. 6, "Organization/Fund-Raising Campaigns," in AUUC Fonds, MG 28, V 154; letter dated 19 September 1963 from NEC, AUUC, Toronto, to all provincial and district committees and branches, AUUC, RCMP translation, Records of CSIS, RG 146, vol. 128; "AUUC Organizational Campaign in 1963," *Ukrainske zhyttia*, 24 April 1963, RCMP translation, Records of CSIS, RG 146, vol. 128; "New Membership Report for Period between X and XI Conventions," AUUC Fonds, MG 28, V 154, vol. 2, "AUUC: 12th National Convention 1966"; and "National Membership Totals since 33rd and 32nd and 33rd Conventions," AUUC Fonds, MG 28, V 154, vol. 5, "National Executive Committee – Minutes."

90 RCMP, "Annual Report for Ontario Concerning the AUUC in 1974 re AUUC – Canada," Records of CSIS, RG 146, vol. 3756, "Association of United Ukrainian Canadians – National Executive Committee Canada," part 21, p. 103.

91 "Membership in All Branches Including Youth Clubs (But Not Children) C. 33rd National Convention," AUUC Fonds, MG 28, V 154, vol. 3, file 6.

6. Children, Youth, and the Post-War Ukrainian Left

1 Mary Skrypnyk, "Little Irene," *Ukrainian Canadian*, September 1981 (special edition in honour of ninety years of Ukrainians in Canada), 60–1. Reprinted from *Ukrainian Canadian*, 1951.

2 Ibid.

3 In 1947 the AUUC National Executive Committee merged all existing youth groups and sports clubs into a single national English-language body called the Youth Division of the AUUC.

4 *Leader's Guide* (Toronto: AUUC National Junior Council, Fall/Winter, 1959).

5 Ibid.

6 Ibid. See also the letter dated 8 May 1952 from AUUC National Executive Committee to all Youth Clubs, Youth and AUUC Choirs, Orchestras, Dancing and Other Groups and Young People, in "E/S Branch and Youth Winnipeg," AUUC Archives, which argues that the Youth Division's purpose was to unite and "build up a powerful youth organization dedicated to the promotion of peace and democracy, to provide the means for progressive education, to the development of the arts (and particularly the arts of the Ukrainian people), to the development of sports and healthy recreation, to organize wholesome social activities, and in all, to build the character of our young generation which is destined to play a most tremendous role in the Canada of tomorrow."

7 "Discussion Memo on Children's Work in the AUUC," n.d., in "Junior Section – Winnipeg" files, AUUC Archives.

8 Resolution on children's work, AUUC Fonds, MG 28 V 154, vo.l 2, "Conventions," file 18, "AUUC: 8th National Convention."

9 *Leader's Guide*, Fall/Winter, 1959.

10 Mary Kardash to Mary Skrypnyk, 21 May 1952, in "E/S Branch and Youth Wpg," AUUC Archives, room 6.

11 "CANADA," *Leader's Guide*, November 1962. Other examples of songs can be found in the aforementioned issue as well as in the November 1962 and September 1963 editions of the guide.

12 Peter Lari Prokop, interviewed by the author, 1999.

13 In its September 1963 issue, for example, the *Leader's Guide* explained the purpose of bazaars and suggested the juniors set up a fish-pond booth at their hall's next bazaar to raise money for the AUUC.

14 *Leader's Guide*, Fall/Winter 1959.

15 *Leader's Guide*, Fall/Winter 1959, November 1962, January 1953, and 15 January 1964.

16 "With Our Juniors," *Ukrainian Canadian*, 1 June 1948; Vera Pauk, "Juniors Have a Busy Year," *Ukrainian Canadian*, 15 April 1961.

17 *Ukrainian Canadian*, 15 April 1948.

18 *Leader's Guide*, Fall/Winter, 1959.

19 File 1, "Correspondence: AUUC – English-Speaking Branches, 1951," in vol. 13, "Correspondence – English-Speaking Branches," AUUC Fonds, MG 28 V 154.

20 "With Our Juniors," *Ukrainian Canadian*, 15 December 1963 and 15 May 1948.

21 Olga Dzatko, "With Our Juniors," *Ukrainian Canadian*, 1 June 1967.

22 Letter from Mary Kardash to Mary Skrypnyk, 21 May 1952, file "E/S Branch and Youth Wpg," found in Room 6, WBA Archives.

23 "1947–48 Annual Report on the Following Mass Language Organizations – Ukrainian, Hungarian, Polish, Russian, Finnish, and Jewish," in Records of CSIS, RG 146, vol. 3757, "AUUC: Case History Canada," part 1.

24 *Ukrainian Canadian*, 15 June 1953.

25 Mary Skrypnyk, interviewed by the author, 1999; "Misha Korol Tours West Provinces," *Ukrainian Canadian*, 1 November 1947; and meeting of 1 March 1949, minutes of Fort William Youth Section, AUUC, housed at AUUC hall, Toronto, Ontario.

26 *Ukrainian Canadian*, 15 August 1952.

27 *Ukrainian Canadian*, January–May, 1953.

28 Letter dated 17 January 1952 from Misha Korol, National Executive Committee, to Mike Mokry, Winnipeg, AUUC Fonds, MG 28 V 154, vol. 12, "Correspondence – English-Speaking Branches," file 29, "AUUC: English-Speaking Branches, 1951." Letter from Bill Harasym and Peter Prokop, National Executive Committee, to Executive Committees and AUUC-sponsored Cultural Groups re "Participating Observer-Delegates from AUUC-sponsored Cultural Groups to the XIIIth AUUC National Convention," AUUC Fonds, MG 28 V 154, vol. 2, "Conventions," file 29, "AUUC: 13th National Convention, 1968."

29 *Forward*, 1954, Stavroff Private Collection.

30 Minutes of meeting on 18 October 1964, Fort William Youth Section, AUUC, housed at AUUC hall in Toronto; Vera Seychuk, interviewed by the author, 30 October 1999.

31 Minutes of meeting on 22 March 1949, Fort William Youth Section, AUUC, housed at AUUC hall in Toronto.

32 Vera Seychuk, interviewed by the author, 30 October 1999.

33 Similarly, girls assisted the women who worked in the kitchens at hall events; the girls of the Edmonton Ukrainian cultural centre in 1960, for instance, assisted with the Mother's Day tea and other events at the hall that year. See for example "Report on Annual Meeting, February 15, 1960, Edmonton Women's Branch," in AUUC Fonds, MG 28 V 154, vols. 11–12, "Correspondence – Women's Branches."

34 1963 National Youth Conference Resolution on Sports, as printed in *Forward*, December 1963; "Proposed Resolutions for the Second National Convention Youth Division AUUC," ca. 1956, AUUC Fonds, MG 28 V 154, vol. 2, "Conventions," file 6, "AUUC 7th Convention."

35 1963 National Youth Conference Resolution on Sports, as printed in *Forward*, December 1963, Stavroff Private Collection.

36 Ibid.

37 Letter dated 15 March 1958 from Donald Kazakoff to National Youth Council, AUUC Fonds, MG 28 V 154, vols. 26–7, "Youth and Related Issues," file 26, "AUUC: Youth Correspondence."

38 Examples include the AUUC track and field meet held at Ville La Salle, Quebec, described in "Greater Montreal Athletes Compete in Track Meet" and "Toronto Slavic Softball Club," *Ukrainian Canadian*, 1 September 1947.

39 AUUC review [Point Douglas, Winnipeg], April 1949, AUUC Archives.

40 Misha Korol, "Our Golden Jubilee," *Forward*, Fall 1957.

41 Meeting, 31 March 1968, Fort William Youth Section, AUUC, housed at AUUC hall in Toronto.

42 Meeting, 1 October 1967, Fort William Youth Section, AUUC, housed at AUUC hall in Toronto.

43 Ibid.

44 Donna Yakimovich, interviewed by the author, 30 October 1999.

45 Vera Seychuk, interviewed by the author, 30 October 1999.

46 Olga Shatulsky, interviewed by the author, 25 May 1998.

47 Peter Lari Prokop, interviewed by the author, 10 December 1999.

48 Olga Berketa Dzatko, unpublished autobiography written in May 2001.

49 For some examples see Olga Shatulsky, interviewed by the author, 25 May 1998; Mary Skrypnyk, interviewed by the author, 1999; Myron Shatulsky, interviewed by the author, June 1998; and Olga Berketa Dzatko, unpublished autobiography written in May 2001.

50 Avakumovic, *The Communist Party in Canada*, 269.

51 Ibid., 270.

52 AUUC Information brief, 15 September 1969, RG 146, vol. 3757, "AUUC: Case History Canada," part 7.

53 "AUUC Youth Division Workshop, March 27–29, 1967," AUUC Fonds, MG 28 V154, vol. 27, file 25, "AUUC – Youth Division Workshop, 1967."

54 Olga Shatulsky, interviewed by the author, 1998.

55 "With Our Juniors," *Ukrainian Canadian*, 15 January 1953.

56 Peter Lari Prokop, interviewed by the author, 10 December 1999.

57 Bob Seychuk, interviewed by the author, 3 August 1999.

58 Olga Berketa Dzatko, unpublished autobiography written in May 2001.

59 "Regina Dancers Win Top Honours," *Ukrainian Canadian*, April 1970.

60 "AUUC Youth Division Workshop, March 27–29, 1967," in AUUC Fonds, MG 28 V154, vol. 27, file 25, "AUUC: Youth Division Workshop, 1967."

61 Unnamed text book, quoted in a report entitled "The Association of United Ukrainian Cdns," compiled by the Research Section, Records of the CSIS, RG 146, vol. 3757, "AUUC: Case History Canada," part 1.

62 *Ukrainske zhyttia*, 6 January 1955, as translated in LAC, Records of CSIS, RG 146, vol. 128, part 1.

63 Myron Shatulsky, interviewed by the author, June 1998.

64 Various labour temple associations owned picnic grounds or made use of farmland for overnight camping excursions and day activities during the 1920s and 1930s.

65 Letter to World Federation of Democratic Youth from Stanley Dobrowolsky, n.d., AUUC Fonds, MG 28 V 154, vol. 11, "Correspondence – Junior Section," file 3, "AUUC: Junior Council – National, 1963–64"; Donna Yakimovich, interviewed by the author, 1999; *Ukrainian Canadian*, 15 June 1961, 15 June 1965, July/August 1971; and membership meeting, 21 February 1965, Fort William Youth Section, minute book, AUUC hall, Toronto, Ontario.

66 AUUC Provincial Women's Committee, records of meetings, November 1959–June 1961–February 1963, in Provincial Women's Committee files, n.d., AUUC Archives; "South Ontario Labour Festival at Palermo," *Ukrainian Canadian*, 1 August 1961; "20,000 Slav Canadians Enjoy Fun, Festivities at 2-Day Picnic Rally: Strengthening the Ties of Unity, Brotherhood," *Ukrainian Canadian*, 15 July 1948; and report dated 16 July 1958, "AUUC Southern Ontario District Festival Picnic," Records of CSIS, RG 146, vol. 3757, "AUUC: Case History, Canada," part 4.

67 See for examples Melody Bileski, Betsy Bilecki, Nancy Kardash, and Carmen Kostaniuk, "Letters from Camp Husavik," *Ukrainian Canadian*, 16 August 1953.

68 Reiter, "Camp Naivelt and the Daughters of the Jewish Left,"; Mishler, *Raising Reds*, 83.

69 Peter Lari Prokop, interviewed by the author, 10 December 1999.

70 "Rival Ukrainian Camps Highway Neighbours," *Globe and Mail*, 4 August 1964. Olga Shatulsky, interviewed by the author, 1998.
71 Olga Shatulsky, interviewed by the author, 1998.
72 Walter Rosiewich, Gordon Lake camp director, "Junior Readers Enjoy Camp Life: Alberta Summer Camp a Rewarding Program," *Ukrainian Canadian*, 15 August 1963.
73 Lucy Nykolyshyn, interviewed by the author, 1998.
74 Steve Karlash, "A Youth Hostel for Palermo Camp," *Ukrainian Canadian*, 1 January 1968.
75 Olga Berketa Dzatko, unpublished autobiography written in May 2001.
76 Speech by Bill Malynychuk, n.d., AUUC Fonds, MG 28 V 154, vol. 2, "Conventions," file 14, "Speeches – AUUC 7th Convention."
77 Letter dated 12 June 1956 from Hannah Polowy, AUUC Vancouver, to Stanley Dobrowolsky, AUUC Fonds, MG 28 V 154, vol. 26, "Youth and Related Issues," file 25, "AUUC: Youth School, Winnipeg, 1956, Correspondence."
78 AUUC Fonds, MG 28 V 154, vol. 26, "Educational Activities," file 8, "AUUC: Applicants, Higher Educational Course, 1950."
79 Olga Shatulsky and Myron Shatulsky, interviewed by the author, 1998; AUUC Fonds, MG 28 V 154, vol. 27, "Youth and Related Issues," file 23, "AUUC: Youth Course, 1952"; AUUC Fonds, MG 28 V 154, vol. 26, "Educational Activities," file 4, "AUUC: Applicants, Higher Educational Course, 1950"; Olga Berketa, "AUUC Youth School," *Ukrainian Canadian*, 1 August 1953; and Michael Korol, "AUUC Doings," *Ukrainian Canadian*, 1 July 1948.
80 Olga Shatulsky, interviewed by the author, 1998.
81 AUUC Fonds, MG 28 V 154, vol 26, "Educational Activities," file 4, "AUUC: Applicants, Higher Educational Course, 1950."
82 For example, students interested in the "Western Workshop for Dance Cadres," which was planned for the summer of 1960, were reluctant to attend because of the dates of the course – they needed to spend the whole summer working to pay for university in the fall. Letter from Betty L. Nahorniak, Youth Council Secretary, to National Youth Division, AUUC – National Executive Committee, 9 June 1960, AUUC Fonds, MG 28 V 154, vol 27, "Youth and Related Issues," file 26, "AUUC: Youth Correspondence." See also Ray Yakimchuk to Stan Dobrowolsky, 7 June 1956, AUUC Fonds, MG 28 V 154, vol. 16, "Correspondence – Branches," file 3.
83 "Report on the 1962 AUUC Youth School, Aug. 5 to Aug. 26," AUUC Fonds, MG 28 V154, vol. 27, "Youth and Related Issues," file 1, "AUUC: Youth Schools, 1961–1962, Alberta, Correspondence, Reports."

84 "Association of United Ukrainian Canadians: Information Brief," 15 September 1969, Records of CSIS, RG 146, vol. 3757, "AUUC: Case History Canada," part 7.

85 Letter from Bill Harasym to "All Registrants for the Eighth National AUUC Youth Seminar and Conference, All AUUC Provincial and District Committees," AUUC Fonds, MG 28 V 154, vol. 27, "Youth and Related Issues," file 30, "AUUC: 8th Youth Conference and Seminar, 1974."

86 Mike Seychuk, interviewed by the author, 1998; and Peter Krawchuk, "The Education of Leading Cadres by the ULFTA, 1920's–1930's," in *The 10th Anniversary Publication of Conference Proceedings of CSULR* ... (CSULR: Toronto, 1996), 32–6.

87 "Association of United Ukrainian Canadians: Information Brief," 15 September 1969, Records of CSIS, RG 146, vol. 3757, "AUUC: Case History," part 7. Although youth made up the bulk of this educational cohort, it should be noted that they was not its sole preserve. Some students were older AUUC members who had already demonstrated promise and loyalty as leaders. Bill Philipovich, for example, who was born in Canada in 1915, graduated from the 1936 HEC and worked as a cultural teacher prior to studying the history of Ukrainian music in Kiev in 1954. When he returned, he continued teaching for the AUUC. For more information see interview with Bill Philipovich by the author, 7 June 1998.

88 Letter dated 8 February 1969 from Sonny Kowalewich to Bill Harasym, AUUC Fonds, MG 28 V 154, vols. 34–5, file 6, "Society Ukraina."

89 Letter dated 22 March 1965 from Ted Kardash to Bill Harasym, Stavroff Private Collection.

90 Letter dated 10 September 1971 from Ron Mokry to National Executive Committee, AUUC, in AUUC Fonds, MG 28 V 154, vol. 30, "Dance Seminars and Schools," file 5, "Folk Dance Seminar – Kiev, 1971–72."

91 AUUC Fonds, MG 28 V 154, vol. 30, "Dance Seminars and Schools," file 9, "Folk Dance Seminar Kiev, 1974."

92 Letter dated 15 August 1974 from Terry Polowy to members of the National Executive Committee, MG 28, V 154, vol. 30, "Dance Seminars and Schools," file 9, "Folk Dance Seminar Kiev, 1974."

93 Letter dated 17 October 1974 from Donna Machuik and Joanne Laslo to Bill Harasym, MG 28, V 154, vol. 30, "Dance Seminars and Schools," file 9, "Folk Dance Seminar Kiev, 1974."

94 Letter dated 15 August 1974 from Terry Polowy to members of the National Executive Committee, MG 28, V 154, vol. 30, "Dance Seminars and Schools," file 9, "Folk Dance Seminar Kiev, 1974."

95 See for examples interviews by the author with Lucy Nykolyshyn (8 August 1998), Bernice Grabish (17 August 1999), E.A. Bilecki (24 August 1999), Clara Babiy (4 November 1999), and Vera Seychuk (30 October 1999).

96 Mike Wos, "Dear UC," *Ukrainian Canadian*, 1 December 1953.

97 "Resolution in AUUC Junior Section Work," AUUC Fonds, MG 28 V 154, vol. 2, "Conventions," file 26, "AUUC: National Junior Council, Sept 26, 1960."

98 Lari Prokop, interviewed by the author, 10 December 1999.

99 "Association of United Ukrainian Canadians: Information Brief," 15 September 1969, Records of CSIS, RG 146, vol. 3757, "AUUC: Case History Canada," part 7.

100 Ibid.; see also memorandum dated 15 December 1951, Records of CSIS, RG 146, vol. 3757, "AUUC: Case History Canada," part 1; and "Resolutions on AUUC Junior Section Work," AUUC Fonds MG 28 V 154, vol. 2, "Conventions," file 5, "AUUC –7th Convention."

101 Draft copy of "Cadre Policy," AUUC Fonds, MG 28 V 154, vol. 3, "Conventions," file 16, "AUUC – 34th National Convention."

102 Letter dated 17 January 1965 from Carol Petrachenko to Stanley Dobrowolsky, AUUC Fonds, MG 28 V 154, vol. 11, "Correspondence – Junior Section," file 17, "AUUC – Juniors, Welland, 1964 65."

103 Julie Dalkie, interviewed by the author, August 1999. See also interview of Vera Seychuk by the author, 30 October 1999, and Bill's response to a survey, AUUC Fonds, MG 28 V 154, vol. 5, files 17 and 18, "AUUC Membership Questionnaire (Canadian Born) 1965–66."

104 Stella, AUUC Fonds, MG 28 V 154, vol. 5, files 17–18, "AUUC Membership Questionnaire (Canadian Born) 1965–66."

105 Kolasky, *The Shattered Illusion*, 196.

106 "Report of the Dynamo Youth Club Year," AUUC Fonds, MG 28 V 154, vol. 27, file 2, "AUUC Youth Club Reports."

107 Response to AUUC Membership Questionnaire (Canadian-born), 1965–66, AUUC Fonds, MG 28 V 154, vol, 5, file 17–18, "AUUC Membership Questionnaire (Canadian Born) 1965–66."

Conclusion

1 Vic Toews, quoted in "Ukrainian Labour Temple Declared National Historic Site," *Winnipeg Free Press*, 5 August 2009.

2 For some examples of the CSULR's activities consult *New Perspectives in Ukrainian Studies and Research: Founding Conference Canadian Society for Ukrainian Labour Research* (Toronto: CSULR, 1986); *Papers Presented at the*

Annual Meetings of the Canadian Society for Ukrainian Labour Research in 1987 and 1988 (Toronto: CSULR, 1990); *The 10th Anniversary Publication of Conference Proceedings of CSULR from 1993 to 1995, as well as Selected Papers Given by Canadians at the Lviv Ukraine Conference Marking the 100th Anniversary of Ukrainian Settlement in Canada That Were Not Published to Date* (Toronto: CSULR, 1996).

3 The *Ukrainian Canadian Herald* was born in 1991 out a merger of the two post-war newspapers the *Ukrainian Canadian* and *Zhittia i slovo* (Life and word) – which was also created out of an earlier merger of the two papers *Ukrainske zhyttia* and *Ukrainske slovo*. Both had been suffering from diminishing circulation and rising publication costs.

Bibliography

PRIMARY SOURCES

Periodicals, Pre–First World War

Chervonyi prapor (Red flag), 1907–8
Robochyi narod (Working people), 1909–18

Periodicals, Interwar Era

Boiova molod (Militant youth), 1930–2
Farmerske zhyttia (Farmers' life), 1925–40
Holos pratsi (Voice of labour), 1922–4
Holos robitnytsi (Voice of working woman), 1923–4
Narodna hazeta (People's gazette), 1937–40
Nasha pratsia (Our work), ca. 1930
Robitnytsia (Working woman), 1924–37
Svit molodi (The youth's world), 1927–32
Ukrainski robitnychi visti (Ukrainian labour news), 1919–37

Periodicals, Second World War and Beyond

Forward, 1950s–1960s
Holos pravdy (Voice of truth), ca. 1940
Leader's Guide, 1950s–1960s
Ukrainian Canadian, 1947–91
Ukrainian Canadian Herald, 1991–Present
Ukrainske slovo (Ukrainian word), 1943–64
Ukrainske zhyttia (Ukrainian life), 1941–64
Zhyttia i slovo (Life and word), 1964–91

Miscellaneous Publications

Album of the Workers Trading Cooperative Limited. Toronto: Workers Trading Cooperative, 1933.

Almanakh TURFDim, 1918–1929. Winnipeg: Labour-Farmer Publishing Association, 1930.

Biuleten ukrainskoho biura tsentralnoho komitetu komunistychnoi partii Kanady. Winnipeg: 1939.

Boyd, John. *A Noble Cause Betrayed ... But Hope Lives On: Pages from a Political Life; Memoirs of a Former Canadian Communist.* Edmonton: Canadian Institute of Ukrainian Studies Press, 1999.

The Case of the Seized Properties of the Ukrainian Labour-Farmer Temple Association: An Appeal for Justice. Toronto: Civil Liberties Association of Toronto, July 1944.

Committee for the Release of Labor Prisoners, *They Fought for Labor – Now Interned!* Winnipeg: Committee for the Release of Labor Prisoners, 1941.

Davies, Raymond Arthur. *This Is Our Land: Ukrainian Canadians against Hitler.* Toronto: Progress Books, 1943.

Dzatko, Olga Berketa. Unpublished autobiography. May 2001.

Fifty Years, 1918–1968: Serving the Community and Canada. Three speeches by P. Prokop, P. Krawchuk, and M.J. Sago to the 13th National Convention of the AUUC on the occasion of the 50th anniversary of the organization and its predecessors, 12–15 April 1968, Toronto: National Committee of the Assocation of United Ukrainian Canadians, 1968.

Forgotten Legacy: Contributions of Socialist Ukrainians to Canada. Winnipeg: CSULR, 1996.

Kardash, William A. *Hitler's Agents in Canada: A Revealing Story of Potentially Dangerous Fifth Column Activities in Canada among Ukrainian Canadians.* Toronto: Morris Printing, 1942.

Kolasky, John. *Prophets and Proletarians: Documents on the History of the Rise and Decline of Ukrainian Communism in Canada.* Edmonton: Canadian Institute of Ukrainian Studies Press, 1990.

Kravchuk, Petro. *Bez nedomovok: Spohady.* Kyiv: Literaturna Ukraina, 1995.

Krawchuk, Peter. *Interned without Cause: The Internment of Canadian Antifascists during World War Two.* Toronto: Kobzar Publishing, 1985.

– ed., *Reminiscences of Courage and Hope: Stories of Ukrainian Canadian Women Pioneers.* Toronto: Kobzar Publishing, 1991.

Manitoba's Program for Total War. Report of the speech delivered by Lieut. W.A. Kardash, MLA, in the Legislature, 16 December 1941. Winnipeg: Workers' Election Committee.

Narady i ukhvaly 4-oho vsekraiovoho zizdu TOUK v ukrainskomu robitnychomu domi, 25–29 sichnia, 1950. Toronto: Association of United Ukrainian Canadians, 1950.

Nashi sproby [Our endeavours]. Winnipeg: Publication of the Students of the Higher Educational Course of the ULFTA, January 1926.

New Perspectives in Ukrainian Studies and Research: Founding Conference Canadian Society for Ukrainian Labour Research. Toronto: CSULR, 1986.

Papers Presented at the Annual Meetings of the Canadian Society for Ukrainian Labour Research in 1987 and 1988. Toronto: CSULR, 1990.

Popovich, M. *Yak robitnyky dopomahaiut sobi v neshchasti: Do 15-richchia isnuvannia i dialnosti robitnychoho zapomohovoho tovarystva*. Winnipeg: Workers Benevolent Association, 1937.

Popovich, M., L. Morris, S. Carr, M. Lenartovych, I.I. Boichuk, eds. *Za bilshovyzatsiu: Polityko-ekonomichnyi ta kulturno-propagandystskyi misiachnyk tsentralnoho vykonavchoho komitetu komunistychnoi partii Kanady, 1931, 1–6*. Winnipeg: Labour-Farmer Publishing Association, 1931.

Prokop, Peter, William Harasym, and Mitch J. Sago. *Change and Challenge in the Ukrainian Ethnic Group*. Toronto: Association of United Ukrainian Canadians, 1967. Prokopchak, P. *Slavnu istoriiu i tradytsiiu maie TURFDim*. Boichuk I., *Borotba za lehalizatsiiu TURFDim*. Speeches at the 17th Convention of the Ukrainian Labour-Farmer Temple Association, 11–12 January 1946, Winnipeg, Manitoba. Toronto: Central Executive Committee, Ukrainian Labour Farmer Temple Association, 1948.

Prokopchak, P. *Sprava oborony ukrainskykh zemel i narodu*. Paper delivered at the 6th Convention of the Association for Aid to the Liberation Movement in Western Ukraine, 22–26 February 1939. Toronto: Democratic Society for the Defence of the Ukrainian People, 1939.

Prokopchak, P. *Za myr – proty viiny: Syla ukrainskoho narodu v yoho yednosti*. Paper delivered at a convention of the Ukrainian Labour-Farmer Mass Organizations, 22 June 1937. Winnipeg: Central Executive Committee, Ukrainian Labour Farmer Temple Association (TURFDIM), 1937.

Prokopchak, Petro, ed. *Almanakh piatdesiatyrichchia zhinochykh viddiliv Tovarystva obiednanykh ukrainskykh kanadtsiv, 1922–1972*. Toronto: Kobzar Publishing, 1976.

Repka, Kathleen M., and William Repka, eds. *Dangerous Patriots: Canada's Unknown Prisoners of War*. Vancouver, BC: New Star Books, 1982.

"Report of the Delegation to Ukraine: Central Committee Meeting – September 16, 17, and 18, 1967," in *Viewpoint*, discussion bulletin issued by the Central Executive Committee, Communist Party of Canada, January 1968.

Resolutions of the Provincial Conference of ULFTA Youth Section, September 1–2, 1934, Toronto: Provincial Secretariat of the Youth Section of the ULFTA, 1934.

Robitnycho-farmerskyi kaliendar na perestupnyi rik, 1928. Winnipeg: Labour-Farmer Publishing Association.

Robitnychyi kaliendar, 1918. Winnipeg: Robochyi narod.

Selected Papers Presented at the National Centenary Conference Marking the 100th Anniversary of Ukrainian Immigration to Canada, Sponsored by the CSULR, Toronto, June9/10, 1990. Also Included Are Papers Presented at Annual Meetings of the CSULR in 1991, 1992, and Others. Toronto: CSULR, 1994.

Six Decades of Progress, 1918–1978: Our Commitment to the Future in a United Canada. Proceedings of the Special Joint Convention, Association of United Ukrainian Canadians and the Workers Benevolent Association of Canada. Winnipeg: AUUC and WBA of Canada, 1978.

The 10th Anniversary Publication of Conference Proceedings of CSULR from 1993 to 1995, as well as Selected Papers Given by Canadians at the Lviv Ukraine Conference Marking the 100th Anniversary of Ukrainian Settlement in Canada That Were Not Published to Date. Toronto: CSULR, 1996.

Tribute to Our Ukrainian Pioneers in Canada's First Century. Proceedings of the special convention of the Association of United Ukrainian Canadians and the Workers' Benevolent Association of Canada (to commemorate the 75th anniversary of Ukrainian immigration to Canada), 23 March 1966. Winnipeg: AUUC and WBA, 1966.

Unite the Youth. Published in honour of the tenth anniversary of the Youth Section, ULFTA. Ca. 1936.

Volynets, M. *Piatnatsiat rokiv TURFDIM, 1918–1933.* Winnipeg: Labour-Farmer Publishing Association, 1933.

Weir, John. *The Case of Canada's Stepchildren: Foreign-Born Canadians Discriminated Against by the Department of Citizenship and Immigration.* Toronto: Canadian Slav Committee, 1961.

Archival Collections

Association of United Ukrainian Canadians (AUUC) Archives, Winnipeg, Manitoba (uncatalogued).

Association of United Ukrainian Canadians (AUUC) Fonds, MG 28, V 154, Library and Archives Canada, Ottawa, Ontario.

Peter Krawchuk Collection, Library and Archives Canada, Ottawa, Ontario.

Records of the Canadian Security Intelligence Service (CSIS), RG 146, Library and Archives Canada, Ottawa, Ontario.

Stavroff Private Collection, Toronto, Ontario (uncatalogued).

Oral History Collections

Preserving the Past: The Ukrainian Labour Temple Oral History Project. AUUC
    Archives, Winnipeg, Manitoba.
Preserving the Past II: The Ukrainian Labour Temple Oral History Project. AUUC
    Archives, Winnipeg, Manitoba.
"Towards a New Path: The History of the Progressive Ukrainian Community
    in Saskatchewan Oral History Project (1976)." Interviews and translations
    by Clara Swityk, accession #R80–550, Saskatchewan Archives Board,
    University of Regina, Saskatchewan.

Secondary Sources

Acker, Joan. "Inequality Regimes: Gender, Class, and Race in Organizations."
    Gender and Society 20, no. 4 (August 2006): 441–64.
Adachi, Ken. *The Enemy That Never Was*. Toronto: McClelland & Stewart, 1991.
Angus, Ian. *Canadian Bolsheviks: The Early Years of the Communist Party of
    Canada*. Victoria, BC: Trafford, 2004.
Ashworth, Mary. "Ukrainian Children." In *Children of the Canadian Mosaic.
    A Brief History to 1950*, 69–80. Toronto: Ontario Institute for Studies in
    Education, 1993.
Auger, Martin F. "The Harikari Club: German Prisoners of War and the Mass
    Escape Scare of 1944–45 at Internment Camp Grande Ligne, Quebec." *Canadian
    Military History* 13, no. 3 (2004): 49–67.
Avakumovic, Ivan. *The Communist Party in Canada: A History*. Toronto:
    McClelland & Stewart, 1975.
Avery, Donald. "Divided Loyalties: The Ukrainian Left and the Canadian
    State." In *Canada's Ukrainians: Negotiating an Identity*, ed. Lobymr Luciuk
    and Stella Hryniuk, 271–87. Toronto: University of Toronto Press, 1991.
– *Reluctant Host*. Toronto: McClelland & Stewart, 1995.
Axelrod, Paul. "Spying on the Young in Depression and War: Students, Youth
    Groups and the RCMP, 1935–1942." *Labour/Le Travail* 1995 (35): 43–63.
Ayukawa, Mona. "Japanese Pioneer Women: Fighting Racism and Rearing
    the Next Generation." In Epp, Iacovetta, and Swyripa, *Sisters or Strangers?*,
    233–47.
Balan, Jars. *Salt and Braided Bread: Ukrainian Life in Canada*. Toronto: Oxford
    University Press, 1984.
Bangarth, Stephanie. "The Long, Wet Summer of 1942: The Ontario Farm
    Service Force, Small-Town Ontario and the Nisei." *Canadian Ethnic Studies*
    37, no. 1 (2005): 40–62.

- "Religious Organizations and the 'Relocation' of Persons of Japanese Ancestry in North America: Evaluating Advocacy." *American Review of Canadian Studies* 34, no. 3 (2004): 511–40.

Beasley, Chris. "Mind the Gap? Masculinity Studies and Contemporary Gender/Sexuality Thinking." *Australian Feminist Studies* 28, no. 75 (2013): 108–24.

Benton-Cohen, Katherine. "Docile Children and Dangerous Revolutionaries: The Racial Hierarchy of Manliness and the Bisbee Deportation of 1917." *Frontiers: A Journal of Women Studies* 24, no. 2 (2003): 30–50.

Berrol, Selma Cantor. *Growing Up American: Immigrant Children in America, Then and Now.* New York: Twayne, 1995.

Bjorkman, Sylvia. "Report on Camp 'W': Internment Camp '100' North of Lake Superior in World War II." *Ontario History* 89, no. 3 (1997): 237–43.

Bociurkiw, Bohdan. "The Federal Policy of Multiculturalism and the Ukrainian-Canadian Community." In *Ukrainian Canadians, Multiculturalism, and Separatism: An Assessment*, ed. Manoly R. Lupul, 98–128. Edmonton: CIUS, 1978.

Bodnar, John. *The Transplanted: A History of Immigrants in Urban America.* Bloomington: Indiana University Press, 1987.

Bosworth, R.J.B. "The Internment of Italians in Australia." In *Enemies Within*, ed. Iacovetta, Perin, and Principe, 227–55.

Bradbury, Bettina. *Working Families: Age, Gender and Daily Survival in Industrializing Montreal, 1876–1914.* Toronto: University of Toronto Press, 1993.

Brittan, Arthur. "Masculinities and Masculism." In *The Masculinities Reader*, ed. Stephen Whitehead and Frank J. Barrett, 51–76. Cambridge: Polity; Malden, MA: Blackwell Publishers, 2001.

Brookfield, Tarah. *Cold War Comforts: Canadian Women, Child Safety, and Global Insecurity, 1945–1975.* Waterloo, ON: Wilfrid Laurier University Press, 2012.

Brunnhuber, Nicole M.T. "After the Prison Ships: Internment Narratives in Canada." *Yearbook of the Research Centre for German & Austrian Exile Studies* 7 (2005): 165–78.

Bullen, John. "Hidden Workers: Child Labour and the Household Economy in Late Nineteenth-Century Urban Ontario." In *Canadian Family History: Selected Readings*, ed. Bettina Bradbury, 199–220. Toronto: Copp Clark Pitman, 1992.

Buse, Dieter K., Mercedes Steedman, and Gary William Kinsman. *Whose National Security? Canadian State Surveillance and the Creation of Enemies.* Toronto: Between the Lines, 2000.

Cameron, Ardis. *Radicals of the Worst Sort: Laboring Women in Lawrence, Massacheusetts, 1890–1912.* Urbana and Chicago: University of Illinois Press, 1993.

Canada's Party of Socialism: History of the Communist Party of Canada, 1921–1976.
  Toronto: Progress Books, 1982.

Candelario, Ginetta. "Working Class Women's Activism in the Dominican
  Republic, 1881–1960." Paper presented at the "Labouring Feminism and
  Feminist Working Class History in North America and Beyond" conference.
  University of Toronto, 29 September–2 October 2005.

Canning, Kathleen. "Gender History: Meanings, Methods, and
  Metanarratives." In *Gender History in Practice: Historical Perspectives on
  Bodies, Class & Citizenship*, 3–62. Ithaca, NY: Cornell University Press, 2006.

Carbado, Devon W. "Colorblind Intersectionality." *Signs: Journal of Women in
  Culture & Society* 38, no. 4 (9 July 2013): 1–42.

Carynnyk, Marco. "Swallowing Stalinism: Pro-Communist Ukrainian
  Canadians and Soviet Ukraine in the 1930's." In *Canada's Ukrainians:
  Negotiating an Identity*, ed. Lobymr Luciuk and Stella Hryniuk, 187–205.
  Toronto: University of Toronto Press, 1991.

Cavell, Richard, ed. *Love, Hate, and Fear in Canada's Cold War.* Toronto: University
  of Toronto Press, 2004.

Charlebois, Justin. "Geographies of Femininities." In *Gender and the Construction
  of Hegemonic and Oppositional Femininities*, 21–41. Lanham, MD.: Lexington
  Books, 2011.

Choo, Hae Yeon, and Myra Marx Ferree. "Practicing Intersectionality in
  Sociological Research: A Critical Analysis of Inclusions, Interactions, and
  Institutions in the Study of Inequalities." *Sociological Theory* 28, no. 2 (June
  2010): 129–49.

Chown, Sarah, and Jaedyn Starr. "Thinking Intersectionally: Understanding
  the Individual and Structural Contexts of Gay Men's Lives." Accessed
  25 June 2014. http://cbrc.net/blog/09-2013/thinking-intersectionally-
  understanding-individual-and-structural-contexts-gay-men%E2%80%99s

Cipko, Serge. *Ukrainians in Argentina, 1897–1950: The Making of a Community.*
  Edmonton, AB: Canadian Institute of Ukrainian Studies Press, 2011.

Cohen, Deborah. "From Peasant to Worker: Migration, Masculinity, and the
  Making of Mexican Workers in the US." *International Labor and Working-
  Class History* 69 (Spring 2006): 81–103.

Connell, R.W. "The Social Organization of Masculinity." In *The Masculinities
  Reader*, ed. Stephen M. Whitehead and Frank J. Barrett, 30–50. Cambridge:
  Polity Press, 2001.

Connell, R.W., and James W. Messerschmidt. "Hegemonic Masculinity:
  Rethinking the Concept." *Gender & Society* 19, no. 6 (1 December 2005):
  829–59.

Connell, Raewyn. *Gender: In World Perspective.* Cambridge: Polity, 2009.

– "Introduction: Master Builders; Research on Men and Masculinities and Directions for Australian Theory and Practice." *Australian Feminist Studies* 28, no. 75 (March 2013): 7–13.

Conquest, Robert. *The Harvest of Sorrow: Soviet Collectivization and the Terror Famine*. New York: Oxford University Press, 1986.

Creese, Gillian. "The Politics of Dependence: Women, Work and Unemployment in the Vancouver Labour Movement before World War II." In *Class, Gender and Region: Essays in Canadian Historical Sociology*, ed. Gregory S. Kealey, 121–42. St John's, NL: Athabasca University Press, 1988.

Crenshaw, Kimberlé. "Demarginalizing the Intersection of Race and Sex: A Black Feminist Critique of Antidiscrimination Doctrine, Feminist Theory, and Antiracist Politics." *University of Chicago Legal Forum*, 1989, 139–67.

Cumbo, Enrico Carlson. "'Uneasy Neighbours': Internment and Hamilton's Italians." In *Enemies Within*, ed. Iacovetta, Perin, and Principe, 99–119.

Darlington, James W. "Farmsteads as Mirrors of Cultural Adjustment and Change: The Ukrainian Canadian Experience." *Great Plains Research* 7, no. 1 (1997): 71–101.

Davis, Kathy. "Intersectionality as Buzzword: A Sociology of Science Perspective on What Makes a Feminist Theory Successful." *Feminist Theory* 9, no. 1 (1 April 2008): 67–85.

Day, Iyko. "Alien Intimacies: The Coloniality of Japanese Internment in Australia, Canada, and the U.S." *Amerasia Journal* 36, no. 2 (2010): 107–24.

Donaldson, Mike. "What Is Hegemonic Masculinity?" In "Masculinities," special issue, *Theory and Society* 22, no. 5 (October 1993): 643–57.

Endicott, Stephen. "Bienfait: Origins and Legacy of the Coal Miners' Strike of 1931." *Prairie Forum* 31, no. 2 (2006): 217–31.

– . *Bienfait: The Saskatchewan Miners' Struggle of '31*. Toronto: University of Toronto Press, 2002.

– ."The Estevan Story, 1931 to 1970." *Canadian Labour* 16, no. 1 (1971): 10.

Epp, Marlene. "Heroes or Yellow-bellies? Masculinity and the Conscientious Objector." *Journal of Mennonite Studies* 17 (1999): 107–17.

– "The Semiotics of Zwieback: Feast and Famine in the Narratives of Mennonite Refugee Women." In Epp, Iacovetta, and Swyripa, *Sisters or Strangers?*, 314–40.

Epp, Marlene, Franca Iacovetta, and Frances Swyripa, eds. *Sisters or Strangers?: Immigrant, Ethnic, and Racialized Women in Canadian History*. Toronto: University of Toronto Press, 2004.

Epp, Stefan. "A Communist in the Council Chambers: Communist Municipal Politics, Ethnicity, and the Career of William Kolisnyk." *Labour/Le travail* 63 (Spring 2009): 79–103.

Forestell, Nancy M. "All That Glitters Is Not Gold: The Gendered Dimensions of Work, Family and Community Life in the Northern Ontario Goldmining Town of Timmins, 1909–1950." PhD diss., University of Toronto, 1994.

Frager, Ruth. *Sweatshop Strife: Class, Ethnicity, and Gender in the Jewish Labour Movement of Toronto, 1900–1939.* Toronto: University of Toronto Press, 1992.

Friends in Need: The WBA Story, a Canadian Epic in Fraternalism. Winnipeg: WBA, 1972.

Gabaccia, Donna R., and Franca Iacovetta. *Women, Gender and Transnational Lives: Italian Workers of the World.* Toronto: University of Toronto Press 2002.

Gabaccia, Donna, Franca Iacovetta, and Fraser Ottanelli. "Labouring across National Borders: Class, Gender and Militancy in the Proletarian Mass Migration." *International Labor and Working Class History* 66 (Fall 2004): 57–77.

Guard, Julie. "Canadian Citizens or Dangerous Foreign Women?" In Epp, Iacovetta, and Swyripa, *Sisters or Strangers?*, 161–89.

– "A Mighty Power against the Cost of Living: Canadian Housewives Organize in the 1930s." *International Labor & Working-Class History*, no. 77 (Spring 2010): 27–47.

Guglielmo, Jennifer. "Italian Women's Proletarian Feminism in the New York City Garment Trades, 1890s–1940s." In *Women, Gender and Transnational Lives: Italian Workers of the World,* ed. Donna R. Gabaccia and Franca Iacovetta, 247–98. Toronto: University of Toronto Press, 2002.

Gulka-Tiechko, Myron. "Ukrainian Immigration to Canada under the Railways Agreement, 1925–30." *Journal of Ukrainian Studies* 16, nos. 1–12 (Summer–Winter 1991): 29–59.

Handlin, Oscar. *The Uprooted.* Boston: Little, Brown, 1951.

Hankivsky, Olena. *Intersectionality 101.* Vancouver, BC: Institute for Intersectionality Research and Policy, Simon Fraser University, 2014.

Heitrich, Megan. "WWII Japanese Internment Camps along the Upper Fraser." *British Columbia History* 44, no. 2 (2011): 5.

Heron, Craig. "Boys Will Be Boys: Working-Class Masculinities in the Age of Mass Production." *International Labor and Working-Class History* 69 (Spring 2006): 6–34.

– "The High School and the Household Economy in Working-Class Hamilton, 1890–1940." *Historical Studies in Education* 7, no. 2 (Fall 1995): 217–59.

Hewitt, Nancy. *Southern Discomfort: Women's Activism in Tampa, Florida, 1880s–1920s.* Urbana: University of Illinois Press, 2001.

– "'The Voice of Virile Labor': Labor Militancy, Community Solidarity, and Gender Identity among Tampa's Latin Workers, 1880–1921." In *Work Engendered: Toward a New History of American Labor,* ed. Ava Baron, 142–67. Ithaca, NY: Cornell University Press, 1991.

Hewitt, Steve. "September 1931: A Re-interpretation of the Royal Canadian Mounted Police's Handling of the 1931 Estevan Strike and Riot." *Labour / Le Travail*, no. 39:159–78.
– *Spying 101: The RCMP's Secret Activities at Canadian Universities, 1917–1997.* Toronto: University of Toronto Press, 2002.
Himka, John Paul. "A Central European Diaspora under the Shadow of World War II: The Galician Ukrainians in North America." *Austrian History Yearbook* 27 (2006): 17–31.
Hinther, Rhonda L. "'Sincerest Revolutionary Greetings': Progressive Ukrainians in Twentieth-Century Canada." PhD. diss., McMaster University (Canada), 2005.
Hinther, Rhonda L., and Jim Mochoruk, eds. *Reimagining Ukrainian Canadians: History, Politics, and Identity.* Toronto: University of Toronto Press, 2011.
Holyck Hunchuck, Suzanne. "A House Like No Other: An Architectural and Social History of the Ukrainian Labour Temple, 523 Arlington Street, Ottawa, 1923–1967." Master's thesis, Carleton University, 2001.
Huard, Victor. "The Canadian Peace Congress and the Challenge to Postwar Consensus, 1948–53." *Peace and Change* 19, no. 1 (1994): 25–49.
Hunt, Karen. "The Politics of Food and Women's Neighborhood Activism in First World War Britain." *International Labor and Working-Class History* 77, no. 1 (2010): 8–26.
– "'Strong Minds, Great Hearts, True Faith and Ready Hands'? Exploring Socialist Masculinities before the First World War." *Labour History Review* 69, no. 2 (August 2004): 201–17.
Iacovetta, Franca. "Defending Honour, Demanding Respect: Manly Discourse and Gendered Practice in Two Construction Strikes, Toronto, 1960–1961." In *Gendered Pasts: Historical Essays in Femininity and Masculinity in Canada*, ed. Kathryn McPherson, Cecilia Morgan, and Nancy M. Forestell, 199–222. New York: Oxford University Press. 1999.
– *Gatekeepers: Reshaping Immigrant Lives in Cold War Canada.* Toronto: Between the Lines, 2006.
– "Gendering Trans/National Historiographies: Feminists Rewriting Canadian History." *Journal of Women's History* 19, no.1 (2007): 206–13.
– *Such Hardworking People: Italian Immigrants in Postwar Toronto.* Montreal: McGill-Queen's University Press, 1992.
Iacovetta, Franca, Marlene Epp, and Valerie Joyce Korinek, eds. *Edible Histories, Cultural Politics: Towards a Canadian Food History.* Toronto: University of Toronto Press, 2012.
Iacovetta, Franca, and Valere J. Korinek. "Jell-O Salads, One-Stop Shopping, and Maria the Homemaker: The Gender Politics of Food." In Epp, Iacovetta, and Swyripa, *Sisters or Strangers?*, 190–230.

Iacovetta, Franca, Roberto Perin, and Angelo Principe, eds. *Enemies Within: Italian and Other Internees in Canada and Abroad*. Toronto: University of Toronto Press, 2000.

Iacovetta, Franca, and Roberto Ventresca. "Redress, Collective Memory, and the Politics of History." In Iacovetta, Perin, and Principe, *Enemies Within*, 379–412.

Izumi, Masumi. "Lessons from History: Japanese Canadians and Civil Liberties in Canada." *Journal of American & Canadian Studies* no. 17 (1999): 1–24.

Jackson, Paul . "The Enemy within the Enemy within: The Canadian Army and Internment Operations during the Second World War." *Left History* 9, no. 2 (2004): 45–83.

Johnston, Ronnie, and Arthur McIvor. "Dangerous Work, Hard Men and Broken Bodies: Masculinity in the Clydeside Heavy Industries, c. 1930–1970s." *Labour History Review* 69, no. 2 (August 2004): 135–51.

Kealey, Greg, and Reg Whitaker, eds. *R.C.M.P. Security Bulletins, Volumes 1–8.* St John's, NF: Canadian Committee on Labour History, various dates.

Kealey, Linda. *Enlisting Women for the Cause: Women, Labour, and the Left in Canada, 1890–1920*. Toronto: University of Toronto Press, 1998.

Kidd, Bruce. "Workers' Sport, Worker Culture." In *The Struggle for Canadian Sport*. Toronto: University of Toronto Press, 1996.

Kinsmen, Gary. "The Canadian Cold War on Queers." In *Love, Hate, and Fear in Canada's Cold War*, ed. Richard Cavell, 108–32. Toronto: University of Toronto Press, 2004.

Klymasz, Robert B., ed. *Art and Ethnicity: The Ukrainian Tradition in Canada*. Hull, QC: Canadian Museum of Civilization, 1991.

Knapp, Gudrun-Axeli. "Race, Class, Gender: Reclaiming Baggage in Fast Travelling Theories." *European Journal of Women's Studies* 12 (2005): 249.

Kobayaski, Audrey. "Within the Barbed Wire Fence: A Japanese Man's Account of His Internment in Canada." *American Review of Canadian Studies* 11, no. 3 (1981): 93–5.

Kocięda, Aphrodite. "Marginalization Is Messy: Beyond Intersectionality | Rabble.ca." Accessed 12 May 2014. http://web.archive.org/web/20140628063348/http://feministcurrent.com/8065/marginalization-is-messy-beyond-intersectionality/ .

Kolasky, John. *The Shattered Illusion: The History of Ukrainian Pro-Communist Organizations in Canada*. Toronto: PMA Books, 1979.

Kordan, Bohdan. *Canada and the Ukrainian Question, 1939–1945: A Study in Statecraft*. Montreal: McGill-Queen's University Press, 2001.

– *Enemy Aliens, Prisoners of War: Internment in Canada during the Great War*. Montreal: McGill-Queen's University Press, 2002.

Kostash, Myrna. *All of Baba's Children*. Edmonton, AB: Hurtig, 1977.

Kravchuk, Petro. *Na novii zemli: Storinky z zhyttia, borotby i tvorchoi pratsi kanadskykh ukraintsiv*. Toronto: National Executive Committee of the Association of United Ukrainian Canadians, 1958.

– *Piatdesiat rokiv sluzhinnia narodu: Do istorii ukrainskoi narodnoi presy v Kanadi*. Toronto: *Ukrainske zhyttia*, 1957.

– *Vony obraly Kanadu: Pershyi period emihruvannia ukraintsiv do Kanady, 1891–1914*. Toronto: Kobzar Publishing, 1991.

Krawchuk, Peter. *The Life and Work of Matthew Shatulsky*. Toronto: Kobzar Publishing, 1991.

– *Mathew Popovich: His Place in the History of Ukrainian Canadians*. Toronto: Canadian Society for Ukrainian Labour Research, 1987.

– *Our Contribution to Victory*. Toronto: Kobzar Publishing, 1985.

– *Our History: The Ukrainian Labour-Farmer Movement in Canada, 1907–1991*. Toronto: Lugus, 1996.

– ed. *Our Stage: The Amateur Performing Arts of the Ukrainian Settlers in Canada*. Toronto: Kobzar Publishing, 1984.

– *The Ukrainians in Winnipeg's First Century*. Toronto: Kobzar Publishing, 1974.

– *The Ukrainian Socialist Movement in Canada, 1907–1918*. Toronto: Progress Books, 1979.

– *The Unforgettable Myroslav Irchan: Pages from a Valiant Life: Dedicated to the 100th Anniversary of His Birth, 1897-1997*. Edmonton: Kobzar Publishing, 1998.

Kukushkin, Vadim. *From Peasants to Labourers: Ukrainian and Belarusan Immigration from the Russian Empire to Canada*. Montreal: McGill-Queen's University Press, 2007.

Kunimoto, Namiko. "Intimate Archives: Japanese-Canadian Family Photography, 1939–1949." *Art History* 27, no. 1 (2004): 129–55.

Lalande, Julia. "The Roots of Multiculturalism: Ukrainian-Canadian Involvement in the Multiculturalism Discussion of the 1960s as an Example of the Position of the 'Third Force.'" *Canadian Ethnic Studies* 38, no. 1 (2006): 47–64.

Lehr, John. *Community and Frontier: A Ukrainian Settlement in the Canadian Parkland*. Winnipeg: University of Manitoba Press, 2011.

Lindström, Varpu. *Defiant Sisters: A Social History of Finnish Immigrant Women in Canada*. Beaverton, ON: Aspasia Books, 2003.

Loewen, Royden. *Family, Church, and Market: A Mennonite Community in the Old and the New Worlds, 1850–1930*. Urbana: University of Illinois Press, 1993.

Loo, Tina. "Of Moose and Men: Hunting for Masculinities in British Columbia, 1880–1939." *Western Historical Quarterly* 32 (Autumn 2001): 296–319.

Luciuk, Lubomyr Y. *In Fear of the Barbed Wire Fence: Canada's First National Internment Operations and the Ukrainian Canadians, 1914–1920.* Kingston, ON: Kashtan Press, 2001.

– *Searching for Place: Ukrainian Displaced Persons, Canada, and the Migration of Memory.* Toronto: University of Toronto Press, 2000.

– "Ukrainians and Internment Operations in Ontario during the First World War." *Polyphony* 10 (October 1988): 27–31.

– *Without Just Cause: Canada's First National Internment Operations and the Ukrainian Canadians, 1914–1920.* Kingston, ON: Kashtan Press, 2006.

Luciuk, Lubomyr, and Stella Hryniuk, eds. *Canada's Ukrainians: Negotiating an Identity.* Toronto: University of Toronto Press, 1991.

Lupul, Manoly R., ed. *A Heritage in Transition: Essays in the History of Ukrainians in Canada.* Toronto: McClelland & Stewart, 1982.

– ed. *Visible Symbols: Cultural Expression among Canada's Ukrainians.* Edmonton: CIUS, 1984.

Lysenko, Vera. *Men in Sheepskin Coats: A Study in Assimilation.* Toronto: Ryerson Press, 1947.

MacKay, Ian. *Reasoning Otherwise: Leftists and the People's Enlightenment in Canada, 1890–1920.* Toronto: Between the Lines, 2008.

Makuch, Andrij. "Fighting for the Soul of the Ukrainian Progressive Movement in Canada: The Lobayites and the Ukrainian Labour-Farmer Temple Association." In *Reimagining Ukrainian Canadians: History, Politics, and Identity,* ed. Rhonda L. Hinther and Jim Mochoruk, 376–400. Toronto: University of Toronto Press, 2011.

Malia, Martin. *The Soviet Tragedy: A History of Socialism in Russia, 1917–1991.* Toronto: Maxwell Macmillan Canada, 1994.

Martynowych, Orest T. *The Showman and the Ukrainian Cause: Folk Dance, Film, and the Life of Vasile Avramenko.* Winnipeg: University of Manitoba Press, 2014.

– *The Ukrainians in Canada: The Formative Years, 1891–1924.* Edmonton, AB: CIUS, 1991.

Marunchak, M.H. *The Ukrainians in Canada: A History.* Winnipeg, MB: Ukrainian Academy of Arts and Sciences, 1982.

Maryn, Sonia. "The Kiew ULFTA Hall: Narrative History." Ukrainian Cultural Heritage Village Project No. 24. Edmonton, 1984.

McBride, Marlene. "The Curious Case of the Female Internees." In Iacovetta, Perin, and Principe, *Enemies Within,* 148–70.

McCall, Leslie. "The Complexity of Intersectionality." *Signs: Journal of Women in Culture and Society* 30, no. 31 (2005): 1771–1800.

McCallum, Todd, "'Not a Sex Question'?: The One Big Union and the Politics of Radical Manhood." *Labour/Le Travail* 42 (Fall 1998): 15–54.

McIntosh, Robert. *Boys in the Pits: Child Labour in Coal Mines*.Montreal and Kingston: McGill-Queen's University Press, 2000.
– "Constructing the Child: New Approaches to the History of Childhood in Canada." *Acadiensis* 28, no. 2 (Spring 1999): 126–40.
McKay, Ian. *Rebels, Reds, Radicals: Rethinking Canada's Left History*. Toronto: Between the Lines, 2005.
McPherson, Kathryn, Cecelia Morgan, and Nancy M. Forestell, eds. *Gendered Pasts: Historical Essays in Femininity and Masculinity in Canada*. Toronto: Oxford University Press 1999.
Merithew, Caroline. "'Love and Solidarity': Generation and Women's Radicalism." Labouring Feminism Conference, 29 September–2 October 2005, University of Toronto.
Messerschmidt, James W. "The Struggle for Heterofeminine Recognition: Bullying, Embodiment, and Reactive Sexual Offending by Adolescent Girls." *Feminist Criminology* 6, no. 3 (July 2011): 203–33.
Miranda, Susana. "An Unlikely Collection of Labour Militants: Portuguese Immigrant Cleaning Women on Strike, Toronto, 1984." Labouring Feminism Conference, 29 September–2 October 2005, University of Toronto.
Mishler, Paul. *Raising Reds: The Young Pioneers, Radical Summer Camps, and Communist Political Culture in the United States*. New York: Columbia University Press, 1999.
Mochoruk, Jim. *The People's Co-op: The Life and Times of a North End Institution*. Halifax, NS: Fernwood Publishing, 2000.
– "'Pop & Co' versus Buck and the 'Lenin School Boys': Ukrainian Canadians and the Communist Party of Canada." In *Reimagining Ukrainian Canadians: History, Politics, and Identity*, ed. Rhonda L. Hinther and Jim Mochoruk, 331–75. Toronto: University of Toronto Press, 2011.
Morelli, Anne. "Nestore's Wife? Work, Family, and Militancy in Belgium." In Gabbaccia and Iacovetta, *Women, Gender, and Transnational Lives*, 327–46.
Moya, José. "Italians in Buenos Aires's Anarchist Movement: Gender Ideology and Women's Participation." In Gabbaccia and Iacovetta, *Women, Gender, and Transnational Lives*, 189–216 .
Nasaw, David. *Children of the City: At Work and at Play*. Garden City, NJ: Anchor Press/Doubleday, 1985.
Nash, Jennifer C. "Re-thinking Intersectionality." *Feminist Review* 89, no. 1 (2008): 1–15.
Nay, Marshall A. *Trailblazers of Ukrainian Emigration to Canada*. Edmonton, AB: Brightest Pebble Publishing, 1997.
Neatby, Nicole, and Peter Hodgins, eds. *Settling and Unsettling Memories: Essays in Canadian Public History*. Toronto: University of Toronto Press, 2011.

Newton, Janice. *The Feminist Challenge to the Canadian Left, 1900–1918.* Montreal: McGill-Queen's University Press, 1995.

Niwayama, Yuukichi. "Caught In-Between: The Life History of a Japanese Canadian Woman Deportee." *Journal of American & Canadian Studies,* no. 28 (2010): 3–28.

Oikawa, Mona. *Cartographies of Violence: Japanese Canadian Women, Memory, and the Subjects of the Internment.* Toronto: University of Toronto Press, 2000.

Ostryzniuk, Natalie. "Savella Stechishin, an Ethnocultural Feminist, and Ukrainian Culture in Saskatchewan." *Saskatchewan History* 51, no. 2 (1999): 12–28.

Owram, Douglas. *Born at the Right Time: A History of the Baby Boom Generation.* Toronto: University of Toronto Press, 1996.

Parr, Joy, ed. *Childhood and Family in Canadian History.* Toronto: McClelland & Stewart, 1982.

Patrias, Carmela. *Patriots and Proletarians: Politicizing Hungarian Immigrants in Interwar Canada.* Montreal: McGill-Queen's University Press, 1994.

– "Relief Strike: Immigrant Workers and the Great Depression in Crowland, Ontario, 1930–35." In *A Nation of Immigrants: Women, Workers, and Communities In Canadian History,* ed. Franca Iacovetta, Paula Draper, and Robert Ventresca., 322–58. Toronto: University of Toronto Press, 1998.

Penfold, Steven. "'Have You No Manhood in You?': Gender and Class in the Cape Breton Coal Towns, 1920–26." In *Gender and History in Canada,* ed. Joy Parr and Mark Rosenfeld, , 270–93. Toronto: McClelland & Stewart, 1996.

Penner, Norman. *Canadian Communism: The Stalin Years and Beyond.* Toronto: Methuen, 1988.

Petryshyn, Jaroslav. *Peasants in the Promised Land: Canada and the Ukrainians, 1891–1914.* Toronto: Lorimer, 1985.

Pipes, Richard. *Russia under the Bolshevik Regime.* New York: Vintage Books, 1994.

Potrebenko, Helen. *No Streets of Gold: A Social History of Ukrainians in Alberta.* Vancouver, BC: New Star Books, 1977.

Prymak, Thomas M. *Maple Leaf and Trident: The Ukrainian Canadians during the Second World War.* Toronto: Multicultural History Society of Ontario, 1988.

Pyke, Karen D., and Denise L. Johnson. "Asian American Women and Racialized Femininities: 'Doing' Gender across Cultural Worlds." In *The Kaleidoscope of Gender: Prisms, Patterns, and Possibilities,* ed. Joan Z. Spade and Catherine G. Valentine, 76–88. Los Angeles, CA: Sage Publications, 2008.

Radforth, Ian. *Bushworkers and Bosses: Logging in Northern Ontario, 1900–1980.* Toronto: University of Toronto Press, 1987.

- "Ethnic Minorities and Wartime Injustices: Redress Campaigns and Historical Narratives in Late Twentieth-Century Canada." Unpublished manuscript, 2005.
- "Political Prisoners: The Communist Internees." In Iacovetta, Perin, and Principe, *Enemies Within*, 194–224.

Rasporich, Beverly. "Vera Lysenko's Fictions: Engendering Prairie Spaces." *Prairie Forum* 16, no. 2 (1991): 249–63.

Reidel, Walter E. "Exiled in Canada: Literary and Related Forms of Cultural Life in the Internment Camps." *Yearbook of German-American Studies* 24 (1989): 73–88.

Reiter, Ester. "Camp Navelt and the Daughters of the Jewish Left." In Epp, Iacovetta, and Swyripa, *Sisters or Strangers?*, 365–80.
- "First-Class Workers Don't Want Second-Class Wages: The Lanark Strike in Dunnville." In *A Diversity of Women: Ontario, 1945–1980*, ed. J. Parr, 168–99. Toronto: University of Toronto Press, 1995.
- "Secular *Yiddishkait*: Left Politics, Culture, and Community." *Labour/Le Travail* 49 (Spring 2002): 121–46.

Roberts, Glenna, and Serge Cipko. *One-Way Ticket: The Soviet Return-to-the-Homeland Campaign, 1955–1960*. Manotick, ON: Penumbra Press, 2008.

Rodney, William. *Soldiers of the International: A History of the Communist Party of Canada, 1919–1929*. Toronto: University of Toronto Press, 1968.

Rooke, Patricia, and R.L. Schnell, eds. *Studies in Childhood History: A Canadian Perspective*. Calgary, AB: Detselig Enterprises, 1982.

Roy, Patricia. *Mutual Hostages: Canadians and Japanese during the Second World War*. Toronto: University of Toronto Press, 1990.

Sangster, Joan. *Dreams of Equality: Women on the Canadian Left, 1920–1950*. Toronto: McClelland & Stewart, 1989.
- "'Robitnytsia,' Ukrainian Communists, and the 'Porcupinism' Debate: Reassessing Ethnicity, Gender, and Class in Early Canadian Communism, 1922–1930." *Labour / Le Travail*, 2005:51–89.

Scherini, Rose D. "When Italian Americans were 'Enemy Aliens.'" In Iacovetta, Perin, and Principe, *Enemies Within*, 280–306.

Schippers, Mimi. "Recovering the Feminine Other: Masculinity, Femininity, and Gender Hegemony." *Theory and Society* 36, no. 1 (1 March 2007): 85–102.

Shields, Stephanie A. "Gender: An Intersectionality Perspective." *Sex Roles* 59, nos. 5–6 (September 2008): 301–11. Accessed 25 June 2014.

Simien, Evelyn M. "Doing Intersectionality Research: From Conceptual Issues to Practical Examples." *Politics & Gender* 3, no. 2 (2007): 264–71.

Smandych, Russell, Gordon Dodds, and Alvin Esau, eds. *Dimensions of Childhood: Essays on the History of Children and Youth in Canada*. Winnipeg, MB: Legal Research Institute, 1990.

Smith, S.E. "Push(back) at the Intersections: Defining (and Critiquing) 'Intersectionality' | Bitch Media." *Bitchmedia*. Accessed 25 June 2014. https://bitchmedia.org/post/pushback-at-the-intersections-defining-and-critiquing-intersectionality.

Spade, Joan Z, and Catherine G. Valentine. Introduction to *The Kaleidoscope of Gender: Prisms, Patterns, and Possibilities*, xiii–xxiv. Los Angeles, CA: Sage Publications, 2008.

Sponza, Lucio. "The Internment of Italians in Britain." In Iacovetta, Perin, and Principe, *Enemies Within*, 256–79.

Srigley, Katrina. "'In Case You Hadn't Noticed!': Race, Ethnicity, and Women's Wage-Earning in a Depression-Era City." *Labour/Le Travail* 55 (Spring 2005): 69–105.

Stanton, John. "Government Internment Policy, 1939–1945." *Labour/Le Travail* 31 (1993): 203–41.

Steedman, Mercedes. *Angels of the Workplace: Women and the Construction of Gender Relations in the Canadian Clothing Industry, 1890–1940*. Toronto: Oxford University Press, 1997.

Subtelny, Orest. *Ukrainians in North America*. Toronto: University of Toronto Press, 1991.

Sugiman, Pamela. "'Life is Sweet': Vulnerability and Composure in the Wartime Narratives of Japanese Canadians." *Journal of Canadian Studies* 43, no. 1 (2009): 186–218.

– "Memories of Internment: Narrating Japanese Canadian Women's Life Stories." *Canadian Journal of Sociology* 29, no. 3 (2004): 359–88.

– "'A Million Hearts from here': Japanese Canadian Mothers and Daughters and the Lessons of War." *Journal of American Ethnic History* 26, no. 4 (2007): 50–68.

– "Passing Time, Moving Memories: Interpreting Wartime Narratives of Japanese Canadian Women." *Histoire Sociale* 37, no. 73 (2004): 51–79.

Sutherland, Neil. *Growing Up: Childhood in English Canada from the Great War to the Age of Television*. Toronto: University of Toronto Press, 1997.

Swankey, Ben. "Reflections of a Communist: Canadian Internment Camps." *Alberta History* 30, no. 2 (April 1982): 11–20.

Swyripa, Frances. "The Politics of Redress: The Contemporary Ukrainian-Canadian Campaign." In Iacovetta, Perin, and Principe, *Enemies Within*, 355–78.

– *Wedded to the Cause: Ukrainian-Canadian Women and Ethnic Identity, 1891–1991*. Toronto: University of Toronto Press, 1993.

Symington, Alison. "Intersectionality: A Tool for Gender and Economic
    Justice." *Women's Rights and Economic Change*, no. 9 (August 2004). https://
    www.awid.org/publications/intersectionality-tool-gender-and-economic-
    justice .

*Tenth Anniversary Publication of Conference Proceedings of CSULR from 1993 to
    1995*. Toronto: CSULR, 1996.

Turnbull, Steve. "Letters from Afar." *British Columbia History* 40, no. 3 (2007):
    13–15.

Valentine, Gill. "Theorizing and Researching Intersectionality: A Challenge for
    Feminist Geography." *Professional Geographer*, 59:1, 10–21.

Weir, John. *Slavs*. Toronto: Canadian Slav Committee, 1949.

Whitaker, Reg. "Official Repression of Communism during World War II."
    Labour/Le Travail 17 (1986): 135–66.

Whitaker, Reg, and Steve Hewitt. *Canada and the Cold War*. Toronto: Lorimer,
    2003.

Whitehead, Stephen, and Frank J. Barrett. *The Masculinities Reader*. Cambridge:
    Polity; Malden, MA: Blackwell Publishers, 2001.

– "The Sociology of Masculinity." In *The Masculinities Reader*, 1–26.
    Cambridge: Polity; Malden, MA: Blackwell Publishers, 2001.

Winker, Gabriele, and Nina Degele. "Intersectionality as Multi-Level Analysis:
    Dealing with Social Inequality." *European Journal of Women's Studies* 18, no. 1
    (1 February 2011): 51–66.

Wiseman, Nelson. "Ukrainian-Canadian Politics." In *Canada's Ukrainians*:
    Negotiating an Identity, ed. Lubomyr Luciuk and Stella Hryniuk, 342–61.
    Toronto: University of Toronto Press, 1991.

Yeo, Eileen. "Editorial: Taking it Like a Man." *Labour History Review* 69, no. 2
    (August 2004): 129–33.

Yuzuk, Paul. "The Ukrainian Communist Delusion." In *The Ukrainians in
    Manitoba*, 96–112. Toronto, University of Toronto Press, 1953.

Zembrzycki, Stacey. "'We Didn't Have a Lot of Money, But We Had Food':
    Ukrainians and Their Depression-Era Food Memories." In *Edible Histories,
    Cultural Politics: Towards a Canadian Food History*, ed. Franca Iacovetta,
    Marlene Epp, and Valerie Joyce Korinek, 131–39. Toronto: University of
    Toronto Press, 2012.

Index

STUDIES IN GENDER AND HISTORY

General Editors: Franca Iacovetta and Karen Dubinsky